SIR EDGAR MacCULLOCH

IN HIS ROBES AS BAILIFF OF GUERNSEY.

GUERNSEY FOLK LORE

A COLLECTION OF

POPULAR SUPERSTITIONS, LEGENDARY TALES,

PECULIAR CUSTOMS, PROVERBS, WEATHER SAYINGS, ETC.,

OF THE PEOPLE OF THAT ISLAND.

FROM MSS. BY THE LATE

SIR EDGAR MacCULLOCH, KNT., F.S.A., &c.

Bailiff of Guernsey.

EDITED BY EDITH F. CAREY.

ILLUSTRATED BY NUMEROUS PHOTOGRAPHS OF OLD PRINTS, ETC.

LONDON:

ELLIOT STOCK, 62, PATERNOSTER ROW, E.C.

GUERNSEY: F. CLARKE, STATES ARCADE.

1903,

"IN WINTER'S TEDIOUS NIGHTS SIT BY THE FIRE
WITH GOOD OLD FOLKS, AND LET THEM TELL THEE TALES
OF WOEFUL AGES LONG AGO BETID."
—K. RICHARD II., ACT V., SC. I.

"LA LEGENDE, LE MYTHE, LA FABLE, SONT, COMME LA CONCENTRATION
DE LA VIE NATIONALE, COMME DES RESERVOIRS PROFONDS OU DORMENT LE
SANG ET LES LARMES DES PEUPLES."—BAUDELAIRE.

AUTHOR'S PREFACE.

Of late years the ancient superstitions of the people, their legendary tales, their proverbial sayings, and, in fine, all that is designated by the comprehensive term of "Folk-Lore," have attracted much and deserved attention. Puerile as are many of these subjects, they become interesting when a comparison is instituted amongst them as they exist in various countries. It is then seen how wide is their spread—how, for example, the same incident in a fairy tale, modified according to the manners and customs of the people by whom it is related, extends from the remotest east to the westernmost confines of Europe, and is even found occasionally to re-appear among the wild tribes of the American Continent, and the isolated inhabitants of Polynesia. The ethnologist may find in this an argument for the common origin of all nations, and their gradual spread from one central point,—the philosopher and psychologist may speculate on the wonderful construction of the human mind, and, throwing aside the idea of the unity of the race, may attribute the similarities of tradition to an innate set of ideas, which find their expression in certain definite forms,—while the historian and antiquary may sometimes discover in these popular traditions, a confirmation or explanation of some doubtful point. Lastly, he whose sole object is amusement, and whose taste is not entirely vitiated by the exaggerated and exciting fiction of modern times, will turn with pleasure to the simple tales which have amused his childhood, and which are ever fresh and ever new.

Much of this ancient lore has already perished, and much is every day disappearing before the influence of the printing press, and the consequent extension of education. This would scarcely be regretted, if, at the same time, the degrading superstitions with which much of these old traditions are mixed up could disappear with them, but unfortunately we find by experience that this is not the case, and that these popular delusions only disappear in one form to re-appear in another, equally, if not more, dangerous.

A desire to preserve, before they were entirely forgotten, some of the traditional stories, and other matters connected with the folk-lore of my native island, induced me to attempt to collect and record them, but I have found the task, though pleasant, by no means easy. The last fifty years has made an immense difference here as elsewhere. The influx of a stranger population, and with it the growth and spread of the English tongue, has

changed, or modified considerably, the manners and
ideas of the people, more particularly in the town.
Old customs are forgotten by the rising generation,
what amused their fathers and mothers possesses
little or no interest for their children, and gradually
even the recollection of these matters dies away.
There are good grounds for supposing that, although
the belief in witchcraft attained its greatest development in the century which succeeded the Reformation,
and was as much the creed of the clergy as of the
laity, other popular superstitions were looked upon
with disfavour, and especially all those customs which
were in any way, even remotely, connected with the
observances of the ancient form of religion. The
rapid spread of dissent among the middle and lower
classes of society within the last half century has
certainly not had the effect of diminishing popular
credulity with respect to the existence of sorcerers
and their supernatural powers, but, by discouraging
the amusements in which the young naturally delight,
and in which the elders took part, it has broken one
of the links which connected the present with the
past.

Doubtless did one know where to look for it much
might still be gleaned among the peasantry, but all
who have attempted to make collections of popular
lore know how difficult it is to make this class of
people open themselves. They fear ridicule, and

cannot conceive what interest one can have in seeking for information on subjects which—whatever may be their own private opinion—they have been taught to speak of as foolishness.

Some of the stories in the following compilation were related to me by an old and valued servant of of the family, Rachel du Port, others were kindly communicated to me by ladies* and others, who had derived their information from similar sources, and whose names I have appended to them, and much is the result of my own research and observation. The subject matter of the following pages, having been collected at various times, and written down as it came to hand, is not arranged as it ought to be, and there are necessarily some repetitions. Whether, after all, the work is worthy of the time that has been spent on it, the reader must decide for himself. Suffice it to say that as far as regards myself it has afforded an occupation and amusement.

EDGAR MacCULLOCH.

Guernsey, February, 1864.

---

* The legends collected by Miss Lane (Mrs. Lane Clarke) were subsequently published by her in the charming little book called *Folk-Lore of Guernsey and Sark*, of which two Editions have been printed.

EDITOR'S PREFACE.

Sir Edgar MacCulloch at his death, which occurred July 31st, 1896, bequeathed his manuscript collection of Guernsey Folk-Lore to the Royal Court of Guernsey, of which he had been for so many years Member and President.

This collection was subsequently handed over to me by Sir T. Godfrey Carey, then Bailiff, and the other Members of the Court, to transcribe for publication : it was contained in three manuscript books, closely written on both sides of the pages, and interspersed with innumerable scraps of paper, containing notes, additions and corrections; as Sir Edgar himself says in his preface, the items were written down as collected, local customs, fairy tales, witch stories, one after the other, with no attempt at classification. In literally transcribing them I have endeavoured to place them under their different headings, as recommended by the English Folk-Lore Society, and have inserted the notes in their proper places ; and I am responsible for the choice of the quotations heading the various chapters. In every other particular I have copied the manuscript word for word as I received it. It took me over three years to transcribe, and was placed by the Royal Court in the printer's hands in February, 1900.

It will be noticed that three sizes of type have been used throughout the book ; Sir Edgar MacCulloch's subject matter has been printed in the largest, the Author's notes to his own text being in the medium, while the notes printed in the smallest type contain additional legends and superstitions, which have been told me, or collected for me, by and from the country people, and which I have added, thereby making the collection more complete. Also, at the end of the book, is an appendix containing a few of the legends collected by myself, which were too long to insert as notes, and a small collection of old Guernsey songs, which I have written down from the lips of the older inhabitants, and which, in one of the last conversations I had with Sir Edgar MacCulloch on the subject, he strongly recommended should be included in any collection of Guernsey Folk-Lore that should ever be published.

I was well aware of the difficulties of the task which I undertook, and how unworthy I, a mere novice, was to edit the work of so eminent an antiquary as the late Sir Edgar MacCulloch ; but it was represented to me that I was one of the very few who took any interest in the fast vanishing traditions of the island, that I understood the local dialect, and that I had had many conversations and much assistance from Sir Edgar MacCulloch during his lifetime on the subject ; and, more especially, that if I did not do it no one else would undertake it, and thus the result of Sir Edgar's labours would be lost to the island. This, I trust may be my excuse for assuming so great a responsibility. I feel I should never have accomplished it without the unfailing assistance and kindness of H. A. Giffard, Esq., the present Bailiff of Guernsey, and John de Garis, Esq., Jurat of the Royal Court, members of the Folk-Lore Committee, who have, in the midst of their own hard work, gone through all the proofs in the most untiring manner, and have helped me in every possible way.

The illustrations are from photographs, collected by myself, of old pictures and views illustrating the Guernsey of which Sir Edgar MacCulloch wrote, and which is now so sadly changed, and it will be noticed that in various instances where Sir Edgar writes of "wooded valleys and cornfields, etc.," in 1864, now (1903) there are nothing but quarries or greenhouses.

I am very grateful to Mr. Grigg, of High Street, for allowing me to use the photographs, taken by his grandson, Mr. William Guerin, of original pictures of Guernsey in his possession; also to Mr. Edgar Dupuy, of the Arcade, and Mr. Singleton, photographer, for the use of photographs done by them of Guernsey scenery.

I cannot conclude without thanking the many friends who have helped me by collecting folk-lore and songs, especially I must mention my cousin, the late Miss Ernestine Le Pelley, who gathered many traditions for me from the west coast of the island, and who, alas! never lived to see the book, in which she took so great an interest, in print. The late Miss Anne Chepmell, who died in 1899, also gave me most valuable assistance, and so have also Mrs. Le Patourel, Mrs. Charles Marquand, Mrs. Mollet, Miss Margaret Mauger, Mrs. Sidney Tostevin, and many others in St. Martin's parish, who have racked their brains to remember for me " chû que j'ai ouï dire à ma gran'mère."

EDITH F. CAREY.

Le Vallon, Guernsey, April, 1903.

CONTENTS.

Part I.

Times and Seasons, Festivals and Merrymakings.

Part II.

Superstitious Belief and Practice.

LIST OF ILLUSTRATIONS.

The Arms of Guernsey, illustrated on the cover, are from a sketch by Sir Edgar MacCulloch himself, drawn many years ago, and then described by him as from the most ancient seal of the island to be found among the records at the Greffe.

ERRATA.

Page 21. For " Fautrat " read " Fautrart."

,,   21. For " entrenir " read " entretenir."

,,   34 (*n*). For " a " read " la."

,,   62. For " ogygiau " read " ogygian."

,,   63. For " Ono Maeritus " read " Onomacritus.'

,,   75-6 (*n*). For " savoir " read " sçauoir."

,,   90. For " ex-communication " read " excommunication."

,,   90. With reference to the note on p. 90 the Editor was
then unaware of the Bull, dated Feb. 13, 1499,
whereby Pope Alexander VI. transferred the Churches
of the Channel Islands from the See of Coutances to
that of Winchester.

,,   114. Add " Les Tas de Pois d'Amont, showing," etc.

,,   164. For " Wishing Well at Fontaine Blicq, St. Andrew's "
read " Les Fontaines de Mont Blicq, Forest."

,,   177 (*n*). For " 1303 " read " 1393."

,,   311. Insert the words " in 1880."

,,   484. For " Tamer " read " Tamar."

Part I.

Times and Seasons.

Festivals and Merry-makings.

CHAPTER I.

Festival Customs.

" Many precious rites
And customs of our rural ancestry
Are gone, or stealing from us."
        —*Wordsworth*.

THE observance of particular days and seasons, and of certain customs connected with them, has been in all countries more or less mixed up with religion. Many of these customs have, it is well known, descended to us from pagan times. The Church, unable altogether to eradicate them, has, in some cases, tacitly sanctioned, in others incorporated them into her own system. At the Reformation some of these observances were thought to savour too strongly of their pagan origin, or to be too nearly allied to papal superstitions. Accordingly we find that in a country like Scotland, where reformation amounted to a total subversion of all the forms which had hitherto subsisted, even such a festival as Christmas was proscribed, and of course with it have fallen all the joyous observances which characterize that season in England. In Guernsey, from the reign of Queen Elizabeth to the Restoration of Charles II., the

Presbyterian form of Church government reigned supreme, and the ministers seem to have set their faces strongly against anything which in their estimation could be looked upon as superstitious. In the reformed churches of Geneva and France, whose discipline the islands had adopted, all Saints' days had been abolished, and, although the greater festivals of Christmas and Whitsuntide were retained, there were those in the insular congregations who would gladly have seen these also discarded. Dr. Peter Heylin, who visited the islands in 1629, tells us how " the Ministers were much heartened in their inconformity by the practice of De La Place, who, stomaching his disappointment in the loss of the Deanery of Jersey, abandoned his native country, and retired to Guernsey, where he breathed nothing but confusion to the English Liturgy, the person of the new Dean (David Bandinel), and the change of government. Whereas there was a lecture weekly every Thursday in the Church of St. Peter's-on-the-Sea, when once the feast of Christ's Nativity fell upon that day, he rather chose to disappoint the hearers, and put off the sermon, than that the least honour should reflect on that ancient festival."

We find that in the year 1622 the Clergy of the Island complained to the Royal Court of the practice that existed in the rural parishes of people going about on the Eve of St. John and on the last day of the year begging from house to house—a custom, which, in their opinion, savoured much of the old leaven of Popery, and which, under the guise of charity, introduced and nourished superstition among their flocks; whereupon an ordinance was framed and promulgated, forbidding the practice under the penalty of a fine or whipping.

"Les Chefs Plaids Cappitaux d'apprés le jour St. Michell tenus le Lundy dernier jour du mois de Septembre, l'an 1622, par Amice de Carteret, Esq., Bailly, présents à ce les Sieurs Pierre Careye, Thomas Beauvoir, Thomas de l'Isle, Thomas Andros, Eleazar Le Marchant, Jean Bonamy, Jean Fautrat, Jean Blondel, et Jacques Guille, Jurez.

"Sur la remonstrance de Messieurs les Ministres de ceste isle, que la vueille du jour St. Jean et celle du jour de l'an se fait une geuzerie ordinaire par les paroisses des champs en ceste isle; laquelle se resent grandement du viel levain de la Papaulté, au moyen de quoy, soubs ombre de charité, la superstition est introduite et nourye parmy nous, au grand destourbier du service de Dieu et manifeste scandalle des gens de bien; desirants iceux Ministres qu'il pleust à la Cour y apporter remede par les voyes les plus convenables—A sur ce Esté par exprès deffendu à toutes personnes qu'ils n'ayent en aulcun des susdits jours à geuzer, ný demander par voye d'aumosne aulcune chose, de peur d'entrenir la susdite superstition, à peine de soixante sous tournois d'amende sur les personnes capables de payer la dite amende, et s'ils n'ont moyen de payer, et qu'ils soyent d'aage, d'estre punis corporellement à discretion de Justice; et quant aux personnes qui ne seront point d'aage, d'estre fouettés publicquement en l'escolle de leur paroisse."

A little later, begging at Baptisms, Marriages, and Burials was prohibited on like grounds, and about the same time sumptuary laws were passed controlling the expenses on these occasions, and limiting the guests that might be invited to persons in the nearest degrees of consanguinity. Dancing and singing were also forbidden, and any persons convicted of these heinous crimes were to perform public penance in their parish church, barefooted and bareheaded, enveloped in a sheet, and holding a lighted torch in their hand.

It is not therefore to be wondered at if many observances and customs, innocent in themselves, came to be forgotten, and this would be more especially the case with such as were connected with the festivals of the Church. Still some few observances and superstitions have survived, and of these we will now endeavour to give the best account we can. We would, however, previously remark that the Guernsey people are an eminently holiday-loving race, and that, notwithstanding their long subjection to Presbyterian rule, and the ascetic spirit of modern dissent, the love of amusement is still strong in them. Christmas Day and the day following, the first two days of the year, the Monday and Tuesday at Easter and Whitsuntide, Midsummer Day and the day after, are all seasons when there is an almost total cessation of work, and all give themselves up to gaiety—and the household must be poor indeed where a cake is not made on these occasions.

But before launching into a description of their ceremonies, festivals, and superstitions, perhaps it might prove of interest if we here attempt to give a slight description of the dress of our island forefathers at different periods, during the last three hundred years, drawn from various sources.

We will begin by an extract from a letter written by Mr. George Métivier, that eminent antiquary, historian, and philologist, to the *Star* of June 20th, 1831 :—

A Guernseyman Three Centuries Ago.

Knows't me not by my clothes ?
No, nor thy tailor."
—*Shakespeare.*

" Suppose we conjure up a Guernseyman in his winter dress—a specimen of the outer man, such as it appeared on high-days and holidays ' sighing like a furnace to its mistress' eye-brow ' in the reign of the most puissant King Henry VIII., and under the long dynasty of the five Westons—(James Guille, the son-in-law of one of them, was then Bailiff). It is probable that the insular gentleman, in the highest sense of that important word, copied the dress of his English and Norman friends, as well as their manner, whether in good or evil.

" Similitude excludes peculiarity : we have therefore nothing to do with Monsieur le Gouverneur, or Monsieur le Baillif, or the most refined in wardrobe matters of his learned assessors. It is certain, however, that the generality of our ancestors—'l'honnête ' and sometimes ' le prudhomme '—derived the materials and cut of their raiment from St. Malo's—whence their very houses were occasionally imported—ready built. We are indebted to a writer of the Elizabethan era for the source of the following portrait.

" *Le cadaù,** the chief article of a Guernseyman's winter costume, exactly resembled, both in name and form, the primitive Irish mantle. Generally composed of wool, or of a kind of shag-rug, bordered with fur, it descended in ample folds till it reached the heels. A surface

---

* A covering or defence. (Celtic.)

of such extraordinary dimensions might have exposed the wearer to some inconvenience in stormy weather: but our fathers, no novices in the art of cloak-wearing, knew how to furl and unfurl this magnificent wrapper, and suit its folds and plaits to all changes of the season. In the first Charles' reign, the Jersey farmers, who still ' bartered the surplusage of their corn with the Spanish merchants at St. Malo's,' were far better acquainted with that long-robed nation than we can now pretend to be. To the *cadaû* was attached a *carapouce**—an enormous hood. If made of serge or good cloth, it was still a *carapouce* ; if the material was coarse—such as friars wore through humility, or mariners and fishermen from motives of economy—the *carapouce* degenerated into a *couaille*. The sea-farer's top-coat affords an instance, not yet quite obsolete, of this island's former partiality for Armorican tailors, dresses, and names—a Tardif and a Dorey will show you their *grigo*. †

" The residence of mind—for our ancestor, this ' fine fleur de Norman,' probably had one—was not forgotten. Muffled up in a voluminous hood, like that of a Spanish *frayle*, it was further protected by the native wig—' la perruque naturelle'—and kept warm by a bonnet, part of the *cadaû* uniform, yclept *la barrette*. The orginal *biread*—a lay mitre, not then peculiar to Ireland—was a conical cap, somewhat resembling the foraging military bonnet. . . . . .

" His Grace, or Holiness—we are a bad hand at title dealing—the Right Reverend Primate of Normandy, having once preached a most godlie and comfortable sermon against long bushy perriwigs, descended from his

---

* *Carabouss bras.* (Breton).

† A wrapper (Celtic). These terms are still used in the country.

pulpit in the Cathedral of Rouen, scissors in hand, then doing merciless execution therewith on King Henry I. and all the princely and noble heads committed to his charge, exhorted them to perpetrate a crime for which that traitor deserved to lose his own.

> ' The people vary too,
> Just as their princes do.'

So sings Nat Wanley, who was no nightingale ; but even when the eighth Harry, and the whole nation, aping him, shore their beautiful locks, in spite of many a fond . wife, what luxuriant male tresses continued to flourish in the Norman Isles ! Our friend of the *Star* may remember the time when the dangling chevelure of our village beaux and ' Soudards de Milice,' though confined with whipcord on working days, was regularly let loose in honour of Sunday and other grand festivals. It is true that burly wife-killing Tudor did interfere. Ah, woe is me ! He requireth from his Normans as well as from his Irish lieges ' conformitie in order and apparel with them that be civill people ' (A.D. 1537). At least, the alteration took place in both places exactly at the same period ; for the censorious terms of this statute were neither applicable nor applied to our ancestors. Indeed, from the size and structure of here and there a yeoman's house, richly overlaid with the golden moss of antiquity, it would seem that the dwellings of our peasantry were very different from the mud-built* and chimneyless cottages of old England. (Such as Jean Lestocq's house in la Vingtaine des Charités, Càtel—the traditional residence of an individual mentioned in a spirited ballad of the year 1371).

---

* At least wattle-built and plastered with mud, if not mud-built altogether. Holinshed exclaims against the *innovation* of chimneys, and regrets that " willow-built houses " are no longer fashionable.

Ruins of an Old Guernsey House, Les Carctiers, St. Sampson's.

" Be this as it may, 'Though the language of such as dwell in these Isles was French, the wearing of their haire long, and their attire was *all after the Irish guise* till the reigne of King Henrie the VIII.' These are the words of Ralph Holinshed, who quotes Leland."

The following description of the dress of the people of Sark in 1673, is taken from a letter in the Harleian MSS. ; it is quoted in full in the "Historical Sketch of the Island of Sark," in the *Guernsey Magazine* for 1874 :—

" Sure I am the genius of the people cannot but be docile, since they are naturally of a courteous affable temper, and the least tainted with pride that ever I saw any of their nation ; that apish variety of fantastic fashions, wherewith Paris is justly accused to infect all Europe, has here no footing, where every one retains the same garb their ancestors wore in the days of Hugh Capet and King Pippin ; so that I can give small encouragement to any of the Knights of the Thimble to transport themselves hither, where cucumbers are like to be more plenty than in the back-side of St. Clement's ; each man religiously preserving his vast blue trunk-breeches, and a coat almost like a Dutch frau's vest, or one of your waterman's liveries. Nor are the women behindhand with them in their hospital-gowns of the same colour, wooden sandals, white stockings and red petticoats, so mean they are scarce worth taking up. Both sexes on festivals wear large ruffs, and the women, instead of hats or hoods, truss up their hair, the more genteel sort in a kind of cabbage net ; those of meaner fortunes in a piece of linen ; perhaps an old dish-clout turned out of service ; or the fag-end of a table-cloth, that had escaped the persecution of washing ever since the Reformation ;

this they, tying on the top, make it shew like a Turkish turban, but that part of it hangs down their backs like a veil."

In Jersey the "fantastic fashions" of Paris seem to have penetrated at an early date, for on the 22nd of September, 1636, a sumptuary law was passed, forbidding anyone, male or female, to put on garments "au-dessus de sa condition;" and also forbidding women to ornament their bonnets with lace costing more than "quinze sols" (a "sol" was worth about a franc) a yard, or to put on silken hoods, the wear of which was reserved for ladies of quality. A short time after this ordinance was passed, a Madame Lemprière, wife of the Seigneur de Rosel, noticed in church, one Sunday, a peasant woman wearing the most magnificent lace in her bonnet. She waited for her after church, tore it off before the whole congregation, covering her with abuse the while; and her friends stood round and applauded her action!

The most picturesque of our island costumes must have been that of the Alderney women in the last century as described by Mrs. Lane-Clarke in her "Guide to Alderney." "A scarlet cloth petticoat and jacket, a large ruff round their necks, fastened under the chin by a black ribbon, or gold hook, and a round linen cap, stiffened so much as to be taken off or put on as a man's hat. On one occasion, when the island was menaced by a French man-of-war, the Governor ordered out all the women in their scarlet dresses, and, disposing them skilfully upon the heights, effectually deceived the enemy with the appearance of his forces."

At about this period the dress of the old Guernsey farmer was "a large cocked hat, and thin 'queue à la francaise,' a long blue coat with brass buttons, flowered waistcoat and jean trousers. Of course this was only for Sundays and festivals. The women wore the black silk plaited Guernsey bonnet, accompanied by a close mob cap underneath, with a narrow muslin border ; plain on the forehead and temples, but plaited from the ears to the chin. A petticoat of black stuff, thickly quilted, the gown—of an old fashion chintz pattern— open in front, and tucked into the pocket holes of the petticoat ; the boddice open in front to the waist, with a coloured or starched muslin handkerchief in lieu of a habit-shirt ; tight sleeves terminating just below the elbow ; blue worsted stockings, with black velvet shoes and buckles."

This description is taken from an old guide book of 1841. The dress was rapidly becoming obsolete then, and has now, like almost every other relic of the past, completely disappeared.

We will now return to the account of our local feasts and festivals.

Beginning with the commencement of the ecclesiastical year—the holy season of Advent—the first day that claims our attention is that dedicated to Saint Thomas, not because of any public observance connected with it, but on account of its being supposed to be a time when the secrets of futurity may be inquired into.

Under the head of " Love Spells " we shall describe the superstitious practices to which, it is said, some young women still resort, in order to ascertain their future destiny.

It is not improbable that some of these observances have been kept alive by the constant communication that has always existed in times of peace between the islands and continental Normandy, not a few young people of both sexes coming over from the mainland to seek for employment as farm servants.

La Longue Veille.

"Meanwhile the village rouses up the fire;
"While well attested, and as well believ'd,
"Heard solemn, goes the goblin story round;
"Till superstitious horror creeps o'er all."
—*Thompson.*

In former days the most lucrative occupation of the
people was that of knitting woollen goods for the English
and French markets. This branch of industry was of
great importance—in fact, after the decay of the fisheries,
which followed the discovery of Newfoundland, it consti-
tuted the staple trade of the island, and the memory of
the manufacture still subsists in the name of "Guernsey
jackets" and "Jerseys," given to the close-fitting knitted
frocks worn by sailors. So highly were the Guernsey
woollen goods esteemed that they were considered a
fitting present for Royalty, and in 1556 Queen Mary[*]
did not disdain to receive from Sir Leonard Chamberlain,
Governor of the Island, four waistcoats, four pair of
sleeves, and four pair of hose of "Garnsey making."[†]
In the accounts of the Royal Scotch wardrobe for the
year 1578, mention is made of woollen hose and gloves
of Garnsey.[‡] In 1586, the keeper of Queen Elizabeth's

---

[*] I am indebted to Mr. Bury Palliser, the accomplished author of "A History of
Lace," for these interesting particulars concerning the ancient staple manufacture of
these islands.

[†] New Year gifts to Queen Mary (Tudor), 1556. Sir Leonard Chamberlain,
"4 waistcoats, 4 paire of slevys, and 4 paire of hoosen of Garnsey making."

[‡] *Scotch Royal Wardrobe*: Three pair of wolwin hois of worsetis of Garnsey.
Six paire of gloves of the same,

wardrobe paid the high price of twenty shillings for one pair of knitted hose " *de facturâ Garnescie.*" It is true that these are described as having the upper part and the clocks of silk. ("Accounts of the Keeper of the Gt. Wardrobe, Elizabeth XXVIII. to XXIX., A.D. 1586 "). And finally the unfortunate Mary Stuart wore at her execution a pair of white Guernsey hose.

The sheep kept in those days in the island were few in quantity, of an inferior breed, described by old writers as having four or more horns, producing coarse scanty wool, far from sufficient to furnish the supply of raw material required to meet the demand of the manufactured article. It was necessary therefore to have recourse to England, but the restrictive laws of that day prohibited the exportation of wool, and it was only by special Acts of Parliament that a certain quantity, strictly limited, was allowed annually to leave the kingdom for the use of the islands. The Governor who could succeed by his representations in getting this quantity increased was sure to win the lasting gratitude of the people.

Men and women of all ages engaged in this manufacture, and time was so strictly economised that the farmer's wife, riding into market with her well stored paniers, knitted as the old horse jogged on through the narrow roads, and the fisherman, after having set his lines, and anchored his boat to wait for the turn of the tide, occupied the leisure hour in fashioning a pair of stockings, or a frock.

In the long winter evenings neighbours were in the habit of meeting at each other's houses in turn, and while the matrons took their places on the " lit de fouaille," and the elderly men occupied the stools set in the deeper recess of the chimney, the young men and maidens gathered together on the floor, and by the dim light of the " crâsset,"* plied their knitting, sang their songs, and told their stories—the songs and tales that appear later on in this collection. Our thrifty ancestors too were well imbued with the wisdom of the old saw that bids one " take care of the pence," and the saving of fuel and oil, which was affected by working in company under the same roof, entered for something in their calculations. These assemblies were called " veilles " or " veillies," and were well adapted to keep up a pleasant neighbourly feeling.

The wares thus made were brought into town for sale on the Saturday, but there was one day in the year when a special market or fair for these goods was held, and that was the day before Christmas. The night previous to that—the 23rd December—was employed in preparing and packing up the articles, and, being the termination of their labours for the year, was made an opportunity for a feast. Masters were in the habit of regaling their servants—merchants treated those with whom they had dealings—and neighbours clubbed together to supply the means of spending a joyous night. It may be that the restraint imposed by the Puritan Clergy—de la Marche, La Place, and others—on all convivial meetings connected in any way with religious observances, caused this occasion for rejoicing—which could not by any possibility be branded with the imputation of superstition—to be more highly appreciated than it would otherwise have been, and to replace in some degree the usual festivities of the season.

EDITOR'S NOTE.—* The Guernsey "crâsset" was very unlike the English "cresset," which was in the form of an iron lantern, filled with inflammable materials. Ours was suspended from a hook or a cord along which it was pulled to the required point, and was rounded at one end and pointed at the other, and filled with oil. It is derived from the Fr. "creuset" from Latin *crux* a cross, because anciently crucibles and all vessels for melting metals were marked with a cross.

Although the manufacture of woollen goods as a staple article of trade has come to an end, and the social " veilles " are no longer kept up, " la longue veille, " or the evening of the 23rd of December, is still observed as an occasion for family gatherings in many Guernsey households, though there is perhaps not one person in twenty who can tell the origin of the custom. Mulled wine, highly spiced and sweetened, and always drunk out of coffee cups, with mild cheese and a peculiar sort of biscuit—called emphatically " Guernsey biscuit"—is considered quite indispensable on this evening, and indeed on all occasions of family rejoicing; while on every afternoon of the 23rd of December the old country people were met riding home from town with their panniers full of provisions for the night. The next day, Christmas Eve, is called the " surveille," and the town on that evening is flocked with pleasure-seekers, buying and eating chestnuts and oranges.

Christmas and New Year.

" Every season
Shall have its suited pastime ; even winter,
In its deep noon, when mountains piled with snow
And choked up valleys from our mansion, bar
All entrance, and nor guest nor traveller
Sounds at our gate ; the empty hall forsaken,
In some warm chamber, by the crackling fire,
We'll hold our little, snug, domestic court,
Plying our work with song and tale between."
—*Joanna Baillie.*

From St. Thomas' Day to New Year's Eve is considered to be a season when the powers of darkness are more than usually active, and it is supposed to be dangerous to be

out after dark.* Men returning home on these nights
have been led astray by the " faeu Bellengier " or Will o'
the wisp, and when they believed themselves to be close to
their own doors have found themselves, they knew not
how, in quite another part of the island.   Others have
been driven almost crazy by finding themselves followed
or preceded by large black dogs, which no threats could
scare away and on which no blows could take effect.
Some find their path beset by white rabbits that go
hopping along just under their feet.

It is generally believed that just at midnight on
Christmas Eve all the cattle kneel and adore the new-
born Saviour. † The considerate farmer will take care
to place an extra quantity of litter in the stall when he
shuts up his beasts for the night, but none would
venture to wait and see the event.   Such prying
curiosity is too dangerous, for it is related how, on one
occasion, a man who professed to disbelieve the fact
remained watching till the witching hour.   What he
saw was never known, for, as he was leaving the stable,
the door slammed violently, and he fell dead on the
threshold.

It is also said that, on the same night, and at
the same hour, all water turns to wine.   A woman,
prompted by curiosity, determined to verify the truth

EDITOR'S NOTES.

* In *Contes Populaires, Préjugés, Patois, Proverbes, etc., de l'arrondissement de Bayeux*,
par M. Pluquet; seconde édition, 1834, it is said : " During the eight days before Christmas
(Les Avents de Noël) apparitions are most frequent, and sorcerers have most power."

† This belief also prevails in Normandy, for M. Du Bois says :—Les paysans sont persuadés
que, la veille de Noël, à l'heure du sacrement de la messe de minuit, tous les bestiaux, et
surtout les bœufs et les vaches, mettent un genou en terre pour rendre hommage à Jésus
naissant. Il serait imprudent, disent-ils, de chercher à s'assurer de ce fait par soi-même ; on
courrait le risque d'être battu."—*Recherches sur la Normandie*, Du Bois, 1843, p. 343. And in
the centre of France and Berry :—"On assure qu'au moment où le prêtre élève l'hostie, pendant
a messe de minuit, tous les animaux de la paroisse s'agenouillent et prient devant leurs
crèches."—*Croyances et Légendes du Centre de la France*, par Laisnel de la Salle. Tome 1er,
p. 17.

of this allegation. Just at midnight, she proceeded to draw a bucket of water from the well, when she heard a voice addressing her in the following words:—

> " Toute l'eau se tourne en vin,
> Et tu es proche de ta fin."

She fell down struck with a mortal disease, and before the end of the year was a corpse.*

Notwithstanding the supernatural terrors of this night, groups of young men and women from all parts of the country flock into town after their day's work is done, and assemble in crowds in the market place, where they regale on oranges and roasted chestnuts. The public-houses profit greatly by their presence; rendered valiant by their potations, and feeling security in numbers, they return home at a late hour, singing in chorus some interminable ditty, which, if goblins have any ear for music, must certainly have the effect of driving them far away.

By those in easy circumstances Christmas Day is now celebrated much as it is in England. The houses are decorated with holly and other evergreens—the same substantial fare loads the hospitable board, presents of meat or geese are sent to poor dependants, and families who are dispersed re-assemble at the same table. It is still customary for the poorer classes among the peasantry,

---

EDITOR'S NOTE.—* In Sark the superstition is that the water in the streams and wells turns into blood at midnight on Christmas Eve, and they also tell you that if you go and look you die within the year. One Sark man said that he was determined to go to the well and draw water at midnight, come what might. So on Christmas Eve he sallied forth to reach the well in his back yard; as he crossed the threshold he tripped and hit his head against the lintel of the door, and was picked up unconscious the next morning. Most people would have taken this as a warning and desisted, but he was obstinate, and the following Christmas Eve he left the house at midnight as before, but as he approached the well he heard a voice saying :—

> " Qui veut voir
> Veut sa mort."

Then at last he was frightened, and rushed back into the house, and never again did he attempt to pry into forbidden mysteries."—From Mrs. Le Messurier, of Sark.

who at any other season of the year would be ashamed to beg, to go about from door to door some days before Christmas, asking for alms under the name of "Noel," in order to be able to add something to their scanty fare; and before grates and sea-coal became so common it was usual to reserve a large log of wood to be burned on the hearth at Christmas. This was called "le tronquet de Noel" and is evidently the same as the Yule log of the North of England.

In the neighbouring island of Alderney, one of the favourite diversions in the merry meetings at this festive season was the assuming of various disguises. Porphyrius, a native of Tyre, and a disciple of Longinus in the year 223 speaks of the "Feast of Mithras, or the Sun, where men were in the habit of disguising themselves as all sorts of animals—lions, lionesses, crows;" and St. Sampson, on his second visit to Jersey, gave gilded medals to the children on condition that they stayed away from these fêtes; so says Mr. Métivier in one of his early letters to the *Gazette.*

On the last night of the year it was customary (and the practice has not altogether fallen into desuetude) for boys to dress up a grotesque figure, which they called "Le vieux bout de l'an," and after parading it through the streets by torch-light with the mock ceremonial of a funeral procession, to end by burying it on the beach, or in some other retired spot, or to make a bonfire and burn it.*

"How often has it been my melancholy duty to attend, sometimes as chief mourner (or mummer), the funeral of old *Bout de l'An!* A log of wood, wrapt

---

EDITOR'S NOTE.—* Hence the country people's term for the effigy of Guy Fawkes on the 5th of November "le vieux bout de l'an,"

up in sable cloth, was his usual representative, when, with great and even classical solemnity, just as the clock struck twelve, the juvenile procession set itself in motion, every member thereof carrying a lantern scooped out of a turnip, or made of oiled paper. . . Ere the law-suit between old and new style was for ever settled, the annual log—Andrew Bonamy is mine authority—underwent the Pagan ceremony of incineration at the Gallet-Heaume."—(Mr. Métivier in the *Star*, March 14th, 1831.)

This is probably one of the superstitious practices against which the ordinance of the Royal Court in 1622 was directed. At the same time, children were wont to go about from house to house to beg for a New Year's gift, under the name of " hirvières " or " oguinane." In so doing they chanted the following rude rhyme :—

> Oguinâni ! Oguinâno !
> Ouvre ta pouque, et pis la recllios.†

---

† " Oguinâni !   Oguinâno !
   Ope thy purse, and shut it then."

There has been much discussion as to the derivation of " oguinâne," from which the Scottish " hogmanay " also comes. Mr. Métivier, in his dictionary, says that it means the annual present of a master to his servants, of a seigneur to his vassals, of a father to his children, and derives it from " *agenhine feoh* " or " *hogenehyne fee* " the present made, or money given, to those who belong to you—a word composed of " agen " one's own—as the English *own*, and " hind " servant, one of the family. And he laughs at the theory propounded by various French and English folklorists that it is derived from the rites of the Druids, and comes from their ancient cry " Au guy l'an neuf "—" the mistletoe (gui) of the New Year "—New Year's Day being the day the pagans went into the forests to seek the mistletoe on the oaks. (See *Notes and Queries*, Series III. Vol. IV. p. 486.) In the *Star* of March 14th, 1831, Mr. Métivier tells us that "as late as the reign of Louis XIV. it was usual for the populace round Morlaix to chant a variety of bacchanalian songs on the last eve of the year, and the chorus or *refrain* of every stanza was precisely what I should never have fancied it to be—our
' Oghin an eit !   Oghin an eit ! '
I am informed by a worthy monk that the good news announced by these mystical words had nothing to do with the religion of Christ, and that, being interpreted, they only tell us that ' the wheat is upspringing - le bled germe.' *Eit* and *od* originally

In Scotland *Hogmanay* is the universal popular name for the last day of the year. " It is a day of high festival among young and old—but particularly the young.* * * It is still customary, in retired and primitive towns, for the children of the poorer class of people to get themselves on that morning swaddled in a great sheet, doubled up in front, so as to form a vast pocket, and then to go along the streets in little bands, calling at the doors of the wealthier classes for an expected dole of wheaten bread. This is called their Hogmanay."*

The first day of the year is with all classes in Guernsey the one most strictly observed as a holiday, and, in all but the religious observance, is more thought of than even Christmas Day. Presents are given to friends, servants and children ; the heads of families gather around them those who have left the paternal roof ; more distant relatives exchange visits ; young people call at the houses

---

implied not wheat only, but every sort of grain and seed. Thus it appears that what at first sight defied all rational conjecture - the ' oguinani, oguinâno,' cry of our small gentry, once formed the immemorial chorus of an Armorican hymn - the pure heathen liturgical relic of some Gaulish festival. The primitive ditty was full of allusions to the increase of light, the revival of vegetable nature, and other seasonable topics. The noisy little heralds of this pleasing intelligence received for their reward an ' oguinâne,' or, as it is now called, ' leurs hirvières ' - an *hibernum donum* or *winter* gift. It is true that a few half-learned lexicographers talk of the mistletoe and 'Au Guy l'An Neuf ;' but the French savans were systematic haters of France's aboriginal languages, and the minor Latin poet who invented this nonsensical interpretation of a word whose etymon he was too lazy to dig for in its native mine has hardly been dead two centuries."

EDITOR'S NOTE.—* The old people of St. Martin's parish still (1866) talk of having in their youth gone to the neighbours' houses on New Year's Eve singing the following rhyme :—

" *Bon jour, Monsieur! Bon jour, Madame!*
Je n'vous ai pas vu acvoûre (encore) *chul* (cette) *an.*
Et je vous souhaite une boudne année,
Et mes irvières s'i'vous plliet."

And a little bowl or bag of pennies was always at hand for gratuities.

of their aged kinsfolk to wish them many happy returns
of the season, and, in many cases, to receive the gifts
that are awaiting them ; and receptions—now become
almost official in their character—are held by the
Lieutenant-Governor, the Bailiff, and the Dean. Cake
and wine are offered to visitors, and the day ends in most
households with a feast in proportion with their means
and rank in society. All the morning the roads and
streets are crowded with groups of persons hurrying from
house to house, hands are warmly shaken, kind words
are spoken, many a little coolness or misunderstanding
is forgotten, and even breaches of long standing are
healed, when neighbours join in eating the many cakes
for which Guernsey is famous, and which are considered
suitable for the occasion. The favourite undoubtedly is
"gâche à corinthes," anglicé "currant cake," also a
kind of soft bread-cake, known by the name of "galette;"
and on Christmas Day a sort of milk-cake, called "gâche
détrempée" is baked early in the morning, so as to appear
hot at the breakfast table ; and so completely is this
repast looked upon in the light of a family feast, that
parents living in the country send presents of these cakes
to their children who have taken service in town. A
younger brother will leave the paternal roof long before
daybreak to carry to his sister, at her master's house, the
cake which the affectionate mother has risen in the
middle of the night to bake for her absent child.

La Grand' Querrue.

" And at the farm on the lochside of Rannock, in parlour and kitchen,
Hark! there is music—yea, flowing of music, of milk, and of whiskey;
Dancing and drinking, the young and the old, the spectators and actors,
Never not actors the young, and the old not always spectators:
Lo, I see piping and dancing!"

—" *The Bothie of Tober-na-Vuolick,*" *by A. H. Clough.*

The parsnip seems to have been cultivated at a very early period in Guernsey, the soil appearing to be particularly well suited to the growth of this valuable root. We have proof that tithe of them was paid in times long anterior to the Reformation, although not claimed in the present day. In order to secure a good crop, it is necessary that the ground should be deeply trenched, and this operation, which takes place at the beginning of the year, and entails a great amount of labour, is, nevertheless, looked forward to with pleasure, as it gives rise to social meetings. The trenching of the soil was formerly, and is still occasionally, effected by the spade alone. This was done by farm labourers and hired men with a peculiar spade called " Une bêque de Guernesi." Made by the country blacksmiths of the island, the handle was of wood, generally ash, and so was the upper portion of the blade, which was heart-shaped, the tip of the blade being of steel. It was a very slow operation, four perches a day being the utmost one man could accomplish, so that it had to begin very early in the year, " whilst eating the bread baked at Christmas," as the old farmers said. But about a hundred years ago the " grand' querrue " or big plough was introduced at Les Fontaines, in the Castel parish, the house of the Lenfesteys. This is preceded by one of

Le Grand' Querrue.

the ordinary size to trace the furrow. The large plough, being an expensive instrument and one that is only wanted occasionally, is often the joint property of several neighbours, who unite together to assist each other in working it. Each brings his quota of labourers, and as many as twenty-two animals have been sometimes seen harnessed to the same plough, to wit, six bullocks and sixteen horses. Every man who is fortunate enough to be the possessor of a beast deems himself bound in honour to produce it on these occasions. The plough is generally guided by the owner of the field, and a furrow is made about twelve inches deep by about eighteen to twenty-four inches wide. As the labour is social, all work with good will and emulation, and the scene is one of great animation. Of course the assistance given is gratuitous, or, to speak more correctly, is to be returned in kind when required. The farmer, however, who avails himself of the labour of his neighbours, is expected to feed them. The consequence is that the " grand' querrue " is made the occasion of a rural feast. The cider, for which the island is famous, circulates freely throughout the day, and the prettiest girls are selected as cup-bearers. Work begins about seven o'clock in the morning; about ten o'clock a sort of luncheon called " mi-matin " is provided; this consists of bread and butter, with cheese, fried cod fish, and strong tea or coffee. At noon the cattle are unharnessed and put to feed, and then comes the dinner of cabbage-soup, a large boiled ham or " pâlette," a breast-piece of pork, and perhaps a round of beef. At two o'clock work is resumed, with a stoppage at four for a " mi-relevée " of tea and currant cake, and occasional intervals for " une petite goutte; " for it is well known that " i'faut prendre une petite goutte pour arrousaï, ou bien j'n'airons pâs d'pànais,"—"one must take a sip to moisten the field, or there will be no parsnips." The day closes with a substantial supper, more beef, more ham, enormous plum-puddings, baked, not boiled, in the old ovens, ("grosses houichepotes") with plenty of cider.

To this feast it is customary to invite the members of the respective families who have not taken part in the labours of the day, and the richer farmers send presents of pudding to their poorer neighbours who are not invited to share in the work. Friends and relations who reside at a distance, or in town, also join the gathering, and the best part of the night is spent in singing, dancing, story-telling, blind man's buff, or the ancient roundelay of "mon beau laurier."*

Shrove Tuesday.

Shrove Tuesday is observed in the usual way, by a general frying and eating of pancakes, and the custom must be old, and one of the superstitious practices which the zeal of the Presbyterian clergy failed in eradicating; for, had it been re-introduced from England, it is not likely that it would have become so universal, or have taken so strong a hold on the minds of the people.

EDITOR'S NOTE.—* One curious custom at the supper or "défrique" was that the men had their meal first, and not till they had finished did the women sit down to have theirs.

The First Sunday in Lent.

In the neighbouring island of Alderney, the first Sunday in Lent is known as " Le Dimanche des Brandons "—a name by which it is designated in old calendars, and which it still bears in some parts of France.* According to the late Mr. John Ozanne (de la Salerie), a native of Alderney, it was also known as " le jour des vitres," this last word having, as he said, in the dialect of Alderney, the meaning of *masks*. This gives rise to the supposition that in days gone by masking formed part of the entertainment. On this day the young people made bonfires and danced round them, especially at " La Pointe de Clanque." This dance was supposed to have had a bacchanalian origin, but was practised up to fifty years ago ; they revolved round these bonfires, and leapt over them, and then, lighting wisps of straw, returned to the town by the fields, throwing about these torches, to the great danger of the thatched roofs.

EDITOR'S NOTES.

* That these customs were also kept up in Guernsey is evident from the following extract from the manuscript note book of Monsieur Elie Brevint, who died in the island of Sark in 1674, aged 87. He says : —" Le premier Dimanche de Caresme s'appelle le jour des Brandons ; à St. Martin de Guernezé les jeunes hommes par esbat portent au soir du dit jour brandons de glie, etc.

In *Les Archives de Normandie*, 1824, p. 164, there is the following notice of " Le Jour des Brandons," which shows that this custom also prevailed in various parts of France. "À Saint Vaast et à Reville, la veille de l'Epiphanie, des centaines d'enfants et même d'hommes, parcourrent les campagnes munis de brandons allumés. Ils crient, ' Taupes et mulots, sortez de mon clos, ou je vous mets le feu sur le dos.' Ou dans quelques autres parties de la Normandie on chante ces vers-ci :

Bon jour les rois
Jusqu'a douze mois
Douz' mois passés
Rois, revenez !
Charge, pommier !
A chaq' petite branchette
Tout plein ma grand' pochette,
Taupes, mulots,
Sortez du clos,
Ou j' vous brul'rai la barbe et l's os !

Good Friday.

On the morning of Good Friday it is the custom
of the young people who live near the sea shore to
make parties to go down to the beach to collect limpets.
When a sufficient quantity of these shell fish has been
taken, a flat stone or rock of sufficient size is selected,
and, after being carefully swept and divested of all
extraneous matter, the limpets are arranged on it
with their shells uppermost. A head of dry furze or
other brushwood is then placed over them and set
on fire, and the limpets are left covered with the
hot embers until they are supposed to be sufficiently
cooked. Bread-cakes, fresh baked—if hot from the
oven so much the better—with an ample supply of
the rich butter for which the island is so famous,
and a few bottles of cider or beer, have been provided
beforehand by the members composing the pic-nic,
and the limpets, now done to a turn, are eaten as a
relish to the simple meal, with a better appetite, and

Le lendemain au soir on allume un nouveau feu qu'on appèle une Bourgulée, et l'on renouvelle
le même chant, qui commence encore par 'Adieu les Rois,' etc. Dans la Commune de Créance,
une grande partie de la population passe presque toute la nuit du premier Dimanche de Carême
à faire la même sommation aux taupes et aux mulots. . . . . Le Dimanche des Brandons
est une date commune et naturelle des actes du moyen age."

The "Dimanche des Brandons" was also kept up in the centre of France with very much the
same ceremonies. See *Croyances et Légendes du centre de la France*, Laisnel de la Salle.
Tome 1er. Page 35.

"At Dijon, in Burgundy, it is the custom upon the first Sunday in Lent to make large fires
in the streets, whence it is called "Firebrand Sunday." This practice originated in the
processions formerly made on that day by the peasants with lighted torches of straw, to drive
away, as they called it, the bad air from the earth."—From *Nori Bourguinons, p.* 148. Quoted
in Brand's *Observations on Popular Antiquities, p.* 57.

more real pleasure than probably a far more elaborate feast would afford.*

Hot cross buns on Good Friday were unknown in Guernsey at the commencement of the present century.

————

Easter.

There do not appear to be any particular customs connected with Easter, but some old people can still remember that in their youth the children in some parts of the country used to go about from door to door begging for eggs.† This was called " demander la mouissole," and was evidently derived from the practice, so common in all parts of Europe, of giving presents of eggs at this season. *Mouissole* is derived from the old Norman word *mouisson*, which means " a bird."

EDITOR'S NOTES.

* " In Sark, on Good Friday it is the custom for boys to go and sail small boats on the ponds or pools by the sea-shore; and these boats are made a good while beforehand, or treasured up of long standing; this custom they never fail to keep up. Numbers of these same boys also go in the afternoon to the Eperqueric drill-ground, to play a game which they call rounders. It is played with a ball and a stick, and somewhat resembles cricket."— From *A Descriptive Sketch of the Island of Sark*, by the Rev. J. L. V. Cachemaille (for many years Vicar of the island), published in Clarke's *Guernsey Magazine*, October, 1875.

† In the country the dinner on Easter Sunday used always to consist of fried eggs and bacon. As an old woman said, " it was the only day we ever tasted an egg." If they could not get fowls' eggs, they even got wild birds' eggs, and fried and ate them !

" In the North of England boys beg on Easter Eve eggs to play with, and beggars ask for them to eat."—*De Ludis Orientalibus*, by Hyde, 1694. p. 237.

" The custom of eating a gammon of bacon at Easter, which is kept up in many parts of England, was founded on this, viz., to shew their abhorrence to Judaism at that solemn commemoration of our Lord's Resurrection."—From *Aubrey*, 1679.

The First of April.

The first of April is not forgotten by children, who amuse themselves on this day by attaching long shreds of paper or bits of rag by means of crooked pins to the clothes of passers-by,* and then crying out as loud as they can bawl, "La Coûe! La Coûe!" or "La Folle Agnès." No one knows the reason of the latter exclamation.

Sundays in May.

On the first Sunday in May the young men and women of the lower orders arise at daybreak and sally forth into the country in groups, returning home with large nosegays generally pilfered from the open gardens that adorn the neat cottages of the peasantry.†

There is reason to believe that this custom was

EDITOR'S NOTES.

* In *Lancashire Folk-Lore* p. 225, it says, "On Mid-Lent or 'Bragot' Sunday it is a custom for boys to hook a piece of coloured cloth to the women's gowns, and a similar custom prevails in Portugal at carnival times."

† "Bourne ('*Antiquit. Vulg.*' chap. xxv.) tells us that in his time, in the villages in the North of England, the juvenile part of both sexes were wont to rise a little after midnight on the first of May, and walk to some neighbouring wood, accompanied with music and the blowing of horns, where they broke down branches from the trees and adorned them with nosegays and crowns of flowers. This done, they returned homewards with their booty about the time of sunrise, and made their doors and windows triumph in the flowery spoil." (Quoted in *Brand's Popular Antiquities*, p. 121).

introduced from England, but in Alderney it appears
to have been a very ancient practice to keep the
first of May as a holiday. Garlands of flowers were
suspended across the street, under which the young
people danced, and the day was generally wound-up
by a sort of pic-nic supper or tea-drinking, to which
each family contributed its quota. The introduction
of late years of a large stranger population into that
island, in consequence of the extensive fortifications
and harbour works undertaken by Government, has
completely changed the primitive character of the
place, and has put an end to this picturesque
custom.

Whitsuntide.

"And let us do it with no show of fear;
No, with no more than if we heard that England
Were busied with a Whitsun morris-dance."
—*Shakspeare.*

Whit Monday, Midsummer Day, and the day on
which Her Majesty's birth is celebrated, are all kept
as holidays, and have long been appropriated to the
mustering and exercising of the Militia.

This institution differs in many respects from what
goes by the same name in England, and is more in
the nature of the "Garde Nationale" of France. It
is of great antiquity, for we find among the Patent
Rolls of Edward III., one dated May, 1337,
appointing Thomas de Ferrers Governor of the Islands,
and giving him directions to enrol all the able-bodied
inhabitants, to supply them with fitting arms, and to

place proper officers over them, in order that they might be able to resist the invasions of the allies of the Scotch, with whom England was then at war, and who had recently made some descents on Sark, and on the coasts of the larger islands. The service is gratuitous and compulsory, for, by the common law, all male inhabitants, from the ages of sixteen to sixty, are liable to be called out, unless prevented by illness, or able to claim exemption on some other legal ground. Nevertheless, with the generality of the people, especially with those of the rural parishes, the service is decidedly popular. An afternoon of ball-practice, or a general review by the Lieutenant-Governor, is looked forward to with pleasure, and the latter occasion is one which affords a treat to all classes of the community. At an early hour the roads are crowded with merry groups, dressed in their best, hastening to the spot where the review is to take place. The country damsels are proud of seeing their lovers set off by their military attire, and when the men are dismissed it is amusing to see the careful wife or the attentive sweetheart produce from the depth of her pocket, or from a hand-basket, a light cap, or wide-awake, to replace the heavy shako, while the young sons and brothers, not yet old enough to be enrolled, dispute who shall have the honour of bearing the weighty musket. The review is generally over by noon, and those who are industrious may return to their work. Most of the men, however, particularly the unmarried ones, prefer making a thorough holiday of it, and for the rest of the afternoon the streets of the town are filled with groups of merry-makers ; the public houses ply a brisk trade, and the evening is often far advanced before the joyous groups think of returning to their own homes.

D

Midsummer.

"At eve last Midsummer no sleep I sought."—*Gay's Pastorals.*

The custom of making bonfires on the hilltops at Midsummer was formerly so general among all the Celtic nations that it is highly probable that it must have existed also in these islands, the aboriginal inhabitants of which belonged undoubtedly to the Celtic race. In Scotland and in Ireland these fires are called Beltein, or Baltein; they are lighted also on May Day, and are supposed to be a relic of the worship formerly paid to the sun, under the name of Bel, or Baal. Throughout Brittany, and in some of the neighbouring parts of Normandy, "les feux de la St. Jean" are still lighted on all the hills. In some parts of Wales and Cornwall the custom is still kept up. That some observances connected with this season still existed in this island in the early part of the 17th Century is certain, from the fact of the Royal Court having promulgated an ordinance in 1622 prohibiting begging on St. John's Eve, "as tending to keep alive superstition," but what these observances were, is now entirely forgotten. It has been asserted that in days gone by "la Rocque Balan," a remarkable and picturesque mass of granite on the plain of L'Ancresse, used to be resorted to at Midsummer, and that the youths and maidens danced together on its summit, where bonfires used to be lit. The burden of an old song—

"J'irons tous à la Saint Jean
"Dansaïr sus la Rocque Balan,"

is quoted as confirmatory of this assertion. Some suppose

that "Balan" has the same derivation as "Beltein;" others say that there was once a logan, or rocking stone, "une pierre qui balançait," on the apex of the rock; but there is also a tradition that the former Priors of St. Michel du Valle caused the merchandise of their tenants and vassals to be weighed, and that the rock derived its appellation from the "balances" used for this purpose.

The most probable and matter of fact solution of the difficulty is that, like many other localities, it took its designation from the person to whom it once belonged, the name "Balan" being that of a family, now extinct, which at one time inhabited this parish.

Every cottage and farmhouse in the island is furnished with what is called a "lit de fouâille" or "jonquière" —now called the "green bed"—a sort of rustic divan generally placed in a recess between the hearth and a window. This, raised about eighteen inches from the ground, is thickly strewn with dried fern, or pea-haulm, and forms the usual seat of the females of the family, when engaged in knitting or sewing, and a very comfortable couch on which the men can repose after the labours of the day. But at Midsummer, after the fresh fern has been cut, the taverns and cottages vie with each other in decorating these seats. A canopy is raised over them, and the whole, floor and all, is thickly carpeted with fresh cut fern, and ornamented with the most brilliant and showy flowers that can be procured, not scattered at hap-hazard, but arranged in formal, and often far from inelegant patterns.* The love

---

EDITOR's NOTE.—* An old country woman described to me a "Lit de Fouaille" she had seen as a child. She described it as being a four-post bed, both mattress and ceiling being one mass of flowers most ingeniously twined together. Each post was garlanded with flowers, and flower curtains hung from the top, woven together, she could not tell how. In the middle sat the girl—silent,

of flowers is almost a passion with every class of the inhabitants, and displays itself in the variety to be found at all seasons in every garden, and the taste with which they are employed in decorations.

It is difficult to say what gave rise to this custom of adorning the "jonquière," but it is doubtless one of great antiquity.* Old people say that in former days it was customary to elect a girl from among the inhabitants of the district, and seat her in state beneath the floral canopy, where under the name† of "La Môme" she received in silence the homage of the assembled guests.‡

---

* See *Folk-Lore Journal*, Vol. I, Pp. 297 and 301.

† Mr. Métivier writes under the heading of "Lit de Fouaille."—"Que de gens instruits, peu versés dans l'étude de notre Calendrier Champêtre, se sont imaginés que le lit de feuilles et de fleurs du solstice d'été—fête aussi ancienne que l'homme lui-même, n'était qu'un lit vert—une jonquière ! L'apothéose de la beauté sur un trone de roses et de lys se retrouvait autrefois dans tous les climats, où le soleil favorisait la culture de ces trésors de Flore. Presque de nos jours, chaque canton de l'île élisait une tante ou cousine. Vouée au silence —'La Môme ;' et cette bonne parente recevait de toute la compagnie l'hommage d'un baiser - c'est une allusion au silence de l'astre du jour et à la naissance d'Harpocrate, le doigt sur la bouche, au milieu d'un carreau de vives fleurs."

EDITOR'S NOTES.

‡ By the courtesy of Mr. J. Linwood Pitts I am able to insert the following note, showing the gradual decadence of the old custom.

"Some sixty or seventy years ago, a Mr. and Mrs. Le Maitre kept a public-house at Le Cognon, near St. Sampson's. At the summer vraicking time, they used to deck the green bed with elaborate floral decorations—a veritable "Lleit de feuilles." A plate was placed in the centre of the bed to receive contributions. The young people used to go there and dance in the evenings after vraicking. Mr. Le Maitre playing the fiddle for the dancers. Mrs. Robin (now seventy-three years old) danced there as a girl."

Stow in his "Survey" tells us "that on the vigil of St. John Baptist every man's door being shadowed with green birch, long fennel, St. John's wort, orpin, white lilies, and such like, garnished upon with garlands of beautiful flowers, had also lamps of glass. . . . "

In "Brand's Popular Antiquities of Great Britain, Vol. I. p. 190, it is said :—"Hutchinson mentions another custom used on this day ; it is "to dress out stools with a cushion of flowers. A layer of clay is placed on the stool, and therein is stuck with great regularity, an arrangement of all kinds of flowers, so close as to form a beautiful cushion. These are exhibited at the doors of houses in the villages, and at the ends of streets and cross lanes of larger towns, where the attendants beg money from passengers to enable them to have an evening feast and dancing." He adds "This custom is evidently derived from the Ludi Compitalii of the Romans; this appellation is taken from the Compita or Cross Lanes, where they were instituted and celebrated by the multitude assembled before the building of Rome. It was the Feast of Lares, or Household Gods, who presided as well over houses as streets. This mode of adorning the seat or couch of the Lares was beautiful, and the idea of reposing them on aromatic flowers, and beds of roses, was excellent."

Perhaps the whole is a remnant of the old May games transferred to this season—perhaps it is an observance connected with the ceremonies with which in many countries, and especially among the Celtic nations, the sun was greeted on his arrival at the summer solstice, and in which branches of trees and bunches of flowers were used to decorate the houses.

———

Midsummer Day in Sark.

In Sark, Midsummer Day is the great holiday of the year, when every youth who is fortunate enough to be the possessor of a horse, or who can borrow one for the occasion, makes use of it. Bedecking both himself and his steed with bunches of flowers, he goes to seek his favourite damsel, who generally sports a new bonnet in honour of the festival, and they often ride about in couples on the horses' backs. They then amuse themselves in racing up and down the roads, and even venture sometimes to cross at a gallop the dangerous pass of the Coupée—a narrow ledge of rock with a precipice on either side,—which connects the peninsula of Little Sark with the main island. In the evening they assemble to drink tea, eat currant cake, and dance. This custom is known by the name of " Les Chevauchées."

EDITOR'S NOTE.—Many charms and spells were also resorted to on the eve and on the day of " La Saint Jean," which will be inserted under their proper heading. Another habit of the young men and girls on Midsummer Day was to go out to the Grand Pont at St. Sampson's, and there have a supper composed of fried ham and eggs and pancakes, and craûbackaûs or crayfish, the latter placed on the table in the pan, and everyone helping themselves with their own fork. The custom was for the girls to be dressed entirely in white, while the men wore white duck or jean trousers, swallow-tailed coats, fancy waistcoats, and shoes adorned with large white bows. The proceedings finished with songs and dances.

Midsummer Day in Jersey.

In Jersey, the fishermen who inhabit the parish of St. John have a custom of circumnavigating at Midsummer a certain rock, called " Le Cheval Guillaume," that lies off their coast, and in the same parish, as well as in some other parts of the island, a very singular practice has long prevailed. It is thus described in Plees' Account of the Island of Jersey. " At Midsummer Eve, a number of persons meet together, and procure a large brass boiler; this is partly filled with water, and sometimes metallic utensils of different kinds are thrown in. The rim is then encircled with a strong species of rush, to which strings of the same substance are attached. When these strings are sufficiently moistened, the persons assembled take hold of them, and, drawing them quickly through their hands, a tremendous vibration is excited in the boiler, and a most barbarous, uncouth, and melancholy sound produced. To render this grating concert still more dissonant, others blow with cows' horns and conches. This singular species of amusement continues for several hours : it is termed ' faire braire les poëles.' " The same custom prevailed in Normandy, from whence it doubtless made its way into Jersey. In the former province it is now on the decline. Being observed on St. John's Eve, it would appear to have a reference to some Christian festival in honour of that saint ; or it may relate to Midsummer Day. Large numbers of the middling and lower classes in Jersey are in the habit of coming to Guernsey for the Midsummer holidays, and the natives of the latter island often choose this season for visiting their friends and relations in Jersey. In the *Athenæum*, September 20th, 1890, it says : "It may not be generally known that in the island of Jersey on St. John's Eve the older inhabitants used to light fires under large iron pots full of water, in which they placed silver articles—as spoons, mugs, etc.,—and then knocked the silver against the iron, with the idea of scaring away all evil spirits. There are now railroads in Jersey, and these old-world practices have probably disappeared."

The day after Midsummer used always to be the day of the fair, held in the Fair-field at the Câtel. It was crowded from the early morning by the entire population of the island, and the hedges round the field, and even the sides of the roads in the vicinity, were filled with French women, selling strawberries, and eggs dyed red with cochineal, and who drove a roaring trade.

August.

On the Sundays in August it was customary, a few years ago, for large crowds from all parts of the island to assemble in the afternoon on the causeway at St. Sampson's called "Le Grand Pont." The favourite mode of proceeding thither was on horseback, but the only object that the visitors seemed to have in view was that of seeing and being seen. It is difficult to ascertain exactly what gave rise to this custom, or indeed whether it is of ancient date. It is certain, however, that the improvement of the roads at the commencement of the present century, and the works carried on at the same time for the recovery of a large portion of land from the sea, in this neighbourhood, concurred in attracting a considerable number of persons to the spot. If the custom existed previously it must have been one of old standing, and may perhaps be traced to a church wake or feast held in honour of St. Sampson, who is said to have been among the first who preached the gospel in the island, and whose name the neighbouring church bears. The calendar commemorates this saint on the 28th of July, and the practice of meeting together on the Sunday following the anniversary of a saint, in the vicinity of the church or chapel dedicated to him, is universal throughout Brittany, where these assemblies are known by the name of "pardons." In some parts of Normandy, too, the custom is observed, and the meetings are known as "Assemblées." If not held on, or near, the actual anniversary of the saint, they are often fixed for some Sunday in August, when, the harvest being over, the peasants have more leisure time for amusements.*

September.

On the Sundays in September it was the custom, at any rate in the early part of this century, to ride out to the "Maison du Neuf Chemin," at St. Saviour's,

---

* EDITOR'S NOTE. "In the southern parts of this nation," says Bourne, "most country villages are wont to observe some Sunday in a more particular manner than the rest, *i.e.*, the Sunday after the day of dedication, or day of the saint to whom their church was dedicated." *Antiq. Vulg.*, chap. xxx.

Maison du Neuf Chemin.

which was kept by a man called Alexandre. There they would eat pancakes, apples and pears, and not come home till dusk. This is the "Mess Alissandre" to whom Métivier alludes in "La Chanson des Alexandriens," "Rimes Guernesiaises," 1831, p. 52.

> " *Vouloüs passair dans l'pu bel endret d'l'île*
> " *Une a' r'levaie sans paine et sans chagrin !*
> " *Tournai mé l'dos ès sales pavais d'la ville,*
> " *Et galoppai sie l'vieil houme du Neuf-Ch'min,* etc.

[TRANSLATION].

" Do you wish to go to the most beautiful neighbourhood of the island
One afternoon without difficulty or trouble?
Turn your back on the dirty pavements of the town,
And gallop out to the old man of the New Path."

CHAPTER II.

Local Customs — Civic, Aquatic, Ceremonial.

" Ordain them laws, part such as appertain
To civil justice, part religious rites."
—*Milton.*

La Chevauchée de St. Michel.

" My parks, my walks, my manors that I had,
Ev'n now forsake me ; and of all my lands
Is nothing left me."
—*Shakspeare*, Henry VI.

BEFORE giving an account of this curious old custom, now abolished, but which seems to have been instituted originally with a view to keeping the highways throughout the island in a due state of repair, it may be as well to say something of the feudal system, as it existed, and indeed, greatly modified of course, still exists in Guernsey. Though, from the loss in the course of many centuries of the original charters, we are left in the dark on many points, and can only guess at the origin of some of the many small manors—or as they are locally termed, "fiefs"—into which the island is divided.

It is known that previous to the Conquest of England by Duke William,[*] Néel de St. Sauveur, Vicomte of Le Cotentin, was patron of six of the ten parish churches in Guernsey—those of St. Samson, St. Pierre Port, St. Martin de la Bellouse, La Trinité de la Forêt, Notre Dame de Torteval, and St. André; and it is probable that he was lord paramount of all the land contained in these parishes. He was one of those barons who conspired against William, and having been defeated by him in the Battle of Val des Dunes, all his possessions were confiscated. On his submission he was again received into favour, and his continental possessions restored, but such does not seem to have been the case with what he held in Guernsey; for the patronage of the churches mentioned above was given by William, a year before the Conquest of England, to the great Abbey of Marmoutier near Tours; and from that time we hear nothing more of the Viscounts of St. Sauveur in Guernsey.

The other four parishes, St. Michel du Valle, Notre Dame du Castel, St. Sauveur, and St. Pierre du Bois, were in the patronage of the Abbey of Mont St. Michel, and the lands in the greater part of these parishes were held in nearly equal proportions between that famous Monastery and the Earls of Chester—those held by the Abbey being known as " Le Fief St. Michel," and those belonging to the Earl being called " Le Fief le Comte." A local tradition says that it was Duke Robert, the father of William the Conqueror,

---

[*] " There were two Nigels (Neel or Niel), Viscounts of Cotentin, and proprietors of St. Sauveur le Vicomte. I have reference to those two charters, the perusal of which exalts conjectures into genuine *facts* It is highly gratifying to possess, at last, extracts from the authentic charters of Robert I. and William II. granted to St. Michel and St. Martin of Tours."- Extract from MS. letter from George Métivier to Sir Edgar MacCulloch, Nov. 1846.

who first bestowed these lands on the Abbey, and on the ancestors of the Earls, but of this there may be some doubt.

These lands were held direct from the Sovereign, to whom these lords were bound to do homage, but in process of time they came to be sub-fieffed by their possessors—that is, divided into smaller manors, which, instead of owing direct allegiance to the Crown, depended on their own lords, to whom they had certain services to render, and dues to pay, and in whose Courts they were bound to make an appearance thrice in the year. These Courts had jurisdiction in civil matters, in causes arising between the tenants on their respective fiefs, and had their seals, by which all written documents emanating from them were authenticated, the seals of the Court of the Priory of St. Michel representing the Archangel trampling Satan under foot, and that of the Fief le Comte, St. George, near whose ruined chapel the Court still holds its sittings. As there was always an appeal from the decision of these Courts to the supreme tribunal of the island, the Royal Court, they gradually ceased to be held, except for the purpose of collecting the seignorial dues, and, by an Order of Her Majesty in Council, the Court of the Fief St. Michel was abolished, the life interest of the seneschal, vavassors, prevôts, bordiers, and other officers of the Court being preserved.

One of the duties of the Court of St. Michel was to see that the King's highway (le chemin du Roi), and certain embankments against the encroachments of the sea were kept in proper order and in due reparation; and in order to insure this they were bound to make an inspection once in three years.

We will now go back and consider the origin of the Fief St. Michel. Among the many fiefs in Guernsey, held in chief from the Crown, one of the most ancient and important is certainly that of St. Michel-du-Valle, extending over the greater part of the northern and western shores of the island. According to a tradition generally accepted by the historians of the island, and which is in part corroborated by documentary evidence, preserved in the "cartulaires" of the famous Abbey of Mont St. Michel in Normandy, and in the Record Office in England, certain monks who had been expelled from that monastery for their irregularities, or had left voluntarily in consequence of reforms in the community which they disapproved of, came .over to Guernsey about the year 966 and established themselves in a part of the island called Le Clos du Valle, which at that period, and until the beginning of the present century, was cut off from the mainland by an arm of the sea, and could only be reached by a way across the sands when the tide had receded. The monks are said to have brought the whole of the western part of the island into cultivation, and to have led such a pious life, and effected such a reform in the manners of the inhabitants, that Guernsey acquired the appellation of "l'ile sainte." * †

---

* According to Mr. Métivier Guernsey was called " Holy Island " in the days of a learned Greek called " Sylla," the friend of Plutarch's grandfather, and he says " that it was the custom for persons to go from the " ogygiau " (Gallic or Breton) Islands, to Delos every century, which means every thirty years. The voyagers also visited the temple of Dodona ; and on their return from Delos " the sacred navigators were conducted by the winds to the Isle of Saturn or Sacred Island (Guernsey), which was peopled entirely by themselves and their predecessors ; for although they were by their laws permitted to return after having served Saturn thirty years, which was the century of the Druids, yet they frequently

---

EDITOR'S NOTE.—† M. de Gerville denies the truth of this tradition. See *Documents Inédits du Moyen Age, relatifs aux Iles du Cotentin*, p. 16,

It is also said that Robert I., Duke of Normandy, father of William the Conqueror, called by some Le Magnifique and by others Le Diable, having been driven by stress of weather to take refuge in Guernsey, when on his way to England with a fleet to assist the Saxon Princes Alfred and Edward in their resistance to the Danish invader Canute, was received and hospitably entertained by the monks, and in return confirmed them in the possession of the lands they had been the means of reclaiming, at the same time constituting the community a priory in dependance on the great monastery from which they had originally come ; a connexion, which although frequently interrupted during the long wars between England and France for the possession of Normandy, existed until the suppression of alien priories in England by Henry V.

Like all other fiefs the priory had its own Feudal Court, by means of which it collected its rents and dues, and which had jurisdiction in civil matters between all its tenants, subject, however, to an

---

preferred remaining in the tranquil retirement of this island to returning to their birth-places." Demetrius, also, says : "Among the islands which lie adjacent to Britain, some are desert, known by the name of the Isles of Heroes. . . . I embarked in the suite of the Emperor, who was about to visit the nearest of them. We found thereon but few inhabitants, and these were accounted *sacred and inviolable.*" Mr. Métivier goes on to say later " Ono Maeritus, an author who flourished five hundred years B.C., in one of his poems speaks of a vessel that conveyed the ashes of the dead between England and Spain, and a celebrated Greek author of undoubted veracity, Procopius, who wrote about 547 A.D., states that the " Breton fishermen of an island subject to the French, were exempt from all tribute, because they conveyed the dead into a neighbouring island." The Breton French fishermen came from Jersey, " La Porte Sainte," and terminated their funeral voyage at Guernsey, " l'Ile Bienheureuse." The ashes of the dead were deposited in our *croutes* and sacred enclosures, within the tombs composed of *five* horizontal stones, which number indicated the resting places of knightly heroes, or noble Gauls."—Métivier in the *Monthly Selection,* 1825, pp. 327 and 452.

appeal to the higher authority of the Royal Court of the island.

The Court of St. Michel-du-Valle consisted of a seneschal and eleven vavassors, who, in virtue of their office and in consideration of their services, held certain lands on the fief. The officers of the Court were a greffier or registrar, four prevôts, who had duties analagous to those of a sheriff, six bordiers, who had certain services to perform in collecting dues and attending the meetings of the Court, and, though last, not least, an officer styled porte-lance—of whom more hereafter. The principal duties of the Court seem to have consisted in legalizing sales of real property, in which tenants on the fief were interested, and settling disputes concerning the same arising among them. But there appear to have been attempts made from time to time to encroach on the prerogatives of the Royal Court, and various ordinances of the latter are in existence restraining the seneschal and vavassors from doing certain acts, and even fining them for having gone beyond their powers. There was one function, however, of the Court of St. Michael which it seems to have exercised without dispute from time immemorial, but which it is impossible to account for—the inspection and keeping in order of the King's highway throughout the island, and of certain of the works for preventing the encroachments of the sea. Possibly it may have originated in marking out the bounds of the Fief St. Michel and its dependencies only, and with this keeping in order the sea defences.* Once in three years, the seneschal and vavassors of the Court were bound to perform this duty, which, judging from their later

---

* See *Gentleman's Magazine Library*, Social Manners and Customs. P. 51, Beating of Bounds at Grimsby.

records, they appear to have considered rather onerous, as we find several Acts of the Court dispensing with the ceremony, the reason given being generally the interruption it caused in agricultural labours, and the loss occasioned thereby, at a time when farmers were far from being in the prosperous condition in which they are at present.

Another very substantial reason was the expense, which had to be defrayed out of the Crown revenue. According to some of our historians, who, however, give no evidence in support of their assertion, this inspection of the roads, commonly known as " La Chevauchée" from the fact of the principal performers being mounted on horseback, was originally annual, and was instituted with a view to having the roads put in order preparatory to the grand religious procession of the Host on Corpus Christi Day, but this origin of the ceremony seems hardly probable, as it is well known that the procession in question is strictly limited in Roman Catholic countries to parishes, and is conducted by the parochial clergy. It is difficult to understand how it came to pass that a subaltern Court, such as was that of the Fief St. Michel, came to be allowed to exercise a quasi jurisdiction over lands which had never been subject to it, but as it was impossible for the Court to proceed to every part of their domain without occasionally trespassing over other manors, what was originally allowed by courtesy came to be looked upon at last as a right. A somewhat similar means of assuring the keeping in due repair of the high roads existed, and probably in a modified form still exists, in the sister island of Jersey, where it is conducted by the vicomte, assisted by two or more jurats of the Royal Court, and the officer, called the

E

"porte-lance," who exercises the same functions as the official bearing the same designation in the "Cour St. Michel." It is known in Jersey as "La Harelle."

But it is time to come to a description of how this. ancient ceremony was conducted in Guernsey. As has been said before, it ought to have taken place every third year, at which time the Court of St. Michael used to meet in the spring to settle preliminaries in fixing the day on which the ceremony was to take place, regulating the costume to be worn by the "*pions*" or footmen in attendance on the Court, and other matters. The month of June was usually chosen, and on the day appointed the Court assembled, with all the officers who were to take part in the procession, at the small Court House adjoining the remains of the ancient monastic buildings still dignified with the name of "L'Abbaye," although the establishment had been for centuries no more than a priory dependent on the famous monastery of Mont St. Michel in Normandy.

The following are translations of a few of the Acts and Regulations of the Court of St. Michael :— *

31 March, 1768. Seneschal nominated by the Governor.

24 May, 1768. The Chevauchée being due to take place on the following 8th of June, the Court has ruled the dress of the pions. A black cap (calotte) with a red ribbon at the back. A ruffled shirt, with black ribbon wristbands, and a black ribbon round the neck. Black breeches with red ribbons tied round the knee. White stockings ; and red rosettes on their

---

EDITOR'S NOTE.*—On the 27th April, 1533. The Court of St. Michel du Valle ordered that the King's Serjeant should " cry in the Market Place for three Saturdays that the Chevauchée would take place in the following month ot May."—*Fief Le Comte MSS.* copied by Colonel J. H. C. Carey.

wands. N.B.—This Act does not seem to have been put in force.

27th April, 1813.—The Chevauchée of His Majesty is appointed to take place on Wednesday, the 9th of the following June, for the reparation of the quays and roads of the King, and it is ordered that it shall be published throughout the parishes of this island, and cried in the Market Place, so that no one can plead ignorance.

The 27th of May, 1813.—Before Thomas Falla, Esq., Seneschal of the Court and Jurisdiction of the Fief St. Michel, present, Messieurs James Ozanne, Nicholas Le Patourel, James Falla, Pierre Falla, Jean Mahy, Richard Ozanne, Nicholas Moullin, Daniel Moullin, and Jean Le Pettevin (called Le Roux), vavassors of the said Court. The Court being to-day assembled to regulate the order to be pursued on Wednesday, the 9th of June proximo,—the day appointed by the Court for the Chevauchée of His Majesty to pass—has ordered that all the pions be dressed uniformly as follows, to wit: Black caps with a red ribbon behind. White shirts, with white cravats or neckerchiefs. Circular white waistcoats, with a red ribbon border. Long white breeches, tied with red ribbon round the knee. White stockings, and red rosettes on their wands.

And Messieurs les prevôts of the Court are ordered to warn all those who are obliged to assist at the said Chevauchée to find themselves with their swords, their pions, and their horses, the aforesaid 9th of June at seven o'clock in the morning at the Court of St. Michael, according to ancient custom, in default of appearance to be subject to such penalties as it shall please the Court to award him. And also shall Monsieur Le Gouverneur be duly warned, and Thomas Falla, Esq., seneschal, and Messrs. Jean Mahy and Nicholas Moullin, vavassors, are nominated by the Court to form a committee so as to take the necessary measures to regulate the conformity of the said act concerning the dress of the pions.

(Signed) JEAN OZANNE, Greffier.

On the above day, conformably to the said Act, all the pions, dressed in the afore-mentioned costume, met at seven o'clock in the morning at the Court of St. Michael, and there also were found the King's officers, vavassors, who had to serve there as esquires. The King's officers and the seneschal each had two pions on either side of his bridle rein, the vavassors were only entitled to one.

They began with a short inspection and a good breakfast on the emplacement east of the Vale Church. After breakfast, the members of the cortège, with their swords at their sides, got on their horses opposite the said Court of St. Michael, where the greffier of the said Court said the customary prayer, and the seneschal read the proclamation, and then they started in the following order :—

The Sheriff of the Vale and his pion.
The Sheriff of the King and his two pions.
The Sheriff of the Grand Moûtier and his pion.
The Sheriff of the Petit Moûtier and his pion.
The Sheriff of Rozel and his pion.
The King's Sergeant and his two pions.
The King's Greffier and his two pions.
The King's Comptroller and his two pions.
The King's Procureur and his two pions.
The King's Receiver and his two pions.
The Lance-Bearer and his two pions.
The Greffier of the Court St. Michel and his two pions.
The Seneschal of the Court St. Michel and his two pions.

The eleven vavassors of the Court St. Michel, and one pion each.

Whilst they are on their march, the five sheriffs carry by turns a white wand in the following order :—

The Sheriff of the Vale, from the Vale Church to the end of Grand Pont.

The King's Sheriff, from the end of Grand Pont, as far as the Forest.

The Sheriff of Grand Moûtier, from the Forest to the King's Mills.

The Sheriff of Petit Moûtier, from the King's Mills to the Douit des Landes in the Market Place, and the Sheriff of Rozel from the last mentioned place to the Vale.

During the procession the lance bearer carried a wand of eleven and a quarter feet long, and any obstacle this wand encountered, stones of walls, branches of trees, etc., had to be cleared away, and the proprietor of the obstacle was fined thirty sous, which went towards the expenses of the dinner. From time immemorial the privilege of the pions,—who were chosen for their good looks—was that of kissing every woman they met, whether gentle or simple, their only restriction being that only one pion was allowed to kiss the same lady, she had not to run the gauntlet of the gang. This privilege of course was invariably exercised !

At the entry of the Braye du Valle the seneschal freed the pions from their attendance on the bridle reins, and gave them authority to embrace any woman they might encounter, recommending good behaviour and the rejoining of their cavaliers at the Hougue-à-la-Perre.

Parish Church of St. Peter Port.
Showing houses demolished to make room for present New Market.

The Chevauchée then went to Sohier, les Landes, la rue du Marais, la Grande Rue, la Mare Sansonnet, les Bordages, la Ronde Cheminée, and les Morets. Arriving at the Hougue-à-la-Perre the pions regained their respective stations on the side of their officers, leading the horses, and there, at ten o'clock, they were met by His Excellency Sir John Doyle, the Lieutenant-Governor and his staff, the horses of which were all decorated with blue ribbons, except those of the said Governor and of his family, who, out of compliment, carried red ribbons, matching those of the Chevauchée. The Bailiff, with his party and John Guille, Esq., also joined them at this spot, uniformly dressed in blue jackets, white trousers, and leghorn hats.

The whole cavalcade then moved on, the Governor and suite at the rear, preceded by the band of the town regiment, dressed as rustics, in long white jackets and large hats with their brims turned down, and followed by six dragoons to bring up the rear. Having passed between eleven and twelve o'clock through Glatney, Pollet, Carrefour, and High-street, they came to the Town Church, where they made the tour around a large round table which had been placed near the westerly door of the said church, which table was covered with a white cloth and supplied with biscuits, cheese, and wine, which had been provided by one of the "sous-prevôts," and the Sheriff and the King's Sergeant, on foot, offered each cavalier who passed the door food and drink.

During this interval the band played serenades and marches.

At noon they proceeded through Berthelot-street to the College fields, and, passing through the Grange, they reached the Gravée; here His Excellency took his leave. The cavalcade passed on by St. Martin's road to the ancient manor of Ville-au-Roi, one of the oldest habitations in the island. The entrance was tastefully decorated with arches of flowers and a crown in the centre, with flags flying, and, on one of the arches, " Vive la Chevauchée." Here, according to old manorial custom, the party was gratuitously regaled with milk. The procession then moved on by Les Câches to Jerbourg, with the exception of the pions, who proceeded to the village of the Forest, and there waited the return of the Court. Here they danced and amused themselves as before, and being rejoined by the cavalcade at the Bourg they moved on by Les Brulliots, and passing Torteval Church arrived at a house called the Château des Pezeries at Pleinmont, where a marquee was erected, and cold meats and wine were prepared for the gentlemen. The pions were seated on the grass in a circle which had been hollowed for them, in the shape of a round table,* and they also had their repast. Here the procession halted till four o'clock, and by this time were joined by many carriages, filled with ladies and gentlemen, who, with a numerous party of all ranks, moved on by Rocquaine, Roque Poisson, below the Rouvets,

---

* As being of the same race and language as Wace, Walter Map and Chrestien de Troyes, who were the first to collect and write of the Arthurian legends,—or, as they are generally spoken of by French writers " *Les Epopées de la Table Ronde*,"—it might reasonably be expected that some traces of these old " romans " that must have so influenced our forefathers should linger among us. This " round table " so carefully hollowed out for the pions may be a relic of " La Table Ronde," of which Wace writes —

" Fist Artus la Roonde Table
" Dont Bretons dient mainte fable."

He goes on to say that Arthur instituted this Round Table in times of peace, for his feudal retainers, so that none might consider himself superior to his fellow knights and squires, for at such a table all must be equal.

Perelle, where a particular stone lies, which they are obliged to go round according to an old custom, from there by the Saint Saviour's Road to the Grands Moulins or King's Mills. On their arrival there they were rejoined by the pions, the mill was put in motion, and the miller came out with a plate in each hand, one containing flour of wheat, and the other of barley, which had been ground that instant by the mill. The miller then placed himself on a large stone, and the procession moved round him ; this custom has prevailed from time immemorial. The procession then continued by St. George, La Haye du Puits, Saumarez, Le Camp du Roy, Les Salines, to the Clos du Valle, to the aforesaid Court of St. Michael, where they arrived about seven o'clock, and where they were again joined by the Lieutenant-Governor, the Bailiff, and some of the principal residents. The Court having been dismissed they all partook of a sumptuous dinner, at which Mr. Seneschal Falla presided. The pions were also handsomely entertained.

The last Chevauchée took place in Guernsey on the 31st of May, 1837, but the description of the procession we have given refers to the one in 1825, and is taken from Jacob's *Annals*, and the *Chronique des Isles*, by Syvret.

The oldest known Act of the Court of St. Michael is the following, dated the 14th of October, 1204 :—

" Les Chefs Plaids Capitaux de la Saint Michel tenus à Sainte Anne en la Paroisse du Sarazin,* par Nicolle de Beauvoir Bailly, à ce présens Jean Le

---

* Now called the Câtel, and the Church of the said Parish is traditionally built on the Castle formerly inhabited by " Le Grand Sarazin," and it was there or thereabouts that the Royal Court used to sit.

Feyvre, Jean Philippes, Martin de Garris, Jean Maingy, Jean Le Gros, Jemmes le Marchand, Pierre de la Lande, Robert de la Salle, Colin Henry, Jurez de la Cour de nostre Souverain Seigneur le Roy d'Angleterre en l'Isle de Guernereye.   Le quatorzième jour du moys d'Octobre, l'an MCCIV. Sur la Remonstrance qui nous a esté faicte de la part des Frères Jean Agenor, Prieur, en la Paroisse de l'Archange de Saint Michel du Valle et ses aliez Pierre de Beauvoir, Pierre Martin, Jean Effart, Jean Jehan, Pierre Nicolle, Pierre du Prey, Jean Agenor, Michel le Pelley, Jean Cappelle et autres Marchands et Manans, tant en la Paroisse du Valle que de Saint Sampson, qu'ils éstoyent grandement empeschez et endomagez concernant le desbordement de la mer, laquelle auroit coupé le Douvre et passage commode entre les dittes Paroisses, entendu qu'il estoit impossible non seulement de faire Procession, mais aussi d'aller traficquer les uns avec les autres aux Landes du Sarazin, s'il ne nous pleust leur permettre et accorder de faire maintenir un certain Pont passant du Valle à Saint Sampson, estant propre et passable de toutes Marées, de Charues, et Charettes, de pied et de Cheval, et à qui il appartiendra de la maintenir en temps advenir. Parquoy ne voulant refuser la Raisonnable remonstrance des avants dits, et 'pour le bien public, nous leur avons appointé Veue sur les Limites les plus célèbres des dittes Paroisses, dans le jour Saint Barthelemi prochain, et advertiront le commun de s'y trouver, pour ouir ce que par nous sera ordonné touchant la ditte edification."

Another copy, which differs from the preceding in the names of the Jurats, finishes by these words, "donné par copie des roles, signé par Colin de la Lande, clerq." According to this copy the names of the Jurats are

" Jean Le Gros, James Le Marchant, Pierre de la Lande, Robert de la Salle, Colin Henry, Raoul Emery, Gaultier Blondel, Guillet Le Febvre." It is noticeable that the first four names of the copy first cited are not among these, and that the last three on this list are not in the Act which we have transcribed.† At the end of the second copy we find the following notice : " N.B.—Mr. Thomas Le Maître, Prevost de St. Sauveur à Jersey en a l'original."

Originally the vavassors* of the Court of St. Michael were twelve in number, similar to the Jurats of the Royal Court, but if you ask why the number for the

---

EDITOR'S NOTES.

* The titles of the eleven vavasseurs are :—(1) Gervaise—(2) Capelle—(3) Soulaire—(4) Maresq—(5) Grent Maison—(6) Garis—(7) Bihon—(8) Agenos—(9) Piquemie—10 (Le Moye—(11) Houët. The titles of the sergeants :—(1) Gaillot)—(2) Bordier Paisson—(3) de la Lande—(4) Roques des Roques—(5) Bourg—(6) l'Ange. The titles of the bordiers : —(1) Béquerel—(2) Rebour—(3) Renost —(4) Ricard—(5) Nant—(6) Salmon—(7) Infart—(8) Scarabie.

† I will here add a copy of the old orders issued by the Cour de St. Michel in 1663, and copied from those issued in 1419. It is taken word for word from a manuscript lent me by Colonel J. H. Carteret Carey, except that in places I have written in full words which are abreviated in the original MSS., such as " par " for " P," " Prevost " for " puost," " présent " for " pnt," que " for " q," " comme " for " coe," " parties " for " pties," " Jour " for " Jor," etc., etc. :—

" 𝔄 𝔗𝔬𝔲𝔰 𝔊𝔢𝔲𝔵 quy ces presentes lettres verront ou orront—Denis Le Marchant, Senechal de la Cour de la prieureté de St. Michel du Val en l'Isle de Guernesey—Salut—comme ainsy soit que Martin Sauvary, comme procureur et attourné des vavasseurs, Sergeans, bordiers, et autres officiers, de la dite Cour acteurs d'une partie eussent fait semondre et convenir pardevant nous en ladite Cour John phylippe recepveur pour lors de la dite Isle de Guernesey et de ladite prieureté du Valle pour très hault et très puissant prince Mon Seigneur Le Duc de Glocester, Seigneur des Isles, et possesseur adonques de toutes les rentes et revenues quelconques appartenans a la dite prieureté en ladite Isle, deffenseur d'autre partie—Lequel attourné que dit est eust declaré et demandé adonques a l'avant dit deffenseur comment iceluy deffenseur recepveur comme dit est debut bailler trouuer et deliurer les debuoirs et deuteys appartenans es dits Officiers de la dite Cour. C'est a ssauoir de temps en temps et toutesfois et quantes qu'il leur appartient de droit et de raison. Sçauoir est les 3 disners par chacun a chascun des plaids Cappitaulx de ladite cour. C'est a sçauoir à la feste St. Michel, à Noel, et à pasques. Item leurs disners toutes fois et quantes que par le dit recepveur seront requis et contraints d'aller reuisiter les Keys de la Coste de la mer et le cours des eaux et que eux en feroient leur debuoir comment de droit et de raison il appartient à leurs offices. Item—toutes fois et quantes que les dits vavasseurs, leurs valets, et seruans et les autres Sergeants et officiers a qu'il appartient iroient en cheuauchée pour reuisiter en ladite Isle leurs debuoirs semblablement—C'est a ssauoir quant eux se sont representés deuant la porte de la dite prieureté et eux doiuent monter a cheval eux doiuent auoir du pain et du vin abondamm_nt et honestement seruis—Item pareillement eux doiuent estre seruis et administrer de pain et de vin par la main du prevost de mon dit seigneur deuant la porte de l'eglise de St. pierre port lequel preuost doit estre présent a la dite cheuauchée ; et doit estre illeques une ronde table mise fournie et garnie bien et honnestement de doublier, pain et vin es coustages de mon dit Seigneur. Item quant eux seront arrivés es portes de pleinmont eux doiuent auoir du pain et a boire et quant eux seront retournes a la dite

last two hundred years has been reduced to eleven, the answer is—"that the devil carried away Vivien." All that is known about Jean Vivien is that he was a vavassor of this Court, and that, in a fit of despair, he drowned himself, early in the seventeenth century. Up to about the middle of the present century three letters " I. V. V." cut by himself on the broken fragment of rock from which he leapt into the gulf, still existed at the end of a footpath, not far from the " Fosse au Courlis "—Curlew's ditch or grave— a spot haunted by witches.

Since then no Christian has dared to replace the

---

prieureté et eux auront ainsi fait leurs debvoir eux doivent avoir a disner bien et honneste-ment tous ensemble es despens et coustages de mon dit Seigneur. Lequel seruice iceux officiers confessoient estre tenus de droit et de raison de trois ans en trois ans par la dignité de leurs offices. Item leurs disners semblablement toutes fois et quant qu'eux taxent les amendes de la dite cour. Item aussi a Noel et a Pasques quant eux rendent et payent les francs tenans (?) C'est a ssavoir les chapons a Noel et les oeufs a pasques. Lesquelles choses et chacune d'icelles en la forme et manière comme dessus est dit et desclaré. Le dit attourné au nom que dit est, proposoit adonques contre le dit recepveur, deffenseur comme dessus est dit ; et qu'a jceux officiers appartenoit de droit et d'antienne coustume a raison et dignitez de leurs offices et cela jceluy attourné offroit a prouver a suffire contre le dit deffenseur et jceluy recepueur deffenseur comme dit est es auant dites parties, propos et callenges dust fait negacion ; et le dit attourné dust prins et offert a prouver à suffire contre le dit deffenseur es quelles parties nous assignames certain jour es premiers plaids de la dite Cour c'est a sçavoir au dit attourné a faire sa preuve et audit deffenseur a la soustenir. Sachent tous que le Jour du Jeudy neufième jour du mois de Juillet l'an de grace mille, quatre cents et trente-neuf, en la dite cour par-devant nous comme dit est les dites parties furent presentes et personellement comparentes, et leurs raisons recitées et alleguées tant de l'une partie que de l'autre. Le dit attourné prouva et informa bien et raisonnablement toute son jntention et propos estre bons et vrays en forme et manière comme dessus est dit, et desclare par le report d'un bon et loyal serment douze preud'hommes de la dite paroisse de St. Michel du Valle, Jures et Sermentez de nostre ofice sur Saintes euangilles de dire et raporter uerité et loyaulté sur les cas, Item en outre et dabondant qu'au Seigneur de ladite prieureté appartient a faire curer et netoyer le fonds du douit du grand maresq appartenant a la dite prieureté, estant a la dite paroisse et en cas qu'aucune ordure soit terre ou pierre cherroit dedans jceluy douit qu'il doit estre netoyé et curé es coustages de ceux a quj la faute seroit trouué après lequel raport de serment fait et raporté a la forme et manière comme dessus est dit nous condanmes (sic) (? confirmames) toutes et chacunes les choses dessus dites et desclarez enfin et par perpetuité d'heritage en sa temps aduenir. En tesmoing desquelles choses nous avons a ces presentes lettres mis et appendu le seell de nos Armes l'an et le Jour de susdit—Les parties a ce presentes.

Collationné à l'original par nous soussignez Senechal et Vavasseurs de la dite cour de St. Michel le vingt et unième Jour du mois de May l'an Mille, six cents soixante et huit.

JEAN PERCHARD, Senechal.	P. LE MARCHANT.	PIERRE LA PERE.
PHILIPPIN PAINT.	JAMES FALLA.	JEAN DE GARIS.
JEAN LE HURAY.	THOMAS de JERSEY.	JEAN FALLA.
WLLIAM LE FAYVRE.	HELLIER de JERSÉ.	JEAMES LIHOU.

⭕ Sceau du
Fief St. Michel
du Valle.

Contre Sceau Initiales du dit Senechal.

suicide Jean Vivien, and, when making the calculation of the symbolic vavassorial stones, his pebble is always omitted. There are but eleven instead of twelve.

———

"Briser La Hanse."

This was a curious civic ceremony which was abolished in the early part of this century. In each of our parishes there are a certain number of functionaries called douzeniers, because the corps in question consists of twelve (douze) members, except in St. Peter Port, where there are twenty, and at St. Michel du Valle, where there are sixteen. When one of these officers was elected, he had to give a feast, to which the electors carried an enormous bouquet of flowers "à deux hanses"—with two handles. The dinner finished and the cloth removed, each man filled his glass, and the abdicating douzenier (le douzenier *déhansé*) broke one of these handles, previously dipping the bouquet into his glass, and drinking the health of the douzenier *hansé*. Then the bouquet went round from hand to hand, each man, while moistening it with the spirit that bubbled in his glass, adding his toast to the newly elected or *hansé* douzenier.

Local Customs—Aquatic.

" Heureux peuple des champs, vos travaux sont des fêtes."
—*St. Lambert.*

Vraicing.

The months of June, July, and August, form one
of the principal seasons for the collection of the sea-
weed with which the rocky shores of Guernsey abound,
and which, from time immemorial, has proved a most
valuable resource to the farmer, not only as affording
an excellent manure for the land, but also, in the
case of the poorer cottagers and fishermen who inhabit
the coast, an unfailing supply of fuel.   Many indeed
of these gain almost their entire livelihood by collecting
the " vraic " as it is locally termed, which they sell to
their richer neighbours for dressing the land, or which,
after drying on the shore, they stack for their winter
firing.   The ashes, which are carefully preserved, always
command a ready market, being considered one of the
best manures that can be applied to the land in
preparing it for certain crops.   The qualities of sea-
weed in general as a fertilizer are so highly appreciated that it has given rise to the agricultural adage
" *point de vraic, point de hautgard* "—no sea-weed,
no stack yard.   It has been remarked that dry seasons
are unfavourable to the growth of sea-weed, and that
rain is almost as essential to its development as it
is to that of the grass of the field—a singular fact,
when we remember that the marine plant has always
a supply of moisture.

Vraicing.

Sea-weed is distinguished into two kinds " *vraic venant* "—drift weed, and " *vraic scié* "—cut weed. The former is that which, like the leaves and branches of a tree, are severed from the place of growth by natural decay, or by the violence of storms, and is thrown up by the action of the waves on the shore. The latter is that which is detached from the rocks by the hand of man, generally with the aid of a small sickle. The collecting of sea-weed, whether drift or cut, is subject to stringent regulations, framed with a view both of preventing dangerous quarrels among those engaged in the occupation, and also of ensuring a regular supply of so precious a commodity by allowing sufficient time for its growth. In Guernsey the Royal Court has always legislated on the subject, but on the coasts of Normandy and Brittany it appears to have been the province of the Church to regulate the matter, and the harvesting of the sea-weed never began until the parish priest had solemnly blessed the undertaking.

Driftweed may be collected at all seasons, but only between sunrise and sunset. It is found left on the beach by the retiring tide, or is dragged on shore by means of long rakes from amidst the breakers that roll in during, or after, heavy gales. This is hard work, and not unattended with danger. The men are frequently up to their waists in the water, and the shelving pebbly beach affords but an insecure footing. The rakes are often wrenched out of the men's hands by the violence of the waves, and hurled back among them, inflicting severe bruises and sometimes even broken limbs. The collecting of the cut weed or " *vraic scié* " is quite another thing. Although entailing a great deal of labour, it is looked upon,

especially in summer, as a sort of holiday. There
are two seasons during which it is lawful to cut : the
first begins with the first spring-tide after Candlemas,
and lasts about five weeks, during the whole of which
time every person is allowed to collect as much as he
wants for manuring his lands. The second cutting,
which is chiefly for fuel, commences about Midsummer
and lasts until the middle of August. Immemorial
usage, strengthened by legal enactment, has consecrated
the first eight days of cutting at this season to the poor.
During this time none but those who are too poor to
possess a horse or cart are allowed the privilege of
gathering the vraic, which, when cut, they must bring
to high water mark on their backs. After this
concession to the less fortunate brethren, the harvest
is thrown open to all. Then it is that the country
people, uniting in parties consisting frequently of two
or three neighbouring families, resort to the beach
with their carts, to watch the ebbing tide, and secure
a favourable spot for their operations. All who can
be spared from the necessary routine work of the farm
attend on these occasions. The younger people adorn
their hats with wreaths of flowers, the horses' heads
are decked with nosegays, and even the yoke of the
patient ox is not without its floral honours. Once
arrived on the sea-shore, not a moment is lost, for
time and tide wait for no man, and first come, first
served. The sickle is plied vigorously, and small
heaps of the precious weed are collected and marked
with a flat pebble, on which the name or initials of
the proprietor are chalked. The men wade across the
" cols " or natural causeways leading to the outlying
rocks, and, when the tide begins to flow, hastily.load
the carts, or the ample panniers with which the horses

are provided, and hurry off to deposit their hard-
earned store above high-water mark. In the meantime
the younger members of the party range along the
beach, turning over the stones in search of that
esteemed mollusc the "ormer" or sea-ear (Haliotis
tuberculata) which, when well cooked—a secret only
known to a native of the isles—is really a delicious
morsel. Not unfrequently crabs of various kinds are
turned out of their hiding places, and hurry off,
holding up their formidable pincers in defiance and
defence, but are soon adroitly transferred to the
"behotte"—a small basket, narrow mouthed and
flattened on one side, which hangs by a belt from the
shoulder of the youth or maiden. Here and there a
larger mass of rock is with difficulty raised, and a goodly
sized conger-eel, disturbed from his snug retreat, glides
away like a snake and endeavours to hide himself in
the grass-like "plize" (Zostera Marina). A blow on
the head stuns him, and he goes to join the captive
ormers and crabs. Perhaps one of those hideous
monsters of the deep, the cuttle fish, is dislodged. His
long tentacles, armed with innumerable suckers, which
attach themselves strongly to anything they touch, his
parrot-like bill and large projecting eyes, staring with
a fixed gaze, are calculated to inspire alarm, but the
trenchant sickle makes short work of him, and his
scattered limbs remain on the spot to form a meal for
the crabs.

The laugh and the jest are to be heard on all
sides—even the brute creation seem to enjoy the
change. The horses, generally quiet, scamper over the
sands and rocks, neighing joyously to one another;
the farm dogs are busy hunting the small crabs that
everywhere abound, or rushing into the water after the

stones thrown by the children. A more animated
scene can nowhere be witnessed, and, when lighted
up by a bright summer sun, none more worthy of
being studied by the artist. The rich colouring of
the rocks, the lustrous bronzed tints of the moist
sea-weed, the delicate hues of the transparent water
as it lies unruffled in the small pools left by the
retiring wave, the groups of oxen and horses with
their shining summer coats, and the merry faces of
the peasantry, form a picture which no true lover of
nature can ever forget. But the tide is rising, and
drives the busy crowd before it. Before, however, they
leave the strand, the younger men choose their
favourite lasses, and lead them, already thoroughly
drenched, to meet the advancing wave. Hand-in-hand
they venture in ; the confiding girl is enticed onwards,
and suddenly finds herself immersed over head and
ears in the water. Some, more coy, feign to fly, sure
to be overtaken and share the same fate. The whole
scene is vividly portrayed by Mr. Métivier in his poem
of the " Sea Weeders " written in 1812.

At last, all re-assemble on the grassy sward that
lines the shore, and join their respective parties. The
careful housewife has baked beforehand a plentiful
supply of " gâche " and biscuits ; the rich golden-
coloured butter has been kept from the market, much
to the annoyance of the thrifty matron in town, who
finds the price enhanced in consequence ; the small
barrel of cider is broached, and all make a hearty
meal. The remaining hours of daylight are employed ·
in carting away the vraic or spreading it out on the
downs to dry, and, when night has set in, many
assemble again at some neighbouring tavern and end
the day with song and dance. The old fashioned

F 2

" *chifournie* " or hurdy-gurdy—the *rote* of mediæval times—has given way to the modern fiddle, but the songs are still those that delighted their ancestors. Most, if not all of them, have been originally derived from France, where it is far from improbable that they are now forgotten except in some remote country villages, but it is curious to find that they are still sung by the Canadian boatmen, and " Belle Rose, au Rosier Blanc" and " A la Claire Fontaine " are as familiar to the American descendants of the Normans as they are to the Guernsey peasant.

Ormering.

Another favourite amusement of the young people in the country, besides the merry-making which accompanies and follows the collection of sea-weed in summer, is the forming of parties to take the ormer, a shell-fish which abounds at low water at the spring-tides in spring and autumn.   The ormer is the *Haliotis tuberculata* of naturalists, and derives its name from its resemblance in shape to an ear—*auris marina*—" oreille de mer." The shell, which was formerly thrown away, is now carefully collected and exported, as it enters largely into the japanned ware manufactured at Birmingham and elsewhere, the lustre of the interior of the shell surpassing in brilliancy and variety of tints that of the best mother-of-pearl.   It is not, however, for the sake of the shell that this mollusc is sought, but for the fish itself, which, after being well beaten to make it tender, and cooked in brown sauce, forms a favourite dish.   Like

the limpet, the ormer adheres strongly to the rock, from
which it requires some degree of strength to detach it,
but it seems to possess considerable powers of locomotion,
and appears to come up from the deep water at certain
seasons of the year, probably for the purpose of depositing
its ova. It is a curious instance of the local distribution
of animal life that, although the ormer is known in
the Mediterranean, and is found all along the western
shores of Spain and France, and in great quantities
on the coasts of Brittany, it has never been discovered
much to the eastward of Cherbourg, nor on the English
side of the Channel.

The localities in which the ormer abounds are the
rocky bays, of which there are so many around our
coast, and there it is found at the proper seasons
adhering to the under surface of the loose boulders.
It is no trifling work to turn over these stones, but
the searcher often returns home laden with several
hundred ormers, and not infrequently he has also
added a crab or a conger to his store.

Sand-Eeling.

The catching of the sand-eel, or "*lanchon*" as it
is locally termed, takes place on nights when the
moon is at her full, and at low water : it is pursued
more as a recreation than as a source of profit. Parties
of young men and women unite and resort to some
sandy bay or creek as the tide is ebbing, armed with
blunted sickles, two-pronged forks, or any instrument
with which the sand can be easily stirred. The fish,

on being disturbed, rise to the surface of the sand with a leap. They are very agile in their movements, but their bright silvery sides, glittering in the moon-beams, betray them to their active pursuers, and before they have time to burrow again in the sand they are caught with the hand and transferred to the basket. It is more easy to imagine than describe the fun and merriment to which this sport gives rise ; how in the eagerness of the pursuit, a false step will place the incautious maiden up to the waist in a pool of water, and subject her to the good natured laughter of her merry companions ; how an apparently accidental push from behind will cause a youth, who is stooping down to gather up the fish, to measure his whole length on the wet sand ; or how a malicious step will splash one or more of the party from top to toe. To the lovers of the picturesque the localities in which this sport takes place add not a little to the charm of the scene. The broad sands of Vazon Bay, those of La Saline and other creeks on the western shores of the island, hemmed in on all sides by reefs of rock, and, above all, that most lovely spot called Le Petit Port, which lies at the foot of the precipitous cliffs of Jerbourg, seen in the full light of the harvest moon, leave impressions on the mind that are not easily forgotten.

Although the coasts of the island abound in fish of various sorts, sea-fishing, as an amusement, is very little resorted to. The reason of this is no doubt to be found in the strong tides and currents and dangerous rocks which surround us on every side, and which render it imprudent to venture out to sea unless under the guidance of an experienced pilot. Of late years, however, the extension of the harbour works into deep water has brought the fish within reach without the risk of hazarding one's life by venturing on the fickle sea, and the "contemplative man's amusement" is becoming daily more and more popular. Crowds of men and boys may be seen in all sorts of weather and at all hours of the day angling from the pier heads, and not infrequently making very fair catches.

Although prawns and shrimps are tolerably plentiful, there are but few who take the trouble of catching them for the market, but the pursuit of these delicate crustaceans is a favourite amusement, and is occasionally indulged in by persons of all ranks, the shores of Herm and Jethou, and the bays of the Pezerie and Rocquaine being the best spots at low tide for the sport. Inglis, in his work on the Channel Islands, remarks " that so various are tastes in the matter of recreation, that he has seen individuals who found as much pleasure in wading for half-a-day, knee-deep among rocks, to make capture of some handfuls of shrimps, as has ever been afforded to others in the pursuit of the deer or the fox."

The Parish Church of S. Peter Port.   A.D. 1846.

Local Customs—Ceremonial.

> " What art thou, thou idle ceremony ?
> What kind of god art thou, that suffer'st more
> Of mortal grief than do thy worshippers !
> Art thou aught else but place, degree, and form ? "
>
> —*Shakespeare.*

Although the doctrines of the Reformation were introduced into Guernsey in the reign of Edward VI., and perhaps earlier, and the Liturgy put forth by authority in the reign of that monarch was translated into French and used in the churches,* it was not until the reign of Elizabeth that the island became wholly Protestant.

Up to this time the Channel Islands had formed part of the Diocese of Coutances in Normandy,† an arrangement which led to much inconvenience in times of war between France and England. Queen

† Boniface IX. being Pope, Clement VII. Anti-Pope in France, and the Bishop of Coutances taking his side, the Bishop of Nantes was appointed by Boniface administrator of the See of Coutances, and the King of England, Richard II., addressed a letter to the Governors, Bailiffs, Jurats, and other inhabitants of Jersey and Guernsey, ordering them to obey the Bishop of Nantes in all spiritual matters. Rymer. Vol. VIII. p. 131.

EDITOR'S NOTE.—* *Comet,* June 29th, 1889.—" At the sale of Lord Crawford's effects, held in London last week, Messrs. Sotheby sold to Messrs. Ellis, of Bond Street, a Prayer Book, translated into French for the special use of Channel Islanders. The book dates as far back as 1553, and was sold for the price of £70. The following is a full description of the book taken from the catalogue :—" 678—Liturgy, Livre des Prières communes de l'administration des sacremens et autres cérémonies en l'Eglise de l'Angleterre. Traduit en Francoys par Francoys Philippe, serviteur de Monsieur le Grand Chancelier d'Angleterre. (Fine copy in blue morocco extra gilt edges by W. Pratt, excessively rare). Sm. 4to. (Paris). De l'imprimerie de Thomas Gaultier, Imprimeur du Roy en la langue Française, pour les Iles de Sa Majesté—1553. The following is the collation of this extremely rare edition, purchased in the Tenison sale for £39. (4) ff. Title, Contents, Epistle to Bp. of Ely. Sig : AI—IV† (4) ff. Preface des Cérémonies en sign. B.I.IV† (14) ff. Table & Kalendar, Proper Psalms and Lessons. Acte pour Uniformité. 4. (184) ff. Texte. The translation was made from the second book of King Edward VI. for the use of the Inhabitants of the Channel Islands."

Elizabeth put an end to this connection in the year 1568,* and attached the islands to the See of Winchester; but it was not until the Restoration of Charles II. that the change took full effect, and that the islands were brought entirely within the discipline of the Church of England by authority of the Bill of Uniformity.

It is well known that it was part of Queen Elizabeth's policy to favour the Huguenot party in France; and that in times of persecution the followers of the Reformed faith always met with an hospitable reception in England. The Channel Islands, lying so close to the coast of France, and speaking the same language as was used in continental Normandy, were naturally chosen as places of refuge in times of persecution by the French Protestants, many of whom—and among them several ministers—resorted thither until more settled times enabled them to return to their own homes. The old Roman Catholic rectors of the parishes in Guernsey, who, apparently, had given a sort of half adhesion to the intermediate order of things, and had been allowed to retain possession of a portion, at least, of the emoluments of their benefices, seem to have disappeared altogether shortly after the excommunication of the Queen by Pope Pius V. in 1570.

The Governor of Guernsey, Sir Thomas Leighton,

EDITOR'S NOTE.—* It was the excommunication of Queen Elizabeth by the Pope that led to the transference of the Channel Islands from the Diocese of Coutances to that of Winchester. Canon MacColl in his "Reformation Settlement" notes as an extraordinary fact that the Bishop of Coutances so far disapproved of that ex-communication as to have offered, on condition that his jurisdiction was allowed, to give institution to those clergy whom the Queen might nominate from the English Universities. In fact, up to the date of the bull of excommunication, the islands remained under the jurisdiction of the Bishop of Coutances, who permitted the use of the reformed Prayer Book, and ruled, apparently without a protest, over a portion of his diocese, in which the claim to supremacy on the part of the Pope was denied.

who favoured the views of the Puritan party in the Church, filled up the vacant pulpits with French refugee ministers, and probably it would have been difficult at that time to find any others.* The same course seems to have been followed in Jersey. These ministers very naturally preferred their own form of conducting divine worship to that of the Anglican Church, and, on the representation of the Governors of both the islands, permission was given by the Queen for the use of the Genevan form in the churches of the towns of St. Peter Port in Guernsey, and of St. Helier in Jersey. This permission was renewed by King James I. on his accession to the throne; and the natural consequence was, that not only the Presbyterian form of worship soon spread into every parish in the islands, but that the Presbyterian discipline and Church government were firmly established, and the authority of the Bishop of Winchester totally ignored. To this discipline the people of Guernsey clung with great pertinacity, and the attempts during the Great Rebellion of the Brownists and other fanatical sects to introduce their peculiar doctrines, met with little or no favour. It was not without some opposition that Episcopacy was brought in, most of the ministers refusing to conform to the new order of things, and

---

EDITOR's NOTE.—* Mr. Matthieu Le Lièvre gives a slightly different version. He says:—
" Parmi ceux qui avaient quitté Guernesey pour échapper au coups de la réaction catholique, se trouvait Guillaume Beauvoir, membre de l'une des familles qui ont joué un grand rôle dans. l'histoire de l'île, et qui occupa lui-même, pendant neuf ans (1572-1581), la dignité de bailli, la première magistrature du pays. . . . Il s'éloigna donc et se refugia avec sa femme à Genève, où il séjourna quelque temps et se fit avantageusement connaître de Calvin et de ses collègues. Rentré dans son île natale après la mort de la reine Marie, il fut frappé de la nécessité d'appeler au plus tôt un homme de tête et de piété pour relever les affaires de la Réforme à Guernesey. Il écrivit donc aux pasteurs de Genève, et à Calvin en particulier, pour leur demander un ministre. La Compagnie des Pasteurs s'en occupa et envoya à la jeune Eglise de Guernesey le ministre Nicolas Baudoin, porteur de deux lettres de recommandation addressées à Guillaume Beauvoir, et signées, l'une Charles Despeville (l'un des pseudonymes de Calvin) et l'autre Raymond Chauvet, l'un des Pasteurs de Genève."—*Histoire du Méthodisme dans les Iles de la Manche*, par Matthieu Le Lièvre, D.D., pp. 38-39.

giving up their livings in consequence.* The people had nothing to say in the matter: they were bound by the Act of Uniformity, but, in deference to their feelings and prejudices, certain practices were allowed to be retained, and certain others dispensed with.

No great objection could be made to a set form of prayer, for something of the kind was in use in the French Reformed Church; but the Litany of the Church of England seems to have given great offence —probably from its close resemblance to some of those used in the Romish Church—insomuch that many persons at first abstained altogether from attending the morning service; and, although in the present day no objection exists to this, or any other part of the Liturgy, it is, perhaps, owing to habits then contracted, and handed down from generation to generation, that so many, especially in the rural parishes, absent themselves from church in the forenoon. The use of the sign of the cross in baptism, in deference to the strong prejudices of the people, who seem to have looked upon it as the Mark of the Beast, was not at first insisted upon, but, in order to counteract this feeling, the thirtieth Canon "On the lawful use of the Cross in Baptism," was inserted at

---

EDITOR'S NOTE.—* Pierre Le Roy's Diary, 24th Sept., 1662. "Il est arrivé dans cette ile une compagnie de cent soldats avec un major, un capitaine, et des officiers, à cause de quelque opposition à l'Acte d'Uniformité. Les ministres n'ont pas voulu s'y soumettre et ont abandonné leurs cures, savoir M. Le Marchant, du Valle et de Saint-Samson; M. Perchard, de Saint Pierre-du-Bois; M. Morehead, de Saint-Sauveur; M. de la Marche, du Câtel, et M. Hérivel, de la Forêt et de Torteval." John de Sausmarez, formerly Rector of St. Martin's parish, was made Dean in 1662, and he and one of his colleagues, Pierre de Jersey, were the first to establish the new ritual. Thomas Le Marchant, who was virtually the head of the Presbyterian party, and as such was especially hated by Dean de Sausmarez, was shut up first in Castle Cornet in 1663, and in 1665 in the Tower of London, till September, 1667, when he was liberated, "ayant donné caution de mille livres sterling qu'il ne présumera pas en aucun temps d'aller dans l'île de Guernesey à moins qu'il n'ait pour le faire une license spéciale de Sa Majesté, et qu'il se comportera à l'avenir comme un respectueux et loyal sujet," etc. He had married Olympe Roland, and his son Eléazar was later Lieutenant Bailiff of Guernsey.—See also *Histoire du Methodisme dans les Isles de la Manche*, par Matthieu Le Lièvre, 1885, p. 112.

the end of the Baptismal Service in the French translation of the Book of Common Prayer printed for use in the islands, and there is every reason to believe that the objection to this practice soon died out.

Probably, kneeling at the Holy Communion was received with little favour, for we find that the first introduction of this practice on the 12th of October, 1662, was thought worthy of a note in a journal kept by a parish clerk and schoolmaster of that day—Pierre Le Roy—who wisely abstained from any comment on the event. To this day appliances for kneeling are rare in many pews, and at the beginning of the nineteenth century most of the congregation remained seated during the singing of the metrical psalms, as is the practice in the Presbyterian churches in Scotland and on the Continent.

Baptismal fonts are of recent introduction, the order to put them up in all the parish churches having been given by the Bishop of Winchester (Dr. C. R. Sumner) on the occasion of his primary visitation to this portion of his diocese in September, 1829, he being the first Prelate of that See who had deigned to inspect the state of the churches in the islands since the time that they were placed under the care of an Anglican Bishop by Queen Elizabeth. Before fonts were provided, the rite of baptism was administered at the altar, the minister, standing within the rail, receiving the water at the proper moment from the clerk, who poured it into his hand from a silver ewer.

In the absence of periodical visits from a Bishop, the rite of confirmation had, of course, become a dead letter. It was administered in 1818, for the first time since the Reformation, by Dr. Fisher, Bishop of

Salisbury, who had been deputed to consecrate two
newly-erected churches by the then Bishop of
Winchester, who was too old and infirm to undertake
the duty himself. Before that time—and indeed for
some considerable time later—it was customary to give
notice from the pulpit, previously to the quarterly
celebration of the Holy Communion, that young persons
desirous of communicating for the first time should
attend in the vestry on a certain day. This notice was,
of course, given in the parish churches in French—
the language of the great majority of the people of
that time—and the word used for "vestry," and which
we have so translated, was "Consistoire." No doubt,
under the Presbyterian discipline, the examination of
catechumens took place before the Consistory, composed
of the minister and elders of the church.

Till a comparatively recent period the Holy Communion was only administered quarterly, and at the
great festivals of Christmas, Easter, Whitsuntide and
Michaelmas. A preparatory sermon was generally
preached at an evening service held on the day
before the communion, and on this occasion a
metrical version of the Decalogue was usually sung
instead of a psalm or hymn. This was a practice
borrowed from the French Reformed Church, as was
also that of singing the 100th Psalm while the non-
communicants were leaving the church, some portions
of the 103rd Psalm while the communion was being
administered, and, just before the final benediction,
the Song of Simeon, "Nunc Dimittis."

Men and women communicated separately, the men
first and the women afterwards,—a relic doubtless of
the time when they were kept apart in the church.
No one thought of leaving the rails until all who knelt

at the same time had communicated, when the officiating minister dismissed them with these words :—

" Allez en paix ; vivez en paix,
Et que le Dieu de Paix vous bénisse."

Or

" Que le Dieu de Paix soit avec vous."

They then retired to make room for others. In parishes where weekly collections were made at the church door for the relief of the poor, it was customary for the minister to say immediately after the final benediction :

" Allez en paix ; vivez en paix ;
Et en sortant de ce temple souvenez vous des pauvres."

All these peculiar customs, which had been handed down from Presbyterian times, are rapidly disappearing. In the days when the celebration of the Lord's Supper was confined to stated days, it was the custom in some of the country parishes to deck out the churches for the occasion with branches of evergreens, as at Christmas. Also, on the day of the communion it was considered irregular to appear in coloured clothes. Black was universally worn, and many old people, both in town and country, but especially in the country, keep to the old custom.

The practice of publishing the banns of marriage immediately after the recital of the Nicene Creed, and not after the Second Lesson, as is done in England, has been retained in Guernsey ; the Act of Parliament of George II., which was supposed to change the custom of the church in this respect, and to do away with the express injunctions in the rubric, not including the Channel Islands in its provisions. In the country parishes, where the cemeteries are in the immediate vicinity of the churches, it is now—though it was not so in former days—the custom to carry the corpse into the church for the reading of the appointed Psalms and Lesson ; but in Town, where the burial-grounds are, for the most part, at some considerable distance from the sacred building, this part of the service was, till of late years, entirely dispensed with. It is customary, however, for the Clergy, sometimes to the number of three or four, to attend at the house of the deceased, if invited so to do, and to head the procession to the church or cemetery. A pious custom existed formerly —which, one is sorry to say, has of late years fallen almost entirely into disuse—no man ever commenced a new work, or even began the usual routine work of the season, without making use of these words " Au nom de Dieu soit ! " Wills and many other legal documents, the books in which the Acts of the Royal Court and of the States of the island are registered, as well as those used by merchants and tradesmen in their business, all commenced with this formula. In many cases it evidently took the place of the sign of the cross. All sittings of the Royal Court and of the States of the island, as well as the meetings of parishioners in the Vestry, and of the parochial councils known as Douzaines, are opened by the recitation of the Lord's Prayer, and closed by the Apostolic Benediction.

Birth and Baptism.

On the birth of a child notice is usually sent to the nearest relations, and as soon as the mother is sufficiently recovered she receives the visits and congratulations of her friends. It is customary to offer cake and wine to the visitors on these occasions. The wine must on no account be refused, but the health of the child must be duly drunk, and the glass drained, for it is considered extremely unlucky to leave a drop behind. The christening feast still retains the ancient name of "*Les Aubailles*" from the white garment or alb—in French "aube"—with which, in the early church, the recipients of baptism were solemnly invested. It is customary for the sponsors to make a present to the child, which usually takes the form of silver spoons, or a drinking cup. Before the re-establishment of Episcopacy at the Restoration there appears to have been only one sponsor of each sex. Of course the rubric which orders that every boy shall have two godfathers, and every girl two godmothers, is now complied with, but the second is invariably styled by the people the "little" godfather or godmother, and is often a child or very young person evidently only put in to comply with the requirements of the church.

The excess of feasting at baptisms and churchings as well as at marriages and funerals seems to have reached to such an extent in the early part of the seventeenth century as to call for repressive measures on the part of the legislature, at that time deeply imbued with a puritanical spirit, and sumptuary laws

G

of a very stringent nature were promulgated restricting the invitations on these occasions to the nearest relations, and prohibiting entirely all dancing, and even almsgiving.

After baptism the child is sent round to its nearest relatives, and the old women say that a present of some sort, preferably an egg, should be placed in the infant's hands, while visitors to the child are always expected to put some money in the infant's hand for luck, and as a token that it shall never want, the value of the gift being of little moment.

It is thought very unlucky to measure or weigh a child, such a proceeding being sure to stop its growth; and it is also supposed to be very unlucky to cover up a baby's face when taking it to the church to be christened, until the ceremony is over.

It is considered peculiarly unlucky for three children to be presented at the font at the same time for baptism, as it is firmly believed that one of the three is sure to die within the year.*—*Communicated by the Rev. C. D. P. Robinson, Rector of St. Martin's.*

EDITOR'S NOTE.—* This superstition still continues, and was told me in 1806 by Mrs. Le Patourel and others.   The doomed baby is supposed to be the one christened *second*, or the middle one, and you still hear women say when their child has been christened with two others, " Oh, but mine was an *end* one."

Betrothals and Weddings.

"As I have seene upon a Bridall day,
Full many maids clad in their best array,
In honour of the Bride come with their Flaskets
Fill'd full with flowers : others in wicker baskets
Bring forth from the Marsh rushes, to o'erspread
The ground whereon to Church the lovers tread ;
Whilst that the quaintest youth of all the Plaine
Ushers their way with many a piping straine."
—*Brown's " Pastorals," written before* 1614.

From the reign of Elizabeth to the Restoration of Charles II., the Presbyterian form of church government, with its rigorous discipline, prevailed in the Island, and the betrothal—" fiançailles "* of persons intending to take upon themselves the holy state of matrimony was a solemn act, performed in the presence of the ministers and elders of the church, and which by an ordinance of the Royal Court of the year 1572, was to be followed by marriage within six months at the latest. The legislature of that day evidently disapproved of long engagements. The promise was usually confirmed by a gift on the part of the bridegroom of some article of value, which was to be held by the bride as an earnest for the performance of the contract, and returned in case the match was broken off by mutual consent. Traces of

---

* " The custom of *flouncing* is said to be peculiar to Guernsey. It is an entertainment given by the parents of a young couple when they are engaged, and the match has received approval. The girl is introduced to her husband's family and friends by her future father-in-law, and the man similarly by hers; after this they must keep aloof from all flirtation, however lengthy the courtship may prove. The belief is that if either party break faith the other side can lay claim to a moiety of his or her effects."—From Brand's *Popular Antiquities of Great Britain.* Vol. II., p. 56.

this custom are still to be observed in the formal
announcement of the engagement to relations, and in
the visits paid to them by the young couple in order
to introduce each other reciprocally to those with
whom they are to be hereafter more closely connected,
as well as in the importance attached to the presents,
locally termed "gages"* (pledges) given by the young
man to his affianced bride.

A round of entertainments usually succeeds the
announcement of the intended marriage, at which in
former days mulled wine used to be " de rigueur,"
as indeed it was at all family merry makings and
occasions of rejoicings.

Among the trading, agricultural, and labouring
classes each party is expected to bring his or her
portion of the articles necessary to set up housekeeping.
The man, for example, provides the bedstead, the
woman, the bed and the household linen, and very
often the crockery and furniture. All, however, is
looked upon as belonging to the wife, and is frequently
secured to her by a regular contract entered into
before marriage, so that in case of the husband getting
into pecuniary difficulties, his creditors cannot lay
claim to the household furniture. The handsomely
carved oaken chests, or large leather-covered boxes
studded with brass nails, which were formerly to be
seen in almost all the old country houses, were used
to contain the stock of linen, and appear to have been
in early days almost the only piece of ornamental
furniture of which the house could boast. This used
to be brought to the bridegroom's residence, with the

EDITOR'S NOTE.—* Usually consisting of half-a-dozen or a dozen (according to the
bridegroom's means) silver spoons, and a pair of sugar tongs, marked with the initials of
bride and the customary " bague de fiançailles."

rest of the articles provided by the bride, a day or two before the wedding, and with a certain degree of form, the bridegroom, or his best man, conducting the cart which contained them,* and the nearest unmarried female relative of the bride carrying the looking-glass or some other valued or brittle article. A similar custom still exists in Normandy and Brittany. It is considered highly unlucky for a bride to take any other way in going to the church to be married than that which she follows when going thither for her usual devotions. Flowers and rushes are invariably strewn in the path of the bride and bridegroom as they leave the church, and before the door of their future habitation.†

On the first or second Sunday after their wedding the newly-married pair appear in church attended by

EDITOR'S NOTES.

* Besides this it was customary amongst farmers for the parents of a bride to give her a cow, and the animal in this case followed the cart.—*From Mr. J. de Garis, Rouvets, St. Saviour's, 1901.*

† Les "gllajeurs"—the wild marsh iris—was always one of the favourite flowers for strewing in front of the bride, and all the water-lanes and marshes were ransacked for it. The wedding festivities generally lasted for two or three days. The house on the wedding day was decorated with wreaths and crowns of flowers, and, as usual, the festivities began with dinner, for which the usual fare was roast beef, roast mutton, a ham, plum pudding, and, of course, "gâche à corinthe," washed down with cider. Then came games, songs, etc., till tea time, and then the tables would be cleared for dancing, while mulled wine, cheese, and Guernsey biscuits would be handed round at intervals. All the relations, friends, and neighbours of course partook of these festivities. A few songs were sung, "Jean, gros Jean," being a "sine quâ non" in the country parishes, and then the mulled wine was handed round in cups, especially at midnight, as the clock struck. The correct formulâ before beginning to drink was

"Cher petit Pêpinot
Quand je te vè
Tu parais bien
Si je te bè, j'm 'en sentirai
Et si je te laisse j'm 'en repentirai,
Faut donc bien mieux bère, et m'en sentir
Que de te laisser, et m'n repentir!
À votre santâi la coumpagnie!"

Very frequently at weddings people who knew what this formula led to put hanging beams from the "pôutre," or central rafter for the men to hold on to! "À mon beau laurier qui danse" was of course always danced at the weddings, "ma coummère, et quand je danse" was another very favourite dance, the steps going to each syllable when sung, and they also danced "Poussette," which entirely consisted of the different inflections of the word "Poussette," "Pou-set-te," alternately chanted smoothly or jerkily. This feasting and dancing was kept up till five or six the next morning, and very often for the next night as well, while on the third day all the old people and non-dancers were asked in to finish up the feast in peace.—*From Mrs. Mollet, Mrs. Marquand, and Mrs. Le Patourel.*

There are certain gifts from a man to his fiancée which are supposed to be most unlucky to accept, as by so doing it would mean that the wedding would probably never take place.

the best man and the bridesmaid, and it is a point
of etiquette for the bride and bridegroom to read and
sing out of the same book, however many books
there may be in the pew.   Among well-to-do people
a series of parties in honour of the young couple
ensue, which in the dialect of the country are called
"reneuchons," "neuches" being the local pronunciation
of the French word "noces."

It appears from an ordinance of the Royal Court of
1625, when the puritanical spirit, which had come in
with the Genevan discipline, was at its height, that the
poor at that time were in the habit of soliciting alms
at weddings, baptisms, and burials.   This practice, as
tending to keep up superstition and as dishonouring
to God, was expressly forbidden by the legislation under

They are a watch and chain, a brooch, and a Bible, and if he should present her with a knife
or a pair of scissors the only way to avert the ill-luck is to pay a penny for them. Should
a girl upset a chair before the wedding her marriage will be delayed for a year.   If a girl
wishes to dream of the man she is to marry she must take some of the wedding cake on the
day of the wedding, pass it through a married woman's wedding ring, or, if possible, the bride's,
(a widow's is of no avail) and put it under her pillow, and dream on it for five consecutive
nights, and the *last* dream will come true.—*From Fanny Ingrouille.*

A correspondent sent the following query in 1857 to "*Notes and Queries*":—"A month or
two back a family, on leaving one of the Channel Islands, presented to a gardener (it is
uncertain whether an inhabitant of the island or no) some pet doves, the conveyance of them
to England being likely to prove troublesome.   A few days afterwards the man brought them
back, stating that *he was engaged to be married*, and the possession of the birds might be
(as he had been informed) an obstacle to the course of true love remaining smooth."   This
was put in the shape of a query, but no answer appeared.   Doves and wild pigeons in
Guernsey are supposed to be most unlucky birds to have in a house, so probably the gardener
had been told that they would bring ill-luck on his future "ménage" if he accepted them.
The country people carry their distrust of them so far that they say that their wings, worn
in a hat, bring misfortune, and they are among the birds whose feathers in the pillows of the
dying prolong the death agony.

"CHEVAUCHERIE D'ANE."

If after marriage a couple do not agree well together, they are admonished by their neighbours
by what, in England, is called "rough music."   In Métivier's Dictionary he describes two young
people, boy and girl, back to back on a donkey, representing the guilty husband and wife.
They were followed by all the idlers of the district singing a scurrilous rhyme, and surrounding
the house of the offending pair, where the song and its accompaniments were kept up all night.
—*Métivier's Dictionary, p. 23.*

Nowadays putting the man and woman back to back on the donkey seems to be discontinued,
but in St. Peter's-in-the-Wood, Miss Le Pelley, a resident in the parish, writes "If the young men
of this parish find out that a man has beaten his wife they form two parties on opposite sides
of his house, at about a distance of one hundred yards from it, and blow conch shells, first one
and then the other in answer.   They keep this noise up for a long time so that the married
couple may feel ashamed of themselves.   I have not heard them just lately (1896), but one
year it was very frequent, and such a nuisance.—See in Brand's *Antiquities*, Vol. 2, p. 129, the
articles on "Riding the Stang" in Yorkshire, said also to be known in Scandinavia.

pain of corporal punishment to the beggar, and a fine
to the giver of alms.*

---

* It is not unusual in the country parishes for the young men of the neighbourhood to assemble around the house in the evening and to fire off their militia
muskets or fowling pieces in honour of the wedding, in return for which they are
regaled with a cup of wine to drink the health of the newly-married pair. If the
marriage is between persons connected with the shipping interest all the vessels in
port make a point of displaying their flags, and a few bottles of wine are
distributed in return among the crews. Marriages among the country people are
frequently celebrated on a Sunday, immediately before the morning service. If
it is the intention of the newly-married couple to attend the service they make it
a point to leave the Church and return after a short interval, as an idea prevails
that if they remained in the Church until the prayers of the day have been begun
the marriage would be illegal.—*From Rev. J. Giraud, Rector of Saint Saviour's.*

Deaths and Funerals.

As soon as a death occurs in a family a servant
or friend is immediately sent round to announce the
sad event to all the nearest relatives of the deceased,
and the omission of this formality is looked upon as
a great slight, and a legitimate cause of offence. If any
person enter a house where a corpse is lying it is
considered a mark of great disrespect not to offer a
sight of it, and it is thought equally disrespectful on
the part of the visitor if the offer is declined, as the
refusal is supposed to bring ill-luck on the house.
When the day is fixed for the funeral a messenger
is sent to invite the friends and relatives to attend,
and in times gone by if those to be invited resided
at any distance it was considered proper that this
messenger should be mounted on a black horse.

Formerly the funeral feast was universal, of late years
it is seldom heard of except in some of the old
country families of the middle classes, among whom
ancient customs generally abide longer than among
the classes immediately above or below them.

The lid of the coffin is not screwed down until all
the guests are assembled, and the person whose
business it is to see to it, comes into the room where
they are met, and invites them to take a last look.
Hearses are almost unknown, even in cases where
the distance from the house to the cemetery is
considerable.   The coffin is almost invariably borne
on the shoulders by hired bearers, but in former days
it was only persons of a certain standing in society
who were considered entitled to this honour; the poor
were carried by their friends, three on each side,
bearing the coffin slung between them.   Care was
always taken that the corpse was carried to the
church by the way the deceased was in the habit
of taking during his lifetime.*

The custom of females attending funerals, which
was formerly universal, has disappeared entirely from
the town, but in the country it is still occasionally
observed, the mourners being attired in long black
cloaks with hoods that almost conceal the face.   The
funeral feast, when there is one, takes place when
the cortège returns to the house of mourning.   A
chair is placed at the table where the deceased was
wont to sit, and a knife, fork, plate, etc., laid before

EDITOR'S NOTE.—* Mr. Allen told me (1896) that attending a short time ago at a funeral in the Mount Durand, the corpse was to be carried to Trinity Church, to which of course the shortest route was *down* the hill, but the widow of the deceased remonstrated so vigorously, saying that she could not allow anything so unlucky to happen to her husband, as that he should start for his funeral *down hill*, that, in deference to her wishes they went *up* the hill and round by Queen's-road.

it as if he were still present.* Tea and coffee, wine, cider, and spirits, cakes, bread and cheese, and more especially a ham, are provided for the occasion. The last-named viand was, in bygone days, almost considered indispensable, and where they kept pigs, —and almost everyone then kept pigs—every year, when the pig was killed, a ham was put away " in case of a funeral " and was not touched till the next pig was killed and another ham was put in readiness; and from thence it comes that " màngier la tchesse à quiqu'un "—" to eat a person's ham "— is proverbially used in the sense of attending his funeral. The first glass of wine is drunk in silence to the memory of the departed, whose good qualities are then dilated upon, but the conversation soon becomes general, and it not unfrequently happens that more liquor is imbibed than is altogether good for the guests. In fact the mourners had generally to be conveyed home in carts.†

From ancient wills it seems that money was some-times left for the purpose of clothing a certain number of poor, and from the ordinances of the Royal

---

* At funeral feasts it was an ancient custom in Iceland to leave the place of the dead man vacant.--See Gould's "*Curiosities of Olden Times*," p 84.

EDITOR'S NOTES.

† Unless the forehead of the corpse is touched after death the ghost will walk. When you go into a house of mourning and are shown the corpse you should always lay your hand on its forehead.—*From Fanny Ingrouille, of the Forest Parish.*

The same idea prevails in Guernsey which we meet with in Yorkshire and many of the Eastern Counties of England that, having your pillow stuffed with pigeons', doves', or any *wild* bird's feathers will cause you to "die hard."—See *Notes and Queries*, 1st Series, Vol. IV.

It is also said that it is unlucky to keep doves in a house, but if they are kept in a cage and anyone dies in the house, unless a crape bow is placed on the top of the cage they will die too.

The country people also believe that no one ever dies when the tide is *rising*. Frequently when talking of a death they will say, "the tide turned, and took off poor —— with it,"— *From Fanny Ingrouille and many others.*

Court prohibiting begging at funerals, or even the voluntary giving of alms on these occasions, it is not improbable that the custom of distributing doles was, at one time, almost general. There is no trace of it in the present day.

Till within the last few years it was almost an universal custom, even among the dissenters, for the members of a household in which a death had occurred, to attend their parish church in a body on the first or second Sunday after the funeral, and the custom is still kept up to a certain extent. If they are regular frequenters of the church they occupy their usual seats, if not, they are placed, if possible, in some conspicuous part of the building, where they remain seated during the entire service, not rising even during those portions of the service in which standing is prescribed by the rubric. This is called " taking mourning," in French " prendre le deuil." Widows remain seated in church during the whole of the first year of their widowhood.

Part II.

Superstitious Belief and Practice.

CHAPTER III.

Prehistoric Monuments; and their Superstitions.

" Of brownyis and of bogillus full is this buke."
—*Gawin Douglas.*

" D'un passé sans mémoire, incertaines reliques
Mystères d'un vieux monde en mystères écrits."
—*Lamartine.*

" Among those rocks and stones, methinks I see
More than the heedless impress that belongs
To lonely Nature's casual work ! They bear
A semblance strange of Power intelligent,
And of design not wholly worn away."
—*Wordsworth, The Excursion.*

THE island of Guernsey still contains many of those rude and ponderous erections commonly known by the name of Cromlechs, or Druids altars. The upright pillar of stone or rude obelisk, known to antiquaries by the Celtic name of Menhir also exists among us. Many of these ancient monuments have no doubt disappeared with the clearing of the land and the enormous amount of quarrying, and many have doubtless been broken up into building materials, or converted into fences and gateposts. But the names of estates and fields still point out where they once existed. Thus we find more than one spot with

the appelation of " Pouquelaye."* " Longue Rocque,"
or " Longue Pierre," and the names of " Les Camps
Dolents," " Les Rocquettes," and " Les Tuzés"
indicate the sites of monuments which have long since
disappeared.

The researches carried on with so much care and
intelligence by Mr. Lukis have clearly proved that the
Cromlechs were sepulchral ; perhaps the burial places
of whole tribes, or at least of the families of the
chieftains.　This does not preclude the popular notion
of their having been altars, for it is well known that
many pagan nations were in the habit of offering
sacrifices on the tombs of their dead.

The following is a list of the principal Druidical
structures, etc., which we can identify, with an account
of the traditional beliefs attached to them of their
origin, etc. :—

The large Cromlech at L'Ancresse called " L'Autel
des Vardes."

The smaller Cromlech in the centre of L'Ancresse,
with a portion of another similar structure to the
east of it.

A small portion of a Cromlech at La Mare ès
Mauves, on the eastern base of the Vardes, almost
in front of the target belonging to the Royal Guernsey
Militia.

---

* The name of "Pouquelaie" given in various districts of Normandy, and in the
Anglo-Norman Isles to megalithic monuments appears to be composed of two
Celtic words, of which the latter, the Breton *lee-h* or *lêh* means a flat stone.
The former of these words—*pouque*, some etymologists say is derived from a
Celtic word meaning, *To kiss*, or *adore*—and thus " Pouquelaie "—*the stone we
adore ;* but many others think with equal probability that *Pouque* is derived
from the same root from whence we get *Puck*, the mad sprite Shakespeare has
so well described in his "Midsummer's Night's Dream." The *pixies*, or Cornish
and Devonshire fairies, and the *Phooka*, or goblin of the Irish, are evidently of
the same family.

"L'Autel des Vardes" et L'Lacrume.

" La Roque Balan."

" La Roque qui Sonne " (destroyed).

" Le Tombeau du Grand Sarrazin," in the district called Fortcàmp (destroyed).

" L'Autel de Déhus," near above.

Small Cromlech at " La Vieille Hougue " (destroyed).

" Le Trépied " or the " Catioroc."

" Menhir " or " Longue Pierre " at Richmond.

* " Creux ès Fées " in the parish of St. Pierre-du-Bois.

" La Longue Roque " or " Palette ès Fées " * at the Paysans.

* " La Roque des Fées " (destroyed).

* " Le Gibet des Fées " (destroyed).

" La Chaire de St. Bonit " (destroyed).

In the Island of Herm there are six or eight mutilated remains of Cromlechs. In Lihou, none are left. In Sark, none are left.

It will be seen that the druidical stones are believed to be the favourite haunt of the fairy folk, who live in the ant hills which are frequently to be found in their vicinity, and who would not fail to punish the audacious mortal who might venture to remove them.

" L'Autel des Vardes " at L'Ancresse.

This consists of five enormous blocks of granite, laid horizontally on perpendicular piles, as large as their enormous covering. Around it, the remains of

---

EDITOR'S NOTES.

* In *Traditions et Superstitions de la Haute Bretagne*, M. Paul Sebillot, says :—" En général les dolmens sont appelés *grottes aux fées*, ou *roches aux fées* ; c'est en quelque sorte une désignation générique (p. 5). Les noms font allusion à des fées, aux lutins, parfois aux saints ou au diable. Comme on le verra dans les dépositions qui suivent, c'est à ces mêmes personnages que les paysans attribuent l'érection des Mégalithes (p. 8.), etc.

In *Croyances et Légendes du Centre de la France*, par Laisnel de la Salle, he says, Tome I., page 100:—" Les fées se plaisent surtout à errer parmi les nombreux monuments druidiques. . . . ou se dressent encore les vieux autels, là sont toujours présentes les vieilles divinités."

a circle of stones, of which the radius is thirty-three feet, and the centre of which coincides with the tomb. Mr. Métivier says in his "Souvenirs Historiques de Guernesey" that this "Cercle de la Plaine," in Norse *Land Kretz*, on this exposed elevation, could not fail to attract the attention of the Franks, Saxons, and Normans, and thus gave its name to the surrounding district.

In it were found bones, stone hatchets, hammers, skulls, limpet shells, etc., etc.

It is perhaps to this latter fact that we must attribute the idea which is entertained by the peasantry that hidden treasures, when discovered by a mortal, are transformed in appearance by the demon who guards them into worthless shells.

"LA ROQUE BALAN."

"La Roque Balan" was situated at the Mielles, in the Vale parish. It is supposed by some to have taken its name from Baal, Belenus, (the Sun God), the Apollo of the Gauls, whom the Thuriens, a Grecian colony, called *Ballen*, "Lord and King," and to whom they dedicated a temple at Baïeux. The custom of lighting fires in honour of Bel or Baal continued in Scotland and Ireland almost to the beginning of this century. In Guernsey, at Midsummer, on the Eve of St. John's Day, June 24th, the people used to go to this rock and there dance on its summit, which Mr. Métivier describes in 1825 as being quite flat. The refrain of an old ballad proved this:

> "J'iron tous à la St. Jean
> Dansaïr à la Roque Balan."

Some people conjecture this rock to be the base of a balancing, or Logan stone, and others again that

H

it was the site where Dom Mathurin, Prior of St. Michel, weighed in the *balances* the commodities of his tenants. But the most probable supposition is that it was named after the *Ballen* family, former residents of this neighbourhood.

Near this rock stood

" La Roque qui Sonne."

This was the name given by the peasantry to a large stone which formerly stood on the borders of L'Ancresse, in the Vale parish. There is no doubt that it formed part of a Cromlech, and it is said that when struck it emitted a clear ringing sound. It was looked upon in the neighbourhood as something supernatural, and great was the astonishment and consternation of the good people of the Clos du Valle, when Mr. Hocart, of Belval, the proprietor of the field in which it stood, announced his intention of breaking it up in order to make doorposts and lintels for the new house he was on the point of building. In vain did the neighbours represent that stone was not scarce in the Vale, and that there was no necessity for destroying an object of so much curiosity. No arguments could prevail with him, not even the predictions of certain grey-headed men, the oracles of the parish, who assured him that misfortune was sure to follow his sacrilegious act. He was one of those obstinate men, who, the more they are spoken to, the less will they listen to reason, and finally the stone-cutters were set to work on the stone.

But now a circumstance occurred which would have moved any man less determined than Hocart from his purpose. Every stroke of the hammer on the stone was heard as distinctly at the Church of St. Michel du Valle, distant nearly a mile, as if the quarrymen

were at work in the very churchyard itself ! * Orders
were nevertheless given to the men to continue their
work. The stone was cut into building materials, and
the new house was rapidly approaching completion
without accident or stoppage. Hocart laughed at the
predictions of the old men, who had foretold all sorts
of disasters.

At last the day arrived when the carpenters were
to quit the house. Two servant maids,—or, as others
have it, a servant man and a maid,—were sent at an
early hour to assist in cleaning and putting things to
rights for the reception of the family, but at eight
o'clock in the morning a fire broke out in the house,
and its progress was so rapid that the poor servants
had not time to save themselves, but perished in the
flames. Before noon the house was one heap of
smoking ruins, but it could never be discovered how
the fire had originated.

Hocart's misfortunes, however, were not at an
end. Some part of the rock had been cut into
paving stones for the English market, and the refuse
broken up into small fragments for making and
repairing roads. In the course of the year the one and
the other were embarked for England on board of two
vessels in which Hocart had an interest as shareholder,
but, strange to say, both vessels perished at sea.

Hocart himself went to reside in Alderney, but was
scarcely settled there when a fire broke out and
destroyed his new dwelling.

---

* I have heard that the strokes of the hammer were heard in the town when
La Roque qui Sonne was broken up. A spot was shewn me some years since as
the site where this stone stood. I cannot exactly define the spot, but know it
was to the east of the Vale Parochial School.—*From John de Garis, Esq., of
Les Rouvets.*

H 2

Smith Street, A.D. 1870.

He then determined on returning to Guernsey, but when close to land a portion of the rigging of the vessel on board which he sailed, fell on his head, fractured his skull, and he died immediately.*

There is another instance given of the ill luck which waits on those who interfere with the Cromlech and disturb the repose of the mighty dead† in the "Legend of La Haye du Puits," which is drawn from an ancient chronicle and published in versified form by "M. A. C.," with extracts from Mrs. White's notes. The legend runs thus :—

In the reign of Henry II. of England Geoffrey of Anjou raised a rebellion against him in Normandy. Not wishing to be a rebel, Sir Richard of La Haye du Puits, a noble Norman knight, fled from thence to Guernsey, and landed in Saints' Bay. He settled in Guernsey and proceeded to build himself a house, which he named after his Norman mansion "La Haye du Puits." Unfortunately for himself, in so doing he destroyed an old Cromlech. All the inhabitants told him that he would in consequence become cursed, and a settled gloom descended upon him. Nothing could cheer him; he felt he was a doomed man. At last he thought that perhaps by resigning the house and dedicating it to God he might avert his fate. So he gave it to the Church, and turned it into a nunnery, making it a condition that the abbess and nuns should daily pray that the curse might be removed from him.

He then set sail from Rocquaine Bay, for France,

---

* From the late Mr. Thomas Hocart, of Marshfield, nephew of the Hocart to whom these events occurred.

EDITOR'S NOTE.—† In *Traditions et Superstitions de la Haute Bretagne*, Vol. I., p. 32, M. Sebillot says : " En beaucoup d'endroits, on pense qu'il est dangereux de détruire les pierres druidiques, parceque les esprits qui les ont construits ne manqueraient pas de se venger." See also " Amélie Bosquet, p. 186 of *La Normandie Romanesque*."

the rebellion being over, and his wife, Matilda, awaiting him in their old home. But on his way his ship was captured by Moorish pirates, and he was taken as prisoner to Barbary. When there, his handsome presence made so much impression on the governor's wife that she entreated he might be allowed to guard the tower where she resided with her maidens.

What was his astonishment when one of them looked out, and, recognising a fellow countryman, called out and told him that she was Adèle, daughter of his old friend and neighbour, Ranulph. She also had been taken prisoner by these pirates, by whom her father had been killed ; she implored him to effect her escape. She handed him her jewels, and with these he bribed their jailers, and he, she, and her nurse Alice, all managed to escape to France. He took her to the Norman " Haye du Puits," and there, according to the old chronicle, he found his wife, Matilda, and all " in a right prosperous and flourishing condition." From there Adèle married a Hugh d'Estaile, a young Norman knight, high in the favour of King Henry.

But the spirits of the Cromlech were not yet appeased. Sir Richard could not shake off the brooding care and haunting night-mares which always oppressed him, though he tried to propitiate heaven by building two churches in Normandy, " St. Marie du Parc," and " St. Michel du Bosq," " for the deliverance of his soul," but it was of no avail, and he died, a wretched and broken-down man. Even the nuns in the Convent of the Haye du Puits were so harassed and distressed, that finally they decided to leave it ; it is said that one unquiet nun haunts the house to this day. Since then it has passed through many hands, but tradition says that for many years it never brought good fortune to its possessors.

"Le Tombeau du Grand Sarrazin."

In the district called Le Tort Càmp, near Paradis, was one of the principal Cromlechs at the Vale, now quarried away, called "L'Autel," or "Le Tombeau du Grand Sarrazin." Who "Le Grand Sarrazin" was, it is now impossible to say. He is also called Le Grand Geffroi, and his ·castle—from whence the name "Le Castel"—stood where the Church of Ste. Marie-du-Castel now stands. He must have been one of those piratical sea kings, who, under the various appellations of Angles, Saxons, Danes, and Northmen or Normans, issued from the countries bordering on the North Sea and the Baltic, and invaded the more favoured regions of Britain and Gaul. The name "Geffroy," (*Gudfrid*, or "la paix de Dieu") seems to confirm this tradition. As to the term "Sarrazin" —Saracen, although originally given to the Mahometans who invaded the southern countries of Europe, it came to be applied indifferently to all marauding bands; and Wace, the poet and historian, a native of Jersey, who lived and wrote in the reign of Henry II., in speaking of the descent of the Northmen on these islands, càlls them expressly "La Gent Sarrazine." Among the many Geoffreys of the North whom history celebrates, there is one, a son of King Regnar, who may be the one celebrated in our local traditions. Charles the Bald yielded to him "a county on the Sequanic shore."

At that time the coast of Gaul was divided into three sea-borders, namely, the Flemish, the Aquitanian, and the Sequanic, called "Sequanicum littus" by Paul Warnefrid, who places one of these islands near it.

That his castle stood at one time on the site of the present church, is confirmed by the discoveries which have frequently been made in digging graves, of considerable masses of solid masonry, which appear to be the foundations of former outworks of the fortress. It is even possible that some portions of the walls of the church may be the remains of the earlier building. There are also in the neighbourhood "Le Fief Geffroi" and "Le Camp Geffroi."[*]

"L'Autel de Déhus."

Quite close to where "Le Tombeau du Grand Sarrazin" was situated, close to the Pointe au Norman, in the environs of Paradis,[†] in the Vale parish, and bordering on the Hougues d'Enfer, is the Pouquelêh de Déhus. This spot, as well as some fields in the Castel parish called "Les Déhusets" or "Les Tuzets," are supposed to be favourite resorts of the fairies.

M. de Villemarqué, in his *Barzas-Breiz*, the work so well known to folk-lorists, tells us that the Bretons gave the imps or goblins, whom they call pigmies, amongst others the name of "Duz," diminutive "Duzik," a name they bore in the time of St. Augustine; and he also says that they, like fairies,

---

Editor's Notes.

[*] Referring to "Le Grand Sarrazin," Dupont says in his *Histoire du Cotentin et ses Iles*, Vol I., p. 140-41 :—"Le personnage ainsi désigné ne peut être que l'un de ces avanturiers Norses qui furent souvent confondus avec les Sarrazins. Wace lui-même appelle les envahisseurs des îles les "*gent Sarrazine.*" Le "Grand Geffroi" était, selon toute vrai semblance le célèbre Jarl *Godefrid* ou *Godefroy* fils d'Hériald. Son père, après avoir détruit l'eglise du Mont Saint Michel fut assassiné par les comtes francs, et pour le venger, il se jeta sur la Frise et sur la Neustrie. Après trois ans de ravage il se fit, en 850, concéder par Charles-le-Chauve une certaine étendue de terre, que le savant danois Suhne conjecture avoir été située dans nôtre province. L'histoire générale, on le voit, confirme donc singulièrement la tradition conservée à Guernesey, en lui donnant une date précise ; et cette tradition elle-même rend à peu près certain le fait fort intéressant, et si souvent obscur, d'un établissement permanent des Normands en Neustrie, plus d'un demi-siècle avant sa prise en possession par Rolle ; elle prouve, enfin, le rôle important que les îles du Contentin remplirent durant ces époques calamiteuses."

[†] Près de Louvigné-du-Désert, est un groupe de dix à douze blocs gigantiques de granite. On a aussi donné le nom de "Rue de *Paradis*, du *Purgatoire*, et de *l'Enfer*" aux intervalles étroits qui séparent ces énormes blocs.—*Traditions de la Haute Bretagne*, par Paul Sebillot, T. I., p. 34.

inhabit Dolmens. Mr. Métivier explains the name "Déhus" or "Dhuss" as the "God of the Dead, and of Riches," the *Dis* of the Gauls in the time of Cæsar, *Théos* in Greek, *Deus* in Latin—le Dus, or le Duc. He says "Our *Dehussets* are nothing but *Dhus i gou*, spirits of the dead and goblins of the deep."

The exterior circle measures sixty feet in diameter, by forty in length, and the direction is from east to west. The enormous block of granite which serves as a roof to the western chamber is the most striking part of it. At the extremity of this chamber is a cell, the outer compartment eleven feet in length by nine in width. The adjoining one is of the same length. On the northern side a singular appendix in the form of a side chamber joins the two smaller rooms just described. There has also been discovered a fifth cell, the roof of which was formed of granite resting on three or four pillars, at the corner of the northern chamber. But the most interesting discovery of all was that of two kneeling skeletons, side by side, but placed in opposite positions, that is to say, one looking towards the north, the other towards the south. Besides these, bones of persons of both sexes and all ages, a stone hatchet, some pottery and limpet shells, were also found inside this place of sepulchre. It was long supposed to be haunted by fairies, imps, and ghosts, perhaps the same spirits who, in the haunted field of "Les Tuzés," are reported to have removed the foundations of the intended Parish Church of the Castel to its present site. There is also a "Le Déhuzel" in the neighbourhood of the Celtic remains near L'Erée.

"Le Trépied, or the Catioroc."

This Cromlech is on a rocky promontory, south-west of Perelle Bay, in the beautiful parish of St. Saviour's. The derivation of its name, " Castiau-Roc" —as it is properly—is from the *" Castelh Carreg"* " Castle Rock " of the Gauls. As one approaches it one is struck by the vestiges of Cromlechs with their circles, and bits of " Longues Roques." In olden days, before so much of the surroundings were quarried away, this must have been only one among many other conspicuous objects down there. The names " La Roque Fendue," " La Roque au Tonnerre," " Plateau ès Roques," " La Pièche des Grandes Roques du Castiau-Roc," which are mentioned in various " Livres de Perquages," are all that remain of these ancient remains. Much to be regretted is the disappearance of the " Portes du Castiau-Roc," which might perhaps have helped us to define with some exactitude where this problematic castle once stood, and perhaps identify it with the fortified mounts of the Celts and Irish. It is noted in our island annals for being the midnight haunt of our witches and wizards. In the trials for witchcraft held under Amias de Carteret in the beginning of the seventeenth century, it was there that his trembling victims confessed to having come and danced on Friday nights, in honour of the gigantic cat or goat with black fur, called " Baal-Bérith " or " Barberi," nowadays " Lucifer." Near this rock was the " Chapel of the Holy Virgin " on Lihou Island, now in ruins, and it is said that the witches even defied the influence of " the Star of the Sea," shouting in chorus while they danced,

> " *Qué, hou, hou,*
> *Marie Lihou.*"

This monument is like the " Tables en Trépied,"

and analogous to the " Lhêch y Drybedh " of the county of Pembroke, in Wales. There were altars in this form and of this description in almost every canton of the island. One, near the Chapel of St. George, is quite destroyed, and there are now no traces left of another between the Haye-du-Puits, and the Villocq. In the environs of the Castiau-Roc bones and arms have been found.*

" LE CREUX ES FAÏES."

This Cromlech is situated on the Houmet Nicolle at the point of L'Erée, (so called from the branch of the sea, *Eiré*, which separates it from the islet of Notre Dame de Lihou). This island, which once had upon it a chapel and a priory dedicated to " Notre Dame de la Roche," was always considered so sacred a spot that even to-day the fishermen salute it in passing.

This Creux is a Dolmen of the nature of those which are called in France " allées couvertes, " perfectly well preserved, and partly covered with earth. The researches which have been made in these ancient monuments of antiquity prove them to have been places of sepulchre. This one consists of a chamber seven feet high, and covered with a roof of two blocks of granite, each fifteen feet long and ten broad. The entrance faces east, and is only two feet eight inches wide, but soon enlarges, and the interior is almost uniformly eleven feet wide.

This is, as its name would lead one to suppose, a favourite haunt of the fairies, or perhaps, to speak more correctly, their usual dwelling place.

---

* See *Archæological Journal*, Vol. I., p. 202, for an engraving of this Castiau-Roc.

It is related that a man who happened to be lying on the grass near it, heard a voice within calling out : " *La païlle, la païlle, le fouar est caùd.*" (The shovel,* the oven is hot). To which the answer was immediately returned : " *Bon ! J'airon de la gâche bientôt.*" (Good ! We shall have some cake presently.

Another version from Mrs. Savidan is that some men were ploughing in a field belonging to Mr. Le Cheminant, just below the Cromlech, when the voice was heard saying " *La paille,*" *etc.* One of them answered, " *Bon ! J'airon de la gâche,*" and almost immediately afterwards a cake, quite hot, fell into one of the furrows. One of the men immediately ran forward and seized it, exclaiming that he would have a piece to take home to his wife, but on stooping to take it up he received such a buffet on the head as stretched him at full length on the ground. It is from here that the fairies issue on the night of the full moon to dance on Mont Saint till daybreak.†

" LA LONGUE ROQUE " OR " PALETTE ES FAÏES."

In a field in the parish of St. Pierre-du-Bois, on the way to L'Erée and in the neighbourhood of the secluded valley of St. Brioc and the woody nook in which the ancient chapel dedicated to that Saint once stood, stands one of those Celtic monuments, many of which are still to be seen in Brittany and Cornwall,

---

EDITOR'S NOTES.

* " La païlle à four, is, in the country, usually a wooden shovel with a long handle. It is used for putting things in the oven when hot, and taking them out when baked."

† This is still believed, for in 1896, when my aunt, Mrs. Curtis, bought some land on Mont Saint, and built a house there, the country people told her that it was very unlucky to go there and disturb the fairy people in the spot where they dance.

My cousin, Miss Le Pelley, writes in 1890 from St. Pierre-du-Bois, saying " The people still believe the Creux des Fées and ' Le Trepied ' to have been the fairies' houses, and as proof one woman told me that when they dug down they found all kinds of pots and pans and china things."

and which are known in those countries by the name of "Menhir." This word in the Breton tongue, and in its cognate dialect the ancient language of Cornwall, signifies "long stone." The name which similar monuments bear in Normandy and Brittany in this island is "longue pierre" or "longue roque," a literal translation of the Celtic name. There must have been at one time many "longues roques" in Guernsey. Another still stands in a field near the road at Richmond. There was in 1581 "la pièche de la longue pierre, la pierre séante dedans,"—a part of the Fief ès Cherfs, at the Castel. There was also "la Roque Séante dans le courtil de la Hougue au Comte," and the "Roque-à-Bœuf dans le Courtil au Sucq du chemin de l'église," near St. George, but these latter have long since disappeared, though a house near the field still bears the name.

Antiquaries are very much divided in opinion as to the original destination of these singular masses of rock; it is not wonderful that they should prove a puzzle and a source of wonder to the unlettered peasantry. How were such immense blocks placed upright, and for what purpose? The agency of supernatural beings is an easy answer to the question, and some such cause is usually assigned for their origin by the tradition of the country. Sometimes they are the work of fairies, sometimes of giants and magicians, and sometimes they are said to be mortals changed into stone by an offended deity for some sacrilegious act, or heroes petrified as a lasting testimony of their exploits.

The Menhir at St. Peter's-in-the-Wood stands in a field at Les Paysans, so called from the name of the extinct family who once possessed it. It is over ten feet in height, and about three feet wide, and the people's name for it, "Palette ès faïes"—the fairies' battledore,—describes it exactly. Tradition says that. in former days a man who was returning homewards at a very late hour of the night, or who had risen before the lark to visit his nets in Rocquaine Bay, was astonished at meeting a woman of very diminutive stature coming up the hill from the sea-shore. She was knitting, while carrying in her apron something with as much care and tenderness as if it had been a clutch of eggs, or a newly-born babe. The man's curiosity was excited, and he determined to watch the little woman. He therefore concealed himself behind a hedge and followed her movements. At last the woman stopped, and great was the astonishment of the countryman when he saw her produce a mass of stone of at least fifteen feet in length, and stick it upright in the midst of the field, with as much ease as if she were merely sticking a pin into a pincushion. He then comprehended that the unknown female could be no other than a denizen of fairy-land, but what could be her object in erecting such a monument ? The people are at a loss in finding an answer to this question. Some say the stone was placed there by the fairies to serve them as a mark when they played at ball.[*]

There is another story told to account for " La Palette ès Faïes." It is well known that Rocquaine

---

[*] From Miss Lane, afterwards Mrs. Lane-Clarke.

EDITOR'S NOTE.—See in *Traditions et Superstitions de la Haute Bretagne* par Paul Sebillot, Tome I., p. 10 and 11, etc. :—" Les Roches aux Fées qui sont vers Saint-Didier et Marpiré (Ille-et-Vilaine) ont été élevées par les Fées ; elles prenaient les plus grosses pierres du pays et les apportaient dans leurs tabliers. . . . Près du bois du Rocher en Pleudihan, sur la route de Dinan à Dol, est un dolmen que les fées, disent les gens du pays, ont apporté dant leurs ' devantières ' (tabliers)."

and its environs was the abode *par excellence* of the fairy folk, and in the valley of St. Brioc two of these fairies once lived. Whether they were father and son, or what other relationship existed between them, is not known, but among the human inhabitants of the valley they went by the names of Le Grand Colin and Le Petit Colin. They were fond of sports, and occasionally amused themselves with a game of ball on the open and tolerably level fields of Les Paysans. On one occasion they had placed their boundary marks, and had played some rounds, when Le Grand Colin struck the ball with such force that it bounded off quite out of sight. Le Petit Colin, whose turn it was to play, called out to his companion, with some degree of ill-humour, that the ball had disappeared beyond the bounds, on which Le Grand Colin struck his bat with force into the ground, and said he would play no more. The bat still remains in the centre of the field, and the ball—an enormous spherical boulder—is pointed out on the sea-shore near Les Pezeries, fully a mile and a half off.[*]

" LA ROQUE DES FAÏES."

A little beyond the village called " Le Bourg de la Forêt " there stood formerly an upright stone, which was known by the name of " La Roque des Faïes,"— the fairies' stone. It was unfortunately destroyed when the road was improved. The people in the neighbourhood were rather shy of passing it at night, as it was believed that the place was haunted, and that fairies held their nightly revels there. Like other stones of a similar nature it was said to have been

---

[*] From William Le Poidevin.

EDITOR'S NOTES.—These two traditions are still told by the country people in 1896.

placed there by the elves to serve as a goal or mark in their games of ball or bowls; and, according to some accounts, the "Longue Roque" at "Les Paysans" in the adjoining parish of St. Pierre-du-du-Bois was the other boundary. It is not at all unlikely that these stones may really have served for such a purpose in days of yore, if not for the fairy-folk, at least for mortals. What is more probable than that the peasantry of the islands should have had the same games as existed until lately in Cornwall under the name of "hurling," and in Brittany under the name of "La Soule," as well as elsewhere, in which the young men of the neighbouring districts met at certain seasons on the confines of their respective parishes, and contended which should first bear a ball to a spot previously fixed on as the goal in each?

It is said that the spot where the stone in question stood was originally fixed on as the site of the Parish Church of the Forest; but that, after all the materials had been got together for the purpose of laying the foundations of the sacred edifice they were removed in the short space of one night by the fairies to the place where the church now stands, the little people thus resenting the intrusion on their domain.*

"Le Gibet des Faïes."

A Celtic monument of the kind commonly known to antiquaries by the name of "trilethon" is said to have existed formerly on the Common at L'Ancresse, near La Hougue Patris. It is described by old people who remember to have seen it in their youth as

---

* From Mrs. Richard Murton, born Caroline Le Tullier.

consisting of three upright stones or props, supporting a fourth, overhanging the others. It was known by the name of "Le Gibet des Fâïes." Near it was a fountain called "La Fontaine des Fâïes," the water of which, although not plentiful, was never known to fail entirely, even in the very driest seasons ; it is said to have been below the surface in a kind of artificial cave formed by huge blocks of stone, and entered by two openings on different sides. The proprietor of the land many years ago broke up the stones for building purposes and converted the fountain into a well.*

OLD FIGURES IN THE CHURCHYARDS OF ST. MARTIN'S AND THE CASTEL.

In the course of some works recently (1878) undertaken for reseating the Parish Church of Ste. Marie-du-Castel, two discoveries were made, which are of great interest. One is a sort of oven or furnace,

---

EDITOR'S NOTE.

STONE ON LA MOYE ESTATE.

* They are still firmly convinced in the Vale parish of the sanctity of Druidical stones, and various stones, which are not generally regarded as being Druidical remains, were pointed out to me by Miss Falla, (whose ancestors for hundreds of years have been landed proprietors at the Vale), as being sacred, and, she added, that her father and grandfathers would have considered it sacrilege to touch them.

Such are the large upright stones in the field Le Courtil-ès-Arbres, immediately opposite the house called Sohier, which is owned by Miss Falla, who said that her uncle, at one time, wished to quarry in that field, but was deterred by his neighbours, who pointed out to him the folly and impiety of meddling with "les pierres saintes.' Beyond the Ville-ès-Pies is a field containing large stones ; it has been extensively quarried, but the stones have been religiously preserved, and are seen on an isolated hillock in the field, their height being intensified by the deep quarries round them.

The cottage which is built on the remains of St. Magloire's Chapel, is supposed to be built on its own old foundation stone, as the workmen when building the cottage, thought it would be sacrilege to interfere with it.

There is a field called La Houmière, opposite an estate called La Moye, which also belonged to the Fallas for many generations, and is now in the possession of Miss Falla's brother. In this field is one solitary upright stone, and to this stone a most extraordinary superstition is attached. It is a grass field and is grown in hay, but for generations the mowers have always been forbidden to cut the hay *round* and *past* the stone till all the other hay has been cut and carted, for if they do, however fine the weather may previously have been, it invariably brings on a storm of wind and rain ! So, taught by experience, it has always been the rule, and still continues, that, though the outer edge of the field may be cut, the stone itself and its " entourage" are not to be touched till the very last, for fear of bringing on the rain in the middle of the hay making.—*(From Miss Falla)*.

which was found below the surface of the floor of
the church, and immediately under the apex of the
westernmost arch, between the nave and the south
aisle. It lies north and south, extending into the
nave; but what appears to have been the mouth
does not reach southward beyond the arch, no part
of it being in the south aisle. If this aisle is really
a more recent addition to the original building, the
mouth of the furnace may have been at one time
in an outer wall. The whole length is eight feet, the
width two feet three inches, and the depth three feet
six inches. The sides are roughly masoned and the
northern end slightly rounded. A length of about
three feet at the south end is arched over with stones,
which have evidently been subjected to great heat.
This part is immediately under the arch between the
nave and the south aisle. The remaining five feet of
the excavation retain no traces whatever of an arch,
and are situated entirely in the nave. The floor of
the excavation is of hard compact gravel, covered with
ashes, among which were several pieces of charcoal
and a few small fragments of brass, perhaps bell-
metal. The northern end seems to have been used
as a sort of ossuary, into which the bones dug up
in making fresh interments in the church were thrown
pell-mell, the remains of no less than nine skulls,
mingled with other osseous remains, having been found
here. These bore no marks of fire, from which we
may conclude that the place had ceased to be used
as an oven or furnace when they were deposited
there. I had forgotten to mention that at the south
end of the excavation was found a tile of about one
and a-half inches in thickness, twelve inches in length,
and nine inches in width; with a notch in it for the

fingers, such as we see in the sliding lid of a box.
A few fragments of moulded tiles were found mingled
with the earth, which the architect believed to be
Roman. With the exception of a few coins, no other
Roman remains have ever been found in Guernsey.
The nave of the church and the westernmost bay of
the aisle had, in olden days, been walled off from the
rest of the building, and served as a sort of vestibule
and place where the cannons and other military stores
belonging to the Militia or trained bands of the parish
were kept. Perhaps the furnace may have been used
for casting balls, of which one at least has been
found in the building. Some think it may have been
used for the casting of a bell, but the bells at present
in the tower throw no light on the subject, having
been re-cast in England about the beginning of the
nineteenth century. There is no appearance of any
chimney or flue leading from the furnace ever having
existed, and the reason of its position within the
church, and the use to which it was put, must, we
fear, ever remain an enigma.

After this long digression we will go on to the
other discovery made at the same time; which
presents another puzzle equally unsolved.

Just within the chancel, at about an equal distance
from the north and south walls, about a foot below
the surface, was found a mass of granite, lying east
and west, and turned over on its left side. It has
all the appearance of a natural boulder somewhat
fashioned by art, and cannot be described better than
by saying that it is in shape like a mummy case,
the back being rounded and slightly curved and the
front nearly flat, with the exception of the upper
portion of the figure, which indicates that it was

I 2

intended to represent a female. The total length is six feet six inches, the width across the shoulders two feet three inches, and the portion corresponding with the head one foot three inches from the top of the forehead to the shoulders. It tapers slightly towards the foot. On each side of the head, extending from the forehead to the breast, are two ridges raised above the surface of the stone, which may have been intended to represent either a veil or tresses of hair. There are no traces of any features remaining, but what should be the face bears evident marks of having been subjected to the action of a hammer or chisel, as also does the right breast.

The stone is altogether too rude and mis-shapen to warrant the supposition that it can have been intended to cover a grave, although its place in the chancel, and its lying with its head to the west, may appear to favour this idea ; but what renders the discovery of this stone more interesting and gives rise to conjecture, is the fact that in the churchyard of St. Martin-de-la-Beilleuse another stone of about the same size, precisely similar in outline, but in a far better state of preservation, exists in the form of a gatepost. In this last the features, very coarsely sculptured, and only slightly raised on a flat surface, are distinctly visible ; a row of small knobs, intended either for curls or a chaplet encircles the forehead, and a sort of drapery in regular folds radiates from the chin to the shoulders and breasts, which are uncovered, leaving no doubt that in this case, as in the stone found in the Church of Ste. Marie-du-Castel, a female figure was intended to be represented. A confused idea exists among the parishioners of St. Martin's that the stone in their churchyard was once

an idol; and it is not many years ago that a
puritanical churchwarden was with difficulty dissuaded
from having it broken up, lest it should once more
become an object of adoration. In fact the stone was
broken in half by his orders, and had to be cemented
together again.

The Church of St. Martin's is called St. Martin-
de-la-Bellouse or Beilleuse, a name which an adjoining
property bears to this day. The meaning of this word
" Bellouse " or " Beilleuse " is unknown; but if, as
some have asserted, the early inhabitants of the
British Isles worshipped a deity of the name of Bel,
it is not impossible that there may have been some
female divinity, with a name derived from the same
source.

It is certainly somewhat remarkable that two stones,
so very similar in character, should exist in connection
with two churches in the same island, and that one
of them should have been found in so singular a
position. One is tempted to believe that both churches
may have been built on spots which had previously
been set apart as places of heathen worship, and that
in the case of Ste. Marie-du-Castel the idol had been
defaced and buried in the earth to put a stop to the
adoration paid to it.

It is well known that up to the end of the
seventeenth century the inhabitants of a district in
the Department du Morbihan, in Brittany, adored
with superstitious and obscene rites a rude stone
image commonly known as " La Vénus de Quinipilly,"
and which was certainly not a Christian image. May
not the stones here described have served also as
objects of worship? The substitution of the Blessed
Virgin for a female divinity is what one may

reasonably suppose to have taken place, and the continuance of superstitious practices in connection with the idol may have led to its defacement and concealment below the floor of the sacred edifice.*

---

* The Antiquarian Society. Proceedings 1879.

EDITOR'S NOTES.

This old figure is still regarded with peculiar affection by the people of St. Martin's. "*La Gran'mère du Chimquière*,"—"the Grandmother of the Churchyard,"—they call it, though I have heard one or two very old people call it "St. Martin," evidently regardless of sex, regarding it as the patron saint of the parish.

Undoubtedly superstitious reverence used to be paid to it to within comparatively recent times, which probably accounts for the churchwarden wishing to have it removed. An old Miss Fallaize, aged eighty, told me that when she was a child the "old people" had told her that it was "lucky" to place a little offering of fruit, flowers, or even to spill a little drop of spirits in front of it, for it was holy—"c'était une pierre sainte" as she expressed it; and an old man named Tourtel, well over eighty, said that when he was a boy it was feared—"on la craignait" much more than they do now.

There is a stone face, very much the same type as that of this figure, over the door of a house at the Villette. It is a house in the district called "La Marette," and belongs to some old Miss Olliviers. They can offer no explanation to account for its presence, but said that the house was covered with creepers, and it was only when some myrtle which covered it was blown down in a gale that it was discovered by their father to be there. Of course it may have belonged to some other old idol which was broken up, and afterwards used for building purposes, but no tradition lingers to account for it in any way.

The earliest account of the Guernsey Cromlechs was contributed to *Archæologia*, Vol. XVIII, p. 251, by Joshua Gosselin, Esq., as follows :—

"AN ACCOUNT OF SOME DRUIDICAL REMAINS IN THE ISLAND OF GUERNSEY, BY JOSHUA GOSSELIN, ESQ., IN A LETTER ADDRESSED TO THE RIGHT HON. SIR JOSEPH BANKS, BART., K.B., P.R.S., F.S.A.

"Guernsey, November 9th, 1811.

"MY DEAR SIR,—A small temporary redoubt was constructed some few years back, on a height near the shore, on the left of L'Ancresse Bay, three miles from the town in this island. The ground on which this redoubt stood, being composed of a sandy turf, was by degrees levelled by the wind, and the edges of some stones were thereby discovered, which, upon inspection, I immediately knew to belong to a Cromlech or Druidical Temple. I send you a drawing of this Temple (plate 18) as it appeared after the sand, which had covered it to the depth of three or four feet, was removed. . . . The largest of the stones weighs about twenty tons. They are supported by stones of the same kind, the highest being about six and a-half feet above the ground. The temple slopes from west to east; the length of it is thirty-two feet, and the greatest width between the supporting stones is twelve feet. The soldiers, who were employed in clearing away the sand, have assured me that there was a stone which closed the entrance into the temple, that some steps led down into it, and that there was a pavement of small pebbles, but I cannot vouch for the truth of these particulars. When I saw the Cromlech there was certainly no vestige of any steps or pavement. There was, however, a quantity of human and different animal bones found in it, likewise some broken pieces of coarse earthen vessels, together with some limpets, such as are on the rocks in the bay, a few cockle shells and land snails. These last might have been blown into it by the wind, when it filled with sand, as there are plenty of them on the adjoining common. Some of the fragments of vessels seem to have been blackened with fire, and bear the appearance of antiquity; a vessel of reddish clay was found whole, which held somewhat more than a quart, and was of the shape of a common tea cup. A flat circular bone of some fish, of the shape of a disk, and about nine inches in diameter, was discovered, together with an old fishhook, the former of which was given by the soldiers to Sir John Doyle. I was only able to procure for myself some of the fragments of broken ware. About eighteen feet distance from the foot of the temple there are remains of a circle of stones which probably surrounded it; they are placed about a foot above the ground, and in general about two feet distant from each other. At about forty-two feet from the temple there appears to have been another circle of stones of a larger size than those of the inner circle, but there are very few of them remaining. As this temple stands upon the top of a hill, it is the intention of some gentlemen in the island to have so much of the sand on each side of it removed, as may render it visible to all the surrounding country.

"We have three more such temples in this island, but not so complete, nor so large, as the one I have just described. One of these is situated near Paradis, at the Clos of the Vale, and is called 'La Pierre du Déhus.' It stands on a rising ground, and slopes towards the east-north-east. The stones are of a grey granite. The supporting, or upright stones, are two and a-half feet above the ground in the inside, and could not be more, as the bottom is rocky; they form a parallelogram in the inside of twelve feet broad.

"Another of these temples is seen at the Catioroc, at St. Saviour's, and the third is situated between L'Ancresse Bay and the Valle Church, and is partly concealed by furze.

"Some years ago I discovered a very large Logan or rocking stone, on a rock at the opposite side of L'Ancresse Bay, which could easily be rocked by a child; but within these three years it has been entirely destroyed, and no vestige of it now remains. An ancient manuscript says that this island was originally inhabited by fishermen, who were Pagans, and used to place large stones one upon another, near the sea shore, on which they performed their sacrifices. The stones of this kind, which are now extant, are certainly all situated near the sea shore, and this circumstance so far corroborates the information given in the manuscript.

"I have the honour to be. Dear Sir,

"Your obliged and very humble servant,

"JOSHUA GOSSELIN."

This article is illustrated by plates drawn by the author, viz., "Temple of L'Ancresse in the Valle Parish, Guernsey," "Plan of the surface of the Temple at L'Ancresse," "Views of the Temple" called "La Pierre du Déhus," from the W.S.W. and the E.N.E. "Plan of the surface of Déhus," North and South Views of the "Temple at the Catioroc," and "The Temple among the Furze between L'Ancresse Bay and the Valle Church."

Çreux des Fàïes.

CHAPTER IV.

Natural Objects and their Superstitions.

"Yon old grey stone, protected from the ray
Of noontide suns. . . . .
And thou, grey stone, the pensive likeness keep
Of a dark chamber where the mighty sleep :
Far more than fancy to the influence bends
When solitary nature condescends
To mimic time's forlorn humanities."
—*Wordsworth.*

" This is the fairy land : oh spight of spights
We talk with goblins, owls, and elvish sprites."
—*Shakespeare.*

THERE are many spots in Guernsey connected with stories and legends besides the Druidical remains. The caverns of the Creux des Fées and Creux Mahié ; the various curiously shaped rocks, formed by the hand of Nature, or by the wearing action of the waves ; the marks of footprints, whether human or diabolical, on various stones; and above all the sacred fountains, which are still regarded as medicinal, have given rise to many a tradition, which, though they lose much of their charm from being translated from the quaint Guernsey French in which they are originally related, we will here endeavour to render.

Le Creux des Fées.

Between the bays of Vazon and Cobo is found the peninsula of Houmet, and here is situated the " Creux des Fées." It is a small cavern, worn away by the action of the sea. The granite surrounding its mouth abounds in particles of mica, which glitter in the sun like streaks of gold. It can only be approached at low tide, and necessitates much scrambling over the rocks which are heaped round the mouth of the grotto. It is said that by a hole not larger than the mouth of an oven, you gain access to a spacious hall, hollowed out of the rock, that in the middle of this hall is a stone table on which are dishes, plates, drinking cups, and everything necessary for a large feast, all in stone, and all used by the fairies, but no one has had the courage to penetrate inside and test the truth of this assertion. It is also believed that beyond it there is a subterranean passage which leads to the bottom of St. Saviour's Church, which is distant more than two miles. This tradition of a subterranean passage leading to a church at a considerable distance is told of other caverns in Guernsey. Of the Creux Mahié, where there is also said to be a passage leading to St. Saviour's Church, of a large cave in Moulin Huet Bay, which is supposed to lead to a passage going straight to St. Martin's Church, and one at Saints' Bay, also supposed to lead to St. Saviour's Church.

Le Creux Mahié.

The whole of the southern coast of Guernsey, from Jerbourg, or St. Martin's Point, to Pleinmont in the parish of Torteval, is extremely precipitous, but abounding in picturesque beauties of no common

EDITOR's NOTE.—" Le groupe le plus important de demeures de fées que j'aie rencontré est celui des Houles (l'anglais *hole*, caverne, grotte)." . . . " Elles se prolongent sous terre si loin, que personne, dit-on, n'est allé jusqu'au fond . . . . parfois on les appelle Chambres des fées. Il y en a où l'on voit, dit-on, des tables de pierre sur lesquelles elles mangeaient, leurs sièges, et les berceaux en pierre de leurs enfants."—*Traditions et Superstitions de la Haute Bretagne*, p. 84.

character. Bold headlands, with outlying granite rocks
rising like pyramids and obelisks from the clear blue
sea, alternating with caves and bays to which access
is gained through deep glens and ravines, some richly
wooded, some hemmed in on both sides by rugged
hills, but through all of which a tiny rill of the
purest water trickles, keeping up a perpetual verdure
—slopes covered in early spring with the golden
blossoms of the gorse, in summer with the purple
bells of the heather, and in autumn with the rich
brown fronds of the withering bracken—cliffs mantled
in parts with luxuriant ivy, in other with many
coloured lichens, and out of every crevice of which
the thrift, the campion, and other flowers that delight
in the vicinity of the sea, burst in wild profusion—
all combine to form pictures which the artist and
the lover of nature are never tired of studying.

The constant action of the waves for unnumbered
centuries has worn out many caverns in these cliffs,
the most considerable of which is that known by
the name of "Le Creux Mahié," or as some old
writers wrote it "Mahio," and it undoubtedly took
its name, so says Mr. Métivier, from its ancient
proprietor, the king of the infernal regions.

> " The Prince of darkness is a gentleman ;
> Modo he's called and *Mahu.*"
> —*King Lear.* Act 3, Sc. 4.

The Hindoos have the same name in their *Maha-
Dêva*, a giant of the family of the dives or demons.*
In the province of Mayo, there is a Sorcerer or
Druid, the Priest of *Mayo*, who lives in a cavern,
and is called "the King of the Waters."

---

* *Recherches Asiatiques*, Tome I., Traduit de l'Anglais,

It is also sometimes called "Le Creux Robilliard," from a family of that name on whose property it was situated. It lies in the parish of Torteval, and is reached by a narrow pathway, winding down the almost precipitous side of a steep cliff, into a small creek worn out by the sea between the headlands. The cave itself, there can be no doubt, must have been formed by the waves wearing away gradually a vein of decomposed rock, softer than that which forms the sides and roof. At some remote period a large portion of the rock which forms the roof of the cavern has given way, and has partially blocked up the entrance, leaving only a long low fissure through which access can be had to the interior, and forming a sort of platform of solid stone, which effectually cuts off any further encroachment on the part of the sea. A steep descent over broken fragments of rock leads down to the floor of the cave, which appears to be nearly on a level with the beach at the foot of the platform. A glimmering light from the entrance enables one to see that the rock arches overhead in a sort of dome, and a bundle of dry furze or other brushwood, set on fire, lights it up sufficiently to bring out all the details. It is a weird sight; as the flickering flames illumine one by one the various masses of rock that are piled up to the roof at the extremity of the cavern, and disclose the entrances to two or three smaller caves. These are, in reality, of no great depth, but they are sufficiently mysterious to have given rise to more than one report concerning them, and there are but few of the peasantry who would be bold enough to attempt to explore their recesses. It is firmly believed by them that there is a passage extending all the way under

ground as far as the Church of St. Saviour's, about
a mile distant as the crow flies; and it is also
affirmed that there is an entrance through a small
hole to an extensive apartment, in the midst of
which stands a stone table, on which are set out
dishes, plates, drinking vessels, and other requisites for
a well-served feast, all of the same solid material.*

There are obscure traditions of the cavern having
been at some early period the resort of men who
lived by stealing their neighbours sheep, and plundering
their hen-roosts, but these traditions cannot be traced
to anything more definite than what is commonly
alleged of all such places, neither are the tales told
of its having been the resort of smugglers more to
be relied on. The difficulty of access to it, either by
sea or land, makes it very improbable that it should
have been used for this purpose ; besides, in former
days, Guernsey was a perfectly free port, nothing that
entered was subject to any duty that it would have
been profitable to evade, and before the establishment
of a branch of the English Custom House, all exports
could be made without the troublesome formalities of
clearance and declaration now required. Of late years
the smuggling of spirits into the island in order to
avoid payment of the local dues in aid of the public
revenue, has been carried on to rather a large extent;
but this has taken place on more accessible parts of
the coast. Possibly, however, tobacco made up in
illegal packages, which would subject it to seizure if
found waterborne, may occasionally have been deposited here for a time, until it could be carried off

---

* This last piece of information was furnished by Caroline le Tullier, of the
Parish of the Forest, wife of Richard Murton.

secretly to the French vessels passing the island in their coasting voyages between Normandy and Brittany.

In a letter dated May, 1665, to one of his friends in Guernsey, from the Rev. John de Sausmarez, who, on the restoration of Charles II., was appointed Dean of the Island, and subsequently Canon of Windsor, he alludes to " Le prophète du Creux Robilliard." Who this prophet was does not appear, but there is every reason to believe that the allusion is to the Rev. Thomas Picot, Minister of the then united parishes of the Forest and Torteval, in the latter of which the Creux Mahié—*alias* Robilliard, is situated ; for in the Assembly of Divines held at Westminster in 1644, articles were exhibited against this clergyman for troubling the Church discipline established in the island, preaching Anabaptist doctrines, and prophesying that in 1655 there should be a perfect reformation, men should do miracles, etc. This conjecture receives some slight confirmation from the fact that it is still remembered in the Forest parish that a Minister of the name of Picot was fond of retiring to caves on the sea-shore for meditation, and one of these caves in particular, that well known one in Petit Bot bay with a double entrance, is still known by the name of " Le Parloir de Monsieur Picot."

Rocks and Stones.

" LE PETIT BONHOMME ANDRELOT, OU ANDRIOU."

"Screams round the Arch-druid's brow the seamew—white
As Menai's foam."
                                                    —*Wordsworth.*

One of the earliest forms of idolatry is undoubtedly
that which was paid to rude stone pillars. These,
whether erected for the purpose of marking the last
resting place of some renowned patriarch or warrior, or
set up with the design of indicating a spot specially
appropriated to religious rites, or perhaps, simply as
a boundary or landmark, came to be regarded, at first,
as sacred, and in process of time, as a symbol of
the Deity himself. Gradually any elevated rock,
and especially if it presented a striking and unusual
appearance, was looked upon with veneration. We
find that this was particularly the case in the north
of Europe, and that the hardy mariners who navigate
the tempestuous seas of Scandinavia, are, even now,
in the habit of paying a sort of superstitious respect
to the lofty "stacks," as the isolated masses of rock
are called, which form the extremity of many of the
headlands, and that, in passing, they salute them,
and throw old clothes, or a little food, or a drop
of spirits, into the sea, as a sort of propitiatory
offering. It is strange to find that the same custom
still exists in Guernsey, notwithstanding that a
thousand years or more have elapsed since the
Northmen first invaded these shores.

Everyone who has visited Guernsey must know the

"Le Petit Bonhomme Andrelot, ou Andriou."

lovely bay of Moulin Huet,* and the remarkable group of rocks, which stretches out into the sea at its eastern extremity beyond the point of Jerbourg. These rocks are called " Les Tas de Pois d'Amont," or " The Pea-Stacks of the East." There being a chain of rocks off Pleinmont which are called the "Tas de Pois d'Aval "—the westerly Pea-Stacks— " Amont " (meaning " en haut ") is the Guernsey word for *east*, *aval* meaning " en bas," their word for *west*.†

Each rock composing the Tas de Pois d'Amont has its own special name. They are " Le Petit Aiguillon," " Le Gros Aiguillon," " L'Aiguillon d'Andrelot," ou " du Petit Bon-Homme."

The united and increasing action of the winds and waves has worn the hard granite rock into the most fantastic forms, and from certain points of view it is not difficult to invest some of these masses of stone with a fancied resemblance to the human form. One of them in particular, when seen at a certain distance, has all the appearance of an aged man enveloped in the gown and cowl of a monk.

So singular a freak of nature has not escaped the attention of the peasantry, and the rock in question is pointed out by the name of " Le Petit Bon-Homme Andriou." The children in the neighbourhood have a rhymed saying :

" *Andriou, tape tout*,"

which may be translated

" Andriou, watch all," or " over all,"

---

† (Par la même raison que le vent d'ouest est le vent d'*aval*, le vent qui vient de la partie la plus haute, la plus montueuse de France, est le vent d'*amont.—Métivier's Dictionary*, page 36).

EDITOR'S NOTE.—* " Moulin Luet," according to Mr. Métivier—" Vier Port "—still in the mouths of the old country people.

and the fishermen and pilots who frequent these parts of the coast show their respect by taking off their hats when passing the point, and are careful to insist on the observance being complied with by any stranger who may chance to be in their company. Formerly it was not unusual with them, before setting sail, to offer a biscuit or a libation of wine or cider to " Le Bon Homme," and, if an old garment past use chanced to be in the boat, this was also cast into the sea.*

There are other rocks on the coast which the fishermen are in the habit of saluting without being able to give any reason why they do so ; and it is not impossible that the honour paid to the little island of Lihou,† on the western coast of Guernsey, by the small craft, in lowering their topmasts while passing, may have originated in the same superstition,

---

† Dr. Heylyn says in his *Survey of the Estate of Guernsey and Jarsey*, published 1656, p. 298 :—" The least of these isles, but yet of most note, is the little islet called *Lehu*, situate on the north side of the eastern corner, and neer unto those scattered rocks, which are called *Les Hanwaux* appertaining once unto the Dean, but now unto the Governour. Famous for a little Oratory or Chantery there once erected to the honour of the Virgin *Mary*, who, by the people in those times was much sued to by the name of our Lady of *Lehu*. A place long since demolished in the ruine of it. " *Sed jam periere ruinæ*," but now the ruines of it are scarce visible, there being almost nothing left of it but the steeple, which serveth only as a sea-marke, and to which, as any of that party sail along they strike their topsail. " *Tantum religio potuit suadere*." Such a religious opinion have they harboured of the place, that, though the Saint be gone, the wals shall yet still be honoured."

---

* There are several legends still repeated by the country people about " Le Petit Bon Homme Andriou.

One is that he was a man searching for hidden treasure among the rocks of the Tas de Pois and that the guardian spirit of the treasure appeared and turned him into stone for his sacrilege.—*Collected by Mr. J. Linwood Pitts, of the Guille-Allès Library.*

Another is that he was an old Arch-Druid, the last of the Druids to hold out against Christianity. Miserable at his brethren's apostacy from the faith of their fathers, he went to live in a cave at the end of Jerbourg Point. His favourite occupation was standing on the rocks of the Tas de Pois and gazing out to sea, for he was passionately fond of the sea and sailors. One day, during a violent gale, he saw a ship in great distress out at sea, so he prayed

although it is generally supposed that they do it out
of reverence to the Blessed Virgin, the ruins of
whose Chapel and Priory are still to be seen on the
isle.   The circumnavigation of a certain rock by the
fishermen of the parish of St. John, in Jersey, on
Midsummer Day, may, perhaps, be traceable to the
same source.

"LA ROQUE MANGI."

La Roque Màngi was a natural granite formation
having a very artificial aspect.   It stood on one of
those sandy downs which extend along the north-
west coast between "Le Grand Havre" and "Les
Grand' Rocques," and consisted of a slender upright
mass of rock of from eight to ten feet in height,
surmounted by a large stone, projecting about half a
foot on every side, resting on the narrowest part of

---

to his gods to stop the storm and save the ship.   They took no notice of his prayers, the
storm still raged, and the ship was driven nearer and nearer to the dangerous rocks on which
he stood.   Then, in desperation, he prayed to the God of the Christians, and vowed that if only
the ship were saved he would tuin Christian and dedicate a Chapel to the Blessed Virgin.   As
he prayed, the gale ceased, and the ship made its way safely to the harbour.   And Andrillot,
after being baptised as a Christian, dedicated a Chapel; some say it is the one of which the
ruins on Lihou Island can still be seen, which is dedicated to "Notre Dame de la Roche;"
others say it was the Chapel, long since destroyed, which was on the Fief Blanchelande in St.
Martin's parish, and which is believed to have stood where the parish school now stands.

Be that as it may, that little figure standing, looking out to sea, petrified there that he may
yet bring good luck and fine weather to his beloved sailors, is still looked upon by them with
fond reverence, and they still throw him in passing their drop of spirits, or doff their flag, for
luck.—*From Mr. Isaac Le Patourel and others.*

"L'Bouan Homme Andriou," as correctly printed in Gray's map.   This is a *petrified Druid,*
or rather Arch-Druid,—An *An Drio*—the Primate of the Unelli, and now the guardian of Moulin
Huet and Saints' Bays, Guernsey; for, according to Rowland, our ancestors called that mighty
Prelate thus, and Toland in his *Celtic Religion,* p. 60, says "The present ignorant vulgar
believes that these enchanters the Druids were at least themselves enchanted by the still
greater enchanter Patrick and his disciples, who miraculously confined them *to the places
that bear their names.*   And let me not be thought over minutious should I notice the
peculiar propriety of the epithet applied by rural tradition to this *most reverend* rock of
ours—"Le Bouan Homme."—bon homme" in France, and "good man" in England, still
denoting a Priest two centuries ago, particularly a priest of the old régime."—*From Mr.
Métivier.*

"LA BELLE LIZABEAU."

Another instance of a traditionally petrified human being is a rock off the Creux Mahié,
standing straight out into the water.   It is called "La Belle Lizabeau," and a little rock
at the foot of it is called "La Petite Lizabeau."   It is said that "Lizabeau" was a
beautiful girl of Torteval, who was turned out of the house with her baby by her infuriated
father.   Mad with despair she rushed to the cliffs and leapt into the sea with her baby in
her arms, and she and her child were turned into the rocks which now stand there.—*From Dan
Mauger, an old fisherman of St. Martin's Parish.*

the supporting stone, and looking at a little distance like a petrified giant. It was destroyed by the proprietor of the land about the middle of the present century in the hopes of finding below it a profitable quarry of granite, in which, however, he was disappointed.

Of this rock a curious legend was related by the neighbouring peasants. It was said that the Devil, having quarrelled one day with his wife, tied her by the hair of her head to the upright stone, and that, in her frantic efforts to disengage herself by running round and round, she wore away the solid granite to the narrow neck which supported the superincumbent head.*

The origin of the name seems doubtful, some tracing it to a family of the name of Maingy, who possessed land in the parish in which the rock was situated. Others, with more probability, attributing it to the " eaten "—" mangé "—(in the local dialect " mângi ") appearance of the stones, where the upper one or head joined the supporting upright.

" La Chaire de St. Bonit."

This was also called " La Chaire au Prêtre," and was situated in the district of the Hamelins, a little to the north of the property known as St. Clair. It was a very regularly formed natural obelisk of about eight to ten feet in height, rising from the summit of one of those hillocks, or " hougues " as they are locally called, which, before the great granite industry took its rise, abounded in St. Sampson's and the Vale parishes, and along the whole western coast. At

---

* From one of the Le Poidevins, of Pleinhcaume.

the foot of the upright rock was a large flat stone, giving the whole mass the appearance of a gigantic chair or pulpit. Seven stone hatchets have been unearthed in its vicinity. It was evidently used by the Druids as one of their sacred chairs, in which their Pontiffs sat to instruct the people. It is probable that towards the end of the seventh century, St. Bonit, Bishop of Auvergne, who was known to have been a great traveller, visited the land previously converted by St. Samson, St. Magloire, St. Paterne, and St. Marcouf, and sat and preached to the people in this erst-while Druid's throne, which henceforth bore his name.

"LA ROCQUE OU LE COQ CHANTE."

This very singular name is given to a picturesque mass of rock which forms the termination of a hill in the parish of Ste. Marie du Castel, and abuts on the road leading from the village of Les Grands Moulins—better known as The King's Mills—to Le Mont Saint. Mr. Métivier gives as his explanation of this name that all this region—from the Mont-au-Nouvel (now called Delancey Hill) to the Castiau Roc—was the centre of the Druids and their observances. "The Eagle," "The Cock," "The Partridge," "The Curlew," were the names of various degrees in Theology[*] among the Druids and among the western sun worshippers. This "Coq" was the Prophet, the "Magician," of the Canton. The Arch-Magician of the King of Babylon was Nergal or "Le Coq." It is said to be a very favourite haunt of the fairies and witches, and it is commonly reported that an immense treasure lies concealed within it. In olden

[*] Christophor : Muyheus apud. Baheum, in Centur. de Script. Brit.

days it was the fashion to walk round it, stamping at the same time, the soil resounded under their feet, they heard, or thought they heard, the monotonous sound of a bell, tolling a far-away knell, and hence the belief of a subterranean fairy cavern and hoards of concealed treasure.[*]

INSCRIBED STONE.

Old people say that there was formerly a very large stone in St. Andrew's parish on which was engraven an inscription in ancient characters. Some men who passed it every day in going to their work at last succeeded in deciphering it, and read as follows:—

> " *Celui qui me tournera*
> *Son temps point ne perdra.*"
> (To him who turns me up, I say,
> His labour won't be thrown away).

This inscription roused their curiosity, and they determined on making a strong effort to raise the stone, fully persuaded that it concealed an enormous treasure. They procured crowbars and levers, and, at last, with much labour and great loss of time, succeeded in lifting it, but who can describe their disappointment when they found nought but the following words, legibly engraved on the other side:—

> " *Tourner je voulais*
> *Car lassée j'étais.*"
> (Tired of lying on one side
> To get turned over long I've tried).[†]

---

[*] From Rachel Duport.

[†] A similar story is told in Scotland. See MacTaggart's *Gallovidian Encyclopædia*, under the article "Lettered Craigs."

See also *Mélusine*, Vol. II., p. 357. Roby's *Traditions of Lancashire*, Vol. I., p. 252, and the same story in *Notes and Queries*, 1st Series. II. 332.

EDITOR'S NOTE.—[*] In *Traditions et Superstitions de la Haute Bretagne*, Tome I., p. 38, M. Paul Sebillot says:—" Presque tous les monuments préhistoriques passent pour renfermer des trésors, il en est de même des gros blocs erratiques qui se trouvent dans les champs ou sur les landes."

Footprints on Stone.

A little inland, about halfway between the points of land which are the northern and southern extremities of the picturesque bay of Rocquaine, there is a rocky hillock known generally by the name of "Le Câtillon," probably from some small castle or fortification which may have existed there in former days. Old people say that the true name of the hill is "La Hougue ès Brinches," from the broom which once grew there in large quantities. At the foot of this hillock, on the northern side, there is a flat stone imbedded in the earth, and on it are the marks of two feet, pointing in opposite directions, as if two persons coming, one from the north, and the other from the south, had met on this spot and left the impress of their footprints on the stone. Of course a story is not wanting to account for these marks. It is said that the Lady of Lihou and the Lady of St. Brioc (or some say the Abbess of La Haye du Puits) had a dispute as to the limits of their territorial possessions, and that, in order to settle the question, they agreed to leave their respective abodes at a certain hour before breakfast, and walk straight forward until they met. The spot where the meeting took place was to be henceforth considered as the boundary, and to avoid any further disputes a lasting memorial was to be placed on the spot.

If the country people are asked who these "Ladies" were, they can give no further information about them, but they evidently consider them to have belonged to the fairy-folk, who have left behind them so many traces of their former occupation of the island. Antiquaries are disposed to look upon the stone as having been placed there to mark the boundary line between the Priories of Notre Dame de Lihou and St. Brioc.

Another story of this rock is that at Pleinmont lived a hermit who was much respected by all the island, and many people came to visit him in his cell, which he never left, except to administer the Holy Sacrament to the dying. He used to be seen kneeling for hours at the foot of a cross upon the cliff; but one night a fisherman, anchored in Rocquaine Bay, saw by the moon's light this hermit cross the sands and meet a tiny shrouded figure which came from the direction of Lihou. They met on this rock, and stood talking there for some time, and then each returned the way he came, and in the morning, when the fisherman came to examine the place, he found the print of two feet. He could not make himself believed when he told the story, until it was discovered that the hermit had disappeared, never to be seen again.*

In the year 1829 a large quantity of coins, amounting, it is said, to nearly seven hundred in number, were dug up at no very great distance from this stone. The greater part were silver pennies, but there were a few copper pieces among them; they were of the reigns of Edward II. of England, and Philip IV. of France. The discovery of this treasure induced some men who lived in the neighbourhood to seek for more, and, under the firm persuasion that the most likely spot to find it was under the stone itself, they resolved on braving the danger which is supposed to be incurred by removing stones which have been placed by the fairies, and devoted a whole morning to clearing away the ground around it with a view to

---

* From Miss Lane.

lifting it. They had, with great labour, succeeded in loosening the stone just as the sun in its zenith marked the hour of noon, an hour when all good workmen cease from their toil to eat their frugal mid-day repast, and to enjoy their siesta under the shelter of a hedge. They felt sure of success, and probably dreamt of the uses to which they would put their treasure, but, alas, for their hopes. When they returned to their work at one o'clock, they found the stone as firmly fixed as ever, and resisting their utmost efforts to remove it. They were more convinced than ever that immense riches lie buried in this spot, but that it is useless to seek for them, and none since that time have been bold enough to renew the attempt.*

" Le Pied du Bœuf."

In the Vale parish there is a large tract of uncultivated land commonly known by the name of L'Ancresse Common. It is said to owe its name of L'Ancresse—the anchoring place—to the circumstance of the neighbouring bay having afforded a refuge to Robert the First, Duke of Normandy, and his fleet, when in danger of perishing in a violent tempest. Our learned antiquary, Mr. George Métivier, is rather disposed to derive the name from the Celtic " Lancreis," " the place of the circle," so many Druidical remains being still to be found on the common as to render it highly probable that one of those circular enclosures, formed of upright stones, in which the Druids are supposed to have held their sacred assemblies, formerly existed here. Along the sea-coast are many eminences, known locally by the name

---

* From Jean Le Lacheur, of Rocquaine.

of "hougues." Their height is not great, but they form picturesque objects in the landscape. Here and there large masses of grey granite covered with lichens rise in irregular forms above the green sward, gay in spring with the bright flowers of the furze and blue-bell, and redolent with the sweet perfume of the wild thyme and chamomile. In some of these rocks may be traced those curious excavations known by the name of rock basins, which antiquaries have considered as artificial, but which geologists are ready to prove to be the work of nature.

Of late years many of these hougues have been quarried for the sake of the stone, which is preferred in London to all others for paving purposes, and if the demand should continue many of these hills will be entirely levelled, and with them will disappear some of the most characteristic features in the scenery of that part of the island. While writing (1853), La Hougue Patris is advertised for sale, and stress is laid in the advertisement on the excellent quality of the stone which it contains. This hougue is situated on the north eastern extremity of L'Ancresse Bay, and is remarkable from the circumstance that a portion of the rock, where it appears above ground, bears marks precisely similar to those which would be left by the hoof of an ox on wet clay. So remarkable an appearance has of course attracted the attention of the neighbouring peasants, who call the rock which bears the impression "Le Pied du Bœuf." Some old people relate that the Devil, after having been driven from the other parts of the island by a Saint whose name is now forgotten, made a last stand on this spot, but that, after a long and desperate conflict, his Satanic Majesty was at last constrained to take flight.

In leaping, he left the marks of his hoofs imprinted on the stone. He directed his flight towards Alderney, but on his way thither alighted on the Brayes rocks, where, it is said, similar marks of cloven feet are to be seen. Whether he got beyond Alderney, or settled down quietly in that island, is a point on which the narrators of the tradition are by no means agreed.

Did we not know that a family of the name of Patris was formerly numerous in the Vale parish,* and that there is every probability that the Hougue derived its name from some member of that family, to whom, in ancient days, it may have belonged; we might be tempted to suppose that the valiant Saint who forced the demon to fly was no other than the renowned St. Patrick himself, especially as, according to some accounts, the Saint was a native of a village in the neighbourhood of the town of St Maloes, within eight or ten hours of this island.

It is true that, with all the self-conceit of the nineteenth century, we are apt to suppose that before the establishment of packets and steamers, communication between the opposite coasts of the Channel was difficult and infrequent, but we have only to open the lives of the British and Irish Saints to see with what ease and rapidity these holy men effected the voyage, with no other conveyance than a stone trough, a bundle of sea-weed, or perchance a cloak spread out on the boisterous waves.

EDITOR'S NOTE.—* The Patris were also a family of note in the parish of St. Martin's in the thirteenth, fourteenth, and fifteenth centuries; a " Ville ès Patrys " was among the numerous subdivisions of this parish. Much of their lands passed into the hands of the Bonamy family through the marriage of Marguerite Patris, daughter of Pierrot Patris, of Les Landes and St. Martin's, to Pierre Bonamy, father of John Bonamy, King's Procureur in 1405, builder of the old Bonamy house of Les Câches, and translator of the " Extente " from Latin into French in 1498.

"The Devil's Claw" at Terbonne

"The Devil's Claw" at Jerbourg.

As the inhabitants of Guernsey may be presumed to be acquainted with the Chronicles of their own Duchy of Normandy, it is not improbable that the following legendary tale, related of Duke Richard, surnamed Sans-Peur, may be known to some of them.

The *Chronique de Normandie*, printed at Rouen in 1576, gives it in words of which the following is a close translation. (Fol. 4. Sur l'an 797). "Once upon a time, as Duke Richard was riding from one of his Castles to a Manor, where a very beautiful lady was residing, the Devil attacked him, and Richard fought with and vanquished him. After this adventure the Devil disguised himself as a beautiful maiden, richly adorned,* and appeared to him in a boat at Granville, where Richard then was. Richard entered into the boat to converse with and contemplate the beauty of this lady, and the Devil carried away the said Duke Richard to a rock in the sea in the island of Guernsey, where he was found."

He is supposed to have anchored at La Petite Porte and leapt up the cliff and landed on the stone near Doyle's Column at Jerbourg, where the print of his claw is still to be seen. As you go along the road from the town to Doyle's Column you see a large white piece of quartz with a deep black splash right across it. It is on the right hand side of the road, just as it begins to rise towards Doyle's Column, at the head of the second vallum, or dyke,

---

* "Ceux qui effleurent tout au galop ne sauront point que, chez les Rabbins, *Lilith*, spectre nocturne, est 'une diablesse' sous la forme de cette 'damoiselle richement aornée,' qui ne fit les yeux doux à notre bon duc Richard, qu'afin de traiter ce nouvel Ixion comme la reine des Dieux avait traité le premier." —*Georges Métivier.*

going down towards La Petite Porte. This stone was
also the termination of the bounds at Jerbourg beaten
by the Chevauchée de St. Michel.

" LE PONT DU DIABLE."

In former days that tract of land lying between
St. Sampson's Harbour and the Vale Church, and
known by the name of " Le Braye du Valle," was
an arm of the sea, which at high water separated
that part of the Vale parish called " Le Clos du
Valle " from the rest of the island. At the beginning
of the present century, Sir John Doyle, then Lieut.-
Governor of the island, seeing the inconvenience that
might arise from the want of a ready communication
with the mainland, in the event of an invading enemy
effecting or attempting a landing in L'Ancresse Bay,
caused the dyke near the Vale Church to be built.
The land recovered from the sea became of course the
property of the Crown, and was subsequently sold to
private individuals, the purchase money being given up
by Government to be employed towards defraying the
expenses of constructing new roads throughout the island.
. Where fishes once swam, and where the husbandman
once gathered sea-weed for the manuring of his land,
droves of cattle now graze, and fields of corn wave.*
From the very earliest times, the want of an easy
communication between the neighbouring parishes
must have been felt, and attempts had been made
to remedy the inconvenience by the erection of rude
bridges. It would be strange, if the Devil, whose
skill in the construction of bridges in every part of
Europe has certainly entitled him to the honourable

EDITOR'S NOTE.—* Of course this was written long before the days of greenhouses and the
tomato-growing industry.

appellation of Pontifex Maximus, had not had a hand in building one of the three principal passages across the Braye du Valle. Accordingly we find that the dyke at St. Sampson's Harbour, known by the name of "Le Grand Pont," is also called "Le Pont du Diable," and old people affirm that it has been handed down as a tradition from their forefathers, that shortly after the building of the Vale Castle, the Devil threw up this embankment, in order to enable him to cross over to that fortress with ease and safety.

Perhaps the bridge may have been built by order of Robert the First, Duke of Normandy, father of William the Conqueror, sometimes called "Robert le Magnifique," but quite as well known by the less honourable cognomen of "Robert le Diable," and, if in the absence of documentary evidence, any reliance is to be placed in the tradition hitherto generally received that the Vale Castle, if not originally built, was at least considerably improved and strengthened by this Prince, it is certainly not going too far to suppose that the bridge may owe its name to him, and not to his Satanic Majesty.

One observance connected with this bridge is worth mentioning. From time immemorial persons from all parts of the island have been in the habit of assembling here on the afternoons of the Sundays in the month of August. No reason is assigned for this custom, but as Saint Sampson is looked upon as the first Apostle of Christianity in this island, and as the church which bears his name is said to have been the first Christian temple erected in the island, and is, in consequence, considered in some respects as the mother church, may not this assembly be the remains of a church-wake, observed in ancient times on the Sunday following the feast of St. Sampson, that is to say, the 28th of July.

Similar meetings are common in Normandy and Brittany, where they are called " assemblies " and " pardons."

The two other principal passages across the Braye du Valle were the bridges called " Le Pont Colliche " and "Le Pont St. Michel." They consisted of rude slabs of stone resting on huge blocks of rock, and were dangerous, both from the sea-weed which attached itself to them, and rendered them exceedingly slippery, and also from the rapidity with which the tide, when rising, flowed in, for both of them were covered at high water. Many and sad were the accidents which had happened to incautious and belated passengers, and it is not wonderful that superstition believed these spots to be haunted by the ghosts of those who had perished in attempting the crossing. The " Pont St. Michel," situated near the Vale Church, where the embankment now is, was held in especial dread. At night the " feu bellenger " or will-o'-the-wisp, was to be seen dancing on the sands, and gliding under the bridge, and even at mid-day, when the sun was shining brightly, unearthly cries of distress would be occasionally heard proceeding from that direction, though no living being could be discovered, by whom they could possibly be uttered.

An old woman, still alive, whose youth was spent in that neighbourhood, has assured me that she has repeatedly heard the cries.

" Le Pont Colliche " was situated about midway between the two others, a little to the eastward of the road which now traverses the Braye. According to tradition, there was once a time when the opening at the "Bougue du Valle"—the channel between the Grand Havre and the Braye—was so small that a faggot, weighted with stone, would have sufficed to stop it.

At that time the passage between the islands of Herm and Guernsey was so narrow that a plank laid down at low water enabled the Rector of St. Sampson's to cross over when his duty called him to perform divine service in the Chapel of St. Tugual. Great quantities of the common cockle *(cardium edule)*, locally known by the name of "cocques du Braye," used to be gathered on the sands at low water. It is said, however, that even before the enclosure of the Braye they had begun to disappear, and their increasing scarcity was attributed to the impiety of an old woman, who, unmindful of the sacred duty of keeping the sabbath holy, was in the habit of searching for these cockles on that day. A similar story is told to account for the rarity of a particular kind of periwinkle *(trochus crassus)* known here by the name of "Cocquelin Brehaut."

A stone, which has evidently served as the socket or base of a cross, and which is said to have come from the Pont Colliche, is still preserved at Les Grandes Capelles.

"THE LOVERS' LEAP."

"Ah me! for aught that ever I could read,
Could ever hear by tale, or history,
The course of true love never did run smooth."

The promontory of Pleinmont forms the south-western extremity of the island of Guernsey, and, to the admirer of the wild and rugged beauties of cliff and rock scenery, affords an ever-varying treat. Lofty precipices, in which the sea-birds and hawks nestle—

K

huge masses of granite piled into fantastic forms—covered with grey and orange-coloured lichens, and gay with the flowers of the thrift and other sea-side plants, large rocks detached from the main-land and tenanted by long rows of the sun-loving cormorant, the ever-restless ocean, now smiling and rippling under a summer sky, now lashed into fury by the wintry blast, all combine to add to the charms of this district.

Many accordingly are the parties which frequent this spot during the summer, and it is probable that some of those who have visited this place may remember a small promontory almost detached from the mainland, and forming the westernmost point of the island. To the southward of this promontory there is a sort of ravine, extending from the table-land of Pleinmont to the edge of the cliff, where a small breastwork of earth and stones has been erected. The reason why this spot, which is by no means the most dangerous along the coast, has been thus protected, is not very apparent. The existence of a small spring of water in the ravine, which keeps up a constant verdure and tempts the cattle turned out to pick up a scanty living on the common to the place, suggests a probable solution of the question ; but the tradition of the peasantry assigns a far more romantic reason for the erection of the parapet than the mere safety of a few stray heifers.

They say that in days long past, the son of a farmer in the neighbourhood formed an attachment for the daughter of a family with whom his own was at variance. His affection was returned by the maiden, and the wishes of the lovers might, in the end, have triumphed over the opposition of the parents, had not the hand of the girl been promised by her friends to one of the richest men in the parish. In vain did the unhappy maiden urge the cruelty of forcing her into a marriage which her heart abhorred. In vain did her lover employ every means in his power to break off the hated contract. Their prayers and representations were treated with scorn, and the preparations for the marriage were proceeded with. The eve of the day appointed for the solemn espousal—a ceremony which in ancient times preceded and was distinct from that of marriage—had arrived. The lovers met by stealth on the cliffs at Pleinmont, and, driven to despair, mounted together on a horse, which they urged into a gallop, and, directing him down the ravine, they fell over the precipice and perished in the waves below. To commemorate the event, and to prevent the recurrence of a similar catastrophe, the barrier was erected.*

* From Miss Rachel Mauger.

" Wishing Well at Fontaine Blicq, St. Andrew's."

CHAPTER V.

Holy Chapels and Holy Wells.

" Thereby a crystal stream did gently play,
Which from a sacred fount welled forth alway."
—*Spenser.*

" For to that holy wood is consecrate,
A virtuous well about whose flowery banks
The nimble-footed fairies dance their rounds
By the pale moonshine, dipping often times
Their stolen children, so to make them free
From dying flesh and dull mortality."
—*Fletcher's " Faithful Shepherdess."*

THOUGH not strictly speaking " Folk-Lore," the ancient priories and chapels of Guernsey are so closely connected with the holy wells that it may be as well here to give some details concerning them. It appears that these chapels must have been of more than one kind. Some were endowed, and had a priest permanently attached to them with probably a certain cure of souls. Others were most likely wayside oratories, where divine service was only performed occasionally by the rector of the parish, or someone acting under him, on certain anniversaries. Some may have been connected with religious guilds or fraternities.

To begin with those churches and chapels known to have been endowed, and which were probably—at least after the suppression of alien priories—under the patronage of the Crown.

A Commission was appointed in the reign of Henry VIII. for the purpose of ascertaining the value of all livings within the kingdom, with a view to the duty called first-fruits, owing on the appointment of every ecclesiastic to a benefice, being henceforth paid to the Crown. From this document we learn that besides the ten parochial churches there were four other benefices—the vicarage of Lihou worth five pounds sterling, that of St. Brioc worth twelve shillings, the chaplaincy of St. George worth sixty shillings, and that of "Our Lady Mares," no doubt Notre Dame des Marais, worth three pounds.

The first of these four, Lihou, was originally a priory dependent on the Priory of St. Michel-du-Valle, which was of itself a dependency of the great Abbey of Mont St. Michel in Normandy. The Prior of Lihou had probably pastoral care of the district comprised in the Fief Lihou, extending along the coast called Perelle,* from L'Erée to Rocquaine Castle, where the district of St. Brioc begins. It also comprised certain possessions in the Castel parish and elsewhere, and its feudal court was held near the western porch of the Castel Church, a little northward of the path leading to it, where are still to be seen three flat stones, which mark the spot.

St. Brioc was situated in the valley leading from Torteval Church to Rocquaine. There is reason to suppose that it had a certain district allotted to it, but its limits are not now known.

St. George was only a chaplaincy, intimately connected with the Fief Le Comte, the court of which

---

* In the *Dédicace des Eglises*, "Notre Dame de Lihou" is called Notre Dame de la *Roche*. Now the word Perelle is a diminutive of Pierre, and we know that in our dialect "pierre" and "rocque" are used indiscriminately, and have the same meaning.

formerly assembled in the chapel, and still meets in its immediate vicinity. The earliest notice we have of this chapel is contained in the Bull of Pope Adrian IV., dated 1155. In the year following Dom Robert de Thorigny—or, as he is sometimes called, "Du Mont"—abbot of the famous monastery of Mont St. Michel, visited this island, and found one Guillaume Gavin established at St. George as chaplain: he was anxious to retire from the world, and, at his request, the abbot admitted him into his community as a monk, and appointed Godefroy Vivier to succeed him as chaplain at St. George. After some time Vivier followed the example of his predecessor, and took the frock at Mont Saint Michel, having previously made over certain lands which he possessed in the neighbourhood of St. George to the abbey which afforded him shelter.

In 1408 the chaplain was Dom Toulley, who obtained an order from the Royal Court prohibiting any one from trespassing on the road leading to the chapel, it being reserved exclusively for persons attending divine service, or sick people visiting the fountain, the small coin left as an offering at the well being doubtless a perquisite belonging to the chaplain.

This chapel was originally endowed with some lands or rents, probably with the territory still known as Le Fief de la Chapelle, which is one of the many dependencies of the Fief Le Comte.

After the Reformation St. George became in some way the property of the de Jersey family,* and by

---

EDITOR'S NOTE.

* The Fief St. George was bought from the Royal Commissioners by Thomas Fouaschin, Seigneur d'Anneville, in 1563, let to Pierre Massey 25th June, 1616, and bought 18th May, 1620, by Nicholas de Jersey, son of Michel, from George Fouaschin, Seigneur d'Anneville, son of Thomas. Nicholas de Jersey's only child Marie married Jacques Guille, 2nd May, 1638, and so brought St. George into the Guille family.

the marriage of Marie de Jersey, an heiress, to
Jacques Guille, which took place about the middle of
the seventeenth century, it passed into the possession
of the latter family, by whom it is still held. This
Marie de Jersey made a gift of the chapel to the
inhabitants of the Castel in about 1675 to serve
as a school house. A more convenient building
was erected in 1736 on the site of an old mill, and
endowed with nine quarters of wheat rente by Marie
de Sausmarez, widow of Mr. William Le Marchant,
and the chapel ceased to be used as a school house.
Bickerings as to rights of way across the estate, under
the pretence that there was a thoroughfare leading
to a public building, ensued, even after the removal
of the school; so finally Mr. Guille ordered the
chapel to be demolished, and only a few ruins are
now left.

The Chapel of "Our Lady Mares"—Notre Dame
des Marais—is thus mentioned in the Extente of
Edward III, "Nostre Sire le Roy n'a rien des
vacations des eglises et chapelles, fors la Chapelle de
Nostre Dame des Maresqs qui vaut XXX lbts en
laquelle iceluy Roy doit présenter en tems de la
vacation, et l'Evesque de Coutance en a l'institution."
The chaplain then in possession, 1331, was Robert
de Hadis.*

The other churches and chapels were not at this

---

* May 10th, 1292.—"Confirmation of a charter which the King has inspected, whereby
Henry III. granted in frank almoin to the Chaplain of the Chapel of St. Mary, Orguil Castle.
Gernescye, the 10th of a rent called Chaumpard in the island of Gerneseye."

Dec. 26th, 1328.—"Grant to John de Etton, King's Clerk, of the Chapel of St. Mary of
the Marsh, in the island of Gerneseye."

Ancient Petition No. 13289.—"To our Lord the King and to his Council shows Ralph the
Chaplain of one of his Chapels called the Chapel des Mareis in the Island of Gerneseye, that
whereas the King has given in alms all the 10th sheaf of his champartz in the said isle to
this Chaplain to sing every day a mass for the King and his ancestors and heirs. Now since
last August the attourneys of the King have disseized him of the tithes of two carues of land,

time in the gift of the Crown, but belonged to alien monasteries, Marmoutiers, Mont St. Michel, and Blanchelande. The chapel itself was, there is very little doubt, situated within the precincts of Le Château des Marais, now better known as Ivy Castle, and the Livres de Perchage of the Town parish of the time of Elizabeth and James I. mention certain fields in the vicinity as belonging to it.

The Hospice and Chapel of St. Julien was situated at the bottom of the Truchot, in the district called Le Bosq, close to the sea-shore. There are many " St. Julians " in the calendar, one of them being considered the special patron of travellers. In the title of his Legende MS. Bodleian, 1596, fol. 4, he is called " St. Julian the Gode herberjoue." It ends thus :—

" Therefore, yet to this day, thei that over lond wende
  Thei biddeth Saint Julian anon that gode herborw he hem
  sende."

Chaucer had the familiar attribute of St. Julian before him when he described his " Francklyn " or country gentleman :—

" An householder, and that a grete, was he :
  Saint Julian he was in his own contré."

The rock on which travellers to the island used to land, now the foundation of the harbour, was " La Roche St. Julien," and probably the hospital, being

---

viz. of the Carue of the Corbines and Suardes and also of the tithes of a place whereof he was never disseized. He prays to be restored thereto, as otherwise he would have nothing to live upon, as his whole rent is only worth £7, and scarcely half that."

(Endorsed) " Go to Otto (de Grandison) and pray for a writ to enquire if the tithes, etc., belong to the Chapel, and if they do, then let them be restored." (No date—but Otho de Grandison was Governor of the Islands 1303-29.)

May 10th, 1382.—" Appointment of Peter Gyon, serjeant-at-arms, and Henry de Rither, supplying the places in Gerneseye of Hugh de Calvyle, governor of the (Channel) Islands, to enquire touching the cessation, through the negligence of the Chaplains, of divine service and works of charity in the Chapel of Marreys in that Island, and touching the sale and removal of its chalices, books, vestments, and other ornaments, and to certify into Chancery. (Vacated because enrolled on the French Roll of this year)."

situated near a landing place, was intended as a refuge for travellers, and therefore dedicated to him. This chapel was founded in the year 1361, the thirty-fifth of the reign of Edward III., at the time when Sir John Maltravers was Governor of the islands. The founder was a certain Petrus de St. Petro, or Pierre de St. Peye, as we find it written in French. Permission was granted him by the Crown to found the said hospital or alms house for a master, brethren and sisters, in a certain spot near *Bowes* (Le Bosq, —this word was evidently Boués, Bois, a wood, with which the word Bouët is also identical), in the parish of St. Peter Port, and to endow it with twenty vergées of land and eighty quarters of wheat rent, out of which certain dues were to be paid to the King. " La Petite École," or parish school, which has from time immemorial been situated in this vicinity, was originally connected with St. Julian. It is generally believed that the school was founded in 1513 by Thomas Le Marchant and Jannette Thelry, his wife.

At the Reformation the chapel and hospital were suppressed, and its revenues and possessions seized by the Crown. The parishioners of St. Peter Port complained to the Royal Commissioners of 1607 of the alienation of this property, which they looked upon as belonging to the parish, but their complaint was not attended to. In the early part of the century there were the remains of an old house, in a late debased Gothic style of the fifteenth century, standing at the bottom of Bosq Lane, which used to be looked upon as the remains of a conventual building. The house in question was a residence of a branch of the de Beauvoir family, whose arms were carved in stone over the principal entrance. The stones forming this entrance were preserved, and are now in the ruins of the Chapel of St. George.

With the exception of the Franciscan Friary, there is no proof of any conventual establishments in the island, though tradition points to La Haye-du-Puits as being the site of an old convent. Doubtless in early times, and before the English had lost Normandy, the great monasteries which held lands in Guernsey may have had priories here. Mont St. Michel we know had the Priory of St. Michel du Valle, and there is some reason to believe that Blanchelande also had some establishment of the kind in the island. How the Abbeys of Marmoutier, La Rue Frairie, Croix St. Lenfroy and Caen, all of which had possessions in the island, managed them, we have no means of knowing, though it was most likely by the machinery of a feudal court.

We will now speak of the Priories of St. Michel du Valle and Notre Dame de Lihou.

A tradition, which may be traced up to the time of Edward II., says that certain monks, driven from Mont St. Michel for their dissolute lives, settled in the Vale parish and founded an abbey about the year 968 A.D. The same authority informs us that they reformed their lives and became famous for their sanctity, and that when Robert, Duke of Normandy, visited the island in the year 1032, having been driven here by stress of weather while on his way to England with a fleet to the help of his nephew, Edward the Confessor, he confirmed them in the possession of the lands they had acquired. The same tradition also says that in the year 1061 certain pirates attacked and pillaged the island, and that their leader "Le Grand Geoffroy," or "Le Grand Sarasin," had his stronghold on the site of what is now the Castel Church. Complaint having been made to Duke William, he sent over Samson d'Anneville, who succeeded, with the aid of the monks, in driving them out. For this service they were rewarded by the Duke with a grant of one half of the island, comprising, besides the Vale, what are now the parishes of the Castel, St. Saviour's, and St. Peter's-in-the-Wood. This grant they divided between them, and the monks, in right of their priory, held that portion of the lands which is still known as Le Fief St. Michel. The rest is now comprised for the most part in the Fiefs Le Comte and Anneville and their dependencies. To the south-east of the Vale Church is an old farm house which still bears the name of L'Abbaye, and which, without doubt, occupies the site of the original priory. Even at the present day, it is easy to trace part of the walls of the earlier edifice, which, however, was in a ruinous state as early as the reign of Henry IV., for we find Sir John de Lisle, Governor of Guernsey, writing to the Privy Council about the year 1406 for permission to use the timber of the building for the repairs of Castle Cornet, and alleging in his letter that the priory had fallen into decay, and giving as a reason for his request that in consequence of the war it was impossible to procure timber either from Normandy or Brittany.

The names of a few priors have survived. It is not quite clear whether a certain Robert, whose name appears as witness to the deed by which Robert, Abbot of Mont St. Michel, during a visit which he made to the island in 1156, appointed Guillaume Gavin, monk, to the chaplaincy of St. George, was Prior of the Vale or not. He is styled in the deed

Priest and Dean of the Vale (de Walo). In 1249 Henry, Canon of Blanchelande, was collated to the Vale Church by special dispensation. About 1307 Johannes de Porta was prior (probably a Du Port, a family of considerable antiquity in the island, and of good standing). In 1312 Guillaume Le Feivre filled the office. In 1323 Renauld Pastey was Prior of the the Vale, and had a lawsuit with the inhabitants of that and other parishes concerning tithes. In 1331 there was another dispute concerning tithes, which was referred to the arbitration of two monks, Guillaume Le Feivre and Jourdain Poingdestre, who had both formerly been priors. In the year 1335 Andreas de Porta, 1364-68, Geoffrey de Carteret, and in 1365 Denis Le Marchant, clerk, was appointed seneschal of the Court of St. Michel.

According to the ballad known as "La Descente des Arragousais," "Brégard" * was the monk in charge of the priory in 1372, and by his intrigues the Vale Castle fell into the hands of the enemy, which was evidently a legend current at the time. Guillaume Paul, alias Règne, in 1478, is the last prior of whom we have found mention.

The Priory of Lihou, as has been already said, was a dependency of St. Michel-du-Valle. The ruins of the church and other buildings are still to be seen. The former was entire at a time long subsequent to the Reformation, and is said to have been destroyed at the command of one of our Governors to prevent the possibility of its serving as an entrenchment in case of an enemy landing on the islet. It appears to have

---

EDITOR'S NOTE.—* The Brégards or Brégearts were a very old family in the Vale and St. Sampson's parishes. Early in the sixteenth century one branch of this family bought land at "Vauvert," St. Peter Port, and became known as "Brégeart, or Briart, alias Vauvert," and finally simply as "Vauvert." A curious instance of change of surname.

replaced a still more ancient building, as many pieces of Caen stone, with well-executed Norman mouldings, are built into the walls. Probably the first building had been destroyed in some of the many inroads to which the island was subjected during the reign of Edward III.

An incumbent of Lihou, with the title of prior, existed until the time of the Reformation.

Now to come to the remaining chapels. The Extente of Edward III. speaks of the King's Chaplain, John de Caretier, who received a salary out of the revenues of the island, and was bound to say mass daily for the King, and for the souls of his ancestors either in the chapel of Castle Cornet or in the chapel of His Majesty's manor of La Grange. It is not exactly known where this manor was situated, but as the estate of the late John Carey, Esq., has always borne this name—the Grange—it is reasonable to suppose that it was thereabouts. The more so, as Richard II. founded the Convent of Cordeliers or Francisian friars on the ground now belonging to Elizabeth College, probably then comprised in the Grange estate. It must be said, however, that there are also reasons for supposing that the King's Grange may have been situated elsewhere, probably in the vicinity of the Tour Gand, a fortress which defended the approaches of the town from the north, and this opinion derives some support from the fact that the Plaiderie, or Court House, is known to have existed in ancient times in this locality, and that in the middle ages a chapel was considered an almost essential adjunct to a Court of Justice.

To return to the Convent of the Cordeliers, it is known that the site of their church, called in Acts of

Court "La Chapelle des Frères," is said to have stood opposite to the entrance of Le Cimetière des Frères, which was the burial ground belonging to this church, and, together with the site of the church, a considerable portion of land appears to have been alienated from the college, probably by the arbitrary act of some Governor of the island. The church consisted of a chancel and nave, the latter, on the building being given for the use of the college, serving as a school-room, and the former being occupied by the master. After its alienation the burial ground fell into the hands of an individual of the name of Blanche, who turned it into an orchard, but, a plague having broken out in 1629, the Court made an order that all who died of that disorder should be buried there, since which time it has served for a cemetery for the Town parish. How the burial ground attached to the Town Church came to acquire the name of "Cimetière des Sœurs" cannot now be known, as there can be no doubt that from time immemorial it was no other than the parochial cemetery. There is no document known to exist which points to any conventual establishment for females in the island, though there are traditions to that effect. There was, however, among many other fraternities, a "confrèrie de frères · et sœurs" connected in some measure with this cemetery, and which may have given it the name. At the Reformation the land and rents due to this fraternity were seized by the Crown, and the list of them is still preserved among the records at the Greffe, with the following heading—"Confessions de rentes dues aux frères et sœurs de la confrerye et fraternité de la charité, fondeye pour la dilyvrance des ames de purgatoyre, par les dis frayres et sœurs,

constytuée, establye et ordonnée, en la Chapelle de
Sepulcre estante dedans le cymetyere de St. Pierre
Port," &c., &c.

This proves the existence of a chapel in the
churchyard, but whether it was the building known
by the name of "Le Belfroi," and which was
demolished in 1787, cannot now be ascertained.
"Belfroi" is the name given in the mediæval ages
to a Town Hall. The edifice known by that name
in St. Peter Port belonged to the Town, and was
used latterly as a store-house for militia requisites.
It is described as having been built of stone, vaulted,
and divided into two apartments, an upper and a
lower, the latterly partly underground. Probably the
lower part of the building was used as a charnel
house, in which the bones of the dead, after they
had lain long enough in the ground to become quite
dry, were piled up; for, among the duties to be
performed by the officiating priest, we find that they
were required to chant a "recorderis" over the bones
of the dead. Such charnel houses are still very
common in Brittany, and many country places
throughout the continent.

Of the other chapels which existed in the Town
parish the memory even has perished. The estate
known as Ste. Catherine may possibly have derived
its name from a chapel dedicated to that virgin
martyr, but all that is known is that there was a
fraternity or religious association under the patronage
of this saint, which was endowed with wheat rents.
Some of the rents seized by the Crown, and afterwards
made over to Elizabeth College, were due to the
"Frerie de Ste. Catherine," and possibly this body
possessed its own chapel. The site of the Chapel of

St. Jacques is well known, and traces of the foundations were still to be seen till comparatively lately. It was situated in a field on the Mon Plaisir estate, on the right hand side of the lane which leads from the Rue Rozel to the back of the Rocquettes, at the head of a little valley, just where the roadway is at the lowest. The orchard to the east of this spot, on the opposite side of the lane, is still known by the name of Le Cimetière, and human bones are still occasionally met with in digging. It had some land attached to it by way of endowment, which was sold by the Royal Commissioners in the reign of Queen Elizabeth, as we learn from the Livre de Perchage, temp. Elizabeth, in which it is called "La Chapelle de *l'ydolle*, St. Jacques," and that Thomas Effard was in possession of land that had belonged to it. From the same document we learn that there was also a chapel called "La Chapelle de Lorette," which, there is reason to suppose, may have been in the vicinity of Candie.

There was also a private chapel, of which we should have known absolutely nothing but for an old contract, still extant, of the early date of 1383, by which Perrot and Jannequin Le Marchant * sell a piece of ground for building purposes to Renolvet Denys. One of the conditions attached to the sale is that no edifice shall be erected on the land thus sold, which can in any manner take away from the view, or deprive the chapel of the manor and hall of the vendors, of light. The property in question was, without doubt, that to the south of the arch, leading to Manor Le Marchant and Lefebvre Street, and it is

---

EDITOR's NOTE.—* Peter and Jannequin Le Marchant were sons of Denis Le Marchant, Jurat and Lieutenant-Bailiff of Guernsey, and Jenette de Chesney, youngest daughter of Sir William de Chesney and Joan de Gorges. The chapel is alluded to in their father's "Bille de Partage," dated 3rd June, 1303.

L

curious that the contract mentions the existence of a
vaulted gateway leading to the manor, at that early
period permission being given to the purchaser of this
ground to build over this arch. An archway still
exists in the locality, and continues to bear the name
of "La Porte," as it did nearly five hundred years
ago.

Now, to come to the only chapel that still exists—
Ste. Apolline. There is no reason for supposing it to
be of such great antiquity as is generally believed. The
vault is pointed, and it is well known that the pointed
arch did not make its appearance in architecture until
the latter part of the twelfth century—say about 1160
—whereas all our parishes are named in documents
anterior to 1066. From the Cartulary of Mont Saint
Michel we learn that in the year 1054 William
Pichenoht, moved by compunction for the many and
great sins he had committed, and desirous of turning
monk, gave, with the consent of Duke William of
Normandy, his lands of La Perrelle with all their
appurtenances to the abbey. These lands were, no
doubt, leased out afterwards by the monks to various
individuals, the abbey retaining the "Seigneurie"
over the whole.

In October, 1392, a certain Nicholas Henry, of La
Perrelle, obtained the consent of the Abbot and monks
of Mont St. Michel, as Lords of the Manor, to the
endowment of a chapel which he had lately erected
on his estate, subject, however to the sanction of the
Sovereign as lord paramount. This permission was
granted by Richard II. in July, 1394. The charter
which is preserved among the island records at
the Greffe authorises Nicholas Henry to endow
the Chapel of *Sainte Marie de la Perrelle* for the

purpose of maintaining a chaplain who was to celebrate
a daily mass for ever, for the safety of the said
Nicholas Henry* and his wife Philippa, for their souls
after they should have departed this life, and for the
souls of all their ancestors, benefactors, and Christian
people generally. Beside the three vergées of land,
which are described as being bounded on the west by
the property of Guillaume Blondel, and on the east by
that of Thomas Dumaresq, both of which families are
still landowners in the district, Nicholas Henry also gave
to the chapel an annual wheat rent of four quarters
due on a piece of ground adjoining. The chapel once
established, other gifts were made from time to time
by pious individuals who took part in the daily service.
In 1485, Johan de Lisle, son of Colas, and Nicholas
de Lisle, son of Pierre, acknowledged in the presence
of the Bailiff and Jurats that they owed jointly the
yearly rent of a hen to the Chaplain of Notre Dame
de la Perrelle; and the latter acknowledged, moreover,
to the annual payment of one bushel of wheat. On

EDITOR'S NOTES.

* The following is a short pedigree of the descendants of Nicholas Henry, derived principally
from MSS. at Sausmarez Manor :—

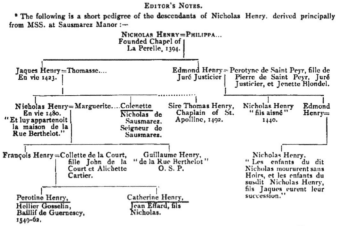

L 2

March 2nd, 1492, Henry Le Tellier, of St. Saviour's, also acknowledged that he owed two bushels of wheat rent to Sire Thomas Henry, who is also mentioned as Chaplain of St. Brioc, in 1477, and as Rector of the Castel, in 1478. He was also styled in an earlier deed, "Dom" Thomas, so was probably also a Benedictine monk, and it is not unlikely that he was grandson of the original founder of this chapel. Its identity with the building still existing is proved by an Act of the Royal Court "en Plaids d'Héritage" of June 6th, 1452, in which the chapel is spoken of as "La Chapelle de Notre Dame de la Perrelle, appelleye la *Chapelle Sainte Appolyne.*" It was then in the possession of Colin Henry, son of Jacques, and grandson of Nicholas, who is described as the founder of the chapel. Forty years later it changed hands, and was in the possession of the Guille family, perhaps by inheritance, for in April, 1496, Nicholas Guille, son of Nicholas, of St. Peter Port, sold the advowson of the chaplaincy to Edmond de Chesney, Seigneur of Anneville, in whose family it probably remained until they * sold their possessions to the Fouaschin family, from whom they came by inheritance into the family of Andros.†

We do not know how the name of Ste. Apolline came to be associated first with that of the Blessed Virgin, and then to have superseded it altogether. Possibly because there were already no less than five places of worship in the island under the invocation

EDITOR'S NOTES.

* Nicholas Fouaschin, son of Thomas, and Jurat of the Royal Court, bought the Manors of Le Comte and Anneville from Sir Robert Willoughby, February 16th, 1509. Sir Robert, afterwards Lord Broke, inherited these Manors from his grandmother, Anne de Chesney, daughter and co-heiress of Sir Edmund de Chesney and Alice Stafford.

† Through the marriage on October 13th, 1660, of Charles Andros to Alice Fashion, only child of Thomas Fashion, Seigneur of Anneville.

of Our Lady—the Churches of the Castel, Torteval,* and Lihou, and the Chapels of Pulias and *Le Château des Marais*, commonly known as Ivy Castle. Saint Apollonia, or in French, Ste. Apolline, is said to have been a virgin of Alexandria, who was burned as a Christian martyr in the year 249.

The chapel is twenty-seven feet long by thirteen feet nine inches wide, and is built of rough unhewn stone, except the heads of the doorways, the jambs of the windows, and the corner stones of the edifice, which appear to have been coarsely wrought. The vault is in solid masonry of small stones cemented with a strong mortar, and if it was ever slated or tiled all traces of the covering have long since disappeared. The interior is stuccoed, and was originally adorned with mural paintings, of which some slight traces are yet to be seen. Figures of angels, and part of a group which seem to have been intended to represent the nativity of our Saviour, are still to be made out. There are three small narrow square headed windows, which may or may not once have been glazed—one in the east gable immediately above where the altar must have stood, and the other two in the north and south walls, near the east end of the building. There is no opening whatever in the western gable, which was surmounted originally by a bell-cote, of which the base only now remains. The hole through which the bell rope passed is still to be seen in the interior. To the south of the chapel is a very ancient and substantially built farm-house, which is traditionally said to have been the residence of the officiating priest. It is quite as probable that it was the manor house of the founder, Nicholas

* See note on page 197.

Henry. In it were preserved the iron clapper of a bell, which is said to have belonged to the chapel, and some wrought stones, which probably formed the supports of the altar slab. A small silver burette, one of a pair, such as are used in the Roman Catholic Church to contain the wine and the water employed in the celebration of the mass, by tradition came originally from this chapel, it bearing the inscription "Sancte Paule ora pro nobis," and on the lid is the letter A, denoting that it was the vessel intended to contain the water. It was in the possession of the ancient family of Guille, whose representative gave it to the Parish Church of St. Peter Port in memory of his father.

In the neighbourhood of Perrelle Bay there is a rock, standing at some little distance from the shore, never covered by the tide, and approachable when the tide is out, called "La Chapelle Dom Hue." The appearance of the natural causeway, or, as it is locally termed "col" or· "pont," which leads to it, would induce one to believe that at some remote period it must have been a narrow neck of low land stretching out into the sea, which divided the bays of L'Erée and La Perrelle, and which has been gradually carried away by the constant action of the waves, leaving only the little hillock we now see. Probably, in ancient times, a small oratory, perhaps a hermitage, had been erected on this spot by a pious founder, "Dom" Hue, who, from his title, must have been a Benedictine monk, and, in all likelihood, a member of the Abbey of Mont Saint Michel, which was in possession of lands in this neighbourhood. There is still a small manor in the parish of St. Saviour's which bears the name of "Les Domaines

Dom Hue," and which we may reasonably suppose belonged originally to the same person, and possibly formed the endowment of the chapel.

The next chapel of which anything definite is known is " Notre Dame de Pulias," otherwise " La Chapelle de l'Epine." The ground on which it stood lies on the sea-shore, to the northward of the promontory of Noirmont, and, though separated from the rest of the parish by an intervening strip of land belonging to the Vale, forms in reality part of St. Sampson's. The Vale parish consists of two distinct portions, the larger of which, called " Le Clos," was, until the beginning of the present century, entirely divided from the rest of the island by an arm of the sea, which extended from St. Sampson's Harbour to the Grand Havre near the Vale Church, and which was only passable at low water. The inhabitants of that part of the parish attached to the mainland of Guernsey, and which is called " La Vingtaine de l'Epine," were thus cut off at times from all access to their parish church, and appear to have made use of this building, as a chapel of ease. It stood close to " La Mare de Pulias," and in this neighbourhood a bit of wall is still shown, which is said to have formed part of the chapel. It is probable that it was under the patronage of the Seigneurs of Anneville, for the earliest notice found of this chapel is in an " extente " of this fief, dated 1405, in which it is stated that the common lands, extending along the shore between ' " La Chapelle de Notre Dame de Pulayes " and the rivulet of St. Brioc at Rocquaine, belong in moieties to the Abbot of St. Michel and the Lord of Anneville. This chapel had an endowment, for we find by the report of the

Royal Commissioners of 1607 that the parishioners of the Vale and St. Sampson's petitioned that it might be restored to them, complaining—

" That whereas their predecessors, the inhabitants of the Vingtaine of the Epine, had in former times built a chapel, with a churchyard, for divine service, by reason of the sea, which doth oftentimes hinder them from going to their parish church of the Valle ; and that since that time His Majesty's Commissioners having considered how necessary that chapel was for them, it hath pleased the late Queen Elizabeth to grant unto them .yearly ten or twelve quarters of wheat, for the maintenance both of the said chapel, and also of a schoolmaster to instruct their children ; notwithstanding all which the said chapel, together with the churchyard, hath been utterly ruinated and the trees beaten down, and the grounds and rents belonging thereunto taken away, to the great grief and prejudice of the said parishioners, and therefore they humbly desire that the said chapel be built again by them that have thus ruinated it, and the rents belonging thereunto, for so necessary a use, be restored unto them again, with the tithes and rights concerning it."

The answer and decision of the Commissioners was not satisfactory. They owned there was probably a chapel of ease on that spot, and they go on to state that, having examined some aged people who dwelt near the place, as well as the Lieutenant-Governor and other officers, they find that ten or twelve quarters of wheat had been given either towards the maintenance of the chapel or of a schoolmaster, and that some had heard divine service said there about the beginning of the reign of

Elizabeth and long before, but they can find no evidence to prove that it was founded or built for a chapel of ease, the complainants accounting for the absence of documentary evidence in support of their claim by alleging that the Governor had taken it away with him. The Commissioners go on to say that on further examinations they have had there was a certain Popish superstitious service used therein, and that wheat rents had been given by certain inhabitants for the saying of a morrow mass upon Sundays, and for such like superstitious uses, and that about forty years previously, the chapel, with all appertaining to it, had been seized for the use of the Queen. The conclusion they arrived at was that the seizure was legal, and should be maintained.

At the north-east extremity of the Clos-du-Valle, near the estate called Paradis, and a little way beyond the cromlech called Déhus or Thus, stood La Chapelle de Saint Malière or Magloire, an early apostle of the island.

All traces of this chapel have long since disappeared, but its site is still pointed out as being that of a little thatch-covered cottage on the side of the hill.* The old farmhouse close by, called " St. Magloire," is said to have been the residence of the priest attached to its service.

It is mentioned as early as the year 1155 in a Bull of Pope Adrian IV. (Breakspear), together with other churches and chapels in Guernsey, as being the property and in the patronage of Mont Saint

---

EDITOR's NOTE.—* Tradition in that part of the island says (so I was told in 1896 by the woman living in the old farmhouse called St. Magloire) that in building this cottage they came upon the old corner stone of the original chapel. Thinking it was sacrilegious to move it, and would entail ill-luck on them and their children, they left it in its place, and there it still remains,

Michel. The only other notice we have of this chapel is the tradition recorded by some of our historians that, at the time of the Reformation, the plate, ornaments, vestments, and records, belonging to the churches in this island, were secretly buried here by the Roman Catholic clergy, with a view to their removal to Normandy when a fitting opportunity should offer, but that one John Le Pelley, a schoolmaster, having by some means got information of the circumstances, dug them up some few years later, and sold them to some Normans of Coutances, who conveyed them away.

Saint Magloire was the nephew and pupil of Saint Samson, and was born in the middle of the sixth century. He succeeded his uncle, Samson, as Bishop of Dol, but after a few years resigned his charge and retreated to Sark, where he founded a sort of monastery or missionary college, and where he died. His remains were translated in the ninth century to Léhon, near Dinan, and afterwards to Paris, where they were deposited in the church which still bears the name of the saint.

Two localities in the immediate neighbourhood of St. Malière bear the singular names of "*Paradis*" and "*Enfer.*" Tradition is entirely silent as to the origin of these names, but it is possible that they may have been in some way connected with the chapel, and with some of the superstitious usages so common among the nations of Celtic origin.

The Chapel of St. Clair was named after the first Bishop of Nantes, who lived in the third century. This chapel stood on the hill a little to the eastward of the farmhouse in Saint Sampson's parish which still bears the name. In clearing the ground for quarries of late years many human bones and a few grave-stones have been discovered there.

It was situated on the " Franc-Fief Gallicien," the tenants of which enjoy to this day an exemption from certain feudal duties, which is said to have been granted to their forefathers by King Edward IV. in acknowledgment of the services rendered by them as mariners in bringing him to this island from Exmouth, when, as Earl of March, he escaped with the famous Earl of Warwick, and their followers from England, after a victory gained by Henry VII. over the Yorkist party in October, 1459.

The Chapel of St. Germain was in the Castel parish, and its holy well, which is still regarded by some as no less efficacious than the fountain of St. George, was situated to the northward of that chapel. All traces of the building have long since disappeared, and all that we know of it is that in the Extents of Queen Elizabeth and James I. a rent payable to the Crown is described as " due on a piece of ground situated near the Chapel of St. Germain."

There is also said to have been a Chapel of Ste. Anne, near the King's Mills, more correctly designated as Les Grands Moulins. St. Anne also had her sacred fountain. The names of " Ste. Hélène," at St. Andrew's, and La Madeleine, St. Pierre-du-Bois, may also have been derived from religious buildings, but of these nothing but the names now remain.

In St. Martin's parish there was a chapel attached to the Priory of Blanchelande, and another, Saint Jean de la Houguette, which very probably was erected on the site now occupied by the parish school.*

In the Extente of the Fief Anneville it is said that

---

* See note on page 197.

the lord has his "Chapelles." It is probable that all
the feudal lords who held the lands direct from the
Crown had the same right of chapel. Such at least
seems to have been the case in Jersey, where some
still exist, and in the Clos-du-Valle, situated in the
Vale parish, is a field called "La Chapelle du Sud,"
west of a field called "Le Galle," on the Crown
lands. Here was probably the site of a now forgotten chapel.

Closely connected with the chapels and churches
are the holy wells. Even in pagan times, before
the introduction of Christianity, it is well known
that a sort of worship was paid to the nymphs or
deities who were supposed to haunt these fountains,
and to whose interference were attributed the cures
effected by the use of these waters. When a purer
faith was preached, and it was found impossible
to wean the minds of the people entirely away
from a belief in the supernatural qualities of these
springs, the early missionaries—whether wisely or
not it is difficult to say—sought to direct the
attention of their converts into a new channel, and
bestowed the name of some saint on these hallowed
spots, who thenceforth was supposed to stand in the
place of the ancient local deity or genius of the well.

Holy Wells.

Holy wells still exist in many parts of the island,
and are resorted to for various purposes, but principally for the cure of erysipelas, rheumatism and
glandular swellings, and inflammation or weakness of

" Wishing Well, Les Fontaines, Castel. "

the eyes. These maladies are all called by the country people "Mal de la Fontaine."

Whether the water will prove efficacious as a remedy is ascertained by noticing the effect produced on applying it. If it evaporates rapidly, passing off in steam, or runs off the swelling like little drops of quicksilver, it is of the right sort, and the sufferer may hope for a speedy cure. Still, there are certain ceremonies to be observed, without which it is useless to make the attempt.

It must be applied before the patient has broken his fast for nine consecutive mornings, and must be dropped on to the affected place with the fingers, and not put on with a sponge or rag. It must be taken fresh from the well every day at daybreak. The person who draws it must on no account speak to anyone either on his way to, or from the fountain, and must be particularly careful not to spill a single drop from the pitcher. It is customary to leave a small coin on the edge of the well, which was doubtless intended originally as an offering to the saint who was supposed to have the spring under his especial protection, and whose name it bore. These wells are said also to be used for purposes of divination. The maiden who is desirous of knowing who her future husband is to be, must visit the fountain for nine consecutive mornings fasting and in silence. On the last day when she looks into the clear basin of the well, she will see the face of him she is fated to wed reflected in the water. Should her destiny be to die unmarried, it is believed that a grinning skull will appear instead of the wished-for face.

The well most in repute is that of St. George, in the parish of Ste. Marie du Castel, but St. Germain and Ste. Anne, at no great distance, have their votaries, and there are also the "Fontaine de St. Clair," near St. Andrew's Church, the fountain of Gounebec in the valley of that name near the Moulin de Haut, two in the parish of the Forest,—that known by the name of "La Fontaine St. Martin," which rises on the cliffs to the westward of the point of La Corbière, and the other at a point between Le Gron and La Planque, where the three parishes of the Forest, St. Saviour's, and St. Andrew's meet. The "Fontaine de Lesset," at St. Saviour's, is also renowned. In the parish of St. Peter Port the fountain of Le Vau Laurent was famous for the cure of sore eyes, and the water of another on the side of the hill below Les Côtils, known formerly as "La Fontaine des Corbins," was supposed to be efficacious in cases of consumption if taken inwardly. "La Fontaine Fleurie," near Havelet, and another in the marshes near the ruined stronghold of "Le Chateau des Marais," commonly known as the Ivy Castle, are also resorted to. The fountains of St. Pierre and Notre Dame are mentioned in early ordinances of the Royal Court. The former is known to have been situated near the Town Church, at a spot called Le Pont Orchon, in the street which still bears the name of "La Rue de la Fontaine." The latter was apparently at the foot of the Mont Gibet, at the upper end of what is now the Market Place. The erection of pumps over most of these springs has deprived them of their ancient prestige, and has effectually removed any curative properties which they may formerly have possessed. Although every spring was not efficacious in all cases, to insure a cure it was necessary to use the water of a particular well, and, in order to choose it to consult certain persons who are knowing in these matters, and who, by an inspection of the part affected are able to tell what particular spring should be resorted to.*

Le Poulain de Saint George.

We have already mentioned the well of St. George as being supreme in its sanctity; indeed we may almost say that its reputation is such that it throws all others into the shade. It stands near the ruined chapel of the same name.

A place of such antiquity and reputed sanctity might naturally be expected to have its legends, though many doubtless have disappeared, but a firm faith still exists in the miraculous properties of the water of the well, and the old people still say that on tempestuous nights, especially during thunder and lightning, the form of a horse, darting flames of fire from its eyes and nostrils, may be seen galloping

---

Editor's Notes.

There are two wells or rather fountains, for it is imperative that they should be fed by a stream of running water, in St. Martin's; one, called "La Fontaine des Navets," is on the right hand side of the cliff above Saints' Bay; it is best approached from the Icart road, by the turning to the left down a little lane, opposite Mr. Moon's cottage. This lane runs just behind Mrs. Martin's pic-nic house. There are two wells in this lane, but the second, the most southerly, is the sacred one.

The other fountain was called "La Fontaine de la Beilleuse," and was situated just east of the church, below the farmhouse, belonging to Mr. Tardif. That again, was a double fountain, of which the southern was the wishing well, but it has now unfortunately been done away with, while the upper one has been converted into a drinking trough for cattle. Both these fountains cured the red swellings known as "Mal de la Fontaine." When I asked why these should be efficacious, and not any other, I was told that it was because they looked east, and were fed by springs running towards the east.—*From Mrs. Le Patourel, Mrs. Mauger, etc.*

See M. Sebillot's *Traditions et Superstitions de la Haute Bretagne,* T. 1, p. 45 :—"Au moment où le Christianisme s'introduisit en Gaul, le culte des pierres, des arbres et des fontaines y était florissant. De l'an 452, date du deuxième concile d'Arles, à l'an 658, concile de Nantes, nombre d'assemblées ecclesiastiques s'occupèrent de la question."

See also *Notions Historiques sur les Côtes-du-Nord,* par Havasque, T. I., p. 17 :—"De l'usage que les druides faisaient de l'eau des différentes sources est venue le culte que les Bretons ont si longtemps rendu aux fontaines. . . . . . Lors de l'établissement du Christianisme, les prêtres les consacrèrent à Dieu, sous l'invocation de la Vierge ou de quelque Saint, afin que les hommes grossiers, frappés par ces effigies, s'acoutumassent insensiblement à rendre à Dieu et à ses Saints l'hommage qu'ils adressaient auparavant aux fontaines elles-mêmes. Telle est l'origine des niches pratiquées dans la maçonnerie de presque toutes les fontaines, niches dans lesquelles on a placé la statue du saint qui donne son nom à la source. C'est pour parvenir au même but que le clergé fit ériger à la même époque des chapelles dans les lieux consacrés à la religion ou au culte."

thrice, and thrice only, round the ruined precincts of the chapel.

Some accounts of the spectral appearance speak only of a horse's head enveloped in flames, without the accompaniment of a body.*

The territory of St. George was also formerly known by the name of " St. Grégoire," and, though Nicholas Breakspear, Pope Adrian IV., numbers " La Chapelle de St. George " among the possessions of St. Michel in his Bull of 1155, Robert de Thorigni calls it " St. Grégoire " in 1156, but in many places the St. George of the legends seems to have been confused with the " Egrégoires," the watcher, " l'ange qui veille," of the old world. It is, according to mythology, " l'Egrégoire " who mounts the white horse that leads to victory, which apparition, in the moment of danger, has roused so many Catholic armies from despair.

The fountain was so much resorted to for divers superstitions formerly, that in 1408 an Act was passed by the Royal Court, at the request of Dom Toulley, Prêtre de St. George, under the Bailiff Gervais de Clermont, that the pathway to the fountain was only open to the faithful on their way to divine service, or to the sick who came to be healed.

We may add that an adjoining field bears the

---

* From G. Métivier, Esq.

" Our Lady and St. George were often partners in worship ; and the latter's holy wells are famous in old legends :—" And the Kynge (of Lybie) did to make a chyrche there of our Lady and of Saynte George. In the whyche yet sourdet a fountayn of lyving water whyche heled the seke peple yᵗ drinken thereof."— *Caxton's Edition of the Golden Legend,* fol. cxi.

EDITOR'S NOTE.—See *Croyances et Légendes du Centre de la France,* by Laisnal de la Salle, Tome I., p, 324.

name of "Le Trépied," a name which is to be found
in other localities in the island, and which indicates
that a primæval stone monument, of the nature of
those commonly called Druid's altars, may have at
one time stood there. These, as has already been
shown, have always had the reputation of being the
haunt of fairies, and sometimes of spirits of a less
innocent nature.

A Legend of St. George's Well.

St. Patrick and St. George, in the days when there
were "saints errant" as well as "knights errant,"
both happened to come to Guernsey, and met on this
spot. St. Patrick had just arrived from Jersey, where
the inhabitants had pelted him with stones and treated
him with such systematic rudeness that the saint,
furious, came on to Guernsey, and there he was welcomed with effusion. Meeting St. George, they began to
quarrel as to whom the island should in future belong.
However, being saints, they decided that it would be
more consistent with their profession each to give
some special boon to the island, and then go their
ways. So St. Patrick filled his wallet with all the
noxious things to be found,—toads, snakes, etc.,—and
went back to Jersey and there emptied it, freeing
Guernsey for ever from all things poisonous, while giving
to Jersey a double share. St. George smote the tiny
stream at his feet, "the waters to be for the healing
of diseases, and a blessing to whoever shall own this
spot. He shall never lack for bread, nor shall he ever
be childless whilst this well be preserved untainted."
Now, many, many years ago, the Guilles, who still
own St. George, inherited it from the De Jerseys, and
it so happened that the lord of the estate had an only

son who was naturally very dear to him. An old friend of the family brought him a canary bird as a pet, and, as one had never before been seen in Guernsey, it was very precious. One day it flew away from its cage, the door being accidentally left open, and was pursued hotly by the child. It made for the well, and apparently flew in, for the child was bending forward, an act which would inevitably have caused him to fall in, when he was arrested by the neighing of a horse behind him. He looked round and saw the fiery head of St. George's charger disappearing among the trees. That look saved him, and the bird was seen perched on the cross above the well, singing loudly. Presently it flew back to its little master, who had been saved by St. George from a watery grave, and a picture of the boy with his canary bird is still to be seen among the Guille family portraits.*

MAIDENS AT ST. GEORGE'S WELL.

There is a curious property attached to this well, that is that if a maiden visits it, fasting and in silence, on nine successive mornings, carefully depositing a piece of silver in the niche as an offering to the saint, she is assured of matrimony within nine times nine weeks, and, by looking into the well with an earnest desire to behold the image of the intended husband, his face will appear mirrored in the water. And, in former times, when the man was identified, the girl gave his name to the priest, who then summoned him before St. George, and, as destined for each other by Heaven, they were solemnly united.

---

* From Miss Lane, afterwards Mrs. Lane Clarke.

There is still a tradition extant of one of the neighbouring girls of the parish, being forbidden by her father to marry the man on whom her heart was set, on the ground of his poverty, declaring that, having seen his face in the well, he was evidently destined for her by Heaven, and that she would claim him as her fate before the priest. On this her father, fearing the exposure and public censure, gave his consent to the marriage.*

There is also a legend told by Mr. Métivier of a country girl stealing out one summer night in the year 1798, to meet her lover near the well, flying home terrified, having seen a troop of bare skeletons grouped round the well, and gazing into the troubled waters.

Connected with the Chapel of St. George was a cemetery, which boasted of many relics, famous for their miracles.

At one time this cemetery was said to be haunted by a beautiful young girl. Every night wailing and crying was heard, and a figure was seen, much mangled, walking about. The cries were supposed to proceed from the tomb of a girl who had disappeared from her home one night in a most mysterious manner, and whose mangled corpse was picked up a few days later near the Hanois rocks, so battered and bruised that it was evidently not a case of suicide. However, in course of time, a grave being opened near hers, some bones were thrown up, and, being handled by an old man who in days gone by had been the murdered girl's lover, a stream of blood oozed out of the dry bone! and with awful shrieks he owned to having been her murderer, and

---

* From Miss Lane, afterwards Mrs. Lane Clarke.

was executed soon afterwards at the " Champ du Gibet " at St. Andrew's.

EDITOR'S NOTES.

With reference to the statement on page 181 that Tortoval Church is under the invocation of Our Lady. In "*A Survey of the Estate of Guernzey and Jarzey* by Peter Heylyn,—1656," p. 320, he says :—"that (church) which is here called Tortevall (is dedicated) as some suppose unto St. Philip, others will have it to St. Martha."

On page 187 it is said that a chapel probably existed on the site of St. Martin's Parish School. In Elie Brevint's MSS. written in the early part of the 17th Century he says :—"Les Havillands de St. Martin ont donné la chappelle pour servir d'eschole, et de la terre auprès deux fois autant que la verd de Serk, comme dit Thomas Robert,"

CHAPTER VI.

Fairies.

POPULAR NOTIONS ABOUT FAIRIES.

IT is not very easy to ascertain precisely what the popular idea of a fairy is. The belief in them seems to have died out, or, perhaps, to speak more correctly, they are no longer looked upon as beings that have any existence in

the present day. That such a race did once exist,
that they possessed supernatural powers, that they
sometimes entered into communication with mankind,
is still believed, but all that is related of them is
told as events that happened long before the memory
of man, and it is curious to see how a known
historical fact—the invasion of the island by Yvon
de Galles in the fourteenth century,—has, in the
lapse of ages, assumed the form of a myth, and
how his Spanish troops have been converted into
denizens of fairyland. Perhaps, as has been suggested
by some writers who have made popular antiquities
their peculiar study, all fairy mythology may be
referred to a confused tradition of a primæval race
of men, who were gradually driven out by the
encroachments of more advanced civilization. According
to this theory the inferior race retired before their
conquerors into the most remote parts of the woods
and hills, where they constructed for themselves rude
dwellings, partly underground and covered with turf,
such as may still be found in Lapland and Finland,
or made use of the natural fissures in the rocks
for their habitations, thus giving rise to the idea
that fairies and dwarfs inhabit hills and the innermost
recesses of the mountains. In the superior cunning
which an oppressed race frequently possesses may
have originated the opinion generally entertained of
the great intelligence of the fairy people—and, as it
is not to be supposed that a constant warfare was
going on between the races, it is far from improbable
that some of the stories which turn on the kindly
intercourse of fairies with mortals, may have arisen
in the recollection of neighbourly acts. The popular
belief that flint arrow-heads are their work—the names

given in these islands—"*rouets des faïkiaux*," or
fairies' spindles, to a sort of small perforated disc
or flattened bead of stone which is occasionally dug
up, and "*pipes des faïkiaux*" to the tiny pipes which
date from the first introduction of tobacco,—their
connection in the minds of the peasantry with the
remains commonly called druidical, and, indeed, with
any antiquity for which they cannot readily account,
are all more or less confirmatory of the theory above
alluded to. Some years ago a grave, walled up on
the inside with stones, and containing a skeleton and
the remains of some arms, was discovered on a
hillside near L'Erée. The country people without
hesitation pronounced it to be "*Le Tombé du
Rouai des Fāïes.*"

One well-preserved cromlech in the same neighbourhood is called "Le Creux des Fāïes" and the
local name of cromlechs, in general "pouquelāie,"
may have some reference to that famous fairy Puck,
or Robin Goodfellow, the west country Pixie, or
Pisky, and the mischievous Irish goblin Phooka.

According to the best accounts the fairies are a
very small people, and always extremely well dressed.
The inhabitants of Sark attribute to them the
peculiarity of carrying their heads under their arms.
They are fond of sporting among the green branches
of the trees, and on the borders of running streams.
They are supposed to live underground in ant hills,
and to have a particular affection for upright stones,
around which they assemble, or which they use as
marks in some of their games, and the removal of
which they are apt to resent by causing injury to
the persons or property of those who are bold enough
to brave their displeasure in this respect. Some are

domestic, living invisibly about the hearth-stone or
oven, but willing to make themselves useful by
finishing the work which the housewife had not been
able to complete during the day. They expected,
however, as a reward for their kind offices that a
bowl of milk porridge should be set on the floor for
them when the family retired to rest. On one
occasion a fairy was heard complaining that the
porridge was too hot and scalded her. The sensible
advice was given—to wait until it cooled.

The few stories about fairies that I have been able
to collect are given in these pages, and are very
much the same as those related in other countries.
Of the more elaborate fairy tale—that which recounts
the adventures of a life-time, and in which a
supernatural being—commonly called a fairy, but
who has little or nothing in common with the fays
who dance on the green sward by the light of the
moon—is the directing influence either for good or
bad,—I have been able to discover only the very
slightest trace.

That such tales did once exist, and that they
were related by nurses to amuse their young charges,
is, I think, sufficiently proved by allusions sometimes
made to Chendrouine, as our old acquaintance
Cendrillon or Cinderella is called, and by the fact
that a friend of mine remembers an old servant
telling him the story of "Pel de Cat," evidently the
same as the English story of "Cat-skin," which
however appears in the French collections of fairy
tales by the name of "Peau d'Ane." All that
my friend could recall to mind were the words in
which the heroine of the tale is welcomed into a
house where she seeks for shelter, and which

have a rythmical cadence that smacks strongly of antiquity :—

"*Entre, paure Pel-de-Cat, mànge, et bés, et séque té.*"

(Enter, poor Cat-skin, eat, drink, and dry yourself).*

But the best informed among the peasantry do not hesitate in expressing their belief that the fairies were a race who lived long before the ancestors of the present occupants of the land had effected a settlement in the island; that the cromlechs were erected by them for dwelling places, and that the remains of pottery which have been from time to time discovered in these primæval structures plainly prove their derivation.

That the fairy race possessed supernatural strength

EDITOR'S NOTES.

* (In St. Martin's there still lingers a version of the English Tom Thumb, the "Thaumlin" or "Little Thumb" of the Northerners, who was a dwarf of Scandinavian descent. I was told the following story in 1896, but the old woman who told me owned that she had forgotten many of the details.)

"LE GRAND BIMERLUE."

Once upon a time a woman had a very tiny little son, who was always called P'tit Jean. He was so small that she was continually losing him. One day he strayed into a field, and was terrified at seeing a large bull rushing towards him, having broken loose from his leash. Hoping for shelter, he ran and hid under a cabbage leaf, but in vain, for the bull ate up the cabbage leaf, and swallowed "P'tit Jean" as well. Soon his mother was heard calling "*P'tit Jean! P'tit Jean! je tràche mon P'tit Jean.*" (P'tit Jean! P'tit Jean! I am looking for my P'tit Jean,") so, as well as he could, he answered "*Je suis dans le ventre du Grand Bimerlue.*" ("I am in the stomach of the "Grand Bimerlue.") Astonished and frightened at hearing these unusual sounds coming from the bull, the woman rushed in and implored her husband to kill "Le Grand Bimerlue," as she was sure he must be bewitched. This was accordingly done, and they cut up the carcase for eating, but the entrails were thrown into the nearest ditch. An old woman was passing by and saw them lying there, so picked them up and put them in her basket, saying—

"*Y en a des biaux boudins pour mon diner.*"

("Here are some fine black puddings for my dinner.")

All the time the boy was calling—

"*Trot, trot le vier,*
"*Trot, trot la vieille,*
"*Je suis dans l'ventre
Du Grand Bimerlue.*"

(Trot, trot old man,
Trot, trot old woman,
I am in the stomach
Of the Grand Bimerlue)."

Hearing these sounds issuing from her basket she hurried home and cut open the stomach of the bull, from whence emerged "P'tit Jean" none the worse for his adventure. He ran home to his mother, who had begun to think that she would never see him again.—*From Mrs. Charles Marquand.*

and knowledge there can be no doubt, or how could
they have moved such enormous blocks of stone?
Whether their strength and extraordinary science was
a gift from Heaven, or whether they acquired these
endowments by having entered into a league with
the powers of darkness, is a very doubtful and
disputed question. Some say they were a highly
religious people, and that they possessed the gift of
working miracles. Others shake their heads and say
that their knowledge, though perhaps greater, was of
the same nature as that possessed in later times by
wizards and witches, who, as everybody knows, derive
their power from the wicked one.*

Some fifty or sixty years since, it was still firmly
believed in the country that the fairies assisted the
industrious, and that, if a stocking or other piece of
knitting was placed at night on the hearth or at the
mouth of the oven with a bowl of pap, in the
morning the work would be found completed and the
pap eaten. Should idleness, however, have prompted
the knitter to seek the assistance of the invisible
people, not only did the work remain undone and
the pap uneaten, but the insult put upon them was
severely revenged by blows inflicted on the offending
parties during their sleep.†

It is asserted by some old people in the neighbourhood of L'Erée that, in days gone by, if a bowl of
milk porridge was taken in the evening to the "Creux
des Faïes," and left there with a piece of knitting
that it was desired to have speedily finished, and a
fitting supply of worsted and knitting needles, the

---

* From Mrs. Savidan.

† From Miss E. Chepmell, of St. Sampson's.

bowl would be found next morning emptied of its contents, and the work completed in a superior manner.*

THE INVASION OF GUERNSEY BY THE FAIRIES.

" Welcome lady! to the cell,
　Where the blameless Pixies dwell,
　But thou sweet nymph! proclaimed our faery queen
With what obeisance meet
Thy presence shall we greet."
—Coleridge.

" In olde dayes of the King Artour
　Of which that Bretons speken gret honour,
　All was this lond fulfilled of faerie;
　The Elf-quene, with hire joly compagnie,
　Danced ful oft in many a grene mede,
　This was the old opinion as I rede;
　I speke of many hundred yeres ago;
　But now can no man see non elves mo."
—Chaucer's " Canterbury Tales."

At a very remote period there lived in the neighbourhood of Vazon a girl of extraordinary beauty. One morning, as was her usual custom, she left her cottage at an early hour to attend to her cows, when, on entering the meadow, she was astonished to find asleep on the grass, under the shelter of a hedge, a young man of very small stature, but finely proportioned, and remarkably handsome. He was habited in a rich suit of grass-green, and by his side lay his bow and arrows. Wondering who the stranger could be, and fascinated by his beauty and splendid appearance, the maiden stood in silent admiration, until he awoke and addressed her. Her person and manners seem to have had as much influence on the youth as his appearance had produced on the damsel. He informed her that he was a fairy from England, and made her an offer of his hand. She immediately

---

* From Mrs. Murton.

"Creux des Fâïes."

consented to unite her destiny with his, and followed
him to the sea-shore, where a barque was waiting,
which conveyed the happy pair to fairyland.

Time passed on, and the disappearance of the
maiden was almost forgotten, when, one morning, a
man who was going down to Vazon Bay at day-break
was surprised to see a numerous host of diminutive
men issuing, like a flock of bees, from the Creux des
Fàïes, and lurking among the reeds and rushes of
Le Grand Marais. He inquired who they were, and
what had induced them to visit the Holy Isle. One,
who appeared their leader, answered for all, and told
the affrighted man, that, charmed with the beauty
and grace of the damsel that one of their companions
had brought from the island, they were determined
also to possess wives from the same country. They
then deputed him to be the bearer of a message to
the men of Guernsey, summoning them to give up
their wives and daughters, and threatening them with
their heaviest displeasure in case of a refusal. Such
an exorbitant demand was, of course, with one accord
refused, and the Guernseymen prepared to defend
their families and drive the bold invaders from their
shores. But, alas! what can poor mortals avail
against supernatural beings! The fairies drove them
eastward with great carnage. The last stand was
made near Le Mont Arrivel, but, wearied and
dispirited, they fell an easy prey to their merciless
enemies, who put every soul to the sword. Their
blood flowed down to the shore, and tinged the sea
to a considerable distance, and the road where this
massacre took place still retains the memory of the
deed, and is known to this day by the name of La
Rouge Rue. Two men only of St. Andrew's parish

are reported to have escaped by hiding in an oven. The fairies then entered into quiet possession of the families and domains of the slain; the widows began to be reconciled to their new masters, the maidens were pleased with their fairy lovers, and the island once more grew prosperous. But this happy state of things could not last for ever. The immutable laws of fairyland will not allow their subjects to sojourn among mortals more than a certain number of years, and at last the dwellers in Sarnia were obliged to bid adieu to the shady valleys, the sunny hills, and flowery plains, which they had delighted to rove amongst and which their skill and industry had materially improved. With heavy hearts they bade adieu to the scene of their fondest recollections, and re-imbarked. But, since then, no Guernsey witch has ever needed a broomstick for her nocturnal journeys, having inherited wings from her fairy ancestors, and the old people endeavour to account for the small stature of many families by relating how the fairies once mingled their race with that of mortals.*

THE FAIRIES AND THE NURSE.

The fairies sometimes avail themselves of the services of mankind, and in return are willing to assist and reward them as far as lies in their power, but woe to the unhappy mortal who chances to offend them!—for they are as pitiless as they are powerful.

It is said that one night a woman, who lived in the neighbourhood of Houmet and who gained her livelihood by nursing and attending on the sick,

---

* Communicated by Miss Lane, to whom the story was related by an old woman of the Castel parish.

heard herself called from without. She immediately
arose, and, looking out, saw a man who was totally
unknown to her standing at the door. He accosted
her, and, telling her that he required her services for
a sick child, bade her follow him. She obeyed, and
he led the way to the mouth of the little cavern at
Houmet, called Le Creux des Fées. She felt alarmed,
but, having proceeded too far to retreat, resolved to
put a bold front on the matter, and followed her
mysterious guide. As they advanced, she was
astonished to find that the cave put on a totally
different appearance—the damp rugged walls became
smooth, and a bright light disclosed the entrance of
a magnificent dwelling.

The poor woman soon comprehended that she had
penetrated into fairyland, but, relying on the good
intentions of her conductor, she followed him into an
apartment where a child was lying ill in a cradle,
whom she was desired to attend to and nurse. She
entered on her new duties with alacrity, and was
plentifully supplied by the fairies with every necessary
and even luxury. One day, however, as she was
fondling the infant, some of its spittle chanced to
touch her eyes. Immediately everything around her
put on a different aspect—the brilliant apartment
once more became a dismal cavern, and squalor and
misery replaced the semblance of riches and
abundance. She was too prudent, however, to impart
to any of the fairy people the discovery she had
made, and, the health of the child being quite
restored, solicited her dismissal, which was granted
her with many thanks, and a handsome compensation
for her trouble.

The Saturday following her return to the light of

day, she went into town to make her weekly purchases of provisions and other necessaries, and, stepping into a shop in the Haut Pavé, was astonished to see one of her acquaintances of the Creux des Fâîes busily employed in filling a basket with the various commodities exposed for sale, but evidently unseen by all in the shop but herself. No longer at a loss to know whence the abundance in the fairies' cavern proceeded, and, indignant at the roguery practised on the unsuspecting shopkeeper, she addressed the pilferer and said "Ah, wicked one! I see thee!"

"You see me—do you?" answered the fairy. "And how—pray?"

"With my eyes to be sure," replied the woman, off her guard.

"Well then," replied he, "I will easily put a stop to any future prying into our affairs on your part."

And, saying this, he spat in her eyes, and she instantly became stone blind! *

There is another version of the preceding, called

The Fairies and the Midwife.

Late one night an old woman was called up by a man with whom she was unacquainted, and requested to follow as quickly as possible, as his wife was in labour and required her immediate assistance. She obeyed, and was led by her guide into a miserable hovel, where everything appeared wretched, the few articles of furniture falling to pieces, and the household vessels of the coarsest ware, and scarcely one whole. Shortly after her arrival, her patient was safely delivered of a child. When she was about to make

---

* From Miss Lane, as related in the Castel parish.

use of some water which stood in a pail, to wash the child with, and had already dipped her hand into it, she was earnestly requested not to meddle with that water, but to use some which stood in a jug close by. She chanced, however, to lift her hand, still wet, to her face, and a drop of the water got into one of her eyes. Immediately she saw everything under a different aspect; the house appeared rich and magnificently furnished, and the broken earthenware turned into vessels of gold and silver.

She was, however, too prudent to express her surprise, and, when her services were no longer required, left the place.

Some time afterwards she met the man in town and accosted him. "What," said he, "You see me! How is this?" Taken unawares, she mentioned what she had done in the cottage, and which of her eyes was endowed with the faculty of beholding him: he immediately spat in it, and destroyed her sight for ever.* †

The Broken Kettle.

Two men were at work in a field near L'Erée, when suddenly their plough stopped, nor would their

---

* From Miss F. Chepmell.

† See Sir Walter Scott's *Lady of the Lake.* Note M:—Many of the German popular tales collected by the Brothers Grimm turn on the circumstance of a midwife being called to assist an Undine, or Fairy.

See also Keightley's *Fairy Mythology,* Vol. 2, p. 182. *Notes and Queries,* 2nd Series, IX. 259.

Mrs. Bray's *Traditions of Devonshire.*

EDITOR'S NOTES.

In *Traditions et Superstitions de La Haute Bretagne,* by Sebillot, almost the same story is told, Tome 1., p. 166. See also Tome 2., p. 89. "Un jour, une sage-femme alla accoucher une fée: elle oublia de se laver la main, et se toucha un œil; ainsi depuis ce temps elle reconnaissait les déguisements des fées. Un jour que le mari de la fée était à voler du grain, elle le vit et cria 'au voleur.' Il lui demanda de quel œil elle le voyait, et aussitôt qu'il le sut, il le lui arracha."

united strength, joined to that of the oxen, succeed in moving it. As they looked about them, wondering what could be the reason of this stoppage, they observed in one of the neighbouring furrows an iron kettle, such as was formerly used for baking bread and cake on the hearth. On approaching it they noticed that it contained a bit which had been broken out of the side, and a couple of nails. On stooping to lift it, they heard a voice desiring them to get it mended, and when done to replace it on the same spot where they had found it. They complied with the request, went to the nearest smith, and on their return to the field with the kettle, which they replaced as directed, continued their work, the plough moving as readily as before. They had completed several furrows when a second time the plough remained stationary. On this occasion they observed a bundle neatly tied up lying near them, and, on opening it, found it to contain a newly-baked cake, quite warm, and a bottle of cider. At the same time they were again addressed by their invisible friend, who bade them eat and drink without fear, thanked them for the readiness with which they had attended to his wishes, and assured them that a kind action never goes without its reward.*

Fairy Neighbours.

The fairies are reported to have regarded some households with particular favour, and to have lived on very neighbourly terms with them, borrowing or lending as occasion might require.

The families of De Garis and Dumont are among

---

* From Miss Lane.

See *Notes and Queries*, 2nd Series, Vol. IX., 259.

those who are said to have been in their good graces,
and it was to a De Garis the following incident
happened.

To the south of the Church of St. Pierre du Bois
there lies a little dell, through which runs a small
stream of water known by the singular name of
" Le Douït d'Israël." This valley is said to have been
in former days a favourite resort of the fairy folk,
and tradition affirms that a very kindly feeling existed
between them and the mortal inhabitants of the land.
A cottage is still pointed out, not far from the estate
called " Le Colombier," which is said to have been
the abode of a countryman and his wife with whom
the fairies were in constant communication.
Frequently, at night, the elves would come and
request the loan of a cart until the morning, and
their request was always complied with willingly, for
it was always accompanied with the following
promise :—

> " *Garis, Garis,*
> *Prête mé ten quériot,*
> *Pour que j'allons à St. Malo,*
> *Queurre des roques et des galots,*
> *Rindelles, roulettes, ou roulons,*
> *S'il en manque j'en mettrons.*"

> (" Garis, Garis,
> Lend your cart now, I pray,
> To go to Saint Malo,
> To fetch stones away.
> Should tires for the wheels
> Or any thing lack,
> We'll make it all right
> Before we come back.")

Permission to take the cart was never refused, for
it was always returned in perfect order, and, if any
injury was done to the metal-work during the

nocturnal journey, it was found the next day carefully repaired with pure silver. But what use was made of it is unknown. Some pretend that a sound of wheels was sometimes heard in the dead of night rolling over the cliffs at Pleinmont, where no horse could have found a footing.*

"LE PETIT COLIN."

Fairies have sometimes been known to enter into the service of mankind, but by what motives they were actuated in so doing is not clear. A certain † "Mess" Dumaresq, of "Les Grands Moulins," once engaged as a farm servant a boy who offered himself. No one knew whence he came, nor did he appear to have any relations. He was extremely lively, active, and attentive to his duties, but so small that he acquired and was known by no other name than that of "P'tit Colin." One morning as Dumaresq was returning from St. Saviour's, he was astonished, on passing the haunted hill known as "La Roque où le Coq Chante," to hear himself called by name. He stopped his horse and looked round, but could see no one. Thinking that his imagination must have deceived him, he began to move on, but was again arrested by the voice. A second time he stopped and looked round, but with no more success than the first. Beginning to feel alarmed, he pushed his horse forward, but was a third time stopped by the voice. He now summoned up all his courage and asked who it was that called, and what was required of him. The voice immediately answered,—

---

* From John de Garis, Esq., and Mrs. Savidan.

† "Mess" is the Guernsey colloquial for "Monsieur," as applied to one of the farmer class.

" Go home directly and tell P'tit Colin that Grand Colin is dead."

Wondering what could be the meaning of this, he made the best of his way home, and, on his arrival, sent for Le Petit Colin, to whom he communicated what had befallen him. The boy replied,

" What! Is Le Grand Colin dead? Then I must leave you," and immediately turned round to depart.

" Stop," said Mess Dumaresq, " I must pay you your wages."

" Wages!" said Colin, with a laugh, " I am far richer now than you. Goodbye."

Saying this he left the room and was never afterwards seen or heard of.

This story is still related by Dumaresq's descendants.*

THE FAIRY BAKERS.

Le Grand Colin and Le Petit Colin, whose names have already been mentioned in connection with La Longue Roque and La Roque où le Coq Chante,

---

* From Miss Lane and John de Garis, Esq.

Mr. Métivier also gives a version of this in an article in one of the French papers, and some notes as to the origin of the legend.

" Ce fut à son retour de St. Pierre-Port, où il avait un tant soit peu trop levé le coude, un Samedi, qu'au moment où il passait " La Roche au Coq," vers minuit, un de nos terriens entendit ces paroles :

" Jean Dumaresq ! Va dire au P'tit Colin que l'Grànd Colin est mort ! "

Or ce Colin, en haut-tudesque *Cole-wire*, est un *troll* ou *guenon*, un gobelin, qui, sous la forme de singe, ou de chat, était persécuté par un maître rébarbatif. Dans la légende norse, le fermier se nomme Platt ; et lorsqu'il revient chez lui, ayant pris, sinon du vin, de la cervoise, il dit à sa ménagère : " Écoute ce qui m'est arrivé ce soir ! Comme je passais Brand Hoy, la Hougue-aux-Balais, la voix d'un troll m'a crié ces mots :

> " Écoute, Platt !
> Dis à ton chat
> ' Que le vieux Surc-Mûre,
> (Rouàne et grond),
> Est mort ! ' "

Aussitôt, notre chat fait une cabriole, et se dressant sur ses pieds de derrière, crie à son tour : " En ce cas-là, il faut que je décampe."

appear to have belonged to that race of household spirits who used to take up their abode on or near the hearth, and who, although rarely making themselves visible to the human inhabitants of the house, were willing, so long as no attempt was made to pry into their secrets, to render occasional acts of kindness to those under whose roof they dwelt, especially if they were honest and industrious.

A man and his wife occupied a small cottage at St. Brioc. The man gained his living as many along the western coasts of the island do. When the weather was favourable he went out fishing. After gales of wind he was up with the first dawn of day to secure his share of the sea-weed which the waves had cast up on the shore, or perchance a spar or cordage detached from some unfortunate ship that had gone down in the storm. At other times he cultivated his own small plot of ground, or hired himself out as a day labourer to some of the

---

See *Lay of the Last Minstrel*, Note S, and a paper on Popular Superstitions, etc., in the *Saturday Magazine*, Vol 10. p. 44. In Brand's *Antiquities*, Vol. 3. p. 44, the following similar story is communicated by T. Quiller Couch, as relating to a Cornish pixy. "A farmer, who formerly lived on an estate in this neighbourhood, called Langreek, was returning one evening from a distant part of the farm, and, in crossing a field, saw, to his surprise, sitting on a stone in the middle of it, a miserable looking creature, human in appearance, though dwarfish in size, and apparently starving with cold and hunger. Pitying its condition, and perhaps aware that it was of elfish origin, and that good luck would amply repay him for his kind treatment of it, he took it home, placed it by the warm hearth on a stool, fed it with milk, and shewed it great kindness. Though at first lumpish and only half sensible, the poor bantling soon revived, and, though it never spoke, became lively and playful, and a general favourite in the family. After the lapse of three or four days, whilst it was at play, a shrill voice in the farm-yard or 'town place' was heard to call three times 'Colman Gray!' at which the little fellow sprang up, and, gaining voice, cried—'Ho! Ho! Ho! My daddy is come!' flew through the key hole, and was never afterwards heard of. A field on the estate is called "Colman Gray" to this day."

neighbouring farmers who were in want of assistance. In short he was never idle.

They lived in a typical old Guernsey country farmhouse, with old walls of grey granite, a thatched roof, small diamond-paned windows, and arched doorways, with its half-door or "hecq." Inside they are all built much on the same pattern. The front door opens into an entrance hall, on one side of which is the "living" room of the house,—parlour and kitchen in one,—with a huge chimney, sometimes adorned with quaint old carvings, as at "Les Fontaines," in the Castel parish, a low hearth stone, a smouldering vraic fire, and "trepied." Still inside its enclosure are stone seats, a large bread oven built in the thickness of the wall, and a hook whereon to hang the "crâset" lamp.

A rack hangs from the low oak ceiling, diversified by its huge centre beam or "poûtre." On this is kept the bacon, and the grease for the "soupe à la graisse," or "de cabôche." A "jonquière," which is an oblong wooden frame about three feet from the ground, is placed in a corner near the fire and if possible near a window, and is used as a sofa by the family. Formerly it was stuffed with rushes, whence its name. Peastraw or dried fern, covered with green baize, now take their place, and it is frequently called the "green bed." A long table and forms, with an eight-day clock by Naftel, Lenfestey, or Blondel, and an old carved chest, which contained the bride's dower of linen in bygone times, is the ordinary furniture of the rooms, whose principal ornament consists of some of the beautiful china brought by sailor sons from the far East or Holland. The floors boast for carpet nothing but earth covered with clean sand, daily renewed.

On the other side of the passage is the best
bedroom, with its four poster, and some still have on
their mantel-pieces the old tinder boxes, with their
flint and steel, and separate compartments for the
burnt rag or tinder. Beyond are the winding stone
steps, built in a curve beyond the straight wall of
the house, and above are more bedrooms, or, in
smaller houses, simply a "ch'nas" or loft.

His wife also was never idle. She was one of the
shrewd, industrious, and frugal race, who were content
with a diet of bacon and cabbage, barley-bread and
cider, and who are, alas, disappearing fast. Night
after night, when her husband had returned home,
and, tired out with the fatigues of the day, had gone
to rest and was sound asleep, she would sit up till
a late hour on the "jonquière" and ply her spinning
wheel by the dim light of the "crâset."

While thus occupied, she, one night, heard a knock
at the door, and a voice enquiring whether the oven
was hot, and whether a batch of dough might be baked
in it. A voice from within then enquired who it was
that stood without, and, on the answer being given
that it was Le Petit Colin, permission was immediately
granted, and the door opened to admit him. She
then heard the noise of the dough being placed in the
oven, and a conversation between the two, by which she
learned that the inmate of the house was called Le
Grand Colin. After the usual time the bread was
drawn, and the mysterious visitor departed, leaving
behind him, on the table, a nicely baked cake, with an
intimation that it was in return for the use of the oven.

This was repeated frequently and at regular intervals,
and the woman at last mentioned the circumstance to
her husband. The fairer sex is frequently accused of

an inclination to pry into secrets and taunted with
the evils which too often result from inordinate
curiosity, but in this instance it was the husband who
was to blame. He was seized with a violent desire
to penetrate the mystery, notwithstanding the earnest
entreaties of his wife—who had a shrewd suspicion of
the real state of the case—that he should leave well
alone. His will prevailed, and it was settled that on
the night when the invisible baker was expected,
the husband should take his wife's place on the
"jonquière," disguised in her clothes, and that she
should go to bed. Knowing that her husband could
not spin, the careful housewife thought it prudent
not to put the usual supply of flax or wool on the
distaff, lest the good man, in turning the wheel,
should spoil it. He had not been long at his post
and pretending to spin, when the expected visitor
came. He could see nothing, but he heard one of
the two say to the other :—

> ' *File, filiocque,*
> *Rien en brocque,*
> *Barbe à cé ser*
> *Pas l'autre ser."*

> (" There's flax on the distaff,
> But nothing is spun ;
> To night there's a beard,
> T'other night there was none.")

Upon which both were heard to quit the house as
if in anger, and were never again known to revisit it.*

---

* From William Le Poidevin, confirmed by Mrs. Savidan.

EDITOR'S NOTES.

Compare in Amélie Bosquet's book *La Normandie Romanesque et Merveilleuse*, p. 130-131,
Le Lutin ou le Fé Amoureux and Webster's *Basque Legends*, p. 55-56.
Paul Sébillot also gives a somewhat similar story, in *Traditions et Superstitions de La Haute
Bretagne*, Tome I., p. 116-117. " Il y avait à la Ville-Douélan, en la paroisse du Gouray, une

THE CHANGELING.

In times long past a young couple occupied a cottage in the neighbourhood of L'Erée. They were in the second year of their marriage, and little more than a fortnight had elapsed since the wife had presented her husband with his first-born son. The happy father, who, like most of the inhabitants of the coast, filled up the time in which he was not otherwise occupied, in collecting sea-weed or fishing, returned one morning from the beach with a basketful of limpets. There are various ways of cooking this shell-fish, which, from the earliest times, appears to have formed a considerable article of food among the poorer inhabitants of the sea-shore, and one of the ways of dressing them is by placing them on the hot embers, where they are soon baked or fried in their own cup-shaped shells. Cooked in this manner they form an appetizing relish to the "dorâïe," or slice of bread-and-butter, which forms the ordinary mid-day meal of the labouring man.

A good fire of furze and sea-weed was flaming on the hearth when the man entered his cottage, and, having raked the hot embers together, he proceeded to arrange the limpets on the ashes, and then left them to cook while he went out to finish digging a piece of ground. The wife in the meanwhile was occupied in some domestic work, but casting a look from time to time on her new-born babe, which was sleeping quietly in its cradle. Suddenly she was

bonne femme qui tous les soirs mettait son souper à chauffer dans le foyer; mais pendant qu'elle était occupée à filer, les fées descendaient par la cheminée et mangeaient son souper. Elle s'en plaignit à son mari, qui était journalier et ne rentrait que pour se coucher. Il lui dit de le laisser un soir tout seul à la maison. Il s'habilla en femme et prit une quenouille comme une fileuse, mais il ne filait point. Quand les fées arrivèrent, elles s'arrêtèrent surprises dans le foyer et dirent, 'Vous ne filez ni ne volez, vous n'êtes pas la bonne femme des autres soirs.' L'homme ne répondit rien; mais il prit une trique et se mit à frapper sur les fées, qui, depuis ce temps-là, ne revinrent plus jamais."

startled by hearing an unknown voice, which seemed to proceed from the child. She turned quickly round, and was much surprised to see the infant sitting up, and looking with the greatest interest at the fire-place, and to hear it exclaim in tones of astonishment :—

> " *Je n'sis de chut an, ni d'antan,*
> *Ni du temps du Rouey Jehan,*
> *Mais de tous mes jours, et de tous mes ans,*
> *Je n'ai vu autant de pots bouaillants.*"

> (" I'm not of this year, nor the year before,
> Nor yet of the time of King John of yore,
> But in all my days and years, I ween,
> So many pots boiling I never have seen.")

She had heard old wives tell how the fairies sometimes took advantage of the absence of the mother or nurse, to steal away a sleeping child, and to substitute one of their own bantlings in its place, and how the only way to cause them to make restitution was to throw the changeling on the hearth, when the fairy mother, unable to withstand the piteous cries of her offspring, was sure to appear, and bring back the stolen infant with her.

She lost no time therefore in catching up the fairy imp, who, knowing the fate that awaited him, set up a fearful yell. Immediately, the fairy mother, without stopping to lift the latch, leaped over the " hecq " or half-door, and, restoring to the trembling housewife her babe uninjured, snatched up her own squalling brat, and departed by the same way she had come.*

Building of the Castel Church.

The parish of Notre Dame du Castel, or, as it is now the fashion to call it, St. Mary de Castro, is the largest in the island, but the church is situated at one extremity of the parish, close on the bounds

---

* From Mrs. Savidan. (Also see Page 225).

of St. Andrew's, to the great inconvenience of many of the parishioners. It is true that in former days they had some relief in the Chapels of Ste. Anne, St. George, and St. Germain, but chapels are not parish churches, and many, while trudging through the miry roads in winter, or toiling up the dusty hill in summer, when some of the great festivals required them to present themselves at the mother church, have inquired how it came to pass that so inconvenient a site had been chosen. The old people, depositaries of the ancient traditions of the place, will answer that originally the foundations were laid in a field called "Les Tuzés," but this was haunted ground, and a favourite resort of the fairies, and that, these little ladies, unwilling to yield up their rights without a struggle, in the course of a single night transported all the tools, stones, etc., in their cambric aprons, to the spot where the Church of St. Mary now stands. Thrice did this happen before the builders gave up their intention of erecting the sacred edifice on the site first chosen.*

THE GUERNSEY LILY.

There is another story told of the fairy man who first came to Guernsey and carried away the beautiful † Michelle de Garis to be his wife. Though, vanquished

---

* From Rachel Duport.

Similar stories are told of the Forest Church, of St. Martin's and the Vale Churches, of St. Brelade's in Jersey. and many others.

See Chambers' *Popular Rhymes of Scotland*, p. 335, and *Notes and Queries*, 2nd Series, IV., 144.

† In those days Guernsey girls were not called Lavinia, Maud, Gladys, and all the ridiculous names with which modern parents disfigure the old Norman surnames, but they were called Michelle, Peronelle,—the diminutive feminine of Pierre, equivalent to the English form Petronilla,—Renouvette, (feminine of Ranulf or Ralph), Oriane, Carterette, Jaqueline, Colette or Colinette, and many other soft graceful old French names.

by his courtliness and grace, she was persuaded to fly
with him back to fairy land, she could not quite forget
the father, mother, and brothers, whom she had left
behind her in their cottage down by Vazon Bay. So
she begged him to let her leave them some slight
token by which to remember her. He thought for a
few moments, and then gave her a bulb, which he
told her to plant in the sand above the bay. He
then whispered to the mother where to go to find a
souvenir of her missing daughter, and, when she went,
weeping, to the search, she found this bulb, burst into
flower, a strange odourless beautiful blossom, decked
with fairy gold, and without a soul—for what is the
scent but the soul of a flower—a fit emblem of a
denizen of fairyland. From that time the flower
has been carefully cultivated in this island, the
"Amaryllis Sarniensis," as it is called, nor will it
flourish, however great the care, in any of the other
islands ; it pines and degenerates when removed from
the soil where it was first planted by the elfin
lover.*

---

* From Miss Lane.

EDITOR'S NOTES.

"LE GIBET DES FAÏES."

This fairy-story is not included by Sir Edgar MacCulloch, but was communicated to me by
the late Miss Annie Chepmell, who most kindly lent me her own manuscript book, in which
she wrote down the legends she had herself collected among the country people. I give it in
her own words.

"For a long time the fairies alone had possession of L'Ancresse, the cromlechs, hougues,
and caves. But evil men rose up, and ambition and the lust of knowledge led them to
cross the sea, and there to learn the mighty art of magic. They returned and quickly
spread the sin of witchcraft in the island, so quickly that the harmless fairies had no time
to accustom themselves to the miseries which were caused thereby, and which they had no
power to remedy. Their hearts fairly broke to see their happy haunts invaded by witches and
wizards, their fairy rings trampled down by the heavy feet of 'sorcières,' and scorched by
the hoofs of their demon partners every Friday night ; and their human friends and pet animals
pining beneath charms and spells. Unable to bear these sorrows, the poor fairies met on
their beloved L'Ancresse, and finding, after much consultation, that they could do nothing
against the disturbers of their happiness, they sadly resolved to get rid of their past by
drinking of the fountain of forgetfulness. There is, or rather was,—for the ruthless quarries
have much diminished its size—a huge pile of rocks rising from the sea at the eastern
extremity of L'Ancresse Bay. At the very top of this granite castle rises a little fountain,

Mermaids.

" I'll drown more sailors than the mermaid shall."
—Shakespeare.

" Thou rememb'rest
Since once I sat upon a promontory,
And heard a mermaid on a dolphin's back,
Uttering such dulcet and harmonious breath,
That the rude sea grew civil at her song."
—Shakespeare.

A belief in the existence of mermaids is not quite extinct, although no tales relating to them appear to have been preserved among the people. An old man, living in the parish of the Forest, of the name of Matthieu Tostevin, whose word might be implicitly relied on, affirmed to Mr. Denys Corbet, the master of the parochial school, that on one occasion, being on the cliffs over-looking Petit-Bôt Bay, he saw a company of six mermaids, or, as he termed them " *seirênes*," disporting themselves on the sands below. He described them as usually depicted, half woman,

cool in the hottest summer, unfrozen in the keenest frost. Its waters have the properties of Lethe—those who drink of them forgetting the past. In a sad procession the fairy tribe moved across the bay, and, after having scaled the steep rocks, clustered round the fountain which was to give them the bliss of unconsciousness. But for them the fountain had no virtue; they drank, and still the past came back, with all its joys and sorrows. In despair at finding even oblivion denied to them, they hastily determined to get rid of life itself. Rushing down the rocks they hurried across the Common to where stood three tall upright stones, with a third resting upon them—a monument of far-off Druid times—and there they hung themselves with blades of grass. So ended the kindly race in Guernsey, the fairy fountain and the upright stones their only monuments."

"There are still a few lingering remnants of fairy lore to be found among the old country people. Old Miss Fallaize, aged eighty, remembers how, in her youth, eatables and drinkables were left outside the door with any unfinished work, and how in the morning the food was gone—but she could not quite remember whether the work was done. But old Mr. Tourtel, over eighty, who was brought up as a boy at an old house at the Mont Durand, now pulled down, said that it was well known that the fairies lived in a ' vôte' (a Guernsey word for the French 'voute,' a vaulted cave), above La Petite Porte. They were a little people, but very strong, and would mend your cart wheels or spokes for you if you would put out some food for them."

Also the woman living in the house called " St. Magloire" opposite the site of his old chapel, said she supposed "Monsieur Magloire" was the first *man* who came to these islands, and when I asked her who were living here when he came, she said "Oh, ' little people,' who lived in the cromlechs."

" Looking down Smith Street, 1870."

half fish. He hastened down to the beach as fast as he could, to get a nearer sight of them, but, on his approaching them, they took to the sea, and were immediately out of sight.

It was doubtless a flock of seals which he saw, for, although these animals are no longer found in numbers on our coasts, a stray one is occasionally, though very rarely, to be seen. They are known to exist on the opposite shores of Brittany and Normandy, and the few specimens that have been taken in our seas are of the same variety as those found on the French coast. It is not improbable that they may have been more common in former days; and it is possible that "Le Creux du Chien," a large cavern at the foot of the cliffs to the eastward. of Petit-Bôt Bay, may have been so named from being the resort of one of these amphibians.*

---

* From Mr. Denys Corbet.

EDITOR'S NOTE.—In Sark as well as in Guernsey they still believe in sirens, and an old man there, who had been a fisherman in his youth, told me of these women who used to sit on the rocks and sing before a storm. In Sark they are considered young and beautiful, but Guernsey fishermen talk of *old* women who sit on the rocks and sing, and the ships are brought closer to the rocks by the curiosity of those on board to hear this mysterious music, and then the storm comes, and the ships go to pieces on the rocks, and the sirens,—whether young or old,—carry down the sailors to the bottom of the sea, and eat them. So the tradition goes.

EDITOR'S NOTES.

* Referring to the legend of the Changeling, as related on pages 219-220, Paul Sébillot also tells a story very similar to this. Tome I. p. 118-119.

"Un jour une femme dit à sa voisine,

—"Ma pauvre commère, je crains que mon gars a été changé par les Margots . . . . . . j'voudrais bien savoir c'qui faut faire."

". . . . . Vous prendrez d's œufs ; vous leur casserez le petit bout, et puis d'cela vous mettrez des petits brochiaux d'bois dedans ; vous allumerez un bon feu ; vous les mettrez autour, debout ; et vous mènerez le petit faitiau à se chauffer aussi."

La femme fit tout cela, et quand le petit faiteau vit les œufs bouillir et les petits bois sauter dedans, il s'écria :

"Voilà que j'ai bientôt cent ans ;
Mais jamais de ma vie durant
Je n'ai vu tant de p'tits pots bouillants."

La femme vit tout de suite que son enfant avait été changé . . . . . . et elle s'écria :

—" Vilain petit sorcier, je vais te tuer ! "

Mais la fée qui était dans le grenier lui cria —

"N'tue pas le mien, j'ne tuerai l'tien ;
N'tien pas l'mien, j'te ren'rai l'tien."

See also Amélie Bosquet, p. 116, etc.

O

CHAPTER VII.

Demons and Goblins.

" Now I remember those old woman's words
Who in my youth would tell me winter's tales,
And speak of sprites and ghosts that glide by night
About the place where treasure hath been hid."
Marlow's " Jew of Venice.'

" Will-a-wisp misleads night-faring clowns,
O'er hills and sinking bogs."

" Let night-dogs tear me,
And goblins ride me in my sleep to jelly,
Ere I forsake my sphere."
—Thierry and Theodoret. Act 1. Sc. 1.

LE FAEU BÉLENGIER.

THAT singular meteor, known by the English as Jack o'Lantern or "Will o' the Wisp," by the French as "Feu Follet," and by the Bretons as "Jan gant y tan" (John with the fingers or gloves of fire), bears in Guernsey the appellation of *Le Faeu Bélengier*—the fire of Bélenger. According to Mr. Métivier "Bélenger" is merely a slight variation of the name "Volunde" or "Velint"—Wayland, or Weyland Smith, the blacksmith of the Scandinavian gods. Bélenger was married to a Valkyrie, daughter of the Fates, so runs the old Norse legend. He was, for the sake of some treasures belonging to him, or under his guardianship, carried away by a certain king as prisoner to an island, where the tyrant cut the sinews of his feet so as to prevent his running away, and then set him to work. Too clever, however, not to be able to compass his revenge, Bélenger managed to kill the two sons of the despot, and fashioned their bones into vessels for the royal table. And then, having maltreated the princess, daughter of his quondam master, he flew away through the air, and the name Bélenger has become identified in popular mythology with any especially clever worker in metals. In English popular tradition the name of Bélenger becomes contracted into Velint, or Wayland Smith, and, according to Sir Walter Scott, " this Wayland was condemned to wander, night after night, from cromlech to cromlech, and belated travellers imagined that they then beheld the fire from his forge issuing from marshes and heaths." The natives of Iceland, descended from our own paternal ancestors of the tenth century, say still of a clever craftsman that he is a " Bélengier " in iron.

In Guernsey they say it is a spirit in pain, condemned to wander, and which seeks to deliver itself from torment by suicide." * Its presence is also supposed to indicate in very many cases the existence of hidden treasures, and many a countryman is known to have made a fruitless journey over bog and morass in the hope of locating the flickering flame. It is also firmly believed by all the country people that if a knife is fixed by the handle to a tree, or stuck in the earth with the point upwards, the spirit or demon that guides the flame will attack and fight with it, and that proofs of the encounter will be

* See Métivier's Dictionary,—Art : Bélengier.

found next morning in the drops of blood found on
the blade. * †

HIDDEN TREASURES.

As we have already stated " Le Faeu Bélengier "
is supposed to indicate the existence of hidden
treasure, and it is well known that when treasures
have been hidden for any considerable time the evil
spirit acquires a property in them, and does all in
his power to prevent their falling into the possession
of mortals. Nevertheless the meteor-like form which
the Bélengier assumes, frequently betrays their place
of concealment as it plays about the spot, and if a
person have sufficient courage and perseverance he
may become the possessor. The wiles, however, of
the demon, and his efforts to retain his own,
frequently prove successful, as the following narratives
will testify. It appears, however, that the guardian
spirit has no power to remove the treasure, unless
the adventure have first been attempted by a mortal.

A country-woman had often observed flames of fire
issuing from and hovering round the earth within
the threshold of her house, and, knowing well what

---

* From Rachel Du Port, and others.

Yorkshire Folk-Lore—*Notes and Queries*, 4th Series. I; 193. "If ever you
are pursued by a Will-o'-the-Wisp, the best thing to do is to put a steel
knife into the ground, with the handle upwards. The Will-o'-the-Wisp will run
round this until the knife is burnt up, and you will thus have the means of
escaping."

EDITOR'S NOTES.

† "Tout le monde connaît ces exhalaisons de gaz inflammable qui brillent quelquefois dans
les endroits marécageux et qui effraient tant les enfants et les vieilles. Ces feux sont appelés
dans nos campagnes La Fourlore, le feu follet, ou le feu errant. Ce sont des âmes damnées ;
et, suivant quelques personnes, ces âmes sont celles de prêtres criminels ou libertins. Elles
cherchent à éblouir les voyageurs, à les entraîner dans les précipices, et à les jeter dans
l'eau. Quand le feu follet, esprit d'ailleurs fort jovial, est venu à bout de son entreprise il
quitte sa victime avec de grands éclats de rire, et il disparaît." *Recherches sur la Normandie*,
par Du Bois, 1815, p. 310.

See also, Fouquet *Légendes du Morbihan*, p. 140. *Le Meu—Revue Celt*, p. 230.
A. Bosquet, pp. 135-143.

they indicated, one day, when all the other inmates
of the dwelling were in the fields busied in getting
in the harvest, she determined on searching for the
treasure. She procured a pick-axe, closed and barred
all the doors to secure herself against interruptions,
and proceeded to work. She had not dug long,
before a violent thunderstorm arose. Though alarmed,
she continued her task, but the rain, which now
began to fall in torrents, drove the field labourers
to seek shelter in the house. By this time the
woman had struck on a brazen pan, which, she had
no doubt, covered the treasure, and was in no hurry
to open to the men who were clamouring at the
door for admission. She was at last obliged to yield
to their entreaties, and, turning her back on the hole
she had dug, unbarred the door. Her dismay was
great, when, on looking back on her work, she saw
the pan turned up, and the whole treasure abstracted.
The demon had seized this opportunity to take
possession of his own.

A man had reason to believe, from the flames
which he had seen hovering about a certain spot,
that a treasure was hidden there. Accordingly, one
night, he took his spade and lantern and dug till
he came to a large jar, which contained what
appeared to him to be shells.* Suspecting that this
might be a stratagem of the evil spirit to deter him
from obtaining possession of the treasure, he carefully
gathered up the whole, and took it home with him.
On examining the parcel the next morning, he found

---

* It is perhaps to the fact that limpet shells are found in the cromlechs,
which are always supposed to be the repository of hidden treasure, that the
idea that buried gold, when discovered by mortals, is transformed by its
guardian spirit into worthless shells, is entertained by the peasantry.

he had judged rightly, for the apparent **shells** of the preceding night had now resumed their **original** form of gold and silver coin.

Another man was less fortunate, for, finding nothing but what he conceived to be shells, he hesitated about removing them, and was effectually deterred by the appearance of an immense animal, resembling a black conger-eel with fiery eyes, coiled up in the hole which he had dug.[*]

" THE VAROU."

The " Varou," now almost entirely forgotten, seems to have belonged to the family of nocturnal goblins. He is allied to the " Loup-Garou " of the French, and the " Were-Wolf " of the English, if, indeed, he is not absolutely identical with them. He is believed to be endowed with a marvellous appetite, and it is still proverbially said of a great eater " Il mange comme un varou." [†]

---

[*] From Rachel Du Port.

"4 Oct. 1586. Procédures contre Edmond Billot, Richard Le Petevin, Nicollas Le Petevin, et Jean Moullin, pour avoir été de nuit fouyr à Ste. Anne, à St. George, et à St. Germain pour chercher des trésors qu'un nommé Baston, des parties de Normandie, leur avoit dit y être déposés,—savoir : trois à St. George, un dans la muraille, un autre enterré dans la chapelle, et un troisième déhors, un à Ste. Anne, et un à St. Germain au milieu du champ."— *Proceedings of the Royal Court.*

EDITOR'S NOTE.—See *Traditions et Superstitions de La Haute Bretagne.* Tome I., p. 39 etc. " On m'a conté à Dinan que lorsque les chercheurs de trésors eurent creusé à la base du Monolithe, il sortit de la terre des flammes qui les forcèrent à interrompre leur travail. On assure qu'à différentes époques on a fait des fouilles sous un meulier de la forêt de Brotonne, dit ' La Pierre aux Houneux' pour y découvrir un trésor ; mais à chaque fois d'effrayantes apparitions les firent discontinuer. . . . . Des ouvriers qui avaient tenté d'enlever le trésor de Néaufle se virent entourés de flammes." A. Bosquet, p. 159-186.

[†] " La veille de la fête de Noël, à nuit close, dans un lieu préscrit par le consentement de la communauté en Prusse, en Livonie, et en Lithuanie, l'affluence des hommes changés en loups est telle que les ravages perpétrés cette nuit-là contre les bergers et les troupeaux sont beaucoup plus graves que ceux des véritables loups. S'insinuant dans les caves, ils y grenouillent et vous

"Aller en varouverie" was an expression used in former times in speaking of those persons who met together in unfrequented places for the purposes of debauchery or other illicit practices. Among the Acts of the Consistory of the parish of St. Martin's, in the time when the island was still under the Presbyterian discipline, is to be found a censure on certain individuals who had been heard to say one night that the time was propitious "pour aller en varouverie sous l'épine."

Varou was originally from the Breton *Varw*—"the dead"—and was identified with the "Heroes" or beatified warriors, who were, by Homer and Hesiod, supposed to be in attendance on Saturn. Guernsey, in the days of Demetrius, was known by the name of the Isle of Heroes, or of Demons, and Saturn was said to be confined there in a "golden rock," bound by "golden chains."

There is the "Creux des Varous," which extends, according to tradition, from Houmet to L'Erée, and is a subterranean cavern formed of rock sprinkled with an abundance of yellow mica, which sparkles like gold; a plot of ground near the cromlech at L'Erée, known as "Le Creux des Fées," still bears the name of "Le Camp du Varou;' and an estate in the parish of St. Saviour's is called "Le Mont-Varou." Old people remember that it used to be said in their youth that "Le Char des Varous"

---

sablent plusieurs tonneaux de bière ou d'hydromel. Ils s'amusent alors à entasser les futailles vides au beau milieu du cellier. Le bon prélat ajoute, que de très grands seigneurs ne dédaignent pas de s'agriger à cette confrèrie maudite. C'est un des anciens adeptes qui initie l'aspirant *varou* ou *garou* dans une ample tasse de cervoise." *Mœurs des Peuples du Nord*, par Olaus Magnus, Vol. VI., p. 46.

was to be heard rolling over the cliffs and rocks on silver-tyred wheels, between Houmet and the Castle of Albecq, before the death of any of the great ones of the earth; and how this supernatural warning was sure to be followed almost immediately by violent storms and tempests. *

HERODIAS.

The 10th of January, in Roman days, was dedicated to the *Fera Dea*, or cruel goddess, of which *Hero Dias* is a literal Celtic interpretation here. She is the queen of the witches, and although Satan himself is the commander-in-chief of the witches, he has a mate who participates in his authority, and leads the dance when his votaries meet to celebrate their midnight orgies · at Catioroc or Rocquaine. This is no less a personage than the dissolute and revengeful woman by whose evil counsel the holy precursor of our Saviour was put to death by Herod. To her, more particularly, is attributed the rising of sudden storms, and especially of those which take the form of a whirlwind. It sometimes happens that during the warm and sultry days of harvest a gust of wind will suddenly arise, and, whirling round the field, catch up and disperse the ears of corn which the reaper has laid in due order for the binder of the sheaves. The countryman doubts not but that this is caused by Herodias shaking her petticoats in dancing—" *Ch'est la fille d'Hérode qui châque ses côtillons,*"—and he loses no time in hurling his reaping hook in the direction she appears to be moving. It is said that this has

---

* Mostly from Mr. George Métivier.

generally the effect of stopping the progress of the whirlwind.

These sudden gusts are locally known by the name of "*héroguiâzes*," and, although there is so easy a means of dispersing them as that indicated above, the man who would venture to throw his sickle or knife at them must be endowed with no small degree of courage.* †

"Le Barboue." §

This was a demon used by old Guernsey nurses to frighten their infant charges. "*Le Barboue*

---

* From Mr. George Métivier.

Father Martin, the oracle of Gaulish divinity, has lavished floods of ink on Herodias. According to him she is the genius of the whirlwind—the "mid-day," as well as a mid-night, demon. Here she continues to "ride on the whirlwind," and "direct the storm." Instead of driving her away with holy water, as our Catholic neighbours do, *we* fling a sickle at "La Vieille" with pious indignation, whenever the eddying straws announce her arrival in the harvest-field.

Near "Le Ras de Fontenay," so infamous for its shipwrecks, the little island of Sain, off Finistère, was dedicated to He'ro Dias. There she presided over the oracle of "Sena," the Hag. Her priestesses were nine shrivelled hags, and their island derived its appellation from the hag, their mistress. None but mariners, suitors for a bagful of favourable wind, were admissible to the presence of these ladies, who spent their time "sur le rocher désert, l'effroi de la nature," in a very edifying manner—brewing storms, manufacturing hail, lightning, thunder, and so forth, and changing themselves into a variety of brutal forms—(Pomponius Mela).

That there is a two-headed serpent which caresses Dame Hérodias on a bas-relief of the temple of Mont-Morillon in Poitou, may be remembered *en passant.*

EDITOR'S NOTES.

†According to the old Latin "Romaunt de Renard," Herodias loved John the Baptist. The jealous King caused him to be beheaded. His head, by her order, was carried to her, and she wished to kiss it, but the head turned away, and blew with so much violence that Herodias was blown into the air. Since then, St. John, faithful to his antipathy, has made her travel for ever in the deserts of the sky, and become the genius of the storm.

Some confound her with "Habunde," who may have been a white lady, or one of those "genii" whom the Celts call "dusi." *Chronique de Philippe Mouskés,* Tome II. Introduction p. 139.

Some also think that Herodias will, if anyone dances at harvest time, bring shipwreck and disasters at sea.—*From Mr. Isaac Le Patourel.*

§ May not this be a corruption of *Barbe Bleue*—the Blue Beard who has frightened so many children both in France and England?

t'attrappera" was quite threat enough to make the naughtiest child repent of his misdeeds. According to Mr. Métivier (See Dictionary, p. 51. *Barboue*), this name "Barboue" is a corruption of *bared meleu*, the spectre which personifies the plague among the Cymri. According to the legends, "Barbaou Hervé" was the wolf who accompanied St. Hervé, a sainted hermit of the country of Léon, 560. He was evidently related to the French "Loup-Garou."

SPECTRAL APPEARANCES.

Many places have the reputation of being haunted by phantoms which make their appearance at the dead of night, not always in a human form, as the spirits of the departed are wont to do when they revisit "the glimpses of the moon," but in the more fearful shapes of beasts and nondescript monsters. "La Bête de la Tour," "Le Cheval de St. George," which has already been spoken of in connection with the well, and "Le Chien Bôdu," are among these.

The "devises," or boundary stones, which served in olden times to mark the limits of some of the principal "fiefs" or manors, but which have now disappeared, leaving only a name to the locality, appear to have been the particular resort of these spectres; and it is not improbable that the superstition may have arisen from the custom, of which traces are to be found in many nations, of sacrificing a victim and burying it where the stone of demarcation was to be set up. It was not, however, these places only which became the haunt of spectres; other spots came in also for their share of these nocturnal and frightful visitors. A lonely dwelling, especially if uninhabited, a dark lane far from any friendly cottage, cromlechs, or spots where these mysterious erections once stood—all these either had, or were likely to acquire, an evil reputation in this respect, and more especially if tradition pointed to any deed of horror, such as murder or suicide, connected with the place or its neighbourhood.

The headless dog which haunts the Ville-au-Roi, and which will be spoken of in the legend attached to that ancient domain, is an instance of these spectres. The best known of them is "Tchi-cô," or the "Bête de la Tour,"—but there are also "La Bête de la Devise de Sausmarez à Saint Martin," which is a black dog supposed to haunt the avenue by Sausmarez Manor. *

"Tchi-co, La Bête de la Tour."

There is no doubt that in early times the town of St. Peter Port was encircled by walls, and fortified—indeed there is an order of Edward III. in 1350, authorising the levy of a duty on merchandise for this purpose. Certain spots, called "les barrières," mark where the gates were situated, and, although all remains of the walls have long since disappeared, it is not difficult to trace the course they must have taken. At the northern extremity of the original

EDITOR'S NOTE.

Then there is the "Rue de la Bête" at St. Andrew's, on the borders of the Fief Rohais. Near this lane there was formerly a prison, so that it is probably full of associations of crime and malefactors. There is also a "Rue de la Bête" near L'Erée, between "Claire Mare" and the Rouvets, where, to this day, people will not go alone after dark, and they still tell the story (so wrote Miss Le Pelley, who lived in that neighbourhood), of a man, a M. Vaucourt, who, driving down that lane in the dark, the "Bête" got up into the cart, which so scared the unfortunate man that he died the next day. There was also a black dog which haunted the Forest Road, clanking its chains. The father of one old woman who told the story, saw and was followed by this beast one night when walking home from St. Martin's to his house near the Forest Church. He was so frightened that he took to his bed and died of the shock very shortly afterwards. There is also "La Bête de la Rue Mase," on the western limits of the Town parish, the "Coin de la Biche," at St. Martin's, between Saints' and La Villette, and in the cross lane running from the "Carrefour David" to the "Profonds Camps," past the house now called "St. Hilda," a small white hare was supposed to be seen on stormy nights, accompanied by "Le Faeu Bélengier."

town, the name of " La Tour Gand" indicates a
fortress of some sort. The southern extremity was
protected by a work called " La Tour Beauregard,"
of sufficient importance to be named, together with
Castle Cornet, in the warrants or commissions issued
by the monarch to those who were intrusted with
the defence of the island.

This fortress stood near the top of Cornet Street,
on the brow of the hill which overlooks the Bordage
and Fountain Street, where now stands St. Barnabas'
Church. Tradition points to a spot at the foot of
the hill, as the place where the execution of heretics
and witches, by burning, used to take place, and
connects with these sad events a spectral appearance
which, even within the present century, was believed
to haunt the purlieus of the old tower.

During the long nights of winter, and especially
about Christmastide, the inhabitants of Tower-hill, the
Bordage, Fountain Street, and Cornet Street used to
be roused from their midnight slumbers by hearing
unearthly howlings and the clanking of heavy chains,
dragged over the rough pavement.

Those who could summon up courage enough to
rise from their beds and peep out of window, declared

EDITOR'S NOTES.

See Pluquet in *Contes Populaires de Bayeux*, p. 16, for an account of a phantom in the
shape of a great dog that wanders about the streets of Bayeux in the winter nights gnawing
bones and dragging chains, called "Le Rongeur d'Os."

See also Sir Walter Scott's note in *Peveril of the Peak*, Vol. II., Chap. I., on the spectral
hound or "Mauthe Doog"—a large black spaniel, which used to haunt Peel Castle in the
Isle of Man.

There is also in Laisnel de la Salle's book *Croyances et Légendes du Centre de la France*,
Tome I. p. 181, a long story of "Le Loup Bron," which in many respects resembles that
of our "Bête de la Tour."

In Sark "they have another superstitious belief, that of the *T'chico*, or old dog, the dog of
the dead, the black or white beast. Several affirm having seen it, and met it walking about
the roads. This dog affects certain localities, and makes its regular rounds, but often it is
invisible." From *Descriptive Sketch of the Island of Sark*, by the Rev. J. L. V. Cachemaille,
published in Clarke's *Guernsey Magazine*, Vol. III., October, 1875.

In Brand's *Antiquities*, Vol. III., p. 330, he identifies the English "Barguest," or " Great
Dog Fiend," with the Norman "Rongeur d'Os," and the "Boggart" of Lancashire, great
dog-spirits, which prowl about in the night-time, dragging heavy chains behind them.

that they saw the form of a huge uncouth animal with large flaming saucer eyes, and somewhat like a bear, or huge calf. This spectre was known as "Tchî-co, La Bête de la Tour."

"Le Chien Bôdu."

This black dog was said to infest the Clos du Valle, and was probably a resident of the Ville Bôdu, which was at one time the slaughter-house of the Benedictine monks of St. Michel du Valle. To see him was taken as a sure sign of approaching death. According to Mr. Métivier, he derived his name from "the German Bohdu, and Gaulish Bodu, which mean the *Abyss*, and the mythological dog of Hades is our 'Chien Bôdu.' " *

Legend of the Ville au Roi.

Although this story is known to everyone, and is to be found in all the local histories and guide books, no collection of Guernsey folk-lore can be considered perfect without it. It is just one of those stories that are calculated to make a profound impression on the popular mind, as showing the special interposition of Providence in preserving a poor and innocent man from the effects of a false accusation, and in causing the nefarious designs of a rich and unprincipled oppressor to fall back with just retribution on his own head.

Whether the story be founded on an occurrence which did actually take place in this island, whether it originated elsewhere, or whether it be a pure invention, it is now impossible to determine. † The

---

Editor's Note.—* In *Croyances et Légendes du Centre de la France* Laisnel de la Salle has a chapter (Tome I. pp. 169-175), on "La Chasse a *Bôdet*," which he describes as "une chasse nocturne qui traverse les airs avec des hurlements, des miculements et des abois epouvantables, auxquels se mêlent des cris de menace et des accents d'angoisse," and he identifies (p. 172), "Bôdet" with the German *Woden*, who is the same as the Scandinavian Odin, Gwyon of the Gauls, the Egyptian Thot, Hermes of the Greeks, and Mercury of the Latins, who filled, in the Teutonic Mythology, the rôle of "Conductor of Souls."

† See note on page 245.

"Old Manor, Ville au Roi."

name of the principal personage in the tale—Gaultier de la Salle—is to be found at the head of the lists of Bailiffs of Guernsey, with the date 1284, but no written evidence has yet been adduced to prove that anyone of the name ever held that office. There is, however, proof of a certain kind that a person bearing this name did exist at some period of the fourteenth century, for, in a manuscript list of Bailiffs, which appears to have been compiled about the year 1650, the writer, who seems careful not to place any on record for whom he cannot produce documentary evidence, appends this note to the name of John Le Marchant, Bailiff from 1359 to 1383:—"J'en ay lettre de 1370 concernant la veuve Gaultier de la Salle."

That no document is known to exist in which this name appears is no proof that Gaultier de la Salle did not hold the office. Previously to the reign of Edward I. it appears to have been the custom for the Warder or Governor of the island to appoint an officer with the title of Bailiff, who combined the functions of Lieutenant-Governor, chief magistrate, and Receiver of the Crown Revenues, and who was generally changed annually. The names of many of these dignitaries have been preserved, but there are still several blanks to be filled up, and it is not impossible that the name of Gaultier de la Salle may some day or other be found as holding this important charge, although probably at a later date than that usually assigned to him—1284.

The estate of the Ville-au-Roi is said to have borne originally the name of "La Petite Ville." * It has now dwindled down to a few fields, but was

---

Editor's Note.—* To this day one of the fields on the adjoining estate of "Le Mont Durant," belonging to Colonel de Guérin, bears the name of "Petite Ville."

doubtless at one period of far greater extent and importance than at the present time. The house, which may probably be assigned to the fifteenth century, is now much diminished in size from what it was, even a few years since, but it still presents an interesting specimen of the architecture of former days. It consisted, when perfect, of a building, forming two sides of a square, with a tower in the angle, where may yet be seen the holes for arrows. It contained a well-wrought newel staircase in stone, leading to a large room, which appears to have been the principal apartment in the house, if we may judge from the careful workmanship bestowed on the handsomely carved granite chimney piece, the traces of stone mullions in the windows, and the ornamental open timber roof, now hidden by a low ceiling. A wall of unusual thickness divides this portion of the building into two parts; and a few steps from the head of the staircase of which we have spoken, lead to the remains of another newel resting on this wall, which evidently formed part of a turret rising above the ridge of the roof, and which could have served no purpose but that of ornament, or perhaps a lookout over the neighbouring country. There are some detached farm buildings, and traces of a wall surrounding the homestead, intended probably to form an inclosure into which the cattle might be driven at night. The remains of an arched gateway at the end of the avenue, leading from the main road, and connecting the western gable of the dwelling house with an out-building, are still to be discerned. This was exactly opposite the principal door of the mansion, which is of good proportions, with a well-executed circular headway in granite, over which is a square

recess in the masonry which doubtless once contained
the armorial device of the original proprietor.   There
is reason to believe this was a member of the De
Beauvoir family, once very numerous and influential
in the island but now extinct, for it was well known
that the family was formerly in possession of this
estate, and the existence of their arms—a chevron
between three cinq-foils—carved in granite on the
mantelpiece of the principal room, is almost sufficient
proof of one of the name having been the original
builder of the house.*   The estate afterwards passed
into the possession of the De la Marche family—also
extinct.   From them it descended to a family of the
name of Le Poidevin.   These last falling into pecuniary
difficulties, the property by the legal process called
" saisie " came into the hands of the present (1859)
proprietor, Thomas Le Retilley, Esq., Jurat of the
Royal Court.

Whilst the recently-abolished manorial Court of
the Priory of St. Michel du Valle still existed, there
was a curious servitude attached to this estate.
When this Court made its periodical procession
through the island to inspect the King's highway
and see that it was kept in due repair, the proprietor
of the Ville-au-Roi was expected to furnish a cup of
milk to everyone legally entitled to a place in the
cortège, and the procession made a halt at the gate

EDITOR'S NOTES.

* There is documentary evidence proving that in the early part of the fifteenth century the
" Ville au Roi " estate belonged to John Thiault, Jurat of the Royal Court. He died, leaving
three daughters, of whom the eldest married Perrin Careye, and thus brought these lands into the
Carey family, where they remained until the year 1570, when Collette Careye, great, great
grand-daughter of Perrin Careye, married Guillaume De Beauvoir, and received the Ville au Roi
estate as her share of her father's property. The property did not remain long in the possession
of the De Beauvoir family, as we find, September 24, 1636, " Monsieur Jean de la Marche,
ministre," its owner, " à cause d'Ester De Beauvoir, sa femme, fille de Collette Careye."

The Reverend John de la Marche, Rector of St. Andrew's and subsequently of the Town
parish, married Esther, daughter of William de Beauvoir and Collette Careye, January 24th, 1616.

P

to demand the accustomed refreshment, which was willingly afforded, although immemorial usage alone could be pleaded for the exaction.

It is now time to come to the legend itself. In the earliest records which the human race possesses—the Holy Scriptures—we read that disputes arose about wells and the right of drawing water from them. Where water is scarce, as it is in some parts of the East, this can readily be understood, but why should any disagreement occur in places where this indispensable element abounds? The answer is simply this. The well is for the most part the property of one person, and situated on his ground, and those who claim a right to the use of it, must necessarily pass over their neighbour's land to get at it. It is clear that this right may be exercised in such a manner as to become vexatious and troublesome.

Gaultier de la Salle had a poor neighbour of the name of Massy, who was the proprietor of a small field containing little more than a vergée of land at the back of the Bailiff's house, but with this land he possessed also the right,—no doubt by virtue of some ancient and binding contract—of drawing water from a well on De la Salle's property. Often had the Bailiff offered to buy off this right,—to give a fair and even liberal price for the piece of ground to which the privilege was attached. Massy was obstinate. His answer to every offer was that of Naboth to Ahab—"The Lord forbid it me that I should give the inheritance of my fathers to thee."

Annoyed at Massy's pertinacious refusal to accede to his wishes, Gaultier de la Salle formed the horrible design of taking away his life, but how was this to

be done without causing suspicion? Open violence,
even in those days, was not to be thought of. Secret
assassination might be discovered. At last the acute
mind of the unworthy Bailiff hit on an expedient
which appeared to him perfectly safe. It was to
make the forms of the law subservient to his wicked
designs, and, under the guise of a judicial proceeding,
to cause the ruin and death of the unfortunate
Massy. Theft was then, and for too many centuries
after, punished with death. If he could succeed in
fixing an accusation of this kind on the innocent
Massy, he flattered himself that there would be no
difficulty in obtaining a conviction, and then would
follow the utmost penalty of the law, and the
consequent forfeiture of the felon's lands and goods
to the King, from whom he hoped to get a grant
or sale of the field. To carry out his nefarious
intention, he hid two of his own silver cups in a
cornstack, and adroitly contrived to cause a suspicion
of having stolen them to rest on his too-obstinate
neighbour. Circumstantial evidence, skilfully combined,
was not wanting on the day of trial, and, notwithstanding his vehement protestations of innocence, poor
Massy was found guilty and condemned to death.
The day fixed for the execution arrived, and the
Bailiff proceeded to the Court House with the
intention of witnessing the death of the unfortunate
victim of his own false accusation. But "the wicked
man diggeth a pit and falleth into the midst of it
himself." Before leaving home, he gave orders to
some of his workmen to take down a certain stack
of corn, and house it in the barn. He had barely
taken his seat in Court, where the magistrates had
assembled for the purpose, as was then the custom,

P 2

" Houses in Church Square, 1825."

of attending the culprit to the place of execution, and seeing their sentence duly carried out, when a messenger, almost breathless, rushed in and exclaimed—

" The cups are found."

" Fool! " cried the Bailiff. " Did I not tell thee not to touch *that* rick. I knew ——." Here he stopped short in confusion, perceiving that he had already said enough to raise the suspicions of those who had heard him.

The Jurats immediately gave orders to stay the execution. The matter was submitted to a searching investigation, and resulted in a full exposure of the Bailiff's nefarious plot. Thereupon Gaultier de la Salle was sentenced to suffer the same punishment that he had intended for the innocent Massy, and his estate was declared to be confiscated to the King, since which time it has borne the appellation of " La Ville-au-Roi." It is said that he was hanged at a spot in the parish of St. Andrew's, where, until the last century, executions * usually took place, and that, on his way to the gibbet, he stopped and received the Holy Sacrament at the foot of a cross, which, though long destroyed, has given its name to the locality " La Croix au Baillif." An old lane bounding the land of the Ville-au-Roi on the north, and which was closed in the early part of last century, when the present high road was cut, bore the singular

---

* The field at St. Andrew's where the executions took place was called " Les Galères," and near it is a lane leading to a water-mill, called " Moulin de L'Échelle," because the miller had, for his tenure, to provide the ladder for the executions.

There is a small piece of land, just off the road which passes the Monnaie, and leads from the Bailiff's Cross Road to the Ecluse Corbin, which is known as " Le Friquet du Gibet,"

name of " La Rue de l'Ombre de la Mort." It had naturally an evil reputation as the resort of phantoms and hobgoblins, and even in the present day it is with fear and trembling that the belated peasant in returning from town passes the avenue of aged elms that leads up to the ruined mansion of the iniquitous judge.

Many will tell you how, at the witching hour of night, they have seen a huge, headless black dog rush out and brush past them, and how those who have been bold enough to strike at the phantom might as well have beaten the air, for their cudgel met with no resistance from anything corporeal. No one doubts that it is the unquiet spirit of Gaultier de la Salle, doomed to wander till the great day of judgment around the field for the sake of which

---

EDITOR'S NOTE.

In the Record Office exists (Assize Roll No. 1165, 17 Edward II., 1323), a petition of " Cecilia, who was wife of Walter de la Sale," for restitution of lands and rentes bought in their name and in that of their children, in the parishes of St. Peter Port and St. Andrew's; " and that these tenements,—on account of the death of the said Walter, who was judicially executed last criminal assizes, now three years past, before Peter Le Marchant, then Bailiff of the Island,—had been seized by the King . . . . Upon the inquisition of 12 men of the parish of St. Peter Port, and 12 men of the parish of St. Andrew's, who depose upon their oath, that the aforesaid Walter was condemned before Peter Le Marchant, Bailiff of the aforesaid Island, for the murder of Ranulph * Vautier, three years ago. An inquisition was made, and on account of the said murder, the said lands were seized into the King's hands, and for this cause, and no other, are still detained . . . . A day given to the said Cecilia for the hearing of her case at Jersey, on which day the aforesaid Cecilia came, and it is determined that the King removes his hand (*i.e.*, restores the land), and that from henceforth she has possession."

The British Museum contains a document, (Add : Ch : 19809) which gives further particulars of " la peticion Cecile qui fut fame Gaultier de la Salle," she claiming the lands, etc., as having been bought with her money " et disante que l'avant dit son mari vint en lylle desus dicte sans nul bien fors son corps." From this document it appears that Cecilia and her husband built the house, presumably that now known as " La Ville-au-Roi," for she claims " une meson séante en la ville de Saint Pierre Port, de laquelle la place fut fiefeye de Jourdan et de Johan des Maons . . . et que du mariage de la dicte Cecile ovecques autres biens pourchaciez par yceluy mariage, fistent la dicte meson." . . . . Signed at St. Peter Port, 10th of October, 1323, before Geoffrey de la + [Hou] gue Guillaume Karupel, Richart Toullay, Guion Nicolle, Renouf de Vic, Henri de la [+ Mule], Guillaume le Genne, Johan Fale, Ranulph leMoigne, de Saint Pierre Port, and Radulph de Beaucamp, Jurats of the King's Court.

The Assize Roll of 32 Edward I (1304), mentions the murder of Brother John del Espin, of the Priory of Lyhou, by Ranulph Vautier and Guillaume Lenginour, who, after having taken refuge in the Church of St. Sampson, and abjured the Islands, were pardoned by the King. Guillaume L'Enginour seems to have been subsequently Gaultier de la Salle's accomplice in

* He seems to have been called " Vautier " or " Gautier " indiscriminately.

+ Letters illegible, but have been supplied from the " Second Report of Commissioners (Guernsey), p. 303, viz,, Names of Officials 5 Ed. III.

he was led into such deadly sin, happy even if so dreadful a penance could expiate his guilt.

THE SPECTRE OF LES GRENTMAISONS.

At no great distance from the thriving village of St. Sampson's, which, thanks to its commodious harbour, the neighbouring granite quarries, and an extensive trade in stone carried on there, bids fair to become a town, stands what was formerly the mansion of a considerable branch of the Le Marchant family,* one of the most ancient and influential in the Channel Archipelago. It is known as "Les Grentmaisons," the name of a family that has been extinct for some centuries, but which possessed lands in this part of the island. The house is situated on the high road leading from St. Sampson's to the

---

the murder of Ranulph Gautier, for the "Lettres Closes" of 1321, mention the restoration of lands to "Guillaume L'Enginour demeurant accusé de la mort de Ranulphe Gautier, tué dit on criminellement, et du vol d'un anneau d'argent au même Ranulphe, et d'un florin d'or à John de Souslemont, Chapelain"; he being willing to stand his trial when called upon.

Among the "Ancient Petitions" No. 4315 contains a request from John du Vivier, Thomas d'Estefeld, and Philip de Vincheles of Guernsey and Jersey, "for protection from the friends of Gaultier de la Salle, his wife, his son, and his relations, who threaten them because he was hanged for the murder of Renout Gautier, murdered in the Castle of Guernsey, by his acquaintances and others who abjured (the Islands), for this deed, such as Master William le Enginour, John Justice, and Christian Hert " . . . .

The Calendars of Patent Rolls for the years 1313-14, contain mentions of "Protections" for "Walter de la Salle, clerk " to "the islands of Gerneseye and Jereseye," and in the Assize Roll of 1319, he is described as "Minister" of Otho de Grandison, then Governor of the Islands.

A Ranulph Gautier was one time bailiff to Otho de Grandison, so the feud between the two may have been of long standing. Gaultier de la Salle was probably a member of one of the many Anglo-Norman families then connected with the Channel Islands. His wife Cecilia was evidently a Guernseywoman, and part of their land in St. Andrew's parish was inherited from Havise, his wife's mother. There is reason to believe that he was the son of a Robert de la Salle, and Agnes his wife, who were landowners in England in the early part of the 14th Century; his son, Nicholas, was King's Receiver to Edward III., in 1372-3.

It is not possible to absolutely locate the lands held by Gaultier de la Salle, but in a British Museum MS. (Clarence Hopper) is quoted a document, then in the Chapter House, Westminster, shewing that part of the "Eschaet " of "Galter de Sale " was the "Clos au Botiller," which particular "Clos " has been identified as part of the territory now known as Le Vauquiédor, and in the petition of Cecilia, widow of Gaultier, she mentions lands bought from "Guillaume et Richard le Hubie." Both the Hubits Lanes and the Vauquiédor estate adjoin that of the Ville-au-Roi, the traditional seat of Gaultier de la Salle.

From documents kindly lent me by Lord de Saumarez, Colonel J. H. C. Carey and Colonel de Guérin.

EDITOR'S NOTE.—* It was bought by the the Reverend Thomas Le Marchant, Rector of St. Sampson's parish, August the sixth, 1055.

town of St. Peter Port, and, although surrounded at the present time on all sides, was, at the beginning of the present century, far removed from any dwelling —none indeed being then in sight but those of the town, distant at least two miles.

At that time the proprietor, who possessed a very handsome dwelling in St. Peter Port, only inhabited the house of the Grentmaisons during the summer months ; and in the winter it was closed and left under the care of a servant, who lived in one of the dependencies. How it had come to acquire the evil reputation of being haunted, or how long it was supposed to have been so, no one could tell, but that it was the resort of troubled spirits no one could doubt. Fearful noises were heard, and lights that could not be accounted for were seen in its deserted rooms during the long winter nights; and belated wayfarers were affrighted by the apparition of a horrible beast, with large glaring eyes, and long shaggy hair trailing down to the ground, which took its nightly rambles round the ancient walls, and seemed to guard the house from intrusion.*

"La Bête de la Pendue."

The western coast of Guernsey, abounding in sunken reefs stretching far out to sea, and exposed to the full force of the Atlantic waves, was, before the establishment of a lighthouse on the Hanois rocks, most dangerous to shipping coming up Channel, and many a gallant vessel, with all its crew, has struck on some hidden danger and gone down in deep water, leaving no traces but what the waves might throw up some days afterwards on the shore, in the form

---

* From Mr. Denys Corbet.

of detached portions of the wreck and cargo, or the dead bodies of the hapless mariners.

The inhabitants of this inhospitable coast are a rugged race of hardy fishermen, for the most part experienced pilots, who know every rock for miles round, not one of which is without its distinguishing name. As might be expected, they are close observers of the weather, and of every sign that may indicate a coming storm. Those in the neighbourhood of L'Érée and Rocquaine declare that they are warned of an approaching tempest by a peculiar bright light which appears some time before in the south-west, and also by a loud roaring, like that of a large animal in great pain, which appears to proceed from a rock known by the name of "La Pendue." They do not attempt to account for this noise, but speak of it as "La Bête de la Pendue." *

THE DOLE OF LOAVES AT LE LAURIER.

In the parish of St. Pierre-du-Bois, there is a house and estate known by the name of Le Laurier, where loaves are distributed to the poor on Christmas Eve and on Good Friday. Nothing certain is known of the origin of this dole, the title-deeds of the property merely containing the following item in the enumeration of the ground-rents due on it:—"*Aux Pauvres de la ditte Paroisse de Saint Pierre-du-Bois, un quartier de froment de rente, à être distribué en*

---

* From Mrs. Savidan and Mrs. Sarre.

According to Mr. Métivier there is also, in the neighbourhood of Lihou, a rock called "Sanbule," a very dangerous place for ships, and sailors say that underneath this rock can be plainly heard the bellowing of a bull. It is conjectured that the "bule" in the name of this cliff is from the English "bull" or the Swedish "bulla," and *san*, from the French *saint*, and that it points to some now-forgotten legend about a holy bull.—See Clarke's *Guernsey Magazine*, September, 1880.

*pain aux dits pauvres, à deux diverses fois; savoir,
deux boisseaux, partie du dit quartier à Noel, et les
deux autres boisseaux à Pâques, comme d'ancienneté.''*

Tradition assigns two very different reasons for the
institution of this charity, one of which is highly
probable. It is that, at some remote period of which
all memory is now lost, the house took fire, and the
proprietor made a vow that if the fire could be
extinguished he would charge his estate with an annual
rent, to be given to the poor in bread. His prayer was
answered, the fire yielding to the efforts of those who
were attempting to put it out, as if by miracle, and
the dole was instituted in conformity with the vow.

The other tradition, which, as it falls into the
domain of the supernatural is, of course, a greater
favourite with the people, is to the following effect.
In times past, long before the memory of the oldest
inhabitants of the parish, the house, for some
undefined reason, but connected, it is surmised, with
some unknown crime of a former proprietor, was
haunted from Christmas Eve to Easter by a hideous
spectre in the form of a black beast like a calf, but
as large as an ox. On Christmas Eve the inmates
of the house were in the habit of leaving the front
and back doors open, and at midnight precisely the
spectre would pass through.

At last, however, the proprietor of the estate
bethought himself of calling in the aid of the clergy,
in hopes that by their powerful help the visits of
this unwelcome guest might be put an end to. Their
prayers and exorcisms soon prevailed in quieting the
phantom, and, by their advice, the annual distribution
of the loaves to the poor was instituted.

It is related, however, that on one occasion the

the owner of the house, instigated by his wife, an avaricious, grasping creature, who would sooner have seen all the poor in the parish die of hunger than bestow a crust on them, withheld the accustomed dole. He paid dear for it, for the house was once more visited by the spectre, which this time made its appearance in the form of a gigantic black sow, accompanied by a numerous litter of pigs, all grunting and clamouring for food, as if they had not eaten for a week. The master of the house was fain to purchase peace by restoring to the poor their rights, but it is said that to her dying day his wife never recovered from the impression this supernatural visit made upon her.

There is a tradition also that at one time a report having been spread abroad that the accustomed alms would no longer be distributed, the poor, who were in the habit of receiving it, assembled at night before the house, formed themselves into a procession, and marched through, entering by the front door, and passing out at the back. The mistress of the house was watching their proceedings from behind the door, and was seen by one of the poor women, who addressed her companion, walking by her side, in these words :—

> " *E't chette-chin, est-alle des nôtes ?* "
> (And that woman there, is she one of us?)

To which the following answer was returned :—

> " *Oh ! Nennin ! quer sa liette nous l'y ôte.* "
> (Oh ! No ! for her snood proves it.)

The "liette" was the riband or snood with which, in days gone by, the cap was fastened on the head, and was apparently a bit of finery quite beyond the reach of the poor who had assembled on this occasion, and only likely to be seen on the head-gear of a person in tolerably easy circumstances. *

THE ENCHANTED HORSE.

A number of young men had met together one evening in search of amusement. One of the party proposed going to a place at some distance, where they were likely to fall in with others as fond of fun as themselves, but, not choosing to fatigue themselves with walking, they determined on using some of their neighbours' horses. A good-looking white horse was grazing hard by in a meadow. One of the party approached, caught, and mounted him. Another got up behind, but still there seemed room for a third : at last, to shorten the story, the whole party, in number above a dozen, found accommodation on the horse's back, but, no sooner were they all well seated, than he set off at full gallop, and, after carrying them through brambles and briers, over hedges and ditches, to a considerable distance, deposited them all in the most muddy marsh he could find, and disappeared, leaving them to find their way home at midnight, in the best way they could. †

THE SPECTRAL CORTÈGE.

One of the most interesting old mansions in

---

* Partly from John de Garis, Esq., and partly from Mrs. Savidan.

EDITOR'S NOTE.—* This story was also told to Miss Le Pelley by an old woman in St. Peter's in 1896.

---

† From Rachel Du Port.

See Keightley's *Fairy Mythology*, Vol. II., p. 294. *La Normandie Romanesque*, p. 128. *Folk-Lore Journal*. Vol. I., p. 292.

EDITOR'S NOTES.

† In *Notions Historiques sur les Côtes-du-Nord*, by M. Habasque, there is mentioned a goblin called *Mourioche*, and it is said "Mourioche qui revêt toutes les formes ; Mourioche, la

Guernsey is that of La Haye du Puits, in the parish
of Le Castel, with its tower rising above the roof, its
handsome "porte cochère" and its pepper box turrets.
It has the appearance of having been built early in
the sixteenth century, and it is known to have been,
in the reign of Henry VIII., the residence of a family
of considerable local antiquity and importance, of the
name of Henry, who had also property in Salisbury,
where they were known by the anglicised form of
their patronymic, Harris. It passed from their possession into that of the Le Marchant family, to one
of whom it still belongs, in the reign of James II.*
It is just one of those sort of places that one might
expect to find some legendary tale or old superstition
attached to; but we are not aware that either La
Haye du Puits, or the neighbouring estate of St.
George, claims any special property in the spectral
appearance, which, from time to time, is seen at Le
Mont au Deval—a steep ascent over which the high
road between the two properties passes. Persons
travelling at night along this road, which in some
parts is thickly overshadowed with trees, have
occasionally met with a funeral procession, preceded,
as is customary in Guernsey, by a clergyman and his
attendant clerk, and composed of the usual carriers,
pall bearers, mourners, and attendant friends. The

---

monture du diable, qui vole avec la rapidité de l'éclair, qui parsément des points lumineux,
et *qui s'allonge tant que l'on veut, assez du moins pour porter quatre personnes.*
"Cinq jeunes filles partirent un soir pour aller chercher un des chevaux de la ferme qui
était dans la prairie. L'une d'elles monta sur le dos de la bête; puis une seconde; alors le
cheval s'allongea, et il y eut place pour la troisième, et les cinq filles finirent par s'asseoir
sur son dos qui s'allongeait à mesure. La monture des filles se mit en marche, et quand elle
fut arrivée au milieu du ruisseau, elle disparut comme si elle s'était évanouie en fumée, et
laissa les filles tomber dans l'eau. Le vrai cheval était déjà rendu à la porte de son
écurie."—*Traditions et Superstitions de La Haute Bretagne*, Tome II., p. 66.

EDITOR'S NOTE.—* It was bought by Joshua Le Marchant from the heirs of Pierre Henry,
June 3rd, 1674.

"Le Coin de la Biche," St. Martin's.

cortège takes its mournful way in perfect silence—and well it may—for, of the many persons who compose it, not one is the bearer of a head !

There are those, it is said, who affirm to having met it, but it is looked upon as of evil augury. The death of some one in the neighbourhood, or of some member of the family of the person who has the misfortune to fall in with it, is believed to follow close upon the appearance of the headless company.*

---

* From Mr. Denys Corbet.

EDITOR'S NOTE.—In Mr. Paul Sébillot's *Traditions et Superstitions de la Haute Bretagne*, Tome I., p. 270, we meet with nearly the same superstition. " Un jour un homme de la Ruée était à dire ses prières. Il vit un enterrement qui passait à quelque distance de lui ; un homme portait la croix, puis venait la chasse, les prêtres et des hommes. Huit jours après, un homme qui était né à la Ruée mourut, et son enterrement eut lieu comme celui que l'homme avait vu."

EDITOR'S NOTES.

"LE COIN DE LA BICHE."

There is a lane leading from the post-box at the "Carrefour David," on the Saints' Bay Road to "La Marette," at the Villette, which was formerly supposed to be haunted by a spectre in the form of an enormous nanny-goat.

As you go along the lane to the Villette, you will see on your right hand side a triangular corner overgrown with weeds and brambles, and, although between two fields, not included in either. This corner is known as "Le Coin de la Biche"—the Corner of the Nanny Goat.

Tradition marks it as one of the proposed sites for St. Martin's Church, but, they say, when the building was commenced, materials, tools, etc., were moved by unknown hands, in the course of the night, to La Bailleuse, its present site, and all attempts to build it there had to be abandoned. Ever since then this corner has borne a bad reputation, and none of the neighbouring proprietors will include it in their fields for fear of ill-luck.

One evening, towards the close of the last century, Mr. Mauger, of the Villette, and some other men, were returning home from vraiking at Saints' Bay. In those days, the road leading to the bay was a water-lane with a very narrow footway and a deep rocky channel, down which the water rushed to the sea. High hedges were on either side, bordered with trees, so that it was a laborious journey for carts to go up and down. When the present road was made, the trees were cut down, and the earth from the hedges used to fill up the waterway. Accordingly, this cart had harnessed to it three oxen and two horses, but even then progress was slow, and it was getting late as they turned into the lane. As they did so, one man said to the other : —

" *Creyous que nous verrons la biche ?* "

(" Do you think we shall see the goat ? ")

" *Si nous la veyons alle nous f'ra pàs d'mà.* "

(" If we see her, she can do us no harm ! ")

was the reply. Almost as he spoke out came a great hairy grey nanny-goat from her corner, and rested her forelegs against the back of the cart. The oxen tugged, the horses pulled, lashed on by the terrified men, who were longing to get out of the lane. But nothing could move the cart while the great beast stood there with her paws on the cart and looked at them. So they finally had to unharness the cattle, and lead them on to the Villette, and leave the cart with all the vraic in it in the lane.

Next morning they brought one ox and one horse, who, "La Biche" being gone, easily pulled the cart home, this part of the country being on level ground.

Another night, Mr. Mauger, of Saints', wanting to go and see his brother at the Villette, took the short cut, which is a tiny lane next to a little shop at the top of the Icart-road, and which comes out nearly opposite "Le Coin de la Biche." He was carrying a torch of "gllic" (glui*—thick straw and resin), and felt that, thus armed, nothing could attack him. As he turned into the lane, he heard the clank of a chain, and, looking down, he saw a large brown beast about the size of a small calf, with enormous red eyes, which it kept fixed on him, walking by his side. He hurried on, and tried by walking in the middle of the lane not to give it room to pass (the lane is barely three feet wide), but it was always there, on the footpath, keeping step with him. When he turned into the broader lane, where its own special "corner" is, it turned away, and he hurried on to the Villette. Determined not to give in to his cowardice, he came home the same way, and there where it had left him was the beast waiting for him. It walked with him, on his other hand this time, still keeping to the footpath, till he got into the Icart-road, where it disappeared.

These stories were told me in 1896 by Mrs. Le Patourel, of St. Martin's, who was a Miss Mauger, of Saints', and she was told them by a relative of hers who was a daughter of the Mr. Mauger to whom these incidents happened. She declared that they were absolutely true.

Our coachman, whose father lived in the neighbourhood at "Les Pages," just above Petit Bôt, told me that his father would never let him go along that lane after dark, and would never go himself, for fear of "La Biche," and many other inhabitants of St. Martin's tell the same story.

Another old man, belonging to one of the most respectable families in the parish, and who had himself been churchwarden for eleven years, told me that in his youth he lived in the neighbourhood of the Villette, and one evening his sister, then a strong young girl of sixteen, rushed in saying she had seen "La Biche." The shock was so great that she took to her bed and died shortly afterwards.

---

* These torches of "glui" were called "des Brandons."

CHAPTER VIII.

The Devil.

"The Prince of Darkness is a gentleman."
—*Shakespeare.*

" 'Tis a history
Handed from ages down; a nurse's tale,
Which children open-eyed and mouth'd devour,
And thus, as garrulous ignorance relates,
We learn it, and believe."

VARIOUS allusions to his Satanic Majesty have already appeared in these pages. He has left his footprints on various rocks; he carried away bodily Jean Vivian, Vavasseur de St. Michel; he fought with St. Patrick at the Hougue Patris; and he enticed Duke Richard in the form of a beautiful woman. He is of course head of the fraternity of wizards and witches, and many references to him occur in all the legends dealing with witchcraft, but there are a few stories dealing with him " in propriâ personâ," and these are collected in the following chapter.

It may be as well to state that his usual manifestation is believed to be in the form of a huge black cat. He takes this shape apparently when he wishes to pass incognito. Black cats in general are looked upon with a suspicious eye, but if seen in the house of anyone supposed to be addicted to magical arts, there is no doubt of their being imps of Satan.

Satan Outwitted.

It was Midsummer Day, the sun was shining brightly, and the country people were hastening in their holiday apparel to the spot where the militia were ordered to muster for a review, when an unfortunate country girl was ordered by her master to weed a large field of parsnips. He promised her that when her task was accomplished she should be allowed the rest of the day to amuse herself; but she soon discovered that this promise meant nothing, for that her utmost exertions would not suffice to finish the allotted work before the evening should close in. She commenced her task with a heavy heart, and often lifted her head as she heard the joyous laugh of the groups of lads and lasses as they passed along the high road on their way to the place of rendezvous. One party followed another, and as they became less frequent, the poor girl lost patience. Her hopes of taking any share in the amusements of the day were nearly at an end. At last she gave utterance to her thoughts, and wished aloud for assistance, were it even from the Devil himself.

Scarcely had she expressed this unhallowed wish, when she thought she heard a slight noise behind her, and, on looking round, saw a gentleman dressed entirely in black, who in the kindest manner immediately addressed her and enquired why she looked so sad, and how it was she was not merry-making with her companions.

"Alas!" she answered, "I must weed the whole of this field before I am released."

"Oh," said he, "is that all? Only promise me the first knot you tie to-morrow morning and I will get your task performed."

The girl easily agreed to these terms, and the gentleman departed.

She resumed her work, but was astonished to perceive that invisible hands were employed in every part of the field, tearing up the weeds and gathering them in bundles. In a very short time the ground was clear, and she went to announce it to her master, who, astonished at the rapidity with which she had executed his orders, gave her permission to spend the rest of the day in amusement.

She went accordingly to the review, and from thence to the " Son," * where she danced the greater part of the evening. As night came on, however, she began to reflect on the adventures of the morning, and to consider that the assistance which she had accepted was most probably not of a very holy nature, and that something more might be meant by the promise which she had made than the mere words implied. She returned home and retired to her bed, but was unable to compose herself to sleep. The more she thought of what she had done the more uneasy did she feel.

At last, in her perplexity, she resolved to rise immediately and seek advice from the Rector of the parish. The worthy clergyman was much alarmed at this open attack made by Satan on one of his flock, but bade her fear nothing, but put her trust in Heaven, go home, and spend the remainder of the night in prayer and repentance, and as soon as morning dawned, before she fastened a single knot, to go to the barn, taking her Bible with her, and,

---

* The old name for the village dances, generally held in some tavern to the sound of that obsolete instrument, the " chifournie."

praying without ceasing, there bind up a sheaf of barley straw.

The girl did as she was advised, and scarcely had she knotted the wisp of straw, when the gentleman in black stood at her side. His looks and voice were no longer so mild and prepossessing as they had been the day before, and the poor maiden, no longer doubting as to the infernal character of the stranger, was near fainting from fright. She was soon reassured, however, when she saw the good minister enter the barn, who, in God's name, bade Satan avaunt. The Devil was not proof against this solemn adjuration, but disappeared with a loud noise, and the poor girl, full of gratitude for her miraculous escape, made a solemn vow to avoid for the future all those places of resort and merry-makings, by which Satan endeavours to tempt the unwary into sin, and to live contentedly thenceforward in that station of life which Providence had allotted to her. *

Satan and the Schoolmaster.

It is good to possess knowledge, but, like all other possessions, the benefit to be derived from it depends on the uses to which it is applied, and there is no doubt that it exposes the possessor to temptations

---

* From Miss Louisa Lane.

In the tales of this nature related in Lower Brittany, the soul that is sold to the evil one is always rescued by the advice or intercession of a holy hermit or priest, see Luzel's *Veillies Bretonnes*, p. 132.

"Quand le diable parait, il est généralement vêtu de couleur sombre, et souvent il ressemblerait exactement à une "manière de monsieur" ou à un gros fermier, si on ne regardait ses pieds, dont l'un au moins est déformé et semblable à un sabot de cheval. Parfois aussi il a des gants de cuir ou des griffes pointues. On lui prête aussi un habillement tout rouge, et le cheval qu'il monte est tout noir."—*Traditions et Superstitions de la Haute Bretagne*, Tome I., p. 179.

which the more ignorant and simple-minded escape—
to say nothing of the envy and calumny which often
follow the man who by his superior acquirements,
rises above the vulgar herd.

In the past century, the parish of St. Michel du
Valle was fortunate in having secured the services of
a man of more than ordinary attainments as its
schoolmaster. Pallot was no common character, and
his studious and retiring habits were but little
appreciated by the surrounding farmers. They
wondered at his superior knowledge, but could not
understand his shutting himself up in his schoolroom
after the labours of the day were over. In their
opinion it would have been far more wise and
natural for him to follow the example of his scholars,
and throw aside his books until the next day. It
was known that his studies were often prolonged far
into the night, and, little by little, it came to be
whispered about that these studies were of a nature
that could not bear the light of day, and, in short,
that the schoolmaster was in league with the powers
of darkness. Pallot felt hurt at the imputation, but
at the same time somewhat flattered at the deference
paid him by his ignorant neighbours.

"Knowledge puffeth up," and of all pride the
pride of intellect is the most dangerous, and exposes
the man who gives way to it to the greatest
temptation. Satan knows well how to make use of
the opportunities which are afforded him to extend
his empire and work the ruin of souls. The
schoolmaster—one whose influence over the youth of
the parish was so great—was a prize worth securing,
and the great enemy of mankind laid siege to him
in due form. His approaches were made with skill,

" Looking up Fountain Street, 1825."

but with little or no success. At last he determined on a desperate expedient—that of a personal interview. The conference lasted for some hours, the most tempting offers were made, but Pallot, now thoroughly on his guard, was firm, and had grace to resist. He had too much regard for his soul to yield in anything to the enemy, and Satan, out of patience, rushed out of the schoolroom, carrying off with him the gate of the inclosure, which was found next morning on a large hawthorn bush on the summit of the Hougue Juas.

The thorn, which was previously green and flourishing, was blasted as if struck by lightning, and, although not killed, never recovered its former beauty, but retained for ever afterwards the same scathed and withered look. *

ANOTHER VERSION OF " SATAN AND THE SCHOOLMASTER."

It is related that in days long past there lived in the vicinity of the Roque Balan, at L'Ancresse, a man of very superior acquirements. It is true that he was commonly suspected of knowing more than was altogether lawful, but as he ostensibly gained his living by instructing the youth of the parish, and as there was no doubt that his scholars profited by his teaching, the neighbouring farmers made no hesitation in sending their sons to him. Among his pupils was one lad of whom he was justly proud, for a prying curiosity and love of acquiring knowledge, joined to a retentive memory and a sharp intellect, had made the boy, in the opinion of many, almost a match for his master. Curiosity and a love of acquiring

---

* From Miss Harriet Chepmell.

knowledge may be good in themselves, but they can be carried too far, and this proved to be the case with the young scholar.

He had noticed some old-looking tomes which his preceptor kept always carefully locked up in an old carved oak chest, and had long felt most anxious to pry into their contents. The clearest hints he could give, and even the openly - expressed wish to be allowed to peruse the hidden volumes, met with no response on the part of his teacher. He determined to watch his opportunity, and to get a sight, by hook or by crook, of the contents of the mysterious books, and one day, when the master had been called away suddenly to make the will of a dying man, and had inadvertently left his keys behind him, the youth seized on them, and, as soon as his back was turned, proceeded to examine the contents of the chest. He lifted one of the ponderous tomes, opened it at hazard, and commenced to read out aloud the first passage which met his eye. Unfortunately this proved to be the spell by which the Prince of Darkness can be summoned to this upper world to do the bidding of his votaries. Great was the terror of the indiscreet youngster when a sudden violent storm arose, which went on increasing in intensity, and Satan in person appeared before him and demanded what he wanted of him. The unfortunate boy knew not what answer to make, nor what task to impose on the demon to get rid of him at least for a time, until the return of the master. Pallot, who was already at some distance from home, hastened back, and entered the house just at the moment when Satan, tired of waiting and enraged at having been unnecessarily called up, had seized on the inquisitive scholar and was on the point of flying off with him. The master, at a glance, perceived how matters stood, and, uttering a hasty spell, arrested the demon in his course. He then proceeded to set him a task, promising him that if he succeeded in accomplishing it before sunset he should be at liberty to carry off his prey.

The Devil made some difficulty in acceding to these terms, but the schoolmaster, determined, if possible, to save his unfortunate pupil, was firm, and not to be influenced either by the threats or cajoleries of the arch-fiend. He caught up a peck-measure containing peas, and scattered them on the floor, handing at the same time a three-pronged pitch-fork to the Devil, and ordering him with that instrument to throw the peas over the door-hatch into the court-yard.

Satan took the fork and set to work with right good will, but soon found that it was labour in vain. Not one pea could he raise from the floor. The sun was fast sinking below the horizon. As the last portion of its orb disappeared beneath the western wave, the enraged and disappointed demon wrenched the door-hatch off its hinges and cast it far away in the direction of Les Landes. There it was found the next morning on a thorn-bush, which had been green and flourishing the day before, but which, since that time, is blasted and flattened almost to the level of the ground, though it still lives and is pointed out as a proof of the truth of this history.*

---

* From Sieur Henry Bisson.

This incident is found in a Breton legend, as told by Dr. Alfred Fouquet in his work *Légendes, Contes, et Chansons Populaires du Morbihan*, apropos

The Devil and the Tailor.

The race of journeymen tailors and shoemakers, hired by the day to make up, at the houses of their employers, the materials that have been provided beforehand, or to patch and mend the clothes and shoes requiring repairs, is not yet quite extinct in the rural districts of Guernsey; although the facility of access to the town of St. Peter Port, afforded by the excellent roads which intersect the island in all directions, and the superior make and fashion of the articles supplied by the tradesmen in town,—to say nothing of the ready-made clothing so generally used in the present day—have had the effect of considerably diminishing the number of men who gain

---

of the first occupant of the lands on which the Château de Herlean was afterwards built. Satan undertook to be the servant of a peasant as long as work could be found for him to do. He accomplished the most difficult tasks with the greatest ease. At last the peasant emptied a sack of millet into the court-yard and ordered Satan to pitch it up to him in the granary with a hay-fork. He acknowledged his inability and was ignominiously dismissed.

A somewhat similar story is also told in *Notes and Queries.* The Vicar of a certain Devonshire parish was a diligent student of the black art, and possessed a large collection of mysterious books and MSS. During his absence at church, one of his servants entered his study, and, finding a large volume open on the desk, imprudently began to read it aloud. He had scarcely read half a page when the sky became dark and a great wind shook the house violently. Still he read on, and in the midst of the storm the doors flew open and a black hen and chickens came into the room. They were of the ordinary size when they first appeared, but gradually became larger and larger, until the hen was of the bigness of a good-size ox. At this point, the Vicar (in the church) suddenly closed his discourse and dismissed his congregation, saying he was wanted at home and hoped he might arrive there in time. When he entered the chamber, the hen was already touching the ceiling. But he threw down a bag of rice which stood ready in the corner, and, whilst the hen and chickens were busily picking up the grains, the Vicar had time to reverse the spell.

Editor's Note.—This story is still believed. It was told me by Miss Falla in 1896.

their living in this way. Although we have no knowledge that the journeyman tailor was ever the important character here that he is in Brittany and even in Normandy, where he is sometimes employed in the delicate office of negotiating marriages between the families of distant hamlets, and where he is often the sole means of circulating the news of the outer world, or carrying the gossiping tales of one village to another, yet even here his presence for a day or two in a house is looked forward to with pleasure as a break in the monotony of the daily family routine; and if he should chance to be what the French call " un farceur," or teller of good stories, he is doubly welcome.

It must be acknowledged that, as a rule, this class of men are not supposed to be very particular as to the exact truth of the stories they put in circulation, and that some of them would be better members of society, if, on quitting their work, they were to go straight home, without thinking it a part of their duty to turn into every house where drink is sold, that they may chance to fall in with on their way.

The hero of the following adventure, if fame does not belie him, is one of this sort, and, although he affirms the truth of the story, there is no corroborative evidence that it is anything more than the dream of a drunken man.

It appeared in a letter from a correspondent to the *Gazette de Guernesey* of the 22nd December, 1873, and is translated literally, omitting only the writer's sensible remarks on the folly and simplicity of those who could give credence to such an invention, and on the superstition which, in spite of education, is still so prevalent among the lower orders. There is no doubt that the story was widely spread and believed in the country, and that the tailor, when questioned about it, asserts it to be true.

He is an inhabitant of the parish of Torteval, and a Guernseyman born and bred, although bearing a name which shews that his family came originally from another country. One evening, as he was returning from his work, a certain tailor, who shall be nameless, and' who bears but an indifferent character, met with an adventure which was far from being agreeable. A man, dressed entirely in black, of a sinister aspect, and mounted on a black horse, met him on his way. This strange looking individual stopped the tailor, and the following conversation took place :

" Hallo, you're a tailor, aren't you ? "

" Yes, sir, at your service," answered the tailor, somewhat alarmed.

" Then I wish you to make me a pair of trousers, which I will come and fetch at your house to-morrow at noon." And, so saying, the stranger went on his way.

" But, sir," cried the tailor, running after him, ' You've forgotten to let me take your measure."

" Bah ! what does that matter ? "

" But, sir, I shall never be able to fit you if I've not got your measure."

" Well then, take it," said the gentleman in black, dismounting from his horse. " There ! "

But imagine the poor tailor's dismay ! There were no legs to be seen. Do, what he would, it was impossible to take a proper measure for trousers under such circumstances. A horrible suspicion flashed through his mind.

" It must be the Devil," thought he to himself.
" How shall I get rid of him ? "

Alarmed, horrified, trembling in all his limbs,
feeling his legs giving way under him, our poor
tailor only got out of the scrape by stammering out
these few words—

" Well, sir, your trousers shall be ready to-morrow
at noon."

" Look to yourself if they are not ready. I shall
come and fetch them at your house," answered the
dark-visaged and black-coated individual, leaping on
his horse and going on his way.

Seized with uncontrollable fear, it is said that the
tailor went straight to the Rector of his parish, and
told him the whole of his adventure. The good
parson advised him to make the trousers, and
promised him that he would not fail to be with
him the next day to be witness to the delivery of
them. Accordingly, the next day, at the hour
appointed, and, but a few minutes after the arrival
of the clergyman, who was beforehand with him,
the Devil knocked at the tailor's door to claim the
trousers ; and the hero of our tale, in delivering
them, heard his Satanic Majesty utter these words—

" If a man of God had not been present in this
house, I would have carried you off also."

RECENT APPEARANCE OF THE DEVIL.

Whatever may be the spread of rationalism in
other places, a belief in the personality of Satan
still holds its ground firmly in the minds of our
peasantry. How can it be otherwise when there are
those who, within the last two or three years, have
had the rare chance of seeing him " in propriâ

personâ; " and this in a locality which, one might suppose, would be about the very last that he would be inclined to honour with his presence? The neighbourhood of L'Erée, it is true, has never borne a very high character. Everyone knows that from time immemorial the hill of Catiauroc and the beach of Rocquaine have been the favourite resort of witches and warlocks, and that their infernal master holds his court there every Friday night, and, seated in state on the cromlech which is called "Le Trépied," receives the homage of his deluded votaries. But who could suppose that he would leave this time-honoured haunt to become the inmate of a Methodist Chapel? Such, however, if we can attach any credit to the statements of the fishermen and others who inhabit this coast, is undoubtedly the case.

Within the last few years the Wesleyans have erected several small chapels in various parts of the island, and, among others, one near a place called "Les Adams." Shortly after the chapel was finished it began to be whispered about that lights were seen in it at hours of the night when it was well known that no one was likely to be there. The light is described by some who had seen it from a distance as if illuminating the whole of the interior, but some fishermen who were bold enough to draw near and look in at the windows could see nothing but a small subdued flame in one corner, which seemed to sink downwards into the earth. A gentleman of strict veracity, formerly residing about a mile from the spot, declared that he had frequently seen the mysterious light. He described it as being of a pale blue colour, and was convinced that it did not proceed from either candle or lamp. He had seen it

" Looking down Berthelot Street, 1880."

from various points, from the rising ground inland, to the east of the chapel, and from the low lands lying along the sea-shore to the west. It seemed to occupy a particular spot in the building, for the light appeared brightest through one of the windows, and fainter through all the others. He had observed it on many occasions immediately after dusk, and at hours when it was most unlikely that any person would be in the chapel for any improper purpose. On drawing near, the light always disappeared. The state of the weather or of the moon seemed to make no difference in it. Curiosity, thus excited, had to be appeased, and, at last, some of the fishermen ventured to approach the chapel and peep in at the windows. What they saw they described as "Le Dain," the name by which his Satanic Majesty is designated when it is thought proper to avoid the more offensive appellation of "Le Guyablle." Sparks of fire issued from his mouth and nostrils, the traditional horns and tail seem to have been discerned, but the cloven feet were hidden by long boots covering the knees, and which, according to some accounts, were red.

His occupation was as difficult to be accounted for as his presence in so unusual a place. It was that of dancing and leaping with all his might and main! Whether the fishermen really saw anything which their fears magnified into a vision of the wicked one, or whether, for reasons of their own, they wished to impose upon the credulity of their neighbours, it is impossible to say. One thing is certain, and that is that persons of the highest respectability, living in that part of the country, vouch for the fact of the lights having frequently been seen in the chapel at hours of the night when it ought not to have been occupied. It does not seem to have occurred to them that many of the mariners on this part of the coast are employed at times in carrying off packages of tobacco to the English and French boats engaged in smuggling, and that, as a temporary depôt may be sometimes required for these goods, the chapel may have been selected for the purpose, in preference to a dwelling house or other private property, the owner of which, in case of detection, might be subjected to much inconvenience. But the neighbouring peasants have their own method of explaining these supernatural appearances.

Some say that they are a judgment on the original founders of the chapel, who, as it is believed and reported, after having collected ample subscriptions towards the building, pretended that the funds were insufficient, and defrauded the workmen whom they had employed of their just dues. Others say that the original proprietor of the land on which the chapel is built, was importuned by his wife to make a free gift of the site, but, being strongly averse to dissent in all forms, could never be brought by her to consent to the alienation; but that immediately on the death of the old man, the widow, who, after a youth spent in frivolity and pleasure, had turned wonderfully pious in her declining years, took measures to make over the ground to the dissenters, and, not content with this, squandered on them large sums of money which ought rightly to have been reserved for her late husband's children by a former marriage. The spirit of the departed could not brook such disregard of his wishes, and such disrespect for his

R

memory, and manifests his displeasure by haunting the spot of which his children ought never to have been deprived.

EDITOR's NOTE.—When in Sark in 1870 I was told by one of the old Sark men, how a Sark fisherman defeated the Devil. This fisherman was supposed to be given to witchcraft, and one day he succeeded in raising the Devil, when Satan appeared and asked him what commands he had for him. The fisherman had nothing to say. Finally he said, " You must carry me where I tell you." They were then on the far end of Little Sark. So the Devil consented, but on the understanding that when they reached their destination, the man, in his turn, should do what Satan commanded. So the man mounted on Satan's back, and first was carried across the Coupée. "*Allez plus loin,*" (Go farther) said the man. Then they went on to the Carrefour, near where the Bel Air Hotel now is. "*Allez plus loin,*" said the man when Satan stopped for a rest. Then they reached the Port du Moulin, where the fisherman's cottage stood. "*Au nom du Grand Dieu—Arrêtez !*" (In God's name—Stop!) At that the Devil had to put him down and fly away shrieking, "for," as the old man concluded his story, "he is powerless when God's name is said."

CHAPTER IX.

Prophetic Warnings and Ghosts.

" Now there spreaden a rumour that everich night
The rooms ihaunted been by many a Sprite,
The Miller avoucheth, and all thereabout
That they full oft hearen the Hellish Rout,
Some faine they hear the gingling of Chains,
And some hath heard the Psautries straines,
At midnight some the headless Horse i meet,
And some espien a Corse in a white Sheet;
And other things, Faye, Elfin and Elfe,
And shapes that Fear createn to itself."
—*Gay.*

" Et chacun croit fort aisément ce qu'il craint."
—*La Fontaine.*

" Now I remember those old women's words
Who in my youth would tell me winter's tales
And speak of sprites and ghosts that glide by night
About the place where treasure hath been hid."
—*Marlowe's* " *Jew of Venice.*'

Prophetic Warnings.

." These true shadows . . . .
Forerunning thus their bodies, may approve
That all things to be done, as here we live,
Are done before all times in th'other life."
—*Chapman.*

IT is a very common belief that events, particularly those of a melancholy nature, are foreshadowed. Unusual noises in or about a house, such as cannot easily be accounted for, the howling of a dog, the crowing of cocks at unaccustomed hours, the hooting of owls, and many other things are looked upon as warnings of evil to come, or, as they are locally termed, "*avertissements.*" This term is also applied to a sort of second-sight, in which a person fancies he sees an image of himself, or, to make use of a Scotch word, his own "wraith." This illusion, arising no doubt from a derangement of the optic nerve consequent on the weakness produced by ill-health, is considered a sure forerunner of death.   Two instances of this, both occurring towards the end of the last century, have come to my knowledge.   In the one case, a young gentleman, slowly dying of decline, was seated near a window, which commanded a view of the avenue leading to the country house in which he resided. Suddenly he saw a figure, which he recognised as his own, standing at the corner of a pathway which led into a cherry-orchard, a favourite resort of his when in health.   His sister was every moment expected to return home from a ride, and, fearing that her horse might take fright at the apparition, he immediately dispatched a servant to meet her, and cause her to return to the house by another way.   He died not many hours afterwards.

In the other instance, a young lady, who was known to be very fragile and delicate, was spending the day at her brother's country-house.   It was summer, and the room in which she was seated with the other members of the family looked out on a parterre gay with flowers.   Suddenly she interrupted the conversation which was going on, by exclaiming:—

"How singular! I see myself yonder in the garden gathering flowers."

Her friends tried to laugh her out of her fancy, but neither ridicule nor reason prevailed. She persisted in saying that she had seen her own likeness in the garden. She grew rapidly worse, and before the autumn was over she passed away.

It occasionally happens that both fruit and blossoms are to be seen at the same time on apple and pear trees. When this occurs it is believed to be a sure presage that a death will follow in the family of the proprietor of the tree within the year. *

Great faith is also put in dreams by our country people, as the following stories will show. They make use of many charms and spells to invoke certain dreams, and those will be told in a future chapter, but the following show the belief that exists in the truth of dreams.

During the late war with France many privateers were fitted out. A man dreamt that if a vessel were sent out to a certain latitude and longitude, that on a certain day it would meet with a rich prize and take it. He realised all his property, bought a ship, equipped and manned it, and sent it out to cruise, in full faith that his dream would come to pass. Time rolled on, and the ship did not appear. The man's friends and neighbours began to jeer at him, but he still felt confident that all would turn out as he had dreamt. His faith was at last rewarded, for one day, when all but he had given up any hope of seeing the vessel again, two vessels were seen in the offing. As they drew near one was recognised as the missing ship, and the other was soon made out, by

---

* From Mr. Thomas Lenfestey and Mr. George Allez.
See *Notes and Queries*, VI. Series, IV., 55.

" Cow Lane."

its rig, to be a foreigner. They came safely into St. Peter Port, and it was then found that the latter was a Spaniard, with a very rich cargo. It turned out that the capture had been made in the very place and at the very time that had been dreamt of.

A country gentleman had occasion to make some alterations in the level of a road in the neighbourhood of his house. He employed two men in the work, a father and son. The materials for the work were to be taken from a gravel pit on the estate, and the work was progressing favourably, when, one morning, the gentleman, on coming down to breakfast, said to his wife that he had had an unpleasant dream, and feared that some accident would happen to the workmen before the day was out. He went out shortly afterwards and cautioned the men, as he had done previously, to be very careful in digging out the materials they were in want of from the overhanging banks of the gravel pit. They made light of his admonition, and he left them. Towards noon the elder of the two workmen left the place to go home to dinner, leaving his son behind. On his return, about an hour later, he found that the bank had given way and buried his son in the rubbish. When, after a considerable time, he was dug out, he was found to be quite dead.

Ghosts.

" That the dead are seen no more, I will not undertake to maintain against the concurrent and unvaried testimony of all ages and of all nations. There is no people, rude or unlearned, among whom apparitions of the dead are not related and believed. This opinion, which prevails as far as human nature is diffused, could become universal only by its truth. Those who never heard of another, would not have agreed in a tale which nothing but experience can make credible. That it is doubted by single cavillers can very little weaken the general evidence, and some who deny it with their tongues confess it with their fears."

—Dr. Samuel Johnson.

The belief that the spirits of the dead are, under certain circumstances, permitted to revisit the places which they were in the habit of frequenting, and the persons with whom they were acquainted while in the body, has too strong a hold on the human mind not to be still an article of popular faith in this island ; but the doings of these disembodied spirits do not differ sensibly from what is attributed to them in other European countries.

The ghost of the murdered man still haunts the spot where he was foully deprived of life, crying for vengeance on his assassin. The murderer's form is seen at the foot of the gibbet where he expiated his crime. The shade of the suicide lingers about the spot where he committed his rash act. The spirit of the tender mother is seen bending over the cradles of her darling children, smoothing their tangled locks, washing their begrimed faces, and lamenting over the neglected state in which they are allowed to remain by a careless or unkind step-dame. The acquirer of ill-gotten wealth wanders about, vainly endeavouring to make restitution. And the ghosts of the shipwrecked mariners who have perished in the waves, roam along the fatal shore, and, with loud wailings, claim a resting place for their remains in their mother-earth.

Some also say that the departing spirit occasionally

takes the form of a bird, and, from a story told us, it would seem that it also sometimes puts on the form of a mouse.

An elderly woman who lived alone in a house in the neighbourhood of Ste. Hélène was found one morning dead at the bottom of a flight of stairs. From the evidence at the inquest it appeared that she had entrusted the latch key of the front door to a workman, who was to come early to the house next morning to do some small job in the way of plastering. It was supposed that before retiring to rest, at her usual hour between nine and ten, she had intended to go to the door to see whether the door was properly latched, and that, in descending the stairs, she had slipped, and, falling forward, had broken her neck.

She had a first cousin, within a week or two of the same age as herself, with whom she had been brought up, and between whom and herself great affection had always existed. About the time that the accident must have happened, this cousin was sitting with his wife, by whom the story was related to me, warming themselves before the fire, previously to getting into bed. They were speaking of the old woman, and the husband remarked that he had not seen her for some days, and hoped she was well, and then immediately made the remark that he had seen a mouse run across the room, coming from the door towards them. His eyesight was very defective, and his wife endeavoured to persuade him that it was impossible that he could have seen anything of the kind, and that, moreover, she had never seen a mouse in that room.

They went to bed and nothing more was thought

about it until the next morning, when the wife, passing
the house where the old woman lived, saw a crowd of
neighbours assembled round the door, and found that
the dead body of her husband's cousin had just been
discovered lying at the foot of the stairs.

The accident in all probability had occurred at the
very time she and her husband were speaking of the
deceased, and when the old man declared he saw the
mouse. She was fully convinced that the spirit of
the old woman had come in that shape to take a
last look and farewell of her kinsman.*

The Robber of the Poor Box.

It is not many years since, that in making some
alterations in the parsonage of St. Michel du Valle,
the workmen found under the flooring of one of the
rooms a few small coins. They remembered that in
the last century, a French priest, who had renounced
his own religion, had been appointed curate of the
parish by a non-resident Rector after having been
duly licensed by the Bishop of Winchester; that, after
leading a most irregular life to the great scandal of
the parishioners, he had one day disappeared suddenly,
and that after his departure the poor box in the
church was found to have been broken open and
robbed of its contents. It was not long before it was
rumoured abroad that mysterious noises were heard
in the dead of the night in the parsonage, as of
someone walking through the rooms and dropping
money as he went. No one doubted that the
sacrilegious robber had left this mortal life, and that

---

* Related to me by Mrs. Andrew Thorn, wife of the old man.
"In many Teutonic myths, we find that the soul leaves the body in the
shape of a mouse,"—*Folk-Lore Journal*, Vol. II., Part VII., p. 208,

his ghost was doomed to revisit the scene of his iniquity, vainly endeavouring to make restitution to the widows and orphans, and to the aged and infirm pensioners of the church, of the money of which he had so unfeelingly deprived them.

The workmen were fully convinced that the coins which they had found were part of those which had been so sacrilegiously abstracted. They dared not retain them for their own use, but brought them to the Rector with a request that they might be given to the poor.*

BURIAL OF THE DROWNED.

In all ages and among all nations the burial of the dead has been looked upon as a sacred duty; and the belief is not yet extinct that until the body is consigned to the earth the spirit is doomed to wander about, seeking rest and finding none.

Great therefore is the guilt of him who, having found a corpse, neglects to provide for its sepulture. "*Les morts recllament la terre, et ch'est leù derouait.*" (The dead claim the earth, and it is their right).

A man who had gone down at low water to visit his nets, found a dead body stretched out on the sands. It was not that of any of his neighbours. A violent storm had raged a day or two previously, and there could be no doubt that some unfortunate vessel had gone down in the gale, and that the body before him was that of one of the crew. It was handsomely dressed, the clothes being of velvet, richly laced with gold. The avarice of the fisherman was excited, and his first thought was to search the pockets. A purse, containing what to a poor man

* From Mrs. Thomas Bell, wife of the Rector of the Vale parish.

was a considerable sum, was found, and, content with
his morning's work, the man hastened home, leaving
the body to be carried away by the next tide. Great
was his astonishment and affright, on entering his
cottage, to see the dead man seated by the fireside,
and looking sternly and reproachfully at him. His
wife, to whom the phantom was not visible,
perceived his trouble, and, pressed by her, he confessed
what he had done. She upbraided him with his
inhuman conduct, and, kneeling down with him,
prayed the Almighty to forgive him his sin. They
then hastened down to the beach, drew the corpse
to shore, and buried it in a neighbouring field. On
their return home the ghost of the drowned man
had disappeared and was never more seen. *

"La Grand' Garce."

" Qu'est qu'tu 'as ? Nou dirait qu'tu 'as veu la
grand' garce." (" What is the matter with you?
One would suppose you had seen the great girl.")

Such were the words with which a gentleman
(Mr. Peter Le Pelley, Seigneur of Sark), in the last
century greeted his sister-in-law, (Miss Frances
Carey, daughter of Mr. John Carey), who had come to
spend a few days with him at his manorial residence
in Sark, on her appearance at the breakfast table the
morning after her arrival. He meant to banter her on
her anxious and haggard look, which she attributed
to a restless night and headache, occasioned in all
probability by crossing the water on the previous day.

---

* From Mrs. Savidan.

EDITOR'S NOTE.—An old fisherman named Mansell told Major Macleane, my informant,
that it is most unlucky to keep a suit of clothes belonging to a drowned man, whether they
have been washed ashore, or by whatever means they have entered your possession; for his
spirit is sure to come back and reanimate his clothes and haunt you. The clothes should
always be burnt or buried immediately.

In reality, although she did not like to acknowledge it at the time, her rest had been disturbed. Having previously locked her door, as was her habit, she had fallen asleep almost as soon as she laid her head on the pillow, but was awakened suddenly,—about midnight, as far as she could judge,—by someone drawing aside the curtains at the foot of her bed. She started up, and saw plainly an elderly lady standing there. She fell back fainting, and when she recovered her senses the figure had disappeared.

It was probably nothing more than a very vivid nightmare, and was followed by no results beyond the effects of the fright which a few days sufficed to remove, but she never again revisited Sark. The question, however, is one which is not unfrequently addressed to a person who has an anxious or startled look, and refers to the apparition of a tall maiden, which is supposed to presage the death of the person who sees it, or that of some near connection.*

---

* From Rachel du Port, who was formerly a servant of Mr. John Carey, and heard it from Miss Fanny Carey herself.

EDITOR'S NOTES.

My cousin, Miss E. Le Pelley, whose great-uncle Peter was Seigneur of Sark, and whose old servant Caroline is still alive and in the service of the Le Pelley family, sends me the following confirmation of the above, which she wrote down from the lips of old Caroline herself. Caroline, as a girl, had one day been teased by some of her fellow servants on the Seigneurie farm, who told her that they would come in and awake her during the night. So she, to prevent such disturbance, locked her door. In the middle of the night she awoke and saw a lady standing at the foot of her bed. She was so frightened that she shut her eyes, but twice curiosity prevailed and she opened them again, and saw the lady gliding away. She had on a crossover shawl, and a beautifully gauffred white cap. Caroline was just going to look again, when she felt something heavy fall on her feet "with a great thump," which so frightened her that she put her head under the clothes, and did not uncover it until the morning, though she could not sleep again. The lady is supposed to be a Miss de Carteret, sister of one of the original Seigneurs of Sark. She had unaccountably disappeared from that room, which was the last spot in which she had been seen.

Old Caroline went on to say that many others besides herself had seen the ghost. Fifty years previously, an old woman living at Havre Gosselin had been terrified by it. The cook, who was fellow-servant with Caroline, had seen it three times.

Henri, an old man-servant, had also often seen it. But the curious thing about the ghost is that it only appears in the room if the door is *locked*.

Caroline was very anxious to tell her mistress, Mrs. Le Pelley, what she had seen, but the other servants dissuaded her, and told her that she had brought it all on herself by locking her door, which she never again dared to do.

"Now," said Caroline, "if only someone had said to her 'In the name of the Great God

"La Fllieur de Jaon."

There is an English saying that "when the gorse is out of bloom, kissing is out of fashion." This is expanded in Guernsey into the following tales.

A man, who had been long suffering from a lingering illness, was at last lying on his death-bed. His wife was unremitting in her attentions, and profuse in her expressions of sorrow at the thoughts of losing him. He did not doubt her affection for him, but ventured to hint at the probability of her looking out for a second husband before the first year of her widowhood should be expired. She warmly repudiated the bare possibility of such a thought entering her mind, and was ready to make a vow that she would never again enter into the married state.

"Well," said the man mildly, "I ask no more than that you should promise me not to wed again while any blossom can be found on the furze."

She gladly made promise. The man died, but it

what tortures you?' the poor lady would have unburdened her soul, and her spirit could have found rest, but no one had the wit or the courage to do it."

As Caroline always ends up her story:—"*Oh mon Dou donc, que j'tai effrdie!*" (Oh my goodness, how frightened I was!).—*From Miss E. Le Pelley.*

· Old Mrs. Le Messurier, who used frequently to go in and "help" at the Seigneurie when the Le Pelleys were there, told me that she was there in February, 1839, the time that Peter Le Pelley was drowned, and the night before "La Grande Garce" was seen walking through the passages, and the tapping of her high heels was heard through the house, while some said she was wringing her hands. Knowing that her appearance in this manner was a sure presage of misfortune, the servants all begged Mr. Le Pelley next day not to set sail for Guernsey, especially as there was a strong south wind blowing, but he would go, and the boat was swamped off the Pointe du Nez, and all perished.—*From Mrs. Le Messurier, of Sark.*

Mr. de Garis, of the Rouvets, told me that he had an old servant who came from Sark, who told him of a lady who appeared at the Seigneurie, if the bedroom door was locked.

In 1565 Queen Elizabeth "conferred on Helier de Carteret and his heirs for ever, in reward of the many services received by herself and her royal ancestors from this family, the aforesaid island of Sark, to be held *in capite*, as a fief haubert, on the payment of an annual rent of fifty shillings." Sir Charles de Carteret, Seigneur of St. Ouen, and of Sark, being heavily in debt, made a provision in his will for the settling of his debts by ordering that at his death the Seigneurie of Sark should be sold. This will bears the date of 1713. During his lifetime he obtained a patent from Queen Anne authorising the above sale. And in 1730 it was bought by Dame Susan Le Gros, widow of Mr. Nicholas Le Pelley. Her son Nicholas inherited it, and it remained in the Le Pelleys' possession until 1852, when, owing to heavy losses incurred in the working of the silver mines in Little Sark, they sold it to Mrs. T. G. Collings, and it is now in the possession of the Collings family.

"Harbour, showing entrance to Cow Lane."

is affirmed that the disconsolate widow, at the end
of twelve months, had discovered by close observation,
and to her great disappointment, that she had made
a rash promise, and that there was not a day in the
whole year when flowers might not be found on the
prickly gorse.

EDITOR'S NOTE.*

* Other Editor's notes on this subject will be found in Appendix A.

In the Castel parish they tell another story based on the same proverb. Here is a house called Les Mourains, in that parish, belonging to the Ozannes. In the middle of the last century, a Mr. Ozanne married a young wife, who died after having given birth to two sons. On her death-bed she made her husband promise that he would never marry, "*lorsqu'il y avait des flieurs sur l' jan.*" He promised, but after her death he married again.

But the poor spirit had not found rest. The nurse, while she dressed and undressed the children, frequently saw her late mistress watching her. The other servants, when in the evenings they stood at the back door talking to their friends and acquaintances, heard the rustling of her silk dress along the passages.

And she so habitually haunted the drawing room that for years it had to be kept locked up, and finally the Rector of the parish had to be sent for, to lay the ghost, which he did, and it was boarded up in a cupboard. The place may be conjectured, for in the drawing room there is still a part boarded up, and at times strange noises are heard, as of a spirit ill at rest.*

* From Miss E. Le Pelley.

CHAPTER X.

𝔚𝔦𝔱𝔠𝔥𝔠𝔯𝔞𝔣𝔱.

"Had learned the art that none may name
In Padua far beyond the sea."

"Tam saw an unco sight!
Warlocks and witches in a dance;
Nae cotillon brent new frae France,
But horn pipes, gigs, strathspeys, and reels,
Put life and mettle in their heels:
. . . . . There sat auld Nick, in shape o' beast;
A towz'e tyke, black, grim, and large,
To gie them music was his charge."
—*Tam O'Shanter*, Burns.

"Wise judges have prescribed that men may not rashly believe the confessions of witches, nor the evidence against them. For the witches themselves are imaginative, and people are credulous, and ready to impute accidents to witchcraft."—*Bacon*.

HE belief in witchcraft dates from so very remote a period, it is so universally spread throughout all the various races that compose the human family, that it is not to be wondered at if it still retains its hold among the ignorant and semi-educated, especially when we find, even in the present day, that persons, who ought by their superior instruction, and by the position they hold in society, to be above such superstitions, are nevertheless, firm believers in judicial astrology, fortune telling, spiritualism, and other similar delusions. Although it is now but very seldom that public rumour goes so far as to point out any particular individual as a proficient in this forbidden art, the persuasion that sorcery does still exist, is by no means extinct. A sudden and unusual malady, either in man or beast, a strange and unlooked-for accident, the failure of crops from blight or insects,—all these, and many more evils, are attributed by the ignorant to supernatural causes ; and, it is probable, will continue to be so as long as there are those who find it their interest to encourage this superstitious belief. For there are individuals, commonly called "désorceleurs" or "white-witches," who pretend to be able to declare whether a person is bewitched or not, and to have it in their power, by charms and incantations, to counteract the evil influence. Of course this is not to be done for nothing ; and cases of this kind, where large sums of money have been extorted from ignorant dupes, have, even of late years, formed the subject of judicial investigation. It is useless to attempt to reason with the lower orders on this subject. They have an answer ready which, in their minds at least, is a conclusive reply to all doubts that may be suggested :—

"Witches and witchcraft are frequently spoken of in the Holy Scriptures ; who, then, but an unbeliever, can doubt that such things are ? "

Guernsey did not escape the epidemic delusion which spread over the whole of Europe in the sixteenth and seventeenth centuries. Here, as elsewhere, a terror seized upon the people, and no man thought himself secure from the machinations of the agents of Satan. The records of the Royal Court of the island contain far too many condemnations of unfortunate men and women to the stake for sorcery ; and the evidence on which the sentences against them were based, as well as their own confessions, extorted under the infliction of torture, and taken down in writing at the time, are still extant. The unhappy individuals were of various ages and conditions, but, judging from the statements of their accusers, and the evidence brought against them, they appear to have been in most, if not all cases, persons of irregular life, subsisting by begging and pilfering, vindictive towards those who offended them, and clever in taking advantage of, and working on, the fears and preconceived notions of their dupes.

They were accused of causing storms to arise, in which the unfortunate fisherman who had refused them a share of his catch, either lost his boat, his gear, or his life; or was so tempest-tossed as to be in danger of losing his wits. Women and children were, by their infernal influence, afflicted with sudden and strange maladies. Oxen, horses, calves, sheep, and swine died unexpectedly, the cows calved prematurely, and either gave no milk, or else blood in lieu of it. Butter would not come, or became rancid even while it was being made, and curds dissolved and turned to whey.

Maggots of unusual appearance, black at both extremities, appeared in prodigious quantities in the beds, and even under the women's caps, and lice were in such numbers that they could be swept away with a broom.

The water in the fountains—usually so bright and limpid—became turbid and unfit for use, and full of tadpoles and disgusting insects. Frogs and black beasts ("*des bêtes noires*"), whatever they may have been, sat by the bedside of those who were under a spell; but all these evils disappear as suddenly as

s 2

they have come, either on the sufferer weakly yielding
to the demands of the supposed sorcerer, or having
courage enough to threaten to denounce him to the
judicial authorities.

It is not to be wondered at that the pretended
wizards and witches should have shrunk from a
judicial investigation at a time when all believed
firmly in their supernatural powers, and when the
examination into the alleged facts was carried on in
a manner so different from the procedure of the
present day, hearsay evidence of the vaguest
description being admitted as proof, and when that
failed, torture being resorted to in order to extort a
confession.

From the evidence given, and the confessions of
the sorcerers themselves, it appears that the means
employed by them to effect their nefarious designs
were various; but two in particular are mentioned.

A peculiar black powder, furnished them by their
master, the Devil, which, being cast on man or beast,
was the cause of serious and unusual maladies; and
certain enchanted articles, introduced furtively into
the beds or pillows of those on whom they wished to
practise their evil arts.

These charms are variously described by the
witnesses as consisting of seeds of different kinds, of
which mildewed or blighted beans seem to have
been the most common, and of feathers, knotted
together with ends of thread or silk twist, and
sometimes made into the shape of a small image.

When the beds or pillows were opened to search
for these articles, it sometimes happened that an
animal was seen to leave the bed, which, after
taking various forms, as that of a black cat, a cock,

a rat, a mouse, or a stoat, succeeded in evading all attempts to catch it, and escaped in a mysterious manner.

Isabell Le Moigne, one of the witches, declared in her confession that this was none other than Satan himself. If these charms were thrown into the fire, they produced a most noisome smell, but, in some instances, the immediate cure of the sufferer was the result. If the person under the influence of witchcraft was uncertain on whom he ought to fix the guilt of bewitching him, there was an infallible method for discovering the culprit.

The house-key was to be placed on the hearth-stone, and the fire heaped around it. As it became hot, the wizard or witch, apparently suffering great agony, would come to the door, and endeavour to force an entrance into the house, offering at the same time to put an end to the spell under which the inmates were bound.

Another means of finding out the guilty party was to roast the heart of some animal—some said that of a black sheep was the most efficacious—with certain prescribed rites and incantations, or to boil it with certain herbs known to the white witch or "désorceleur," who, of course, could not be expected to give his valuable advice and services for nothing.

According to the confessions of the unfortunate victims of the superstition and credulity of their times, to which allusion has been made above, the doings of Satan with them were just such as we read of in the accounts of prosecutions for witchcraft in other countries. A desire to be revenged on some persons who had given them offence seems to have been the first motive.

" North Arm, Old Harbour, showing back of Pollet."

The Devil then appeared to them in the shape of a black dog, cat, or other animal, sometimes under one likeness, sometimes under another; offered his services, invited them to attend the "Sabbath," which was generally held in some weird, out-of-the-way locality; furnished them with a certain ointment, which was to be rubbed on the back and stomach; after doing which, they found themselves carried through the air, with extraordinary velocity, to the appointed place of meeting, where they found other wizards and witches, and a number of imps in the shape of dogs, cats, and hares. They were unable to recognise the other sorcerers on account of their all appearing blackened and disfigured, but they knew who they were by their answering to their names when the roll was called over by Satan before entering on the business of the night.

They commenced by adoring their infernal master in a manner which it is not necessary to describe minutely. They then danced back to back, after which they were regaled with bread and wine, which Satan poured out of silver or pewter flagons into goblets of the same metals. They all agreed in describing the wine as being inferior to that usually drunk; and they asserted that salt was never seen at these feasts. The Devil, before dismissing the assembly, gave them a certain black powder, of which we have spoken before.

The favourite form assumed by Satan on these occasions seems to have been that of a large black dog, standing upright on his hind legs, but he sometimes appeared in the shape of a he-goat.

Isabell Le Moigne described him as a black dog of large size, with long erect horns, and hands like those of a man. Deeds were done at the Sabbath which will not bear being spoken of ; but there are circumstances which lead one to suppose that the poor deluded wretches of women may, in some cases, have been deceived by designing men, who enticed them from their houses at night, and, under assumed disguises, abused their credulity.

All sorcerers were marked by Satan in some part or other of the body, and the mark thus made was insensible to pain, and bloodless.

One of the witches asserted that the Devil, before her enlistment into his service, required of her the gift of some living animal, and that she presented him with a young fowl. The next night at the Sabbath, whither she was conveyed through the air after having duly anointed her body with the ointment given her by the Devil, she was made to renounce the Holy Trinity, and to promise obedience to her infernal master. It appeared also from the confessions that if the servants of Satan refused to do his behests, they are beaten and otherwise maltreated by him.

It is clear from the evidence given in many of the trials for witchcraft that the accused, in a majority of cases, were persons who trafficked on the ignorance and credulity of the people, and who encouraged the idea of their being possessed of supernatural powers so long as they found it profitable to do so.

Even in the present day there are people who are afraid to refuse to give alms to a beggar, lest an evil eye should be cast upon them ; and who can say how many deaths of cattle and pigs, attributed to witchcraft, may not have been caused by poison adroitly administered out of revenge for a supposed injury ?

In their nocturnal flights through the air to their appointed place of meeting with the Demon, witches were said to utter loud cries ; and persons may, perhaps, still be found ready to affirm that in tempestuous nights, when the wind was howling round their dwellings, they have been able to distinguish above all the tumult of the elements, the unearthly cry of "*Har-hèri* *! *qué-hou-hou!* *Sabbat! Sabbat.*" This cry is attributed to the "*gens du hocq*" or "*gens du Vendredi,*" as they are called by those whose prudence deters them from speaking of "sorciers" and "sorcières," lest the use of such offensive epithets should give umbrage. It is believed, too, that in their assemblies on Friday nights on the hill of Catiôroc, around the cromlech called "Le Trepied," or on the sands of Rocquaine Bay, they dance to a roundelay, the burden of which is "*Qué-hou-hou! Marie Lihou!*" Some suppose that these words are uttered in defiance of the Blessed Virgin Mary, in whose honour the church and priory were erected and dedicated by the name of Notre Dame, Ste. Marie de Lihou. They are now a heap of shapeless ruins, but the place must have been looked upon as one of peculiar sanctity, for even down to the present day French coasting vessels passing by salute it by lowering their topmast. It is not then to be wondered at if the infernal sisterhood— one of whose chief amusements, as is well known, is the raising of storms in which many a proud vessel goes down—should take a particular delight in insulting

---

* *Kè, Guè* or *Tiè* and *Hou* are epithets applied to the Diety in the Bas Breton. MS. Note by Mr. George Métivier.

"*Sabot-Daim*—a witch hornpipe." (Idem.)

the "Star of the Sea," the kind and ever-watchful guardian of the poor mariner.

. Wizards and witches are supposed to have the power of navigating on the sea in egg-shells, and on the blade-bones of animals. It is to prevent this improper use of them that the spoon is always thrust through the egg-shell after eating its contents, and that a hole is made through the blade-bone before throwing it away.

It is believed that witches have the power of assuming the shape of various animals, and many stories turn on the exercise of this supposed faculty. The favourite forms with them appear to be those of cats, hares, and "cahouettes"* or red-legged choughs. It is not easy to conjecture how this beautiful and harmless bird got into such bad company; perhaps its predilection for the wild and unfrequented cliffs and headlands, where the witches are supposed to hold their unholy meetings, may have gained it the reputation of being in alliance with them.

In Guernsey, as elsewhere, a horseshoe, nailed on the lintel, door, or threshold, or on the mast or any other part of a ship or boat, is supposed to be a

---

* Mr. Métivier, in his *Dictionnaire Franco-Normand*, has a long article on "cahouettes." He says :—

"They play, in neo-latin mythology, a very interesting part, even to-day some traces of which are to be found. Wizards and witches, according to the councils, disguised themselves formerly as 'cahouets' and 'cahouettes.' Raphaël, Archbishop of Nicosie, capital of the island of Cyprus, in the year 1251, excommunicated all the 'cahouets' and the 'cahouettes' as well as those who supported and encouraged games of chance.—*(Constitutions, ch. 15).* And the Council of Nîmes, thirty years after, treats in the same manner witches and sooth sayers, 'coavets' and "coavettes,"

"In the hierarchy of Mithras, that type of the rising sun which bewitched the Gauls, the deacon, or minister was entitled 'corneille' or *rook*; and on the

sure preservative against witchcraft, and, although a black cat is one of the most frequent disguises assumed by Satan's imps and servants, the household in which a cat without a single white hair is domesticated, is thought to be highly favoured, as none of the infernal gang will venture to molest it. As some persons are fully persuaded that every black cat, however tame and well-behaved it may appear to be, is in reality in league with the Prince of Darkness, it may be that any interference on the part of others of the fraternity is contrary to the rules established among them, and resented accordingly, the old saying that " two of a trade cannot agree," holding good in this case.

Allusion has been made to those who have an interest in encouraging a belief in witchcraft, and there is no doubt that persons who, for some· reason or other, enjoy the unenviable reputation of dabbling in this forbidden art, now that they have no longer the fear of the stake and faggot before their eyes, and have only the minor terrors of a Police Court to dread, are not altogether unwilling to brave the latter danger if, by working on the credulity of the

---

first day of the year, according to Porphyry, the initiates disguised themselves severally as beasts and birds."

Mr. Métivier ends by citing two authorities on ancient traditions concerning these birds.

" Le corbeau est consacré à Apollon, et il est son ministre *(famulus),* voilà pourquoi il possède la faculté de prédire." *Gérard Jean Voss, liv.* 3, *sur l'Idolâtrie.*

" Je crois que ces cérémonies se célébraient près de Coptos, ville dont le nom était si fameux, et d'où vient l'Egypte. Dans les environs de cette cité, on voyait deux corbeaux, c'étaient les seuls . . . . Et il y avait là l'image d'Apollon, auquel les corbeaux étaient consacrés."

La corneille est le symbole de l'amour conjugal." *Nicolas Caussin, Jésuite, natif. de Troyes, Notes sur Horapollo. Paris,* 1618, p. 165.

ignorant and superstitious, they can extort money, or even command a certain amount of consideration as the possessors of supernatural powers.

Few would venture in the present day to acknowledge openly that they could injure their neighbours by the exercise of unholy arts ; but many may be found who pretend to a secret knowledge which may be used for beneficent purposes.

The difference, however, between a true witch—the servant of Satan—and what is commonly called " a white witch," has never been clearly defined. The latter is known in Guernsey by the name of " désorceleresse " or " désorceleur," for the art is quite as frequently, if not more frequently, exercised by men than by women. The persons who practise it pretend to be able to declare whether man or beast is suffering from the effects of witchcraft, to discover who it is that has cast the spell, and, by means of spells and incantations, to counteract the evil influence. It is clear, however, that one who is in possession of such powers must himself have a very intimate and profound knowledge of the arts he is fighting against, and that, if offended, he may perhaps be tempted to practise them. The " désorceleur " thus is as much feared as trusted, and as, of course, he cannot be expected to give his valuable services for nothing, the profession is often found to be very remunerative, large sums of money, besides presents in kind, being sometimes extorted from the superstition and fears of the credulous dupes.

There is no doubt, however, that some of these pretenders have some skill in the cure of the diseases to which cattle are liable, and even that some of the minor ailments to which the human race are subject, are occasionally relieved by them, especially those—and among ignorant, uneducated people they are not few—which arise out of a disordered imagination. The habits of close observation which those of his profession acquire must needs give the " désorceleur " a great insight into character ; his cunning will soon teach him how to work on the fears and credulity of those who come to consult him, and his experience will guide him into the best way of exercising his knowledge.

How far the so-called white-witches are believers in their own supernatural powers is an open question. It may be that, in making use of certain forms or practices which they have learned from others, they may be fully persuaded in their own minds of their efficacy, it may be that in some cases they are labouring under a sort of hallucination.

A noted bone-setter, who, it is said, was occasionally resorted to when man or beast was supposed to be under evil influence, or when it was sought to discover the perpetration of a theft, used to account for his pretended knowledge of the anatomy of the human body by asserting solemnly that this know-ledge had been revealed to him in a vision from Heaven, and he had repeated this story so often that it was evident to his hearers that he had come at last to believe fully in the truth of what he said.

The rustic bone-setter is not necessarily a " désorceleur," although, as in the instance just noticed, the two professions may be combined; but he is skilled in the cure of those somewhat mysterious ailments known as " une veine trésaillie," which seems to be a sprain or strain, and "les

côtaïs bas," which may be defined as that sort of
dyspeptic affection which the lower orders call a
" sinking of the stomach " or " all-overness." This
ailment is supposed popularly to be caused by the
ribs slipping out of their place, and is cured by
manipulation and pushing them gradually back into
their proper position. The efficacy of friction properly
applied in reducing a sprain is well known, and
accounts for the frequent success of the bone-setter
in the treatment of " veines trésaillies."

Some of these practitioners—old women as well as
men—pretend to have the gift of causing warts to
disappear by counting them, and asking certain
questions of the persons applying to them for relief.
The principal information they seem to wish to arrive
at is the age of the person; and this known, they
predict that the warts are likely to disappear within
a certain time. As these unsightly excrescences affect
more particularly young persons, and as it is known
that they frequently disappear naturally at that age
when youth is passing into manhood, it is not
unlikely that this fact may have been observed, and
the knowledge of it turned to account. It is believed
that those who possess the secret may impart it to
one, and to one only; but they must receive neither
fee nor reward for so doing; for if they do, or if
they tell it to more than one, they lose their power
of curing. They must not receive money for their
services, but if a cure is effected they are at liberty
to take a present.

As might be expected, fortune-telling forms no
small part of the white-witch's profession, although
all do not practise it, and some confine themselves
to this particular branch alone. Cards seem to be

"Town Harbour, from an old picture."

now the principal means used for prying into the secrets of futurity, but other appliances have been used, and may, perhaps, still be used by some, such as the detection of a thief by means of a Bible and key.

A sort of rhabdomancy, or divination by small rods, shuffled together with certain ceremonies and charms, and then thrown on the ground, was used by a sort of half-demented creature called Collas Roussé, about the end of the last century.

He is said to have had a good deal of shrewdness, to have been very quick at repartee, and to have had great facility in expressing himself in rhymed sentences. He appears to have believed that he was really in possession of supernatural knowledge, and as his assumption of extraordinary powers gained credence with the vulgar, he found it an easy task to make a profit of their credulity. It is reported of him that when brought to justice for some gross act of imposition, he had the audacity to threaten his judges with the effects of his vengeance. His threats, however, did not deter the magistrates from sentencing him to exposure in the cage on a market day, with his divining apparatus by his side. He bore his punishment bravely, and entertained the multitude who crowded to see him with rhyming remarks. Another species of rhabdomancy is the use of the divining rod, the efficacy of which is fully believed in, not only for the discovery of springs of water, but also for the revealing of the spot where treasure has been concealed ; and, if the stories that are told are all to be depended upon, there is evidence sufficient to stagger the sturdiest unbeliever.

A country gentleman, now dead, whom nobody who knew him took for a conjurer, was particularly renowned for his skill in this art. Not only could he tell by means of the rod where a spring of water was to be found, and to what depth it would be necessary to dig before coming to it, but he could also discover in what part of a field or house money or plate had been hidden. In order, however, to perform this last feat, it is necessary that the rod should be previously touched with metal of the same kind as that to be sought for. It is only in the hands of some few favoured individuals that the rod works, and even then it does so in various degrees; with some, being violently agitated, with others, moving slowly, and sometimes imperceptibly. The art of holding the forked stick may be taught to anyone, but unless a natural aptitude exists, the rod remains inert in the grasp of the holder.

A portion of the confessions of some of the unfortunate victims who suffered at the stake in 1617, translated from the records preserved in the Register Office of the Royal Court of Guernsey, will be given as a specimen of the absurdities to which credence could be given in a superstitious age.*

It must not, however, be forgotten that the island did not stand alone in this belief. No part of Europe seems to have escaped the absurd dread of witchcraft, which, like a pestilence, spread from one nation to another, and from which even the most learned of the age, men of profound thought, did not escape. One curious fact may be noticed; the

EDITOR'S NOTE.—* These are also given in full, in French, with an English translation, by Mr. J. Linwood Pitts, F.S.A., (Normandy), in his *Witchcraft and Devil-Lore in the Channel Islands*, etc., 1886.

T

practices imputed to the accused, who were for the most part of the lowest and most ignorant classes of society, and to which in numberless instances they confessed, appear to have been nearly identical in all countries. The inference is that they must have been handed down from a very remote period, and that they were in use among the pretenders to magical arts and supernatural powers among our pagan ancestors; just as in the present day we find similar ideas and practices existing among savage tribes, and in semi-civilised countries where the light of Christianity has not yet penetrated. It is well known how difficult it is to wean a people from their primitive belief, and how prone they are to cling to it in secret. Is it not possible that some secret society may have existed for ages after the spread of the Gospel in which heathen practices may have been perpetuated?

Trials for Witchcraft, and Confessions of Witches.*

15TH MAY, 1581.

Katherine Eustace and her daughter were accused by common consent of practising the art of witchcraft in the island.

The wife of Collas Cousin deposed that having

EDITOR'S NOTE.—* The documents which follow are translated from the Records of the Royal Court preserved at the Greffe. Sir Edgar MacCulloch had copied out the depositions of the witnesses on loose sheets of paper, evidently meaning to incorporate them into his book. The " Confession of the Witches " in his MS. follows his essay on Witchcraft.

refused to give milk to the accused, saying that there were poorer people to whom she would rather give, her cow then gave blood instead of milk.

Johan Le Roux deposed that having been seized with great pains in his knee, he believed himself to be bewitched by Katherine Eustace, so his wife went to the latter and threatened to denounce her to the Royal Court; after that he got better.

28TH OCTOBER, 1581.

Robert Asheley, found dead in the garden behind St. Peter Port parsonage, suspected of having committed suicide by shooting himself with an arquebus. This having been proved according to the law, the Court, after hearing the speech made by Her Majesty's Procureur, found that the said Robert Asheley shall be carried to some unfrequented spot and there buried, a heap of stones being placed on his body,* and thus he shall be deprived of burial in the spot where Christian remains are placed; and that all his goods shall be confiscate to Her Majesty the Queen.

25TH FEBRUARY, 1583.

Collas de la Rue is accused of using the arts of witchcraft, and of grievously vexing and tormenting divers subjects of Her Majesty.

Matthieu Cauchez deposed that his wife being in a pining languorous condition, having heard that Collas de la Rue was a wizard, and knowing that

---

EDITOR'S NOTE.

* See in " Hamlet," where the priest refuses Christian burial to Ophelia as a suicide, and commands : —" Shards, flints, and pebbles should be thrown upon her."

It has been conjectured that these heaps of stones were placed upon graves, more especially of criminals and suicides, to keep the spirit in the earth, and prevent the ghost from walking. Hence the modern gravestone.

he frequently visited his house, he asked him if he could help his wife. Collas replied :—

"As to her she is an 'in pace' (sic), she will not live much longer."

De la Rue came to the place where his wife lay ill, and caused the bed to be reversed, putting the bolster at the foot; she died three hours afterwards.

James Blanche affirmed that having failed in a promise he had made to De la Rue, the latter swore he should repent. His wife soon afterwards became swollen all over, in which state she remained for some considerable time. He finally went to De la Rue, and consulted him as to how to cure his wife, and he gave him a decoction of herbs to be used as a drink, by which his wife was cured.

Thomas Behot deposed that on returning from fishing, he refused to give some fish to the son of Collas De la Rue. The son said he was a "false villain," and complained to his father, who on that said, "*Tais-toy, il n'en peschera plus guères.*" ("Be quiet, he will not catch many more.") That same day he was taken ill, and became so swollen that he could not rest between his sheets—(en ses draps). After having been ill for a long time, his wife unsewed his mattress and found therein several sorts of grains, such as broom, "alisandre" "nocillons" or "nerillons de fèves," (black beans?), the treadles of sheep, pieces of laurel, rags with feathers stuck into them,* and several other things. His wife threw it

EDITOR'S NOTE.—* In a letter called "Voudouism in Virginia," quoted by Mr. Moncure D. Conway in his book on *Demonology and Devil-Lore*, Vol. l., p. 69., the following similar superstition is noticed. "If an ignorant negro is smitten with a disease which he cannot comprehend, he often imagines himself the victim of witchcraft, and, having no faith in 'white folks' physic' for such ailments, must apply to one of these quacks. A physician residing near this city (Richmond), was invited by such a one to witness his mode of procedure with a dropsical patient for whom the physician in question had occasionally charitably prescribed. On the coverlet of the bed on which the sick man lay, was spread a quantity of

all into the fire, and such an awful smell arose from the flames that they were obliged to leave the room, and immediately his swelling disappeared. The same day he was taken with such violent pains that he thought his last hour was come. Whereupon his wife put the key of their front door in the fire, and, as soon as it began to get red hot, Collas de la Rue, who had not been invited, and who had not put foot inside their house for six years, arrived there before sunrise, and said that he would undertake to cure him, but that it would be a lengthy operation, that he would have to refer to a book that he had at home, by which he had cured several people, Matthieu Cauchez among others, and that also he (the witness) would be cured. So Collas made him some poultices of herbs, but they did not cure him. With great difficulty he dragged himself to St. Martin's Church (au temple de St. Martin), where De la Rue said to him :—

"I am glad to see you here, and yet not entirely glad, for you are not yet cured."

When the deponent replied that he soon hoped to be on the sea again, De la Rue replied :

"Do not go, for you will not return without great danger." ("N'y vas pas, car à grand' peine en reviendras tu.")

However, he persisted in going, and encountered such bad weather that he and all the crew were

---

bones, feathers and other trash. The charlatan went through with a series of so-called conjurations, burned feathers, hair, and tiny fragments of wood in a charcoal furnace, and mumbled gibberish past the physician's comprehension. He then proceeded to rip open the pillows and bolsters, and took from them some queer conglomerations of feathers. These he said had caused all the trouble. Sprinkling a whitish powder over them he burnt them in his furnace. A black offensive smoke was produced, and he announced triumphantly that the evil influence was destroyed and that the patient would surely get well. He died not many days later, believing, in common with all his friends and relatives, that the conjurations of the 'trick doctor' had failed to save him only because resorted to too late."

nearly drowned. And returning very ill, and his malady continuing, his wife again unsewed his mattress and there found an image made of a bone-like substance and apparently all gnawed, (d'une manière d'os tout rongé) which he took to the magistrates, and afterwards got better.

Collas De la Rue also told him that Collas Rouget had gone to Normandy to seek a cure. Had he only consulted him first, he need not have gone so far to be cured. In conclusion he said that on his conscience he believed and affirmed the said De la Rue to be a wizard.

Richard de Vauriouf deposed that having had several differences with Collas De la Rue on the subject of his cattle, which had caused him annoyance, De la Rue said to him :

" You are very strong and active, but before long you will not be thus, and you will be humbled after another manner." (" Tu es bien robuste et fort, mais avant qu'il soit guères ce ne sera pas ainsy, et tu seras autrement abaissé.")

Very soon afterwards the said Vauriouf was taken ill, and so was one of his daughters, and he was weak and languishing for more than a month.

Pierre Tardif, who had had some law-suits with Collas De la Rue, deposed that thereupon his daughter was taken ill, and her mattress being searched they found several . . . . (here and in various places the record is torn) . . . . of several kinds, and being . . . . made principally of a coloured silken thread and of . . . . of broom, of beans cut up, two of them being black . . . . a pin stuck in a piece of rag and . . . . After having taken advice he (Tardif) had thrashed De la Rue . . . . after having

" Royal Court House."

given him two knock-down blows, his daughter was
all right again. After which she was again taken ill,
so he searched for De la Rue, and, having found
him, he again thrashed him, this time drawing blood,
and shortly after that his daughter was cured. In
conclusion he also deposed upon oath his belief that
De la Rue was a wizard.

. . . . deposed as to having heard Collas De la Rue
say that he had means to silence those who spoke
ill of him ("qu'il avait des moyens de faire taire
ceux qui parloient mal de luy."

(The record is here again torn, and the trial apparently did not conclude, but in 1585 the proceedings
against Collas De la Rue were recommenced and many
of the same witnesses appeared).

The Trial of Collas de la Rue resumed.

17th December, 1585.

Collas Hugues appeared in person and showed his
child to us in the Court. This said child cannot talk
except at random and with an impediment in its
speech that none can cure ; and he declares his
conviction that his said child is "detained" (detenu)
by some wizard, and he will take his oath that it is
Collas De la Rue who "detains" him, inasmuch
that the latter threatened him that he would afflict
him through his most precious treasure (du plus
cher joyau qu'il peut avoir). On this declaration,
Her Majesty's Procureur testified to us that the said
De la Rue had formerly been imprisoned for sorcery,
and now, that though he had not always been
proved guilty, yet that to all outward appearance he
had practised the art of witchcraft, and so much so,
that new complaints being made against him, he had

demanded the arrest and the confiscation of the goods of the said De la Rue, which was granted.

On the 25th of December an investigation was ordered.

DECEMBER, 1585.

James Blanche affirms that on a certain day, having promised to go for a day's work to the aforesaid De la Rue, and not having done so, that he was heard to say to one of his people, that he, Blanche, should repent, and that soon afterwards his wife was seized with an illness which lasted for nearly a year. So that, finding the said De la Rue near "La Croix Guerin," * he asked him if he could give him something to cure his wife. Then the said De la Rue took an apple, which he broke into six parts, of which he retained one, and gave the remaining five pieces to the said Blanche to carry back to his wife, forbidding him at the same time to eat a mouthful. Notwith-standing, when he quitted De la Rue, he ate the said apple, and at that moment the said De la Rue appeared before him, he having not yet reached his own house, and taxed him with having eaten the forbidden apple, and the same day his wife was cured. He, Blanche, says that this is a man given to threats, and is much suspected and generally denounced as being a wizard, and he has even heard that people have called him "sorcier" to his face and he has not resented it.

DECEMBER, 1585.

Jehennet des Perques deposed that at divers times the said Collas De la Rue went to the fishermen and foretold to them when they should have fine weather

EDITOR'S NOTE.—* The old name for the cross roads at St. Martin's, near where the village Post Office now stands.

and when they should have storms. . . . . He was
commonly reported to be a .wizard. He also deposed
that on a certain day, he being at the house of Collas
Henry, where the said De la Rue had quarrelled with
the wife of Collas de Bertran, who had called him
" sorcier " (wizard), he threatened her that she
should repent, and that the said Mrs. de Bertran fell
in descending the stairs (cheut aval les degrez)
and bruised herself from head to foot.

Several witnesses depose that Collas De la Rue is
a man much given to threats, that various persons
have fallen ill after having been threatened by him,
and that he cured them at his will.

He was sent back to prison.

It appears that Collas De la Rue was executed,
for, in a lawsuit against Denis de Garis for concealing
a treasure that he had found in his house, it is said
that the aforesaid treasure was found on the day of
Collas De la Rue's execution, that is to say the
25th of March, 1585-6.

24TH NOVEMBER, 1602.

Marie Roland is accused of sorcery.

John Sohier witnesses that the aforesaid Marie,
having been with him one day at the house of the
Henry's, together with Joan Henry, whose child lay
ill, she confessed to having bewitched the child, and
on being asked in what manner, said that she had
put its clothes one night by the stream (auprès du
douit) and that she and her master the Devil then
entered into the house of the said Henry by the
chimney, and found the said child by the hearth,
and with a splinter she pricked the child, and it
was bewitched for three months.

10TH APRIL, 1613.

An inquest on the suspicions of witchcraft against Olivier Omont, Cecile Vaultier, his wife, and Guillemine Omont, their daughter.

Jacques Bailleul deposed that having refused alms to Olivier Omont his son was taken with a pain in his ear which lasted twenty-four hours, that the doctor said that he could not understand it (qu'il n'y connaissait rien), that he believes that Olivier is a wizard.

Guillemine Le Pastourell affirms that Omont came begging from her, and she said that he was stronger than her and that he could gain his bread if necessary without begging, that the next day she was taken ill, that she remained ill for three weeks, that Omont, having come again, gave her some bread, and after that she recovered. During her illness all her cattle died. She believed it was from some spell cast by the said Omont.

Marie Sohier witnesses that the day after the death of her husband Olivier Omont came to her house demanding bread. She replied that having numerous children to feed she could not spare him any, that he went away grumbling. At that very moment her daughter Marguerite, aged six years, was taken ill, and when they gave her some bread she threw it away and ate cinders by the handful. That her daughter Marie, one year old, was taken ill one hour after the departure of Omont, and she had remained ill for two years. That having met Omont at the Mont Durand she threatened to throw a stone at him, and called him "sorcier," that on returning home she gave a lump of white bread to her child, who ate it all, and since then is quite well. She believes that the said Omont was the cause of the sickness of her children.

Philippin Le Goubey witnesses that Olivier Omont having begged for cider from his wife, she refused him, and was instantly afflicted with grievous pains; that he entreated the said Omont several times to come into his house to see his wife, but that he always refused; that one day he forced him to enter, and he put one foot in the house and the other out, and then he fled; that rushing after him he threatened to denounce him to justice if he would not cure his wife; that then he said that she would be well again in a fortnight, but that he could not cure her at that moment; that he forced him to return to the house, and that, when there, he threatened to keep him there until he was delivered up to justice; that at that very moment his wife was cured of the worst of her pains; that having shortly afterwards come into the town to make a notification of these things, he found that the said Omont had already taken a boat and fled from the country.

Pierre Simon, of Torteval, being at the Hougue Antan,* met Olivier Omont lying with his face against the ground. He tried to awake him, shook him, and heard a buzzing (un bourdonnement) but saw nothing. Feeling rather frightened he left him and went on towards the Buttes† of Torteval, and then came back to the place where he had left him. Omont suddenly awoke, having his mouth full of mud,

---

* This is a hill at Torteval, on which, says Mr. Métivier, our ancestors used to light signal fires near the "Hougue Hérault," where the northern King *Herolt* made his signals.   He says the name is derived from the Breton *An Tat,* "the old Father," a name for the God of the Gauls; in Swedish it is *Anda,* the spirit, or *Onda,* the evil one.   See Notes in *Rimes Guernesiaises.*

† These were the mounds of earth where they practised with the cross-bow before the introduction of muskets.   The "Buttes" still exist in some parishes,

and his face all disfigured (défiguré). Omont having been questioned replied that he had fallen from the cliff, and that Pierre Nant had seen him fall.

Several people witnessed that having refused alms to Omont and to his wife, their cattle fell ill and died, their cows gave blood instead of milk, or gave nothing at all, their sows and their cows miscarried, and misfortunes happened to their wives.

29TH JUNE, 1613.

Thomas Mancell witnessed that his wife having refused alms to Omont, their cow fell ill, and they were obliged to kill it. Jean Hamon, who flayed the cow, cut it at the shoulder, and "there issued a black beast as large as a little 'cabot' (a small fish). Its throat was such that one could easily insert the tip of one's little finger, and it had two little wings" ("en sortit une beste noire, grosse comme un petit cabot, dans la gueule duquell on aurait bien mis le bout du petit doigt et avait deulx petites ailes.")

Jean Le Feyvre, of the Mielles,* witnesseth that one morning he found Cécile, wife of Omont, near the Chapelle de l'Epine, where she was searching, he could not tell for what, and where she remained for a long while without his being able to perceive that she found anything, and she did not perceive that he was watching her; and he having asked her shortly afterwards whether it was she that he had observed at such an hour near the chapel, she denied

---

* *Mielles*, in Normandy, Brittany, and the Channel Islands, means the "waste lands on the sea-shore." In the Vale parish alone there were two estates called "Les Mielles." See Métivier's *Dictionary*, *Mielles*.

it, and that afterwards he asked her again whether it was she who was in that neighbourhood, and she replied in the affirmative, and then he started fine rumours, (ung beau bruit) saying that she was dancing on the thorn which grows in the aforesaid neighbourhood.

29TH MAY, 1613.

Thomasse, wife of Collas Troussey, deposes that one night, her husband being on guard at the Castle, she was awakened by a frightful noise, like cats squalling, and she dared not cry out on account of Olivier Omont, who was sleeping in the same corridor as herself, though the miauling of the cats still continued. When her husband was returned from his patrol, she dared ask Omont if he had not heard the cats, to which he replied Yes, but there was nothing for her to be afraid of, that they would do her no harm. That another night, her husband being also there, she had heard Omont call "Cats! cats!" and on asking him if he had cats in his wallet (en son bisac,) he replied "No," and that the noise seemed beneath where she lay, but that he was afraid that they would eat the fish that was on the table.

Olivier Omont, his wife and daughter, were all banished from the island.

30TH JUNE, 1613.

An enquiry was held on Laurence L'Eustace, wife of Thomas Le Comte, suspected of being a witch.

Jean Hallouvris witnesses that for four years he has driven his cart. As the wheels passed close to Laurence she dropped several strings and twists of

" High Street, 1850,"

Sketched from an Old Picture by the late Mr. A. C. Andros.

rushes (quelques colliers et nattes de pavie) * that she was carrying, at which she was very angry. Two days afterwards, one of his bullocks set off running as if it were mad, and then fell down stone dead, and the other bullock died the next day.

Pierre Machon deposes that he has heard Laurence swear "By God's ten fingers" ("Par les dix doigts de Dieu"), and with oaths and blasphemies call devils to her assistance.

Christine, wife of Pierre Jehan, says that her first husband, Collas Henry, having had a quarrel with Laurence Le Comte, one of their children, aged two years, was taken with an illness which lasted for twelve months. When the attack first came on, he jumped high into the air, that, before being taken ill he walked very well, but that afterwards, all that year he crawled on his hands and knees. That, having had a quarrel with the said Laurence, and having put some curds to cool, (des caillebottes à refroidir), she found them the next day just like bits of rag (que de la mêque), and that on the following Monday the child was seized with terror, and cried out that someone was pulling his nose. That, as soon as she went to Laurence's house, the child got better, but, on her return, fell ill again, and finally died.

Laurence L'Eustache, wife of Thomas Le Comte, was also banished from the island.

On the 17th of May, 1617, began the trial of Collette du Mont, widow of Jean Becquet, Marie, her daughter, wife of Pierre Massy, and Isebel Becquet, wife of Jean Le Moygne.

EDITOR'S NOTE.—* Pavie used to be grown in ponds arranged for the purpose, and was used for making pack-saddles, horse-collars, mats, etc. It is a reed.—*From John de Garis, Esq.*

James Gallienne witnesses that one day, having quarrelled with Jean Le Moigne, husband of the aforesaid Isebell, the said Le Moigne said to him :—

" You are always seeking to pick quarrels with me, and you say that my wife is a witch, but before six months are over you will be very glad to come and implore me to help you ; " that immediately his wife fell into a lingering illness, and, doubting not but that it was the effect of a spell, opened all the mattresses and found all kinds of filth and bits of feather, which he has showed to several people; and in some quite new pillows which he had at home he found a large quantity of worms. He says that about six years ago, one of his children being ill, he was putting a pillow under his head, found it hard, and, on unripping it, found it full of dirt. While they unsewed it they heard a flapping noise as of the wings of a cock, and the said child declared that he saw this cock ; that, having shut all the doors, they tried to find what it really was, and that, having hunted and ransacked the house, they saw first a rat, then a weasel, which slipped through the holes of the pavement (sortit par les pertius de la dalle). And at the end of two or three days he was asked why he had beaten the said Isebell Becquet. He replied that he had not touched her, and soon after that he was advised to try whether she was a witch, by putting the key of his front door (de son grand huis) in the fire, which he did. When the said key had been nearly two days in the fire the said woman arrived at his house, without asking whether he were at home, and begged of him seven to nine (sept à neuf) things which he refused her, she

U

wishing at all hazards to come in further (entrer plus outre) to see the sick child, which he would not allow.

Item. Deposeth that his wife having rebuked the said Isebell because her children annoyed those of the said Gallienne, she went away very vexed, and the next day one of his oxen broke its neck, his mare miscarried, and his wife was taken ill.

Item ; that the children of the said Isebell said one day to the children of the said Gallienne, that if their mother was ill it was because she had spoken rudely ; that some time afterwards, Mrs. Gallienne being in bed in her room, the door being shut and simply a sky-light (une luquerne *sic*, lucarne) open, she felt something like a cat, which, little by little, crept on her chest as she lay on her bed. Having shaken it to the ground, she heard one or two growls, on which, astonished, she began to threaten it that if it was a wizard or a witch she would cut it to pieces (que le couperoit en pièces), it returned by the said sky-light.

Thomas Sohier said that Jean Jehan having summoned him to come and make his will, he complained that the said Isebell was killing him for having refused to make a jacket for her son. That some little time afterwards James Gallienne, having a sick daughter, caused her bed to be unripped, out of which came a sort of animal like a rat (une manière de bête comme un rat), which hid itself in some wood and was hunted for throughout the house ; that on the following day, having met the said Isebell, he noticed her face all torn (déchiré *sic*). On asking her the cause she said it was from " du mal d'Espagne," (cantharides, the

Spanish fly used for making blisters) ; that on that he asked James Gallienne if he had not beaten her, who replied in the negative ; that, being the other day at the house of the said Gallienne, giving evidence to this, his wife fell down as if dead, and on returning to consciousness, said that she was bewitched.

Item. Testifies that in the bed of the aforesaid daughter (of Gallienne), were found twenty-one or twenty-two spells (sorcerons).*

Many other depositions told the same story. Oxen and calves died, cows and mares miscarried, sheep fell dead, children and women were taken ill, no cream was found on the milk, curds would not " make," cows dried up, or only gave blood. Worms were bred in the beds, or even under the women's caps. They were black at both ends, or sometimes had two heads. Frogs and black beasts (des bêtes noires) haunted the paths of the bewitched persons. Fountains were full of insects, black pimples appeared all over the bodies of the afflicted persons, and lice, in such abundance that they had to use a broom to sweep them away. On the witch being threatened the sick person recovered.

The trial was resumed on the 6th June, 1617.

Marie, wife of James Gallienne . . . .

deposed. . . Item ; that for nearly ten years her eldest daughter Rachel had been bewitched ; that, having unsewed her mattress, by which was some straw,†

EDITOR'S NOTES.

* (See footnote to p. 308). Some had a goat's hair intwined, others a flaxen thread.
  Mr. J. Linwood Pitts, in his pamphlet on *Witchcraft in the Channel Islands*, points out, page 6, " that the natural tendency of wool and feathers to felt and clog together, has been distorted, by widely different peoples, into an outward and visible sign that occult and malignant influences were at work.

† " Il y avoit de *l'etrain* "—a Guernsey-French word—from the old French *estrain, estraine,* lat. strannu.—See Métivier's *Dictionary* " Etrain."

something was seen lurking in the said straw, and Jean
Le Gallez, being present, said that it looked to him
like a black cat, and sometimes like a cock, and then
like a mouse, and then like a rat, that it—whatever
it was—hid in some wood which was in the house,
which was immediately rummaged and moved, but no
one knew how to capture it (ne sçurent tant faire
que de le prendre). That her husband saw it like a
cock, and her daughter like a mouse; that on opening
the mattress they found within it many spells (force
sorcerons) and also beans with which were mingled
black grains as if mildewed,* which beans or grains
having been put in a porringer (une écuelle) in
the presence of various women who were there, it
dissolved in their presence, and they did not know
what became of it (cela fondit en leur presence
et ne sçurent que devint.) That the said Isabell,
having come to the house at the end of two or
three days, and asking for seven or nine sorts of
things, and trying to force an entrance into the place
where the child was lying ill, all which things were
refused her by her husband, so she then went away,
and her face was all cut; and went to her
husband and said that she would not stay while
Isebell Becquet was there, and she believes that she
is a witch.

On the 4th of July, 1617, these three women,
Collette Dumont, widow of Jean Becquet, Marie,
her daughter, wife of Pierre Massy, and Isebell
Becquet, wife of Jean le Moigne, were convicted by
the Royal Court of Guernsey of having practised
the damnable art of sorcery, and of having thereby

Editor's Note. —* " Des graines noires comme de la neisle " (an old French word *nèle*, from
Latin *Nigella*)—Métivier's *Dictionary* " *Nele.*"

caused the death of many persons, destroyed and injured much cattle, and done many other evil deeds. They were condemned to be tied to a stake, strangled, and burnt until their bodies were totally consumed ; and their ashes to be scattered abroad. The sentence added that, previous to execution, they were to be put to the torture* in order to force them to declare the names of their accomplices.

First, the said Collette, immediately after the said sentence had been rendered, and before leaving the Court, freely acknowledged that she was a witch, but would not particularise the crimes which she had committed ; whereupon she was conducted with the others to the torture-house, and, being put to the question, confessed that the Devil, when she was still young, appeared to her in the form of a cat,† in the parish of Torteval, it being yet day, as she was returning from tending her cattle ; that he prevailed upon her by inviting her to revenge herself on one of her neighbours with whom she was on bad terms in consequence of some injury done to her by his cattle ; that on subsequent occasions, when she had quarrelled with anyone, he again appeared to her in the same form, and sometimes in that of a dog,

---

EDITOR'S NOTE.

* The manner in which torture was administered in Guernsey is thus described by Warburton, herald and antiquary, *temp.* Charles II., in his *Treatise on the History, Laws and Customs of the Island of Guernsey,* 1682, page 126,

"By the law approved (*Terrien,* Lib. XII, Cap. 37), torture is to be used, though not upon slight presumption, yet where the presumptive proof is strong, and much more when the proof is positive, and there wants only the confession of the party accused. Yet this practice of torturing does not appear to have been used in the Island for some ages, except in the case of witches, when it was too frequently applied, near a century since. The custom then was, when any person was supposed guilty of sorcery or witchcraft, they carried them to a place in the town called *La Tour Beauregard,* and there, tying their hands behind them by the two thumbs, drew them to a certain height, with an engine made for that purpose, by which means sometimes their shoulders were turned round, and sometimes their thumbs torn off ; but this fancy of witches has for some years been laid aside."

† Mary Osgood, one of the "Salem Witches" tried in 1692, confessed that "when in a melancholy condition she saw the appearance of a cat at the end of the house, which cat proved to be the Devil himself. See *Demonology and Devil-Lore,* Vol. II., p. 315.

inducing her to revenge herself against those with whom she was displeased, and persuading her to cause the death of men and beasts ; that the Devil having come to invite her to the Sabbath, called her, without its being perceived by others, and gave her a certain black ointment,* with which, having stripped, she rubbed her body nearly all over, and, having dressed herself again and gone out of doors, she was immediately carried through the air with great velocity to the place where the Sabbath was held, which was sometimes near the Torteval parish churchyard, and sometimes on the sea-shore near Rocquaine Castle ; that, being arrived there, she met frequently as many as fifteen or sixteen wizards and witches, with devils, who were there in the form of dogs, cats, and hares ; that she could not recognise the wizards and witches, because they were all blackened and disfigured, although she heard the Devil evoke them by name, and remembers among others, the wives Calais and Hardy. She confesses also that at the opening of the Sabbath, the Devil, in making the evocation, began sometimes by her name ; that her daughter Marie, wife of Massy, at present under condemnation for the same crime, is a witch, and that she has taken her twice to the Sabbath with her. She does not know where the Devil has marked her. She says that at the Sabbath they adored the Devil, who stood upon his hind legs . . . in the form of a dog, that afterwards they danced back to back, and after having danced they drank wine, but of what colour she does not know, which

---

* The Witches' Sabbath being a travesty of all Christian holy rites and ceremonies, the "black ointment" evidently represented the chrism.

" Castle Cornet, 1660."

the Devil poured out of a flagon into a silver or pewter goblet; but that the wine did not seem so good as that which is usually drunk, that they also ate white bread, which the Devil presented to them, but that she has never seen any salt[*] at the Sabbath.

She confesses that the Devil had charged her to call in on her way for Isebell Le Moigne, when she went to the Sabbath, and that she has done so several times; that on leaving the Sabbath the Devil invited her to perpetrate many evils, and that, for this purpose he gave her certain black powders, which he ordered her to throw on such persons and beasts as she pleased; and that with this powder she did much evil, which she cannot now call to mind, but she remembers that she threw some over Mr. Dolbel, the minister of the parish, and by this means was the cause of his death. With the same powder she bewitched the wife of Jean Manguès, but denies that her death was caused by it. She says that she touched the side, and threw some of this powder on the wife,[†] since deceased, of Mr. Perchard, who succeeded Mr. Dolbel as minister of the parish, thereby causing her death and that of her unborn babe. She cannot say what offence the deceased had given her. She says that on the refusal of Collas Tostevin's wife to give her some milk, she caused her cow to run dry by throwing some of the powder

---

over it, but that she cured the cow afterwards by giving it bran mixed with grass, which the Devil had given her, to eat.

The confession of her daughter Marie, wife of Pierre Massy, is much to the same effect, with this exception, that she seems to have been in the habit of meeting the Devil in the form of a dog, and that he changed her into an animal of the same species at the time of their interviews.

The third of these unfortunate wretches, Isebell, wife of Jean Le Moigne, enters, in her confession, into some additional details.

It was in the semblance of a hare, and in broad daylight, that the Devil appeared to her for the first time, and incited her to avenge herself on her sister-in-law, La Girarde, with whom she had quarrelled. At first she resisted the tempter, but he appeared to her a second time, again in the road next her house, and on this occasion left with her a packet of black powder, which she kept. A third time the demon appeared, in the same form, urging her, if she would not give herself to him, to make him a present of some living animal, whereupon she gave him a chicken, and he appointed her to meet him the next day before sunrise at the Sabbath, promising to send someone to guide her there. Accordingly old Collette Dumont came that night to her house, and gave her some black ointment, with which she rubbed herself. She was then carried over hedges and ditches to the place of meeting near Rocquaine Castle. She was received and welcomed by the Devil in the form of a dog, with long erect horns (avec de grandes cornes dressées en hautt), and hands like those of a man. He caused her to go down on her knees and renounce the Almighty in these words: "I deny God the Father, God the Son, and God the Holy Ghost." ("Je renie Dieu le Père, Dieu le Fils, et Dieu le Saint Esprit"). After this, she was made to adore the Devil and invoke him in these terms: "Our great Master, help us!" ("Nostre grand Maistre, aide nous!") and also to enter into an express covenant to adhere to his service. At the conclusion of this ceremony, the same acts of license, dancing and drinking (again bread and wine in mockery of the Holy Sacrament), took place as are described by Collette Dumont, widow Becquet, in her confession. On this occasion Isebell Le Moigne entered into a pact with Satan for one month only; but subsequently the agreement was extended to three years. She stated that Satan treated Collette Dumont with marked respect, always evoking her name first, styling her "Madame, la vieille Becquette," and giving her a place by his side. She also said that one night, when she was at the Sabbath, the Devil marked her on the thigh. The mark thus made having been examined by women appointed for that purpose, they certified that they had thrust pins deep into it, and that Isebell felt no pain therefrom, nor did any blood follow when the pins were withdrawn.

According to her account, the Devil appeared occasionally in the form of a he-goat, and when they took leave of him, they all had to kiss him, that he inquired of them when they would return, and exhorted them to adhere to him and do all the evil in their power. He then took them all by the hand and they departed in different directions. She asserted also that it was the Devil who had been seen in the forms of a rat and a stoat in the house of James Gallienne, whose child she had bewitched; that she was in the neighbourhood of the house at the time; and that the Devil, having resumed the form of a man, came to her and beat her severely about the head and face, which ill-treatment she attributed to her having refused to go with him to Gallienne's house. She said that she never went to the Sabbath except when her husband was gone out to sea for the night, fishing.

The depositions of the witnesses, taken down very minutely in the three cases above cited and in many others of a similar nature, have been preserved, and throw a good deal of light on the popular ideas of the day in respect to sorcerers and their doings.

WIZARDS AND WITCHES.

There are some families in Guernsey whose members have the reputation of being sorcerers from their birth. These individuals require no initiation into the diabolic mysteries of the " Sabbat," Satan claiming them as his own from the very cradle. They are, however, furnished by him with a familiar, generally in the shape of a fly, so that the phrase *" avoir une mouque"* is well understood as meaning that the person of whom it is said is one of the infernal fraternity. Indeed, in talking of persons who are addicted to magical arts, it is reckoned highly imprudent to speak of them as *" sorciers "* or *" sorcières,"* or to call them by the now almost-forgotten name of " Quéraud." * By so doing you give offence, and,

---

* Mr. Métivier derives this word " quéraud," meaning enchanter, or " maître sorcier," from the old French *charay, caral*, meaning magical type or letter. " In dog Latin *Caraco* was the writer or engraver of occult characters, and in the old French version of " Le Roman du Lancelot du Lac " it says that " Morgain, la seur au Roi Artur, sceut des enchantements et des *caraulx* plus que nulle femme."

what is of still more consequence, you put it in their power to injure you. It is, however, quite safe to speak of them as "*gens du Vendredi*," * or "*gens du hoc*." †

Satan does not always wait for their death to claim their souls as his own, but sometimes carries them off bodily; and a former schoolmaster of the Vale, who, from his eccentricities, had acquired the reputation of being a wizard, having disappeared mysteriously, and having never been seen again, is commonly believed, to this day, to have been spirited away.

Those who are born sorcerers have the faculty of transporting themselves at will wherever they please, but those who seek admission into the fraternity, and are initiated into the diabolical rites, are furnished by their infernal master with a certain ointment with which they anoint every part of their bodies before undertaking their aerial journeys. They are also supposed to be able to introduce themselves at night through the chinks and crevices of the buildings into the sheds in which the cattle are housed, for the purpose of milking the cows, not only thus depriving the owner of his property, but also worrying and alarming the poor animals, whose altered looks in the morning shew the ill-treatment to which they have been subjected. An old horse-shoe nailed on the door or lintel, or a

---

* Friday nights being always the nights appointed for the "Sabbat."

† Mr. Métivier translates this word *Hoc* as the great feast given by the enemy of mankind to his familiars, the wizards and witches. Like most of the words and customs connected with witchcraft it had originally a sacred meaning, for he says that the Hebrew word in the seventh verse of the second Psalm, translated "the decree" is "the Hoc," and means:—The law imposed by a King on his subjects from which there is no appeal.

naturally pierced flintstone pebble attached to the key of the stable door, are both considered efficacious in warding off these attacks—but an infallible method of driving off the witches is to suspend wreaths of the bramble from the rafters. Witches and wizards travelling, not on land, but through the air, finding these unexpected obstacles in their way, get scratched.*

After having rubbed themselves over with this ointment they are then instructed to pronounce without intermission the words " *Roule, roule, par dessus ronces et buissons.*" ("Roll, roll, above brambles and brakes ").

This was discovered in the following manner :—A prying valet, who lived in the service of a gentleman who was a wizard, of which fact he was nevertheless ignorant, was one day amusing himself by peeping through the key-hole of his master's bed chamber. He observed his master make use of the ointment, and heard distinctly the words which he pronounced, immediately after which he became invisible. Wishing to try the effect of the unguent on his own person, he entered the room, and went through the process of anointment, but when he came to pronounce the magic formula, he made use of the word " dessous " instead of " dessus " ("under" instead of "over.") Perhaps he was an Englishman, to whom the French " u " was an insurmountable difficulty. Be this as it may, he had reason to repent bitterly of his indiscreet curiosity, for, no sooner were the words out of his mouth, than he felt himself lifted up, and carried at a fearful rate through furze brakes and bramble hedges, while at the same

* From George Allez, Esq.

time he had the mortification to see his master
gliding along through the air, several feet above the
bushes, and laughing heartily at his misfortunes. At
last, dreadfully scratched and torn, and more dead
than alive, he arrived at the spot where the infernal
troops had their rendezvous, but was too much
frightened to notice what took place there, only too
happy to escape without being forced, against his will,
to enrol himself among them. His curiosity, however,
was effectually cured, and he vowed nevermore to
pry into his master's secrets.*

The following is another instance of the use of
this infernal ointment. It is related that a lady of
St. Pierre-du-Bois was astonished at the long time
her husband remained in his private apartment, and
her curiosity at last induced her to watch him.
Accordingly she one day concealed herself in the
room. Her husband came in shortly afterwards, and,
after stripping off all his clothes, proceeded to anoint
himself from head to foot with a certain ointment,
after which he repeated the words "*va et vient*" ("go
and come"), and immediately disappeared. Anxious
to know whither he was gone, she went through the
same ceremony, and no sooner had she repeated the

---

* From Miss Elizabeth Chepmell.

EDITOR'S NOTES.

* A very similar story is told in M. Paul Sebillot's *Traditions et Superstitions de la Haute
Bretagne*, Tome I., p. 277.

"Une femme avait deux enfants, quand elle, les avait couchés, elle sortait, et ils ne la
revoyaient que de matin. Un des enfants, qui commençait à être grand, fit mine de
s'endormir, il vit sa mère aller sous le lit, se mettre toute nue, et se frotter d'onguent, puis
dire, avant de partir :

" Par sur haies et bûchons (buissons) Faut que je trouve les autres où qu'ils sont."
Le gars, dès que sa mère fut partir, se frotta aussi avec l'onguent et dit :—" Par en travers
haies et bûchons. Faut que je trouve les autres où qu'ils sont." Mais, comme il s'était
trompé en répétant ce qu'il avait ouï dire, il passa à *travers* les ronces et les haies, et arriva
tout sanglant au rendezvous des sorciers. Il les trouva qui dansaient, et qui chantaient, et
sa mère était avec eux."

"Old Harbour."

mysterious words than she found herself on the
summit of Pleinmont, in the midst of a large
concourse of people. A table was set out, covered
with a variety of viands of which some present
invited her courteously to partake. Previously,
however, to touching anything, she, like a good
Christian, repeated aloud the words "*Au nom de
Dieu soit, Amen*, ("In the name of God, Amen"). No
sooner had the sacred name passed her lips than she
found herself alone. All had disappeared, and the
only signs which remained of any living beings having
been on the spot besides herself were recent marks of
cloven feet indented on the sward in every direction.

The Aerial Journey.

There is a story told of two men who were
neighbours and inhabitants of the parish of St.
Saviour's, that their occupation—that of quarrymen—
took them frequently to the Vale parish, where the
finest qualities of granite are to be procured. The
distance they had to traverse before arriving at their
destination was considerable, and the road in some
places, rather lonely.

Leonard Sarre, who was of a companionable nature,
thought that the tediousness of the way would be
considerably lessened by having someone to talk to,
even if it were only his fellow workman, Matthew
Tostevin, whose taciturnity and reserve were proverbial.
Often, when setting off in the early morning to go to
his work, he would, as he passed Tostevin's door,
look in and offer his company. The answer was
invariably the same :—

"Go on, I shall be there as soon as you, though
I shall not leave home for an hour to come."

When Sarre arrived at the quarry where they worked he was frequently astounded at finding Tostevin already there. The way which Sarre took was the very shortest and most direct. He was confident that Tostevin could not pass without his perceiving him, and any other road would entail at least half-an-hour's extra walking to accomplish. There was evidently a mystery, and Leonard was resolved to fathom it.

At last, in answer to his repeated enquiries, Matthew told him that he was willing to let him into the secret. He bade him place his foot on one of his, clasp him tightly round the waist, shut his eyes closely, and, above all, on no account whatever, to utter a word.

Leonard Sarre did as he was directed, and immediately felt himself lifted into the air and carried along at a fearful rate. In his fright he forgot the injunctions that had been given him, opened his eyes, and, finding himself far above the earth, cried out in terror "*O, mon Dieu !*" The holy name dissolved the unhallowed spell, at least so far as poor Leonard was concerned. He fell; fortunately it was into one of the most boggy spots of La Grand' Mare, so he escaped with a few scratches and bruises, a thorough ducking, and a tremendous fright. What became of Matthew Tostevin is not known.

· It was not until many years had rolled over his head that Leonard Sarre ventured to relate his perilous adventure, and then Tostevin had long been dead.*

---

* From John De Garis, Esq.

W

The Countrywoman and the Witch.

The barren and rugged hill of Catiauroc, situated near the sea-shore in the parish of St. Saviour's, is the noted and favourite haunt of wizards and witches. Once every week on the Friday night they resort thither, and grand assemblies, at which their infernal master presides in person, are held at other seasons, particularly on St. Thomas', or the longest night, and on the eve of Christmas.

Though the power of sorcerers in doing harm is very great, yet they themselves are subject to all the accidents and infirmities of life, nor can their supernatural skill extricate them from any difficulty they may chance to get into.

A countrywoman left her cottage one morning at daybreak to look after her cows. In passing through a furze brake that led to the meadow she thought she perceived, by the yet imperfect light, what appeared to her a bundle of clothes thrown on the top of a hedge. On approaching nearer she was astonished to recognise a lady from the town, whose dress was so entangled in the brambles that it was impossible for her to extricate herself, or to descend from her elevated situation, and who was so exhausted that she had scarcely sufficient strength left to beg for assistance. It immediately occurred to her, that the lady in her aërial journey to the Catiauroc that night had kept too close to the earth, and thus had been caught by the bushes, but, remembering that there are some persons with whom it is better to be friends than enemies, she immediately drew near and assisted the lady to descend, at the same time expressing her surprise at seeing her in such a singular position, and begging her to walk into her cottage and rest herself.

"No," said the lady, thanking her, "I must now make the best of my way home. Mention to no living creature what you have seen this day, and all will go well with you, but bitterly will you repent your folly if you disobey this injunction."

She then left the countrywoman. It is not easy for a man to keep a secret from his wife, but it is almost impossible for a woman to conceal anything from her husband.

The secret weighed on the poor woman's heart and rendered her miserable, till at last she flattered herself she had discovered an expedient by which she might ease her mind without disobeying the commands put upon her. She therefore one morning desired her husband to follow her into the garden and stand at some little distance from her. She then addressed herself to a tree, and related to this inanimate object what she had seen, but the secret of course reached, as was intended, the ears of her husband. The subterfuge availed her nothing; before the close of day she was struck with deafness, and never, to her dying day, did she recover her hearing.

The old woman of the Castel, who related this story to Miss Lane, said that the woman was her great-aunt, and remembered having seen her when very young.

Stories very similar in their general features to the preceding are far from uncommon in the country, and in all the sorceress is represented as a lady of rank.

A countryman met a lady entangled in the brambles on the top of a hedge. He disengaged her, and was promised that as long as he kept the secret he should find every morning, under a stone which she pointed out to him, a piece of money.*

MAGIC BOOKS.

" O Faustus, lay that damnèd book aside
And gaze not on it, lest it tempt thy soul,
And heap God's heavy wrath upon thy head !
Read, read the Scriptures :—that is blasphemy."
—*Tragical History of Doctor Faustus*, by Christopher Marlowe.

Many persons, although not absolutely considered as wizards, are looked upon with no favourable eye from their supposed possession of books relating to the black art, by the study of which they are thought to be able to control the elements, to produce strange effects either for good or bad on the bodies of man and beast, to discover hidden secrets, treasure, etc.

These books are generally known by the name of *Albins*, probably derived from that famous professor of magic, Albertus Magnus, many of whose formulas for raising the Devil, etc., they are said to contain.

They are also called " *Le Grammaille* " or "*Grand-Mêle*," † and a distinction is made between the *Grand-Mêle* and the *Petit-Mêle*.

Among the effects which the possessors of these books are said to be able to produce is that of causing persons to walk in their sleep, and to direct their steps towards any point to which the dabbler in magic may wish them to go, but in order to

---

* From Miss E. Chepmell.

---

† Mr. Métivier in his dictionary translates *Grand-Mêle* as *Grimoire*, or the book by which sorcerers pretend to raise the dead, being derived from the old Norse word *grima*, a spectre, a witch, a word which is, he says, also the origin of "*grimace*." The *Grand-Mêle* of the Guernsey folk was literally the *big* book, just as the *Petit-Mêle* was the little book, *Mêle* being nothing but a survival of the Gothic *Meli*—a writing, discourse, or song. Also *Ma'l*, with the Norsemen, as *Veda* with the Hindoos, and as *Scripture* with us, was simply the collective name of all the holy books.

accomplish this, it is necessary that he should have previously drawn blood from the person on whom he intends to practise his unlawful art. So small a quantity however as that produced by the scratch of a pin is amply sufficient for the purpose.

These books are said to be indestructible. If thrown on the fire they remain unconsumed, if sunk in the sea, or buried in the earth, they will be found again the next day in the cupboard or chest from whence they were taken.*

THE PRIOR OF LIHOU.

The small islet of Lihou lies on the western coast of Guernsey, from which it is separated by an arm of the sea. An ancient causeway, which is uncovered at half-tide, affords an easy access to the main-land, but it is dangerous to attempt the passage when the tide is flowing, for the coast is so flat that the water rises with great rapidity, and many accidents have occurred. A church, the ruins of which are still to be seen, existed here until the Reformation. It was

---

* From Elizabeth Matthieu.

EDITOR'S NOTES.

* Nowadays the people, in speaking of the "bad books" as they frequently term them, call them the "*Grand Albert*" and the "*Petit Albert*," the former being undoubtedly derived from "Albertus Magnus." The "Petit Albert" is an abridgment of the larger book, and is supposed to be comparatively harmless, and, with proper precautions, some say it may even be used by good Christians. The country people to this day believe these books to be imperishable, and many is the tale they tell of how they will neither drown, nor burn, and how in particular, one old wizard's books at Saints' Bay had to be buried, and part of the funeral service read over them, to keep them from reappearing on their accustomed shelf.

Our old nurse, Margaret Mauger, has often told me the story of the books belonging to an extremely clever old gentleman who owned an estate in the country. At his death, when his daughters came to divide his large library, they were horrified to find many "witch books" and atheistical books included in it. These they set aside to be burnt, and also a great many harmless but dull histories, biographies, and sermons, which they did not wish to keep, and made one huge bonfire. But (and it was one of the daughters who vouched for the truth of this story) the good books would not burn with the bad books! A frightful smell arose, and thick columns of black smoke, but none were consumed, and they all had to be re-sorted, and made into two separate piles,—the sheep and the goats—and then they all burnt readily enough.—*From Margaret Mauger.*

" In Denmark and some neighbouring countries it is believed that a strange and formidable book exists, by means of which you can raise or lay the Devil—called the *Book of Cyprianus.* The owner of it can neither sell, bury or burn it, and if he cannot get rid of it before his death he becomes the prey of the fiend."—*Demonology and Devil-Lore*, by Moncure Conway, Vol. 2., p. 282.

dedicated to Notre Dame de la Roche, and was served by a prior, who was appointed by the Prior of St. Michel du Valle, a dependency of the great Abbey of Mont St. Michel-au-peril-de-la-Mer, in the Bay of Avranches. The isle is to this day looked upon with such veneration by the Norman and Breton sailors employed in the coasting trade, that they never pass it without saluting, by lowering their topmasts, and there is reason to believe that it was a favourite resort of pilgrims. A house belonging to a family of the name of Lenfestey, and situated at Les Adams, is said to have been, in former days, the residence of the priest who officiated at Lihou. A free-stone let into one of the exterior walls has a rough delineation of a church incised on it, which is said to represent the Priory Church of Lihou as it formerly existed.*

Stone supposed to represent the ancient Priory at Lihou.

EDITOR'S NOTE.

* Mr. S. Carey Curtis, who is an architect, has made some very interesting plans of the ruins of Lihou Priory, and has shown their correspondence with the architecture of the building depicted on this stone. I will quote his exact words:—

"There is built into the wall of a house, on the Paysans Road, a sculptured stone, which corresponds so exactly with what might have been the Chapel of Lihou that I have, on the plan, restored the chapel on those lines. All the principal features work in exactly, the tower,

A few years ago the remains of a skeleton were discovered in sinking a well on the property, to which a certain number of houses in the neighbourhood have a right of resorting for water. Many persons who have gone to draw water at night have heard groans, thrice repeated, as if from a person expiring, and these have generally been followed by the death of some near relation of the hearer. Three days after Mrs. Savidan heard the groans, a boat, in which were two of her relations named Le Cras, was capsized in a storm and both perished.*

Notwithstanding the sanctity of the place, however, the old proverb of "The nearer the church, the farther from God," might at one time have been applied to it, for it is related of one of the priors that he was addicted to the black art. Neither the fear of God, nor the censures of the church, could wean him from the fascinating study of magic, and the *Grand-Mêle* was far oftener in his hands than the Bible or breviary. But wizards, it is well known, have often been the victims of their own art, and so it chanced with the profane Prior of Lihou.

One morning, taking advantage of the receding tide, he crossed over to Guernsey to seek an interview with

---

the windows, the roof, etc.,—all except the door, of which there is positively no trace; but possibly, in view of the various coats of paint on the stone, it is merely a fancy of one of the many artists who have retouched it. Of the ruins which remain there is sufficient to show what its measurements once were. Of the tower, about twelve feet is still standing, a large portion of the north wall, and several smaller pieces; these all show that it consisted of a nave about thirty-four by twenty-three feet inside measurement, and a choir or sanctuary about thirty-four by twenty feet. There is enough of the north wall still standing to shew where the spring of the vaulting began, and thus, approximately, the height of the walls and roof. The corner of the chancel arch pier is a Caen stone, with a plain beading on it; there is also trace of a porphyry column on the south side of the sanctuary, and under the site of the altar is a paving of Malachite green and buff tiles, some of which still remain; they measure six and a quarter inches square and were laid alternately."

The lettering has been explained as standing for " H . . . Dominus Lihou Mel," " H . . . priest of Lihou Mel, (as Lihou was called in ancient times) in 1114."

---

* From Mrs. Savidan.

another adept in necromancy, the priest of the neighbouring Chapel of Ste. Apolline. He was accompanied by his servant, to whom he had entrusted a ponderous tome, containing the formulas by which he performed his incantations, and to whom he had given strict orders on no account to open the volume or read a word which it contained.

The visit over, the prior prepared to return to his convent, and walked along leisurely, knowing as it was then spring tide that two or three hours must elapse before the returning waves could bar the passage to the islet. The servant lingered behind, and when he arrived on the beach found his master already half way over. His curiosity had been vividly excited by the repeated injunctions of his master that he should abstain carefully from opening the book. He began to think that it must contain something very wonderful, and that, as but few minutes must elapse before their arrival at the convent, when the mysterious volume would, without doubt, be instantly demanded by the prior, if he did not seize this opportunity of acquainting himself with its contents, no other occasion might ever present itself. He yielded to the temptation, opened the book, and began to read. The prior by this time had arrived at about the middle of the causeway, and was astonished to find the tide rising rapidly and threatening to cut off his further progress, either backwards or forwards. He felt that some unnatural agency was at work, and, guessing how matters stood, looked back to the shore which he had just left, and saw his faithless servant comfortably seated on a heap of dried sea-weed, with the fatal volume spread open on his knees. He was reading aloud, and the prior caught enough of the words to know that his attendant had hit upon the spell which causes the tides to rise out of their usual course, and, moreover, that he was reading most leisurely.

In great fright he called out to the man to read on quickly to the end, as he knew that then the waves would stop and return to their proper limits. The servant was too much absorbed in his reading to pay any attention to the directions given him, and the waves had by this time reached above the prior's waist. In mortal agony he called out for the second time : —

"If thou canst not read forwards, read backwards!" The roaring waves this time effectually drowned his voice. The servant read on, but long before he had arrived at the end of the incantation, the sea had covered the profane priest, and the demon whom the magic lines had evoked carried off his prey.*

---

* From Dr. Lukis, to whom the story was told by an old woman at l'Erée.

EDITOR'S NOTES.

A somewhat similar story was told me in 1896 by Mrs. Le Patourel, who had heard it from her mother-in-law. A schoolmaster, either at St. Pierre-du-Bois or at Torteval, was given to witchcraft, and owned one of these "bad books." He took it one day to his school and, by an oversight, left it on his desk. It was a lovely day, and, impatient to be out, he omitted to lock it up, and hurried home to get his dinner. Whilst in the middle of eating it, quite suddenly a terrific storm came on, such thunder and lightning as had never before been seen in the country, and was most unaccountable in such a hitherto lovely weather. It seemed to be at its worst just over the school. Terrified, remembering the book he had left there, he rushed back and there he found one of the boys reading this book out loud. He snatched the book from his hand, and asked him to show him where he had begun, and where he had read to, and then began at once to real *backwards* from where the boy had left off. As he read, the storm began to lull, and when he reached the place where the boy had begun to read, the storm had stopped as suddenly as it begun. (This is possibly another version of the story of "Satan and the Schoolmaster," related in the chapter on the Devil.)

Mrs. Le Patourel also knew a man who had once owned a "*Grand Albert*" and used it, and, repenting, tried to burn it, but it is well known that if you have once used one of these books you can never rid yourself of it, try as you will. He heated his oven red hot, and put the book within it. Two minutes afterwards he looked up and saw the book, unsinged even, in its old place on the dresser. My cousin Miss Le Pelley sends me a story told her by an old servant Judy Ozanne, how some very religious people, going into a house found a "*Grand Albert*" on the poûtre (the centre beam) in the kitchen, so they threw it into the fire, but in vain, for "it went back to its old place and stayed there!"

A Wizard on the West Coast.

We all know how dangerous it is to possess books which treat of the arts of magic and sorcery, or to tamper in any way with these forbidden practices.

It came to the ears of a former rector of St. Pierre-du-Bois or Torteval, that one of his parishioners, of the name of Sarre, not only owned such books, but was in the habit of reading and studying them. Indeed, if there was any truth in public rumour, many of Sarre's neighbours had been sufferers from the improper use he made of the knowledge thus unlawfully acquired. The good rector thought it his duty to remonstrate with his parishioner, and to point out to him the sinfulness of his conduct, and the danger he was incurring of forfeiting both body and soul to the Prince of Darkness; but all his good advice was, for a long time, treated with contempt. At last, what the rector's charitable remonstrances had been unable to effect was brought about by Sarre's own fears. The presence of a large black cat, which followed him wherever he went, and was with him night and day, began to alarm him. It was useless to attempt to drive the beast away; it cared neither for threats nor blows. In short Sarre began to be seriously alarmed lest his assiduous study of the forbidden volumes should, at last, have brought, if not Satan, at least one of his familiars, to dog his steps continually, and to watch an opportunity of seizing on his prey.

Under these circumstances he thought it most prudent to get rid of the books, and, with this intent, went one night to the extreme verge of low-water mark at spring-tides, dug a hole in the sand, and buried the accursed volumes. The rising tide soon covered the spot, and Sarre returned home with his mind at ease. His feeling of security was not destined to be of long duration, for, on entering his door, he was met by the black cat, who, erecting his tail, and rubbing himself against his master's legs, manifested his joy at seeing him again. The next object that his eyes rested on were the books he had just buried, carefully placed on their accustomed shelf, and as dry as if they had never left it. A profound melancholy seized him ; he ceased to occupy himself in his usual avocations, and wandered about the cliffs and sea-shore in a disconsolate state, till, at last, he disappeared. Those who were charitably disposed, surmised that, in his despair, he had thrown himself over one of the lofty precipices of Pleinmont into the sea, but there were not wanting others who suggested that the master, into whose service he had entered, had at last claimed his own, and carried him off bodily.*

The Wizard's Death.

A certain man of the name of Robin, who lived near Les Capelles, in the parish of St. Sampson's, had risen from being a day labourer to be the possessor of what, in Guernsey, passes for a considerable landed estate. Riches are sure to create envy, and more particularly is this the case when a man has been prosperous in the world and has arrived at a rank and station to which he was not born. The poor hate him because he has acquired a title to consideration, which his origin, as humble as their own, can never confer. The rich pretend to despise him because

---

* From Mrs. W. T. Collings, wife of the late Seigneur of Sark,

he is wanting in the accidental circumstance of birth. All concur in attributing his success in life to luck, to want of honesty, to anything but intelligence, industry, and good conduct. It will not, therefore, be thought surprising if calumny was busy at work to blacken the character of one, who, like Robin, had been so fortunate in his undertakings. He was openly spoken of by his neighbours as being addicted to sorcery.

It was well known that he possessed the art of taming the most refractory bulls, and it therefore followed as a matter of course that he had also the power of bewitching other cattle. Sometimes, when a cow was sick, and all the usual nostrums of the village farrier had failed in effecting a cure, recourse was had, as a last resort, to Robin, who was generally successful. What conclusion was more natural, than that he, who could so easily remove a malady, had also the power of inflicting it? Besides, it was whispered about by some of those who contrive to be well informed of all that passes, even in the most secret recesses of their neighbours' houses, that Robin would sit for hours together, shut up in his private room, with a pack of cards before him, with which he appeared to be playing some game. No adversary was seen, but what game can be played by one man alone? It was clear to the most obtuse that another was present, although invisible to mortal eye, and who could this be but the great enemy of human souls?

At last old age came on; Robin became more and more infirm, and was at last confined to his bed. During his illness his attendants were much annoyed by the continual creaking and cracking of an ancient oaken press, which stood in the corner of the room, and which he would not allow them on any account to open or meddle with. Of course they all thought that this chest contained untold gold, for he was known to be extremely avaricious—in fact he was one of those "who would cut a double * in two" as the saying is. He was frightfully hard on all his workmen, exacting every moment of their time. So far did he carry this, that it is said he only allowed them five minutes to take their noon-day meal, which, according to the universal custom at that time, was furnished by the employer, and eaten at his table. It was commonly believed that one source of his wealth was the discovery of a buried treasure in one of his fields. There was a well on his property which was intermittent, at times overflowing, and at others not having above an inch or so of water in it. It was supposed to conceal a treasure, and a man was sent down to examine it, but no sooner had he begun to bale out the water than it returned with such violence that he was obliged to be drawn up to avoid drowning. When Robin was dying, his son urged him to give something to the poor, but his constant answer was :—

"*Je n'en counis pouïnt.*" ("I do not know any.")

His last hour was, however, rapidly approaching, and he desired the press to be opened, and certain books which it contained to be thrown on the hearth where a large fire was blazing. His orders were obeyed, but, to the great astonishment of the servants and attendants, instead of being consumed in the

---

* A *double* is the smallest copper coin in Guernsey currency, value one-eighth of a penny.

flames, the books extinguised the fire!* Fresh faggots
were, by the orders of the dying man, heaped on
the hearth, and kindled, and, at last, the mysterious
books, if not consumed, at least disappeared. The
press had ceased to creak from the moment the
books were taken out of it, and shortly afterwards
Robin breathed his last.

A storm of unusual violence was raging at the
time, but the most singular circumstance remains yet
to be told. A crow of unusual size was seen to
hover over the house, and finally alighted on the
roof, and, it is said, that on the day of the funeral,
as the corpse was leaving the house, it flew down
and perched on the coffin. In vain did the bearers
endeavour to drive it off; it held its ground, and
even when the body was lowered into the grave it
would not quit the station which it had chosen, but
suffered itself to be covered with the mould by the
sexton. †

THE WITCH OF CAUBO.§

Among the many bays with which the sea-coast of
Guernsey is indented, few have a wilder aspect than

EDITOR'S NOTE.—* In *Traditions et Superstitions de la Haute Bretagne*, Tome I., p. 304,
M. Sebillot tells the story of a priest, who, at the request of a penitent "sorcier," tries to
burn *Le Petit Albert*:—"Il le mit dans le foyer pour le brûler; mais le livre sautait dans
le feu comme s'il avait voulu en sortir. Le prêtre le repoussait dans les flammes avec sa
canne, et il brûla longtemps sans se consumer."

† From Miss Elizabeth Chepmell, Nancy Bichard, and Rachel Duport.

EDITOR'S NOTE.

† "In German Switzerland, a crow perching on the roof of a house where a corpse lies, is
a sure sign that the dead is damned." Swainson's *Folk-Lore*, p. 84.
"In Germany ravens are believed to hold the souls of the damned, sometimes to be the
evil one himself." Idem., p. 90. "The raven was indeed, from of old endowed with the holy
awfulness of the Christian dove in the Norse mythology. Odin was believed to have given
this bird the colour of the night, that it might the better spy out the deeds of darkness."
Demonology and Devil-Lore, by Conway, Vol. 2., p. 368.

---

§ Caûbo = "Sic Armorici Coet-Bo = La Baie du Bois, Sinus Sylvestris, il y
a une Coet Bo sur la côte du Bretagne." MS. note by Mr. Métivier.

that of Caûbo; not that it is surrounded with bold cliffs and precipices, like those of the southern coast, for, on the contrary, the sea is only prevented from inundating the neighbouring land by the banks of sand and shingle which the ever-restless waves have thrown up, or by the sea walls which the industry of man has raised to form a barrier against them.

Its charm consists in the wildness of its scenery *— the rugged promontory of "La Roque du Guet," surmounted by an old watch-house and battery to to the south; the point of land known as "Les Grandes Roques," with its outlying reefs, the scene of many a wreck, to the north; the chain of rocks stretching right across the bay to the westward, and seeming to bar all access to the land. All this, whether seen when, with a westerly wind, the heavy waves are sweeping in with resistless force from the broad Atlantic, or when, on a calm summer's day, the sun's rays "like light dissolved in star-showers" pour down on the brilliantly blue water, from which the innumerable jagged peaks arise, from any of which one might expect to "have sight of Proteus rising from the sea, or hear old Triton blow his wreathèd horn." The shores are alternately picturesque and rugged, or else smiling valleys of green fields overhung with trees, and with a few old thatched houses in the background, and, until lately, were inhabited almost exclusively by a race of poor hardy fishermen, to whom every passage through the intricate and rugged rocks of the bay are well known, but who are by no means exempt from the

---

EDITOR'S NOTE.—* It must be remembered that none of Sir Edgar's MSS. are dated later than 1874, and therefore that none of the greenhouses, surburban villas, and workmen's cottages which have so spoilt our island scenery were then built.

superstitions that seem to attach particularly to a sea-faring life.

Of late some extensive quarries have been opened in the hills that lie eastward of the bay, from one of which the dark granite steps leading to the western entrance of St. Paul's Cathedral were hewn. The quarries have brought other labourers to reside in the neighbourhood, and it is from a brother of one of these—a Cornishman—that the following particulars have been obtained.

The quarryman now in question, when he first determined on seeking work at Caûbo, had much difficulty in finding a cottage to suit him; but, at last, tempted by the low rent asked for one, which had remained untenanted for a long time, he made up his mind to take it. Other labourers had lived formerly in the house, but generally, after a short residence, they had left it as soon as they could find a decent excuse, without assigning any definite reason. The quarryman had not been long settled in his new habitation when he and his family began to be alarmed by strange and unaccountable noises, particularly at night. He spoke to some of the neighbours on the subject, and, at last, with some difficulty— for it was evident that there was a great unwilling- ness to speak on the subject,—he ascertained that the house had the reputation of being bewitched, and that an old woman living in the immediate vicinity was commonly reported to be the cause of the nightly disturbances. Some of the previous tenants went so far as to say that on stormy nights, when the wind was blowing a full gale from the south-west, and all were gathered round the hearth, lamenting the sad condition of the poor mariners and fishermen out at sea, and praying for the safety of the shipping exposed to the pitiless blast, they had seen the old sorceress come down the chimney in a cloud of smoke and soot, pass through their midst, and vanish through the key-hole, causing all the doors in the cottage to slam, and leaving a villainous smell behind her. Other tales, no less veracious, are told of her.

A woman, scrupulously clean in her person and attire, against whom the witch had a previous grudge, chanced to make use of some not very complimentary expressions in speaking of her, and instantaneously her clothes were covered with vermin of the most loathsome description. A neighbour, who had offended her, was never able, either by fair means or foul, to get his cattle past the witch's dwelling, but was obliged to take another and much longer way in leading them to and from their pasturage, to the grievous loss of his time and temper.

Two strong horses, harnessed to the empty cart of another man with whom the sorceress had lately had a quarrel, though urged by word and whip, were unable to move it an inch forward. It was well known to all that it was by means of books of magic that she was enabled to perform these and still greater marvels ; and her brothers, good respectable men, who were aware of her evil deeds and ashamed of the disgrace her conduct brought on the family, finding that all their remonstrances were in vain, and that they could not persuade her to abandon her evil courses, had attempted to destroy the books, and so deprive her, in some degree, of her power of doing mischief.

On one occasion, during her absence from home,

they got possession of the unhallowed volumes, and, lighting a large fire on the hearth, placed them in the midst of the flames, and heaped up fuel around them, until, to all appearance, they were reduced to a heap of ashes.

They were rejoicing in the success of their undertaking, but, alas, their joy was of short duration. They soon found that all their labour had been in vain, and that they had consumed their fuel to no purpose ; for, chancing to cast their eyes on the top of an old chest of drawers which stood in one corner of the room, where the books, when not actually in use, were. always to be found, what was their dismay to see them lying there uninjured and looking as if they had never been touched. Fire, it was clear, had no power over them. So they determined to try what effect the other elements, earth and water, might have. It chanced to be one of the lowest spring-tides in the year, so they carried the books down to dead low-water mark, dug a deep hole in the sand, placed the books in it, and watched until the flowing tide had covered the spot with three or four feet of water.

They then returned home, and on entering the cottage naturally turned their eyes towards the usual resting-place of the books. There they were, without a vestige of sand on them, and as dry as bones. After these two attempts they gave up all hopes of ever getting rid of the unholy tomes ; indeed it is well known that there is but one method of destroying such books ; it is by burying them with their owner when death shall have delivered the world from his or her presence.

It is fortunate that there are men and women who have the gift of counteracting the spells of wizards and witches; and it so chances that not many doors from the house where the witch of Caûbo dwelt there resided an old man whose knowledge enabled him to frustrate her evil designs, and whose services were readily given to those who may require them. These things are said to have happened as lately as the year 1874, and are a proof that, in some quarters at least, and notwithstanding the boasted enlightenment of the nineteenth century, faith in witchcraft is as rife as ever. Can it, however, be wondered at, if ignorant peasants. should believe in what they think they have Scriptural warrant for considering an article of faith, when learned men and educated women are found ready to give in to all the delusions of spiritualism.

THE WITCH OF THE VILLE-ES-PIES.*

There lived in the last century at La Ville-ès-Pies, in that part of the parish of St. Michel-du-Valle known as "Le Clos," an old lady, whose maiden name it is not necessary to recall any more than that of the really worthy man who had the misfortune to be joined with her in the bonds of wedlock. Suffice it to say that both belonged to respectable families. It was notorious, however, to all the neighbourhood that she was addicted to the execrable practice of witchcraft; indeed she. made no mystery of it, for she was proud of the fear she inspired, and clever enough to turn it to her own advantage;

---

* A MS. note by Mr. Métivier explains this name by saying that this was an old residence of Friars, robed in black and white, and hence known as "Les Frères Pies,"—the Magpie Friars.

knowing well that the time was past when the
suspicion alone of being an adept in the black art
was sufficient to condemn a person to the stake.

The place whither she was said to be in the
habit of resorting to meet her infernal master, and
to dance and revel at night with others, who, like
herself, had entered into a league with the Prince
of Darkness, was that group of rocks and islets near
Herm, known by the name of "Les Houmets
d'Amont."*

On these occasions she was in the habit of
attiring herself in her very best array, and a pair of
silver slippers formed a principal part of her
adornment. How she came, in her nocturnal flight,
to drop one of them, is not known, but it was
picked up on one of these rocks by a fisherman,
recognised as her property, and honestly returned to
her. Perhaps the finder did not like to run the
risk of appropriating the precious metal to his own
use.

It is said that, not content with serving Satan
herself, she laid a spell on her children as soon as
they were presented to her after their birth, and so
consecrated them for ever to the service of her infernal
master.

The husband, a good pious man, by some means
discovered this, and, when his wife was on the point
of being delivered of her last child, a son, he begged
the midwife in attendance to be careful, as soon
as the child made its appearance, and before the
unnatural mother could set eyes on it, to sign it

---

* "Houmet, from the Swedish holm, is a peninsula, or a grazing ground
down near the water.—Métivier's Dictionary.

with the holy sign of the cross. This precaution saved the infant. The unholy mother's spell had no power over him, and, as he grew up, he was enabled, by God's grace, and by the pious teaching of his father, to withstand all the temptations which were laid in his way by his brothers and sisters, who depicted to him in glowing terms the amusements they indulged in, when, in the form of hares, they frolicked on moonlight nights around the mill which stands on the hill around the Ville-ès-Pies.*

The Sick Princess and the Wizards.

In ancient days, (in what reign is not mentioned), when the island was as yet but thinly peopled, and considerable tracts of country were destitute of habitations, a peasant and his wife, who had been passing the day in town, were overtaken on their way home by a violent storm of wind, rain, and thunder. They pressed forward, hoping to reach their cottage before night should set in, but, the storm increasing, they were fain to seek shelter in an old ruin that stood by the roadside.

Scarcely had they entered, before they heard on all sides of the building the cries of "Ké-hou-hou," which are uttered by the sorcerers when on their nocturnal flights. They then remembered that it was Friday, the day on which the powers of darkness have the most power, and that all the wizards and witches of the island were reported to hold their weekly meetings in that place. It was too late to think of retreating, but they were not yet discovered, and there were still

---

* From Mr. Thomas Hocart Henry.

hopes of their escaping detection. Fear quickened
their invention. Looking round they saw an oven,
into which they both crept, and the woman, by
spreading her black petticoat over the entrance,
effectually concealed them. They had scarcely time
to do this, before a tumultuous crowd of wizards
entered the building. They conversed with great
delight on all the mischief they had caused, and
appeared to derive much pleasure from the misfortunes
which afflicted mankind.

One of them mentioned the illness of the King of
England's only daughter, which the most eminent of
physicians of the realm had been unable to cure, or
even to discover the cause of. "Neither will they,"
said one, who appeared to be the chief, with an
infernal laugh, "for I alone know the cause and the
remedy."

They pressed him to tell, but for a long time he
refused. At last, wearied out by their entreaties, he
said—"A hair, which this Princess has accidentally
swallowed, has twined itself round her heart, and,
unless speedily removed, must cause her death. There
is but one means of cure—a piece of skin of pork
with some of the bristles attached to it, must be
well secured by a string. Let the Princess swallow
this, and the hair will become entangled in the
bristles, and may thus be drawn up."

Shortly afterwards the meeting broke up, without a
suspicion that their conversation had been overheard,
and as soon as the day dawned, the countryman
and his wife returned to town and made known their
adventure to the authorities. A boat immediately
set sail for England, with a messenger bound for
the King, and the advice of the wizard being

" Mill Pond at the Vrangue."

followed, the Princess was soon restored to health. A considerable sum of money was sent over as a present to the man and woman by whose means the discovery had been made, with which they were enabled to buy a farm and stock it.

The manner in which they had acquired their riches soon became known, and, tempted by the hopes of gain, a man concealed himself in the oven of the ruined house near the Catioroc one Friday night. He had not long lain there before the wizards entered, but before a word was uttered they made a strict search through the house, and soon discovered the trembling man, whom they obliged to take the oaths of allegiance to their infernal master, to the eternal ruin both of his soul and body.* †

A Witch in Disguise.

Sorcerers have the power of taking the forms of different animals, but when thus disguised cannot be wounded but by silver.

A Mr. Le Marchant, " des grent mesons," had often fired at a white rabbit which frequented his warren, but without success. One day, however, beginning to suspect how the case really stood, he

---

* From Miss E. Chepmell.

* See an incident somewhat similar in Chambers' *Popular Rhymes of Scotland*, in the tale of Sir James Ramsay, of Bamff.

See also Suzet's *Veillées Bretonnes, Comte de Cocherard et Turquin*, p. 258, and *Folk-Lore Record*, Vol. III., part I., p. 40.

EDITOR'S NOTE.—† This story is also told in *Folk-Lore of Guernsey and Sark*, by Louisa Lane-Clarke (2nd Edition, 1890, p. 21). She makes certain alterations in the narrative and her version of the cure for the Princess is :—" If they cut a small square of bacon from just *over the heart*, tied it to a silken thread, and made the Princess swallow it, then jerked it up again, the hair would stick to it, and come away from *her heart*, and she would recover."

On the 16th May, 1900, the late Mrs. Murray-Aynsley read a paper on " Guernsey Folk-Lore," to the Folk-Lore Society of England, and she also quoted this story, evidently taken from Mrs. Lane-Clarke's version, only told in slightly different words,

detached his silver sleeve button from his wrist-band, loaded his gun with it, took a steady aim, and fired.

The rabbit immediately disappeared behind the hedge. He ran up, and, hearing some person groaning as if in great pain on the other side, looked over and recognised a neighbour of his, a lady of the Vale, who was lying with her leg broken and bleeding profusely from a fresh wound.

COLLAS ROUSSÉ.*

Une histouaire du bouan vier temps.

A story of the good old times.

Un bouan houme et sa femme avaient autefais une p'tite ferme ès environs du Vazon; Collas Roussé et sa femme, Nency Guille, étaient des gens tranquilles, qui faisaient d' leux mûx pour elvair leu famille, mais i' l'taient r' nomaï pour changier leux forme à volontaï.

An honest man and his wife had formerly a little farm in the neighbourhood of Vazon ; Collas Roussel and his wife, Nancy Guille, were quiet people, who did their best to bring up their family properly, but they were noted for being able to change their forms at will.

Une belle séraïe d'étaï nou vit un biau lièvre dans l' gardin du Probytère qui dansait autouar d'une vaque qu' était la fiquie.

One fine summer's evening people saw a fine hare in the rectory garden, which was dancing round a cow which was tethered there.

La vaque se mins a r' gardaïr le lièvre qui toute suite se bûti su ses dœux

The cow began to look at the hare, who at once rose up on his hind legs, gam-

---

* The above Guernsey story of animal transformations I found cut out and placed with Sir Edgar MacCulloch's MSS. in its Guernsey-French form. I think it better to give both the Guernsey-French and its English translation, the former being the language in which all these old stories are handed down to us.

pattes de derriere faisant des pernagues coum si voulait invitaïr la vaque à dansaïr d'auve li. Les gens n' savaient pas qui en craire ou qu'est que vela qui voulait dire. Ls' uns disaient que ch'était Collas Roussé ou sa femme, d'autres pensaient q'nou f'rait mûx de l' tiraï, d'autres enfin disaient que l'lait d'la vaque s'rait gataï et q'la vaque jamais n'vaudrait sa tuache.

Le lecteur, Pierre Simon, qui s'trouvait la par écanche, s'en fut tout doucement pres du lièvre, l'attrapi et s'mis à l'frottaï à r'brousse pel, les uns li criaient d'li teurtre le cô,'l' s'autres d'li rompre les gambes, " et pis nou verrait bien vite si chen 'tait pouint Collas Roussé ou sa femme." L's 'uns disaient qu'ils avaient vœu le lièvre v'nir dret du Vazon, mais qu'il avait ieux la malice, de prendre un ch'min detournaï, d'autres vaisins étaient d'avis de prendre le prumier lait d'la vaque et de l' mettre à bouidre su une bouane fouaïe d'vrec et

bolling as if he wished to invite the cow to dance with him. The people did not know what to think or what it could all mean. Some said that it was either Collas Roussel or his wife, others thought it would be better to fire at it, and the others finally said that the cow's milk would be spoilt and that she would never be worth slaughtering.

The clerk, Pierre Simon, who was there by chance, crept quietly near the hare, caught it, and began to rub up its fur the wrong way. Some cried out to him to wring its neck, others to break its legs, " and then we will see very quickly whether it is Collas Roussel or his wife or no." Some said that they had seen the hare come straight from Vazon, but that it had had the artfulness to take a circuitous route. Other neighbours advised that the first milk the cow should give after this should be taken, and put to boil on a good

q'nou verrait bientot Collas Roussé et sa vieille v'nir d'mandaï une goutte de lait bouailli ; c'h'tait là la vraie manière d'les decouvrir. Pierre Simon fut bien bllamaï de toute la contraie pour avé laissi la bête écappaï, mais i disait pour raison qu'les lièvres étaient sujets à des maux d' têtes coum d'autres personnes et que ch'tait pour chunna qu'il l'avait frottaï. Il aïmait la soupe de lièvre coum d'autres, mais que ch'nérait pas étaï bien d'sa part de prendre avantage d'la paure bête.

Le bouan vier Mêssier en pâlant d' l'affaire disait : "Je n' voudrais pas dire du mà' d' personne, seit keriature ou cheva', mais j'ai mes pensaïes au sujet de Collas Roussé et sa femme, l'annaie passaie coum j'allais r'muaïr nos bêtes de bouan matin qu'est que j'vis sinon daeux biaux lièvres a rôguer ma raie-grasse. J'fis du bruit, et i s'en furent couarant d'vier le Vazon, et un matin

vraic fire, and that one would soon see Collas Roussel and his old woman come and ask for a cup of boiled milk. That was the best way of finding them out. Pierre Simon was much blamed by all the country side for having allowed the beast to escape, but he said, as an excuse, that hares were subject to headaches as much as other people and it was for that that he had rubbed it. He liked hare soup as well as anyone, but that it would not have been right of him to take advantage of the poor beast.

The good old herdsman in talking over the affair said : "I would not speak ill of anyone, be it creature, man, or horse, but I have my own ideas on the subject of Collas Roussel and his wife. Last year as I was moving our cattle early in the morning, what should I see but two fine hares nibbling my rye grass. I made a noise, and they ran off towards Vazon, and one

j'mécryi "Tu devrais en aver honte Collas."

Eh bien, chu jour là is'en furent derriere le prinseux, trav'sirent le belle, et, j'n' ments pouint, j' cré qui passirent par d'sous l'us. Mais terjous, que j'aie tort ou raison, ni Collas ni sa femme n'ont peux me r'gardaïr en fache d'pis chu jour-là.

Jamais n'ou ne me fra craire que g'nia point bien de qué que nous n'serait expliquer. J'en ai ouï d'bien des sortes d'pis m'en jâne temps. Jai souvent ouï la raeue du prinseux tournaï a mignet que g'niavait fils d'âme par dehors ; j'ai vaeux not' cat aquand i' ventait gros assis l' dos tournaï au faeu, guettant l'us et la f'nêtre coum si s'attendait à véer quiq'un entraïr, et parfais i poussait de drôles de cris, j'vous en reponds, et not t'chen s'mauchaï derriere ma caire quand j'disais mes perières, parfais i' braq'tait dans s'en dormir coum s'il' tait a s'battre d'auve d'au-

morning I cried out "You should be ashamed of yourself, Collas."

Well, on that day they went behind the cider press, crossed the court-yard, and, I am not lying, I believe that they passed under the door. But ever since, whether I am wrong or right, neither Collas or his wife, have been able to look me in the face.

Never will you make me believe that there are not many things that are not explained to us. I have heard of all sorts since my young days. I have often heard the wheel of the cider press turn at midnight, when there was not a soul about. I have seen our cat when it blew hard, sitting with his back turned to the fire, watching the door and the window as if it expected to see some one enter, and sometimes it uttered curious cries, I assure you, and our dog would hide himself behind my chair when I said my prayers. Sometimes he barked in his

tres t'chens ; o'ch'est m'n avis que des câts et des t'chens vés l's affaires d'une autre manière que nous, et j'cré que ch'est grand piti que tous cheux qui s'dementent de changier de forme n'aient affaire à yeux."

UN LURON.

sleep, as if he were fighting with other dogs. Oh, it is my opinion that cats and dogs see things in a different way to what we do, and I think it is a great pity that all those who deny that people can change their forms, cannot refer to them."

A TRIFLER.

THE MILLER AND THE DUCK.

A miller, one day passing by his mill-pond at the Vrangue, was attracted by the noise and struggles of a very beautiful duck. He soon perceived that something was wrong, and that, unless the bird was speedily relieved, it must perish. He accordingly, with some difficulty, succeeded in extricating the duck from the water, and took it into the mill, where, after wiping it dry, and endeavouring to to arrange its ruffled feathers, he deposited it in a place of safety and left it. Returning shortly afterwards, he was astonished to find its place supplied by a very beautiful and richly-dressed lady, who thanked him for his humanity, and assured him, but for his assistance, she must inevitably have been drowned, promising him at the same time, that as long as he kept the adventure secret, he should, whenever he was in want, find a sum of money deposited on his mill stone.*

---

* From Miss E. Chepmell.

* The transformation of princesses into ducks by magical arts is a very common incident in the fairy tales of Norway and Sweden and Denmark. See Thorpe's *Yule-tide Stories.*

Mahy de la Catte.

An old sea captain, of the name of Mahy, who for many years had navigated a cutter between Guernsey and England, had, at last, by industry and perseverance, amassed a sufficient competency to enable him to give up his arduous and dangerous profession, and pass the remainder of his days in peace on shore. At least, so he hoped, but, alas! the expectation of happiness, which poor mortals indulge in, is often doomed to be disappointed, and often by apparently trivial causes. Who could have guessed that a cat would have embittered the remaining days of the old sailor? Yet so it was. The mischievous tricks of this imp of Satan rendered his life almost unbearable; not a moment's rest could he enjoy in his own house. In vain did he attempt to drive the troublesome brute away. If ejected by the door, she returned immediately by the window, or down the chimney. It was useless to attempt to catch her; she never slept, and her activity was so great that she escaped every blow aimed at her. One day, as he was sitting by his fireside, the tricks of the cat became unsupportable; if he dozed off for a moment, his wig was twitched off his head; if he laid down his pipe, puss was watching her opportunity to give a sly pat and knock it off the table; the moment his glass of grog left his hand, it was sure to be upset. At last his patience being quite exhausted, he seized the poker and gave chase, but with as little effect as ever. Puss contrived to elude him, and managed so well that blows, aimed at her, fell on the furniture and crockery. After leading him several times round the room, she

"Old Mill House at La Vrangue, at the beginning of the Nineteenth Century."

escaped into the passage, and seated herself on the
" hecq " or half door, which was formerly to be
found in almost every house. Mahy seized a gun
that was lying on the bacon-rack, and aimed at the
cat, exclaiming at the same time, " Now I have
you ! " The cat paused, turned round, and, in a
voice which domestic jars and curtain lectures made
by far too familiar to him, said, very quietly and
distinctly, " Pas *acouäre* " (" Not yet.")

He then, for the first time, remembered that he
had never seen puss and his wife at one and the
same moment, and the unpleasant truth flashed
across his mind that his good woman was one of
those who frequent the weekly entertainments given
by his Satanic Majesty on Friday nights at Catioroc,
Pleinmont, le Cimetière de Torteval, and elsewhere.

Soon afterwards, Mrs. Mahy's identity was revealed
in another manner. It is well known to housekeepers
who retain the good old custom of having their linen
washed and ironed at home, that an amount of
gossip, scarcely to be credited, goes on on these
occasions. The women employed, moving as they do
from house to house, pick up all the news that has
arisen during the week, and, meeting every day with
fresh companions, retail what they have heard, and
gather new information in return, from every direction.
Of course the characters of the neighbours, and even
of their employers, are not spared, and for this latter
reason, perhaps, it is that a certain degree of mystery
frequently pervades these conversations, and that
listeners and evesdroppers are discouraged. A sort of
freemasonry prevails, and it is only by a rare
accident that the scandal and gossip retailed at the
washing tub or ironing board find their way to the

parlour. Great, therefore, was the astonishment of the discreet and prudent workwomen, whose avocations took them to the houses in the neighbourhood of Madame Mahy's dwelling, to find that their most confidential communications were repeated, and could in most cases be traced to that good lady. They had never detected her listening; they felt convinced that none among them could be so treacherous as to betray their secrets. They determined to keep a sharp look-out, and at last the mystery was solved. A young ironer, of more keen observation than her companions, had remarked that, in whatever house they worked, the same old tabby cat was to be seen seated before the fire, and apparently dreaming away her existence. Her suspicions were aroused. She watched puss closely, and was convinced at last that, even when apparently dozing, pussy was listening attentively to what was going on. She was not long in forming a plan to prove whether her conjectures were correct. She took up a flat iron from the hearth, and, under the pretence of cleaning and cooling it on the mat, approached the unsuspecting cat and suddenly applied it to her nose. Puss jumped up and suddenly disappeared with a yell, which, as the conclave of gossips declared, resembled far more the cry of a woman in pain than the miauling of a cat. Next day it was rumoured abroad that poor Madame Mahy, while sitting before her fire, had been overtaken with sleep, and falling forward had burnt her face severely on the bars of the grate! "You know," said the old woman who related the story, " that Capt. Mahy never passed for a conjuror. He ought however to have had more wit than to tell these stories to his friends over a glass of grog,

for, although he did not say that he had recognised
his wife's voice, or that he did not believe that she
had dozed over the fire, they had already made the
remark that Mrs. Mahy and the cat had never been
seen together, and were not long in drawing their
conclusions and publishing them to the world. The
story soon found its way to those hot-beds of gossip,
the public bake-houses, and from thence over all
the town." *

THE TRANSFORMED WIZARD.

It is one of the greatest characteristics of wizards
and witches that they have the power of assuming
any form they please.

A man, who kept a large number of cows, observed

---

* From Miss Martineau, to whom the story was related by Mrs. Jonathan
Bichard, of L'Ancresse, and also from Rachel Du Port.

EDITOR'S NOTE.
TWO WITCHES AND TWO CATS.

In the Vale parish, very many years ago, lived a father and daughter, Nico and Denise
Roberts. Denise was an extremely pretty girl, and Pierre Henry, the richest man in the
parish, wanted to marry her. There were two old maiden ladies who were neighbours of the
Roberts', and were excessively jealous of all the attention and admiration Denise received.
They both considered that they were still young and fascinating, and one was considered to
have designs on old Roberts, and the other on Pierre Henry himself.

They both had the reputation of being witches by all the neighbours, principally because
they were never seen without two black cats, and they even used to go so far as to take
these two cats with them, when, in the evenings, as was their frequent custom, they would
take their knitting and go and sit for hours in the Roberts' kitchen. Denise used to implore
her father not to encourage "*ces daeux vieilles |sorilles,*" * knowing well that they were
trying to poison his mind against Pierre Henry, but he paid no attention to his daughter, as
they amused him by telling him all the gossip and scandal of the place, and he used to sit
and let them whisper to him on one side of the hearth, while Pierre and Denise sat on the
other; but all the time the two latter were talking, they were annoyed by the cats brought
in by old Margot and Olympe Le Moine, and this went on evening after evening. If Pierre
tried to move his chair nearer to hers, one of the cats would climb up and manage to thrust
its claws in his leg. If he bent forward to whisper to her, the other cat would jump on her
shoulder, and prevent Denise from attending to what he was saying. After some time he
grew convinced that all this could not be accidental, so, one evening, just as the largest of
the two cats had perched itself on Denise's shoulder at the most inopportune moment, he
whispered in its ear "*Margot, tu quérràs*" ("Margot, you will tumble down.") At that
moment, Margot Le Moine, who was sitting at the other end of the room, fell off her chair
in a dead faint, and the cat gave a yell and darted up the chimney. This finally convinced
old Roberts as to the true character of his friends, and he swore that never again should
these two "*quéraudes*" darken his doors, and, soon after, Denise Roberts and Pierre Henry
were married.†

* Métivier translates *sorille* as a term of reproach, derived probably from the
Bas-Breton *soreih*, wizard, *sorelhés*, witch.

† From Mrs. Charles Marquand, who had heard it from Denise Roberts' first cousin.

that they were gradually pining away, that they failed to give the usual quantity of milk, and that no care that he could bestow on them availed aught in improving their condition. One or two of them had already died, and he feared that all the others would soon follow their example. The summer had set in, and at · that season the cows are left out all night in the field, but when in the early morning the farmer went to look after them, he generally found them thoroughly exhausted, and looking as if they had been hard driven all night.

At last he began to suspect that the poor animals were under the influence of some spell, and he determined to watch, in order to discover, if possible, what means were used to bring the cows into the condition in which he found them. It seems rather a singular circumstance that wizards and witches, with all their cleverness, do not appear to be able at times to see things which are passing under their very eyes. Perhaps their eagerness to do mischief blinds them to the danger of discovery. At all events, the farmer, who had concealed himself, as soon as the daylight had well departed, in a cattle shed that stood in one corner of the field, remained undisturbed, with his eyes intently fixed on the cows, who were lying down, quietly chewing the cud.

About midnight his attention was attracted by a large black dog, which jumped over the hedge separating his field from that of a neighbour with whom he had lately had a quarrel. The dog approached the cows, stood up on his hind legs, and began to dance before them, cutting such capers and somersaults as the farmer had never seen before. No sooner had the cows seen the dog than they also stood upright,

and imitated all his movements. The farmer crept
stealthily out of the field, went home, loaded his gun
with a silver coin, which he cut into slugs,—for it
is a well known fact that no baser metal than silver
will wound a sorcerer,—returned to the field, where he
found the dance still going on as fast and furious
as ever, and fired at the dog, which ran off howling,
and limping on three legs.

The next day his neighbour was seen with his arm
in a sling, and it was given out that, in returning
from the town the previous evening, he had fallen
accidentally over a heap of stones, and so broken it.
The farmer had his own ideas, but wisely kept them
to himself. His neighbour had had a lesson ; he
found that he had to deal with a resolute man ; the
cows were allowed to remain unmolested, and soon
recovered their pristine health and strength. This is
said to have occurred in Jersey.*

La Dame au Voile.

Some years have now elapsed since a family had
reason to suppose that recourse had been had to
magic arts in order to injure them. Their health
declined, their cattle fell sick and died, their crops
failed, and everything went wrong with them. It was
but too plain that they were bewitched, and no
chance remained of any amelioration of their condition
unless they could discover the author of their
misfortunes. They therefore determined, by the advice
of a friend skilled in white witchcraft, to perform
a charm for the purpose of obliging the wizard or
witch to show himself. This charm is popularly

---

* From Reuben Wilkins.

called " *Une bouïture* " or " boiling," and consists in setting certain ingredients to seethe in a large cauldron. The pot, duly filled, was accordingly placed on the hearth with all the prescribed ceremonial.

No sooner did it begin to simmer than six mice entered the room, walking in procession, two and two, and all deeply veiled. As soon, however, as the pot boiled, the mice disappeared, and in their place stood a lady whom they all knew full well.

Her name we have not been able to discover, our informant being evidently unwilling to compromise herself by mentioning it, but she was well known to the market women by the name of "La Dame au Voile," and bold would have been the farmer's wife who would have refused to let her have her wares at her own price.

Another version of the story says that the mice were caught and carried to the office of "Le Procureur du Roi," and that in the presence of this legal personage they resumed their own shapes, and appeared as three ladies and three women of the lower orders. *

CASE OF A MAN WHO WAS BEWITCHED.

A man of the name of Collenette, living in the Castel parish, had sold a lot of furze to another countryman, who was one of the drummers of the North Regiment of Militia, but did not receive payment for it at the time of striking the bargain. Some days afterwards, Collenette, on his way to his work, was met by a neighbour to whom he owed a small sum of money, who put him in mind of his

---

* From Miss Martineau, to whom the story was related by an old servant,

debt. He excused himself for the time, promising to pay as soon as ever he should receive his money for the furze he had sold. He then proceeded to his work, which was that of a quarryman, but the very first blow he struck the stone caused him to start back in affright, for he distinctly heard a voice proceeding from the rock, which said to him :—

"Thou hast told such an one that I did not pay thee for the furze. Thou shalt suffer for this to the last day of thy life, but that day is still distant."

He looked about to see if any one was concealed near, from whom the voice could proceed, but saw no one. He then returned to his work, but every minute the same words rang in his ears. At noon he ate his meal, which he had brought to the field with him, and then, as labourers do, lay down on the grass to sleep. No sooner had he closed his eyes than he was roused by the beating of a great drum close to his ears. He started up, but could see nothing, and whenever he lay down the drumming re-commenced.

This state of things continued, and the poor man, worn out by fatigue and fright, fell into a lingering illness.

If by chance he fell asleep, he was soon awakened by a sensation which he described as being as though a calf passed over his body, immediately after which he seemed to be violently lifted from his bed and thrown on the floor. It is even asserted that articles of furniture, which were in the same room with him, were thrown about without any visible agency.

His friends and neighbours kindly visited him, and endeavoured to divert his mind from dwelling on his misfortunes, but all to no avail. Whether in

Victor Hugo's " Haunted House " at Pleinmont.

company or alone, he was equally tormented. At last, one night, he escaped the vigilance of his friends, and the next morning was found on the sea-shore, entangled in the mooring ropes of a fishing boat, and drowned in two or three inches of water.*

JEAN FALLA AND THE WITCHES.

Nowhere is the life of a fisherman to be envied. In summer, when the sea is calm, the days long, and the nights comparatively warm, it may be endurable. The amateur may find pleasure in sailing over a sunny sea, and the excitement of drawing in the lines or nets laden with fish may prove a sufficient compensation for many minor hardships; but the man whose means of subsistence depend on his precarious gains, who must brave the perils of the waves at all seasons, at all hours, and in all weathers, is to be pitied.

The coasts of Guernsey abound in fish of all sorts, and the earliest authentic records of the island prove that for many centuries the fisheries have been of great importance, and one of the main sources of wealth to the inhabitants.

Considering the great number of boats kept, the dangerous nature of the coast, the numerous rocks, the intricate currents and strong tides, it is wonderful that so few accidents occur. The fishermen are skilful navigators, and have full confidence in themselves; they fear not the usual dangers of a sailor's life, but they dread the supernatural influences that may be brought to bear against them.

They—or even some member of their family—may

---

* From Rachel Du Port.

have, perhaps quite unconsciously, offended some old crone who has it in her power to injure them in various ways. By her evil arts she may cause their lines to become inextricably entangled in the sea-weed, or to come up laden with dog-fish, blue sharks, and such-like worthless fish. Happy indeed may the poor fisherman consider himself if the old woman's spite confines itself to such trifling annoyances, for has she not also the power to raise storms? Is it not on record how Collette Salmon, wife of Collas Du Port, caused the loss of a boat and the death of the whole crew, merely because one of them asked her more than she thought was right for three miserable dog-fish? Is it not well known how, when that noted witch, Marie Mouton, was banished from the island for her evil doings, the cutter that landed her at Southampton encountered a most terrific gale on its return? And how the captain and crew were ready to depose upon oath that during the height of the storm they had seen Marie, sometimes perched on the top of the mast, and at other times astride on the jib-boom, tearing the sails to shreds and tatters? Who could be incredulous enough to resist such testimony as this? Certainly not Jean Falla. He was a bold fisherman. Every rock and shallow from the Hanois to the Amfroques were thoroughly well known to him. By night or day could he steer his way through their most intricate passes. He was not aware of having any enemy, but witches are easily provoked to anger, and unwittingly he may have offended one of the sisterhood. If he had done so, he had cause to repent his involuntary fault, and to his dying day he never forgot the fright he had to undergo in consequence.

He had left his moorings in the Bay of Les Péqueries early in the morning. A more beautiful day had never risen on Guernsey. The sun shone, a light breeze just ruffled the surface of the sea, the tide served, fish were plentiful on the coast, and everything promised an abundant catch. He sailed out alone, reached the fishing ground, took his marks carefully, cast out his lines, and then anchored to await the turn of the tide when the fish begin to bite. It was not long before the gentle rocking of the boat and the warmth of the atmosphere began to make him feel drowsy, and, knowing that an hour or two must still elapse before he was likely to catch anything, he yielded to the influence, and was soon sound asleep.

How long his sleep lasted he was never able to say, but the impression on his mind was that scarce a quarter of an hour had elapsed before he was awakened by one of the most terrific storms that he had ever experienced. The boat was rolling fearfully, and rapidly filling with water. To hoist a sail, to slip the cable, and to turn the boat's head in the direction of the land was his next endeavour, but at this critical moment his courage almost failed him. In the howlings of the storm he heard a peal of unearthly laughter above his head, and, looking up, was horrorstruck at discerning, in the fast flying scud, the form of an old woman perfectly well known to him, who appeared quite at home in her elevated situation. She was accompanied by many others who were strangers to him, but she was the leader of the party, and it was evident that his fright and embarrassment were the cause of their uproarious merriment. Who she was, he could never be prevailed upon to say, and, no doubt, in this he acted wisely.

The wind fortunately favoured him. He made for the land, reached his moorings in safety, ran his boat up high and dry on the beach, and leaped ashore. A fresh peal of laughter from his aërial tormentors spurred him on.

His house was at no great distance from the shore, but the way to it by the road was circuitous. He took, therefore, a short cut across the fields, passed over one or two hedges without accident, jumped over another and alighted astride on the back of a cow that was quietly chewing the cud on the other side, regardless of the turmoil of the elements. The poor beast, roused so suddenly from her repose, started up and rushed madly across the field, carrying her terrified load with her. The middle of the field was crossed by one of those deep cuttings which are made for draining the marshy lands of that district, and the cow, brought suddenly to a stand, precipitated the unfortunate Jean Falla head over heels into the muddy ditch.

Again the unearthly laughter resounded. A less resolute man than Jean would have lost all presence of mind, but he remembered that he was within a few perches of his own house. He scrambled out as well as he could, reached his cottage door, which was fortunately open, entered, closed the door behind him, and fell exhausted on the floor. Another prolonged peal of laughter dying away in the distance was heard outside, but Jean, once under his own roof, felt himself safe.

It was some time, however, before he recovered from his fright, and, whatever his real feelings towards

them may have been, he was observed from that
time forward to treat all old women with marked
deference and respect.[*]

The Bladebone.

Every careful and prudent person, before throwing
away either the bladebone of an animal, or an empty
egg-shell, makes a hole in it, and the reason assigned
for this practice is to prevent an improper use being
made of either by witches; for it is firmly believed
that they have the power of employing both the one
and the other as vessels to convey them across the
seas. No matter how tempestuous the weather may
be, how high the billows may be rolling, the magic
bark makes its way against wind and tide, with
more speed and greater certainty than the best
appointed steamer that was ever launched. Those
who avail themselves of these means of conveyance
seem to possess the power of making their vessel
assume the appearance of a handsome well-rigged
ship. It is related that in days long past, a
respectable inhabitant of the neighbourhood of La
Perelle Bay, went out with the early dawn, after a
stormy night, to collect the sea-weed which the
waves might have cast on the shore, or to pick up
perchance, some fragments of wreckage, which are
not unfrequently stranded on that dangerous coast
after a heavy gale from the westward.

He was surprised to see, in the yet uncertain
light of the morning, a large ship in the offing
bearing down upon the land. He watched it atten-

---

[*] From my father, to whom the main incidents were related by Sieur Jean
Falla himself.

tively, expecting every moment to see it strike on one of the many sunken rocks that render the navigation of our seas so difficult and perilous. To his astonishment the ship, as it neared the shore, appeared to diminish rapidly in size. He was alarmed, but curiosity got the better of fright, and he stood his ground manfully. The vessel at last stranded close to the spot where he was standing, and, by this time, it was reduced to the dimensions of one of those toy boats, with which the children amuse themselves in the pools left on the beach by the receding tide.

A man of dwarfish stature stepped on shore, and the countryman then perceived that the mysterious vessel had assumed the form of the bladebone of a sheep, enveloped in a mass of tangled sea-weed. Nothing daunted, he addressed the mysterious stranger, and asked him whence he came? What was his name? Whither was he going? The stranger either was, or pretended to be, ignorant of the language in which he was addressed, but to the last question answered: " Je vais cheminant "—(" I am going travelling)."

He is said, however, to have remained in the island, to have built himself a house on a spot called " Casquet," * in the neighbourhood of the

---

* According to Métivier's *Dictionary*—" Casquet "—(from the Latin *Casicare*) means " Over-fall Rock," and is the same as the *Casus Rupes* of Hearne and Leland.

EDITOR'S NOTE.—* The name of the house is " La Perelle," " Casquet " is a nick-name. After the erection of a lighthouse on " Casquet" or " Les Casquets," the fishermen keeping their boats in Perelle Bay, nick-named the house " Le P'tit Casquet," because the inhabitants were in the habit of sitting up late, and consequently there was light to be seen in the house when they returned from sea late in the evening.—*From John de Garis, Esq.*

place where he landed, and to have become the progenitor of a family which bears the name of "Le Cheminant," and of which many of the members were famous for their skill as smiths.

It is not unlikely that in this tale we have the remains—strangely altered by passing through the mouths of many successive generations—of some one of the numerous legendary stories of . the early British saints, who, according to some of the hagiographers, were in the habit of navigating from Brittany to Cornwall, and from Wales to Ireland, on their mantles, in stone troughs, or on bundles of sea-weed.[*]

A WITCH'S FORESIGHT.

It is generally believed that those who practise unlawful acts, however clever they may be, are generally quite unable to foresee what is likely to happen to themselves. That this is not invariably the case the following story will show.

A woman, who had the reputation of being a sorceress, contrived to live in comparative ease and comfort by begging from door to door, few venturing to send her away without an alms for fear of incurring her displeasure, and bringing down some misfortune on themselves or their households. She presented herself one morning at the house of a farmer in easy circumstances, whose wife was one not likely to be imposed upon, and not by any means remarkable for liberality towards the poor. The witch's well-contrived tale of distress failed to

---

[*] From George Métivier, Esq., and Mrs. Savidan.
See in Thorpe's *Northern Mythology*, Vol. I., p. 179, how Oller crosses the sea on a bone.

Old Market Place and States Arcade.

make an impression on the hard heart of the farmer's wife, and the beggar was dismissed without even a kind word : indeed, it is even said that the odious epithet " *Caïmande* " * was applied to her. On turning her back on the inhospitable door, she was heard to mutter between her teeth, " You shall repent of this."

It was a fine morning in spring, and a hen that had hatched an early brood of chickens, had brought them out into the sun, and was clucking over her callow brood, and scratching the earth in search of seeds and insects for them. The farmer's wife was looking on with complacency, and already calculating in her mind what the brood was likely to fetch in the market. The proverb tells us that we must not reckon our chickens before they are hatched. It seems that it is not wise to reckon on them even after they are hatched. And this the farmer's wife found to her cost ; for, scarcely was the witch out of the farm-yard, before one of the chickens fell on its side, gave a kick or two, and died. Its example was soon followed by all its brothers and sisters, and, last of all, the bereaved mother also departed this life. The farmer's wife was at no loss to whose evil agency to impute this untoward event, and hastened at once to consult an old neighbour, a wise woman, who had the reputation of knowing how these unholy spells were to be counteracted, and what means were to be adopted to prevent the sorceress from doing any further mischief. She was advised to

---

* Métivier derives this word—meaning " beggar "—from the old French word " *guermenter* " to complain. The old Bas-Breton word was " *c'harm* "—to utter cries.

lose no time in returning home ; to extract carefully the hearts of all the chickens, as well as that of the hen ; to stick new pins or nails into them, and to roast or fry them over a brisk fire, when, she was assured, that not only would the witch be made to suffer unheard of agonies, but that all power would be taken from her to do any further mischief.

The farmer's wife hastened home to follow the instructions given her by the wise woman, but found, to her dismay, that the sorceress had profited by her short absence from home to re-visit the farmyard, and that she had carefully removed every heart from the carcases.*

FORTUNE TELLING.

Persons who have the temerity to wish to pry into the secrets of futurity are frequently punished for their curiosity by the exact fulfilment of the prediction, although it may appear to be such as could by no possibility come to pass. The following story may be taken as an instance.

A young man applied to a woman, who pretended to be able to foresee events, to tell him what was likely to happen to him hereafter. She foretold that he had not long to live, but that he should be hanged, drowned, and burnt. Not knowing how it was possible that all these evils should come upon him, he made light of the prophecy, but the event proved the truth of the soothsayer's prediction. One night, having allowed his fire to go out, and having no means at hand to rekindle it, he ran across the fields to the nearest habitation to beg a light. On his return, in jumping over a ditch, his foot caught

* From Charlotte Du Port.

in some brambles, and he fell head foremost into the water, his legs at the same time became so entangled in the bushes that he remained suspended, and the torch which he held in his hand setting fire to his clothes, he perished, as the fortune-teller had predicted, by hanging, drowning, and burning.*

* From Rachel Du Port.

EDITOR'S NOTE.

Other Editor's Notes on this subject will be found in Appendix B.

Compare "Damasc, Seigneur d'Asnières, excommunié par Hugues de Saint-Calais, Evêque de Mans (A.D. 1136-1144). Damasc, averti qu'il périrait par le feu et par l'eau, ne fit qu'en rire; mais un jour, traversant en bateau la Sarthe pendant un orage, il fut foudroyé et noyé."—La Suze.—*Magazin Pittoresque*, 34me année, p. 312.

CHAPTER XI.

Charms, Spells, and Incantations.

" This, gathered in the planetary hour,
With noxious weeds, and spell'd with words of power,
Dire stepdames in the magic bowl infuse."
—*Dryden.*

" Begin, begin; the mystic spell prepare."
—*Milton.*

S long as the popular belief in witchcraft exists—and with all the boasted light and civilisation of the nineteenth century it still holds its ground—there will be found those who imagine that the evil influence of the sorcerer may be averted by a counteracting spell, or by certain practices, such as carrying an amulet about one's person, nailing a horse-shoe to the door of a house or the mast of a ship, etc.

With the ignorant and unlearned it is often useless to reason: they cannot understand nice distinctions, and if their faith be shaken or destroyed on one point, who can tell where the current of unbelief will stop? That there are persons who, by their illicit arts, can cause sickness to man or beast is firmly credited, but as there is no evil without a remedy, it is equally an article of popular belief that there are also those who are in possession of the necessary knowledge and power to counteract the evil designs and practices of the sorcerer.

As may readily be supposed these last are cunning
and unprincipled wretches, who trade on the folly
and superstition of their ignorant neighbours, and
who, doubtless, are often the cause of the malady of
the unfortunate cow or pig, which they are afterwards
called in to advise about. Various charms and
ceremonies are resorted to on these occasions, whereof
the most potent appears to be that known as "*la
bouïture,*" which consists in setting a number of
ingredients to seethe together in a cauldron, of which
the principal is the heart of some animal stuck full
of pins. It is not easy to arrive at a correct
knowledge of what is done, for great secrecy is
generally observed, and the actors in these superstitious follies are afraid to divulge what takes place.
The object of the charm seems to be either to avert
the evil, or to discover the author of it. In the
latter case, it often leads to serious misunderstandings
between neighbours. There are, however, certain
charms of a more innocent character, which can be
resorted to without the intervention of a cunning man.

Shortly after the Rev. Thomas Brock took possession of the Rectory of St. Pierre-du-Bois, about
the beginning of the nineteenth century, he was returning home one night from town, where he had been
detained until a late hour. It was midnight when
he reached the parsonage, and in the imperfect light
he thought that he saw a number of persons
assembled near the church porch. Astonished at so
unusual a sight, and wondering what could possibly
be the cause of such an assembly at that hour, he
tied up his horse to the gate, and stepped over the
stile into the churchyard. On drawing near he was
witness to an extraordinary ceremony. Several of his

parishioners, among whom he recognised many of the better sort, were walking in orderly procession round the church, and touching every angle as they passed. He addressed them and inquired what they were doing, but not a single word could he get in answer to his questions. Perfect silence was preserved until they came to the church-porch, where they all knelt down and recited the Lord's Prayer. This was repeated more than once, and at last they left the place without satisfying the legitimate curiosity of their pastor. Determined to fathom the mystery, he called the next day on some of the principal actors in the ceremony, and then learnt, not without some difficulty, that it was intended to remove a spell that was supposed to be hanging over the son or daughter of one of the parties, and that a single word spoken by any of the persons engaged in the solemn rite, would have effectually broken the charm.

In reference to this charm it may here be mentioned that an old servant of the Rev. W. Chepmell, Rector of St. Sampson's and the Vale, was suffering from an ulcer in the leg. To cure it she went round the church, stopping at each of the angles, and repeating a certain prayer. The Rev. H. Le M. Chepmell, D.D., who was a child at the time, remembers the circumstance, but does not know what the prayer was that was used on the occasion.

The forms which follow, and which, for the benefit of those who are unacquainted with French, have been translated as closely as possible, were found in a book of memoranda, household and farming accounts, recipes for medicines, etc., which once belonged to Sieur Jean Lenfestey, des Adams, in the parish of St. Pierre-du-Bois. It was written about the end of the last, and beginning of the present, century. The mystical words used in some of the spells have been given just as they were found in the manuscript. They appear to be a curious jumble of Hebrew, Greek, and Latin, very much disfigured by having passed through the hands of ignorant, unlettered transcribers, or, perhaps, by having been transmitted orally from one to another, and, at last, taken down from dictation. It is quite impossible to say how long these spells and charms have been in use among the peasantry, whether they have been handed down by tradition from times before the Reformation, or whether—which is far more probable—they have been introduced in comparatively recent times by some of the farm-labourers, who, in times of peace, come to the island from the neighbouring coasts of Normandy and Brittany in search of work. It is only on the latter supposition that the invocation of St. Blaize and St. Nicodemus, the saying of a Mass, and the reciting of *Paters* and *Ave-Marias* can be accounted for, the indigenous population having been so thoroughly reformed as to have lost all recollection of these matters.

To Remove any kind of Spell, and Cause the Person who has Cast it to Appear.

Choose one of the animals whose death has been caused, taking care that there is no sign of life remaining in it: take out its heart, and place it in a. clean plate: then take nine thorns of "noble épine " * and proceed as follows :—

Pierce one of the thorns into the heart, saying :—

---

* Probably a corruption of "aube-épine."

The " Groignet."

Adibaga, Sabaoth, Adonay, contra, ratout prisons preront fini unixio paracle gasum.

Take two thorns and pierce them in, saying:—*Qui susum mediotos agres gravoil valax.*

Take two more, and in placing them say:—*Laula zazai valoi sator saluxu paracle gassum.*

Take two more, and say in placing them:—*Mortuis cum fice suni et per flagelationem domini nostri Jesu Christi.*

Then place the last two thorns with these words:— *Avir sunt devant nous paracle tui strator verbonum ossisum fidando.*

Then continue saying:—" I call on him or her who has caused the Missal Abel to be fabricated: cease from thine evil deed; come, nevertheless, by sea or by land, wherever thou art; show thyself to us without delay and without fail."

(Note: that if thorns of the "noble épine" are not to be procured, one may have recourse to new nails).

The heart, being pierced with thorns, as directed, must be put into a small bag and hung in the chimney. The next day it must be taken out of the bag and put upon a plate; then pull out the first thorn, and place it in another part of the heart, pronouncing the same words as were said at first; then take out the two next thorns with the fitting words, and so on with the others in due order, replacing them as we have directed, and being careful never to stick a thorn again into the same hole. This is to be done on nine consecutive days; nevertheless, if you wish not to give any respite to the malefactor, you may compress the nine days into one, observing the order above prescribed. At the last operation, after having pierced in the thorns or nails with the fitting words, you must make a large fire, place the heart on a gridiron, and put it to roast on the live embers. The malefactor will be obliged to appear and to beg for mercy; and if it be out of his power to appear within the time you appoint, his death will ensue.

ANOTHER METHOD.

Kill a pigeon; open it and pluck out its heart. Stick new pins all round the heart. Put water to boil in a small pot, and when it is boiling throw the heart in it. You must have ready a green turf to serve as a cover to the pot, and must put it on with the earth downwards.

The pot must boil for an hour. Be careful to keep up a good fire of wood or charcoal, and at the end of the hour throw the heart into the burning embers. See that all the doors, windows, and other openings of the house are closed. The sorcerer will come and call and knock at the door, demanding to speak with you; but you must not open to him until you have made him promise to do what you wish.

ANOTHER MEANS OF CAUSING A SORCERER TO SHEW HIMSELF.

Take the tails of two fresh-water eels, with the inner bark of an ash tree, that which is next the wood. Buy twenty-six new needles, and put all to burn together with flower of sulphur.

If you wish to see the sorcerer by daylight you must take the roots of small and large sage, with the pith of the elder and daffodil bulbs. Put the whole to boil together in vinegar, and make your arrangements so that it shall boil a quarter of an hour before noon. As soon as the first bubbles begin to rise the sorcerer will make his appearance. In. this experiment you must leave the door open. It is done simply with the view of knowing the malefactor.

To Avert all Sorts of Spells and Enchantments.

Take a sheep's heart, pierce nails into it, and hang it in the chimney, saying :—*Rostin, Clasta Auvara, Chasta, Custodia, Duranee.* These words must be said over the heart every day, and eight days will not have elapsed before the sorcerer who has cast the spell will come and beg you to remove the heart, complaining that he feels great pain internally. You can then ask him to remove the spell, and he will request you to give him some animal to which he may transfer it. You may grant what he asks, otherwise he will burst asunder.

A Preservative against Spells, to be Hung Round the Neck.

Take nine bits of green broom, and two sprigs of the same, which you must tie together in the form of a cross (×); nine morsels of elder, nine leaves of betony, nine of agrimony, a little bay salt, sal-ammoniac, new wax, barley, leaven, camphor and quick-silver. The quick-silver must be inclosed in cobbler's wax. Put the whole into a new linen cloth which has never been used, and sew it well up so that nothing may fall out. Hang this round your neck. It is a sure preservative against the power of witches.

To Win at Play

On St. John's Eve gather fern before noon. Make a bracelet of it in the form of these letters—H U T Y .

To Make Peace between Men who are Fighting.

Write on the circumference of an apple the letters H A O N and throw it into the midst of the combatants.

To Stop Bleeding.

Touching the part affected, say :—*Place* + + + *Consummatum* + + + *Resurrexit.*

To Cure a Burn.

Repeat these words thrice over the burn, breathing thereon each time :—

" *Feu de Dieu, perds ta chaleur,*
Comme Judas perdit sa couleur,
Quand il trahit notre Seigneur,
Au jardin des oliviers." *

To Stop a Fire that is Burning a House.

Make three crosses on the mantel-piece with a live coal, and say :—" *In te Domine speravi, non confundar in æternum.*"

To Cause a Person to Love You.

Take four-leaved clover and place it on a consecrated stone ; then say a Mass over it, put it into a nosegay, and make the person smell it, saying at the same time " *Gabriel illa sunt.*"

Another Means.

On St. John's Eve gather clecampane (alliène de campana), dry it in an oven, reduce it to powder

---

EDITOR'S NOTE.—* Another form is as follows :—
Brulure, brulure, mollis ta chaleur,
Comme Judas perdit sa couleur
En trahissant notre Seigneur.
—*From John de Garis, Esq.*

with ambergris, and wear it next your heart for
nine days. Then endeavour to get the person whose
love you wish to obtain, to swallow a portion of it,
and the effect is sure to follow.

To Prevent a Sportsman from Killing any Game.

Say:—"*Si ergo me quæritis, sinite hos abire.*"

To Cure a Horse that has the Vives or the Gripes.*

Say:—"Our help is in the name of the Lord,
who made the Heavens and the Earth. In the name
of God, Amen! St. Nicodemus, who tookest down
our Lord Jesus Christ from the cross, deign by the
permission of God to cure this horse (name the
colour), belonging to (name the owner), of the vives
or gripes (as the case may be)."

Then let all who are present say the Lord's Prayer
nine times.

Another Form.

"Horse (name the colour), belonging to (name the
owner), if thou hast the vives, or the red gripes,
or any other of thirty-six maladies, in case thou be
suffering from them: May God cure thee and the
blessed Saint Eloy! In the name of the Father,
and of the Son, and of the Holy Ghost, Amen!"

Then say five "*Paters*" and five "*Aves*" on
your knees.

---

* This charm must have been long current in Guernsey, for the invocation
with which it commences is a strictly Presbyterian form, being the sentence
with which the services of the Reformed French Church invariably began.

The mention of "*Paters*" and "*Aves*," and the invocation of St. Eloy in
the second charm, points clearly to a Romish origin, and render it very doubtful
whether the charm could ever have been resorted to in Guernsey within the
last two or three hundred years. St. Nicodemus might still be recognised, but
St. Eloy has long been entirely forgotten, and probably not one in a thousand
of our peasantry has the slightest idea of what is meant by the words "*Pater*"
and "*Ave.*"

To Remove a Fish Bone from the Throat.

Say :—" Blaise, martyr for Jesus Christ, command thee to come up or go down."

To Prevent a Dog from Barking or Biting.

Say three times, while looking at the dog :—
" Bare—Barbare ! May thy tail hang down ! May St. Peter's key close thy jaws until to-morrow ! " *

Quick-Silver a Protection against Witchcraft.

A belief in the efficacy of quick-silver in counteracting the evil eye, and averting the injurious effects of spells, is very universal among the lower orders; and there are many persons who will never venture beyond their threshold without having in their pocket, or hung round their neck, a small portion of this metal.

A fisherman, who for some time had been unsuccessful in his fishing, imagined that a spell had been cast upon him. No man was better acquainted with the marks by which the fishermen recognise the spots where the finny tribe are to be found in most abundance. None was better acquainted with the intricate tides and currents which render the rocky coasts of the island such a puzzle to navigators, or knew better when to take advantage of them to secure a plentiful catch of fish. His tackle was good, he used the best and most tempting bait, and yet, under the most propitious circumstances, with the most favourable conditions of tide, wind, and weather, day after day passed and he took next to nothing. Winter was coming on, and a longer

Editor's Note.—* Many of these charms are to be found almost word for word in *Croyances et Légendes du Centre de la France*, by Laisnel de la Salle, Vol. I., p. 291-330., etc,

continuance of bad weather than is usual at that season, combined with the worthless quality of the fish caught when he did venture out between the gales,—in short, a continued run of ill-luck,—confirmed him in the idea that he was bewitched.

He confided his fears to an old man of his own profession, who had the reputation of knowing more than his neighbours, and particularly of being able to give advice in such cases as this, where there was reason to suppose that some unlawful influence was at work.

The old man listened to his tale, confirmed him in the idea that some evil-disposed person, in league with Satan, had cast an evil eye on him, and ended by counselling him always to carry quick-silver about with him. With this precaution he told him that he might defy the spells of all the wizards and witches that ever met on a Friday night at Catioroc to pay their homage to Old Nick.

The fisherman took the old man's advice, and procured a small vial containing mercury, which he placed carefully in the purse in which he carried his money, when he was fortunate enough to have any.

Strange to say, from that moment his luck turned, and, a succession of good hauls rewarding his industry, the fisherman soon found himself in possession of what, to him, was a goodly sum of money, and in which not a few gold pieces were included. These were, of course, carefully deposited in the purse containing the precious amulet, to which he attributed his good luck and his deliverance from the spell, which, he no longer doubted, had been cast upon him.

Alas ! his confidence in the charm was destined

Old House at Cobo.

to be, for a time, rudely broken. One night, in manœuvring his boat, an accidental blow from some of the gear shattered the bottle containing the quick-silver. What was his dismay the next morning, on opening his purse, to perceive that all his gold was turned into silver, and that the silver coins bore the appearance of vile lead! He was in despair, concluding very naturally that he had fallen into the power of some prince of magicians, and that henceforth he was a ruined man. He again consulted his old friend, whose experience this time proved of more practical use than his former advice. The wise man soon saw what had caused the apparent change in the coin, and recommended him to go without delay to a silversmith, who soon removed the quick-silver with which the precious pieces were coated, and restored them to their pristine brightness.*

The Cure of Warts, etc.

There are certain old men and women who, without pretending to any supernatural knowledge, are nevertheless supposed to possess the power of causing those unsightly excrescences (warts) to disappear, merely by looking at, and counting, them. Some mystery, however, is attached to the operation. They may not impart their secret, neither may they receive money for their services, although there is no reason why they should refuse any other present that may be offered. There is no doubt that the hands of growing boys and girls are more often disfigured by these excrescences than those of adults, and that, at a certain age, they are apt to disappear almost

---

* From Mr. John Le Cheminant.

suddenly. Perhaps this has been noticed by the persons who pretend to the art of removing warts, and that they do not undertake the cure unless they perceive certain indications of their being likely to disappear before long by the mere agency of natural causes. Nevertheless, the cases in which a cure has been effected after all the usual surgical remedies have been resorted to in vain, are quite sufficiently numerous to justify a belief in the minds of the vulgar of a possession of this extraordinary gift.

The operation, whatever it may be, is designated by the word "*décompter*," which may be translated "to uncount," or "to count backwards."

The process by which a wen, or glandular swelling, known in our local dialect as "*un veuble*," is to be removed, is expressed by the same term, but in this there is no mystery which requires concealment. The charm is well known, and may be used by anyone. It is as follows. The person who undertakes the cure must begin by making the sign of the cross on the part affected, and must then repeat the following formula :—" *Pour décompter un veuble.*" * " *Saint Jean avait un veuble qui coulait à neuf pertins. De neuf ils vinrent à huit; de huit ils vinrent à sept; de sept ils vinrent à six; de six ils vinrent à cinq; de cinq ils vinrent à quatre; de quatre ils vinrent à trois; de trois ils vinrent à deux; de deux ils vinrent à un; d'un il vint à rien, et ainsi Saint Jean perdit son veuble.*"

The second day the operator must begin at "eight," the day after at "seven," and so on until the whole nine are counted off, when, if a cure is

---

* From Mrs. Dalgairns and Rachel Duport.

A A

not effected, it must be set down to some neglect
or want of faith in one or the other of the parties
concerned, for no one can venture to doubt the
efficacy of the spell.

It will, doubtless, have struck the reader that in
this, as well as in other charms, the number nine
plays a conspicuous part. This may possibly be
connected in some way with the practice of the
Church of Rome, which, on certain special occasions,
orders solemn prayers and ceremonies for nine
consecutive days.

In most farm-houses there were formerly to be found
one or more old oak-chests, sometimes very richly
and quaintly carved. In some places where they
had been taken care of, they were in excellent
preservation, but, in the majority of cases, they had
given way to those more modern articles of furniture—
chests of drawers and wardrobes—less elegant, perhaps,
but more fashionable, and decidedly more convenient.
Now there are few or none to be met with, the
revival of the taste for rich and elaborate carving
having led to a demand for these ancient specimens
of the skill of our forefathers to be remodelled into
sideboards, cabinets, and other similar articles of
furniture. When these old coffers had ceased to be
thought worthy of a place in the bettermost rooms
of the house, they were frequently to be found in
the stables or outhouses, serving as cornbins, or
receptacles for all sorts of rubbish. Still they were
sometimes remembered, for old people would tell of
their efficacy in curing erysipelas, or, as it is locally
termed, "*le faeu sauvage.*" The chests chosen for
this purpose were those ornamented with Scriptural
subjects or figures of Apostles and Saints, and the

cure was supposed to be effected by opening and shutting the lid of the coffer nine times, so as to fan the face of the patient.

One of the many mysterious ills to which poor human nature is subject, is known as "*la maladie de la nère poule.*" This is to be removed by procuring a perfectly black hen, and swinging her round the head of the sufferer three times.

To cure an equally undefined affection known as "*le mal volant*" the patient must also take a black hen, and, holding her in both hands, must rub that part of the body in which the pain is felt. The hen used in this incantation must be bought; if a gift, the charm would fail of its effect. After having been used it must not be kept or put to death, but given away. The classical reader will not require to be reminded that cocks were sacrificed to Æsculapius.

CELTS.

These interesting relics of the aboriginal inhabitants of the island are called by the country people "*fouïdres,*" *i.e.* thunderbolts. It is firmly believed that the house which has the happiness to possess one of them will neither be struck by lightning nor consumed by fire.

It is believed that animals that are sick can be cured by giving them water to drink in which a celt has been dipped.

ANOTHER COUNTER-CHARM FOR WITCHCRAFT.

When a person has reason to believe that either himself or any of his belongings is under the influence of a spell, he should procure the heart of an animal—that of a black sheep is supposed to be

A A 2

the most efficacious,—and, having stuck it over thickly in every part with new pins or nails, put it down to roast before a strong fire. Care must, however, have been taken previously to close up all means of entry into the house, even to stuffing up the key-hole. The heart no sooner begins to feel the influence of the fire than doleful cries are heard from without, which increase more and more as the roasting goes on. Loud knocks are next heard at the door, and urgent appeals for admission are made, so urgent that few have the heart to withstand them. No sooner, however, is the door opened than all the clamour ceases. No one is seen outside, and, on looking at the heart, it is found to be burnt to a cinder. The charm has failed, and those who tried it remain as much under the influence of the sorcerer as ever, with the additional certainty of having offended their enemy without a chance of pardon or pity on his part, nay, they know that they have only exposed themselves to greater persecution in revenge for the pain they have made him suffer; for it is universally believed that the wizards or witches are irresistibly attracted to the place where this counter-spell is being performed; and that, while it lasts, the tortures of the damned are suffered by them. What would occur if the spell were persevered in and the door kept closed is not generally known, but it is thought that as the heart dried up before the flames, the sorcerer would wither away, and that, with the last drop of moisture, his wicked soul would depart to the place of everlasting torment.[*]

---

[*] From Charlotte Du Port.

THE SEIGNEUR OF ST. GEORGE AND THE DÉSORCELLEUR.

It is related that towards the end of the eighteenth century a number of country people were assembled in a farm-house in the parish of Ste. Marie-du-Castel, for the purpose of putting into practice the counter-spell described in the preceding paragraph, or one of a similar nature; for it is believed that the same end may be attained by setting a cauldron on the hearth, and boiling the heart with certain herbs, gathered with some peculiar precautions, and known only to the "*désorcelleurs*," as the white-witches who generally conduct these ceremonies are called in the local dialect. The doors of the house, as is required in these cases, had been carefully closed and fastened, and the charm was, to all appearance, progressing favourably, when a knock was heard at the door. No one answered, for fear of breaking the spell, but all remained in breathless and awe-stricken silence, believing firmly that their incantation was working favourably and in accordance with their wishes. The visitor on the outside, who could plainly see that the house was not untenanted, grew impatient at not being admitted, and called out with a loud and authoritative voice, to know why an entrance was refused him. The voice was that of a gentleman residing in the neighbourhood, the Seigneur de St. George, a magistrate universally respected for his integrity, and beloved for his benevolence. The inmates of the dwelling durst no longer keep him out; the door was at last unbolted, but, as the common belief is that the first person who applies for admission after the spell has begun is the sorcerer, the assembled peasants were at their wits' end to account for his presence.

The gentleman was not long in perceiving how matters stood. He lectured the assembly soundly on their folly and superstition, and, recognising among them the "*désorcelleur*," whom he well knew to be a designing knave, making his profit out of the credulity of his neighbours, he drove him out of the house with some well-applied stripes from a dog-whip he chanced to have in his hand.

It is not known whether the Seigneur de St. George succeeded in convincing any of his neighbours of the folly of believing in witchcraft; it is rather thought, on the contrary, that from that day forward they considered him wiser than need be! *

———

Love Spells.

"A love-potion works more by the strength of charm than nature."
—Collier, *On Popularity.*

Under the head of Holy Wells mention has already been made of a means resorted to by maidens to ascertain who their future husbands are to be, but this is not the only manner by which this most interesting information is to be obtained.

St. Thomas' Night, La Longue Veille, Christmas Eve, and the last night of the year, are all seasons in which it is supposed that the powers of the air, devils, witches, fairies, and goblins, are abroad and active, and accordingly, these days, like Hallowe'en in Scotland, are chosen for the performance of spells

———

* From W. P. Métivier, Esq.

Old Manor House, Anneville.

by which some of the secrets of futurity may be
discovered.

Some of these charms must be performed alone—
others are social, but all require strict silence.   As
to the social spells, it is easy to conceive that when a
number of girls are met together to try their fortunes,
the charm is frequently broken, either by the fears of
the superstitious, or the laughter of the incredulous.
We will begin with the solitary spells.   On St.
Thomas' Night the girl who is desirous of knowing
whom she is to marry, must take a golden pippin,
and, when about retiring to rest, must pass two pins
crossways through it, and lay it under her pillow.
Some say that the pippin should be wrapped up in
the stocking taken from the left leg—others that this
stocking should be taken off last and thrown over
the left shoulder.   Which is right, we have no means
of ascertaining, but doubtless the efficacy of the spell
depends on following the correct formula.   It is then
necessary to get into bed backwards, and repeat the
following incantation thrice :—

" *Saint Thomas, Saint Thomas,*
Le plus court, le plus bas,
Fais moi voir en m'endormant
Celui qui sera mon amant,
Et le pays, et la contrée.
Où il fait sa demeurée,
Et le métier qu'il sait faire
Devant moi qu'il vienne faire.
Qu'il soit beau ou qu'il soit laid
Tel qu'il sera je l'aimerai.
Saint Thomas, fait moi la grâce
Que je le voie, que je l'embrasse."
" *Ainsi soit il.*"

Not another word must be spoken, and, if the rite has been duly performed, the desired knowledge will be communicated in a dream. There are different versions of the words to be repeated. One of them avoids a direct invocation of the Saint, and begins thus :—

> " *Le jour Saint Thomas,*
> *Le plus court, le plus bas,*
> *Je prie Dieu incessamment*
> *De me faire voir en dormant*
> *Celui qui doit être mon amant, etc.**

Another charm consists in placing two fronds of agrimony, each bearing nine leaflets, crosswise under the pillow, and securing them by means of two new pins, also crossed. The future husband is sure to appear in a dream.†

The name of the future husband may be discovered by writing the letters of the alphabet on a piece of paper, cutting them apart, and, when getting into bed, just after extinguishing the light, throwing them into a basin or bucket of water. Next morning the bits of paper which float with the written side

---

* See *Notes and Queries*, IV. Series. Vol. VIII., p. 506. *Derbyshire Folk-Lore.*

On St. Thomas' Eve there used to be a custom among girls to procure a large red onion, into which, after peeling, they would stick nine pins, and say :—

> " Good St. Thomas, do me right,
> Send me my true love this night,
> In his clothes and his array,
> Which he weareth every day."

Eight pins were stuck round one in the centre, to which was given the name of the swain—the " true love."

The onion was placed under the pillow on going to bed, and they would dream of the desired person.

† From Miss Lane.

uppermost indicate the name. This charm is efficacious on Midsummer Eve.*

The trade of the husband that is to be may be guessed at by throwing the white of a raw egg into a glass of water, and exposing it to the rays of the noonday sun at Christmas or Midsummer. The egg in coagulating assumes curious and fantastic forms, and these are interpreted to denote the trade or profession of him whom the girl who tries the charm is destined to marry. A sort of divination to the same effect is also practised by pouring molten lead into water.

A spell which requires to be performed in society is as follows. On any of the solemn nights about Christmastide, when spells are supposed to be efficaciously used, a number of girls meet together and make a chaplet in perfect silence, by stringing grains of allspice and berries of holly alternately, placing, at intervals of twelve, an acorn, of which there must be as many as there are persons in the company.

This chaplet is twined round a log of wood, which is then placed on the blazing hearth, and, as the last acorn is being consumed, each of the young women sees the form of her future husband pass between her and the fire.*

Another social spell consists in making a cake, to which each person in the company contributes a portion of flour, salt, and water, together with a hair from her own head, or parings from the nails. When the cake is kneaded—an operation in which all must take a part—it is placed on the hearth to bake. A

---

* From Miss Lane.

table is then set out in the middle of the room, and covered with a clean cloth. As many plates are laid out as there are persons present, and as many seats placed round the table, each girl designating her own. The cake, when thoroughly baked, is placed on the board, and the girls watch in solemn silence until the hour of midnight, when, exactly as the clock strikes twelve, the appearances of the future husbands are seen to enter, and seat themselves in the chairs prepared for them; each girl, however, seeing only her own husband that is to be, those of her companions remaining invisible to her. Should anyone of the party be destined to die unmarried, instead of the appearance of a man, she sees a coffin. The spell is broken, should a single word be uttered from the moment when the ingredients for the cake are first produced, until the whole of the ceremony is completed.*

The charmed cake may also be used by a person alone, in which case the manner of proceeding is as follows. The cake, which should be composed of equal quantities of flour, salt, and soot, must be made and baked in secret and in silence. On retiring to rest it must be divided into two equal portions, one of which must be eaten by the person who tries the charm, but no water or other liquid is to be drunk with it. The other half is to be wrapped up in the garter taken from the left leg, and placed under the pillow. At midnight the form of the future husband will stand at the bedside and be seen by his intended bride.†

---

* From the late Miss Sophy Brock and Rachel Du Port.

† From Miss Lane.

The Consequences of a Love Spell.

It must not be supposed that these love charms can always be tried with impunity. Like all other forms of divination they are sinful, and instances are on record in which punishment has followed the unhallowed attempt to pry into the secrets of futurity so wisely hidden from our mortal ken. It would seem that not merely the wraith or similitude of the destined husband can be made to show itself, but that, by some unexplained and mysterious agency, the actual presence in the body can be completed, at whatever distance the man may at that moment be. To the unfortunate individual who is made the victim of these practices the whole appears the effect of a frightful dream, attended with much suffering. It is related that an officer, thus forced to show himself, left behind him a sword, which was found by the young woman after his departure, and carefully hidden away. In process of time he came to the island, saw the girl, fell in love with her, and was married. For many years they lived happily together, until, one day, in turning out the contents of an old coffer, he found at the bottom of it the identical sword which had disappeared from his possession in so unaccountable and mysterious a manner. The memory of the frightful dream in which he had endured so much flashed across his mind. In a frenzy of passion he sought his wife, and, upbraiding her with having been to him the cause of dreadful suffering, and of having put him in peril of his life by her magical practices, plunged the sword into her breast.*

---

* From Rachel Du Port.

* See *Les Veillées Allemandes*, by Grimm. *La Veille de St. André*, Vol. I., p. 201.

WITCHES AND THE WHITE-THORN.

There appear to be some superstitious notions with regard to the connection of witchcraft with the white-thorn. Witches are suspected of meeting at night under its shade. An old man of very eccentric habits not many years since still inhabited the ruined manor house of Anneville, once the residence of the ancient family of de Chesney, sold in 1509 to Nicholas Fashin, and subsequently passing by inheritance into the Andros family, in whose possession it still remains.

He passed with his neighbours for a wizard, although he only professed to be a " *désorcelleur* " or white-witch, and was said to have been in the habit of taking those who applied to him to be unbewitched to a very old thorn-bush, which had grown up within the walls of an ancient square tower adjoining the house, and there, before sunrise, making them go through certain evolutions which were supposed to counteract the spells which had been cast upon them.*

The hawthorn, or at least such specimens of the tree as are remarkable for their age, their size, or their gnarled branches, seems to be associated in the minds of our peasantry with magic and magical practices. The wizards and witches, when, in their nocturnal excursions they take the form of hares, rabbits, cats, or other animals, assemble under the shadow, or in the vicinity of some ancient thorn, and amuse themselves with skipping round it in the moonlight. The " *désorcelleur* " who pretends to the power of counteracting the spells of witches, and

---

* From the present proprietor of Anneville.

freeing the unfortunate victims of their art from
their evil influence, resorts with the sufferer to some
noted thorn-bush, and there goes through the ceremonies and incantations which are to free the
sufferer. A large and very old tree, on the estate
of a gentleman in the parish of St. Saviour's, was,
in days gone by, constantly resorted to at night for
the purpose of cutting from it small portions of the
wood to be carried about the person as a safeguard
against witchcraft. It is essential to the efficacy of
this charm that the part of the branch cut off
should be that from which three spurs issue.*

William Le Poidevin was told by his grandmother
that the "blanche-épine" is "le roi des bois;" the
wood must not be employed for common uses. A
boat or ship, into the construction of which it
entered, would infallibly be lost or come to grief.†

DIVINING ROD.

The following extract from a work published in
London in 1815, but which is now very rarely to be
met with, gives so good an account of the manner in
which springs of water are believed in these islands to
be discovered by means of the divining rod, that we
have no hesitation in copying it at length.

The work bears the following title : " General View
of the Agriculture and Present State of the Islands of
Normandy subject to the Crown of Great Britain,

---

* From George Allez, Esq., who calls the tree he speaks of " aube-épine," but
declares it was not a hawthorn. May it not be a mountain ash or rowan tree?

† Among the Blakeway MSS. in the Bodleian Library I found noticed these
superstitious cures for whooping-cough.

" Near to Button Oak, in the Forest of Bewdley, grows a thorn in the
form of an arch, one end in the county of Salop, the other in Stafford. This
is visited by numbers in order to make their children pass under it for the
cure of the whooping-cough."—*Notes and Queries*, IV. Series, III. 216.

Oratory Window, Anneville.

drawn up for the consideration of the Board of
Agriculture and Internal Improvement," by Thomas
Quayle, Esq.

The passage in question will be found at p. 31.
Baguette Divinatoire.—"The opinion still prevails in
Jersey, of a power, possessed by certain individuals, of
discovering by means of a rod of hazel or of some few
trees, in what spot springs of water may be found. A
respectable farmer in the parish of St. Sauveur is
persuaded that he is endowed with this faculty, of
which he says he discovered himself to be possessed in
consequence of observing and imitating the ceremonies
employed for a similar purpose by an emigrant priest.
The farmer, on repeating these himself, found them
equally efficacious, and afterwards received from the
priest instructions for his exercise of the water-finding
art.

He first removes from his person every particle of
metal. A slender rod of hazel, terminating in two
twigs, the whole about ten inches in length, is taken
into both hands, one holding each twig. The forked
point of the rod, and palms of the hands, as closed,
are turned upwards. The operator then walks forward,
with his eye directed on the forked end of the rod.
When he approaches a spot where a spring is
concealed, the elevated point of the rod begins to wave
and bend downwards; at the spot itself it becomes
inverted.

On the 28th of August, 1812, these ceremonies were
practised in the presence of three gentlemen, then and
still unconvinced of the existence of any such power.
The farmer had, at their request, civilly left his
harvest, and repeated his practice for their satisfaction.
He first held the rod over his own well, where it did

not bend, in consequence, as he asserted, of the spring not being perennial. He then slowly walked forward with the rod of hazel held in his hands; at a particular spot, near his own dwelling, the forked end of the rod began to be agitated and droop downward; at length, as he proceeded, it became nearly or quite inverted. He then marked the spot, walked away, and, setting off in another direction, returned toward the same spot. When he arrived near it, the end of the rod again began to droop, and, at the spot, was, as before, inverted. When he was proceeding, the persons present carefully watched his hands, but could not discern any motion in either, or any other visible means by which the rod could be affected. One of them took the rod into his own hands, and, repeating the same practice over the same ground, the rod did not bend.

"Whether under the designated spot a spring exists or not was not examined; probably there may, quite apart from any virtue in the *Baguette divinatoire.*

"On several occasions the farmer has been requested to seek for water, and it has not only been found, but nearly at the depth which he indicated. He is a man of good character, of simple manners, obliging and communicative. Being in easy circumstances, he exercises his art without reward. The priest had communicated some rules, to enable him to judge of the exact distance of the water from the surface. These, he observes, proved fallacious, and the only guide he has for judging of the depth of the water, is his observation of the distance between the spot at which the forked end of the rod begins to be agitated, and that at which, when he arrives, the rod becomes wholly inverted."

It will be observed that Quayle does not assert
that he himself saw the farmer practise his art, but
merely that it had been witnessed by three gentlemen
in 1812. The copy of Quayle's work, however, from
which the extract was made, contains a very
interesting marginal note in pencil, in the handwriting
of a former owner of the book, Peter Le Pelley, Esq,
Seigneur of Sark, who was, unfortunately, drowned
by the capsizing of a boat in which he was crossing
from that island to Guernsey in March, 1839. He
says :—

"I have seen it practised by Mr. Moullin, of *Le
Ponchez*, at Sark and Brechou ; and at Brechou the
forked stick became so inverted that it split at the
fork. He did it in my presence on gold, silver, and
water, and the rod inverted over them. He first
rubbed his hands with the substance to be sought
for, and, if water, dipped his hands in it, and held
his two thumbs on the extremity of the forks. That
there is a virtue in the using of the *Baguette
divinatoire* is incontestable, the reason I deem unknown. May not electricity or magnetism be
concerned in it? It turned in the hands of some
Sarkmen who previously were ignorant of possessing
that power. *Ergo* it is independent of the will.

"On Mr. Moullin's indication, who told me I should
find water at twenty to twenty-two feet at Brechou,
I had a well dug. The men blasted all the way
through the solid rock without finding any water,
and at nineteen to twenty feet, on making a hole
with a jumper, the water sprang up and filled the
well. Mr. Moullin found a ring that had been lost
by means of the *Baguette divinatoire*."

Brechou, mentioned in this note, is a small islet

or dependency of Sark, more generally known by the
name of l'Ile des Marchants, a name it derived
from some former proprietors, members of the ancient
Guernsey family of Le Marchant ; and for those
who are unacquainted with the art of quarrying, it
may not be amiss to explain that a "jumper" is
an iron tool with which holes are bored in the rock
for the purpose of blasting it with gunpowder, and
so facilitating its removal piecemeal.

The writer of the present compilation had an
opportunity of witnessing experiments with the
divining rod, when attending, in September, 1875, at
Guingamp, in Brittany, a meeting of the "Association
Bretonne," a combination of the Agricultural and
Archæological Societies of that Province. The place
where the experiments were made was a piece of
grass-land at the head of a small valley, and the
course of an underground stream seemed to be traced
by the deflections of the rod, until it pointed almost
perpendicularly downwards over a certain spot in the
garden of a neighbouring *château*, where, we were
told, there was no doubt a strong spring would be
found at no great distance from the surface, which,
taking into consideration the nature of the locality,
seemed highly probable. It is certain that in the
hands of some who had never seen the experiment
performed before, and who at first professed incredulity,
the rod appeared ready to twist itself out of their
grasp as soon as they drew near to the place where
water was supposed to be, while with others, who
were disposed to believe only the evidence of what
they witnessed with their own eyes, the mysterious
twig remained perfectly still. No attempt at deceit
could be detected. The persons who made the

experiment were gentlemen, and men of education, although, as Bretons, not perhaps quite free from that tinge of superstitious feeling which is so characteristic of all Celtic nations. The writer is bound to add that, neither in his own hands, nor in those of his companion and fellow countryman, was the slightest effect produced, although they were carefully instructed how to hold the rod, and they went over the very same ground where, in the hands of others, the rod had been visibly affected.

It is not irrelevant to add that in Cornwall, and other mining countries, the divining rod is said to be used for the purpose of discovering and tracing veins of metalliferous ore.

Bees Put in Mourning.

Few insects besides the bee and the silk-worm have been pressed into the service of man—at least in such a manner as to be looked upon as domesticated—and of these the bee, from its superior intelligence, and the striking fact of its living in community, with the semblance of a well-organised government, has, from the earliest times, attracted the attention and excited the interest of mankind. It is asserted by those who keep these useful insects, as well as by naturalists who have made them their especial study, that they recognise their masters and the members of their families, and that these may approach them with impunity when a stranger would run great risk of being stung. If this is really the case, it is not difficult to conceive how, among a people rude and ignorant, and yet observant of the phenomena of nature, the bee should come to be regarded with particular respect. It is probably from a feeling of this kind that the custom arose of informing the bees when a death occurs in a family. The correct way of performing the ceremony is this. One of the household must take the door-key, and, proceeding to the hives, knock with it, and give notice to the bees in a whisper of the sad event which has just taken place, affixing, at the same time, a small shred of black crape or other stuff to each of the hives. If this formality is omitted, it is believed that the bees will die, or forsake the place. The same custom exists in other countries, but in Guernsey it is also thought proper to give them notice of weddings, and to deck the hives with white streamers.

A swarm of bees ought not to be sold for money, if you wish it to prosper. It should be given or exchanged for something of equal value. A money price is, however, sometimes agreed for, but in this case the sum must not be paid in any baser metal than gold. In following a swarm of bees, besides beating on pots and pans to make them settle, it is customary to call out to them "*Align'ous, mes p'tits, align'ous.*" *

---

* From J. de Garis, Esq., J. L. Mansell, Esq., and others.

EDITOR'S NOTE.—Various Editor's Notes on the subject of Charms and Spells will be found in Appendix C.

CHAPTER XII.

Folk Medicine and Leech Craft.

"A certain shepherd lad,
Of small regard to see to, yet well skill'd
In every virtuous plant and healing herb,
That spreads her verdant leaf to th' morning ray."
—*Comus.*

IN days gone by, before the invention of Morrison's pills, Holloway's ointment, and other infallible remedies, no farm was without its plot of medicinal herbs, skilful combinations of which—secrets handed down from one old wife or village doctor to another—were supposed to be capable of curing all the ills to which poor suffering humanity is heir, to say nothing of the various diseases affecting horses, oxen, swine, and other domestic animals.

Nine varieties of herbs was the number usually cultivated, a number which, like three and seven, is generally supposed to have some occult and mystic virtues. As to the herbs themselves it is not easy at the present day, when old traditions are rapidly passing away, to obtain a correct list of them, but the following is as correct as we can make it.

La Poumillière, or Helleborus viridis. Métivier, in his Dictionary, page 401, says of this plant that it was originally held in great veneration by the Greeks

St. Peter Port Harbour, 1852, showing the Old North Pier.

and Romans. He also says that it was used in cases
of consumption in cattle by our local veterinary
doctors. They pierced the dewlap or the ear of the
affected animal, and inserted in the hole one of the
small roots of this plant. This induced an abundant
suppuration, which sometimes proved beneficial.

La Cassidone, or French lavender. Boiste, in his
dictionary, says that its flowers and leaves promote
salivation. There is a proverb to the effect that:

> " *L'hyssope tout ma' développe*
> *La cassidoune tout ma' détrone.*"

Le Rosmarin, or rosemary. It is considered
unlucky not to have a plant of rosemary in one's
garden, but it is a plant that should never be *bought*,
but grown for you, and presented by a friend and
well-wisher.

La Petite Sauche, or small-leaved sage.

Le Grànd Consoul, or comfrey. Of this the root
is the part used.

La Rue. Rue, which was supposed to have a
potent effect on the eyes, and bestow second sight.

L'Alliène, or wormwood.

La Marjolaine, or marjoram, and

La Campana, or vervain, the "holy herb" of the
Druids.

This list by no means exhausts the plants possessed
of healing powers.

George Métivier, in his *Souvenirs Historiques*,
chapter IV. and II., speaks of a sacred briar, called
"pied-de-chat," worn as a waist-belt as an infallible
talisman against witchcraft. When a man was
afflicted with boils, he had to pass, fasting and in
silence, for nine consecutive mornings, under an arch
of this same briar. The green sprigs of broom,

however, are believed to be equally efficacious in averting the evil influence of spells.

In planting a bed of the smaller herbs, to render them thoroughly efficacious they should be planted under a volley of minor oaths, such as "goderabetin" or "godzamin." It is not expedient that the oaths should be too blood curdling.

George Métivier alludes to this, and says he himself knew old gardeners who made a constant practice of this prehistoric method, and quotes Pliny, Vol. X., p. 77 : "He was enjoined to sow (basil) with curses and oaths, and then, so that it should succeed, to beat the ground."

KING'S EVIL.

That the belief in touching for King's Evil prevailed in the island is evident from the following extracts.

"Extraits des Comptes des Diacres de l'Eglise de la Ville, contenus dans un Livre en la possession du Procureur des Pauvres de cette paroisse, endossé 'Aux Pauvres de la Ville.'"

"Le Vendredy, 24 Aout, 1677, l'on a trouvé dans le tronq la somme de deux cents vingt livres tournois en or, argent, sols marquez, et doubles. Item, vingt et quatre livres tournois, qui ont été données à la veuve de Nicolas Corbel pour son enfant, qui est incomodé des ecrouëlles, et qui s'en va à Londres pour estre touché de sa Ma^{té}."

"Le 26 Aout, 1678, a été tiré hors du tronq la

EDITOR'S NOTE.—"MAL DE POULE."—In St. Martin's parish lived an old woman who had an infallible cure for sick headaches. The patient was put to bed, and a live chicken, with its beak stuffed with parsley, enveloped in a cloth, was tied on his head. She then muttered a prayer over it, and tied it again, still more firmly, round the patient's forehead. As the chicken died the headache ceased.—*From Miss Thoume,*

sõe de trente livres tournois, qui ont été delivrés à
Caterine de Garis, fẽme de Jean Hairon, pour aller
en Angleterre y faire toucher par Sa Majesté une
fillette qui est affligée des ecrouëllés.   La d$_{te}$ sõe
luy ayant été allouée par consentement des officiers
de l'Eglise."

" Le 26me de Mars, 1688, par ordre de Messrs. les
Collecteurs des Pauvres de la Ville, j'ay balay a
Anne, fẽme de Pierre De Lahee, 12 livres tournois
pour luy aider à aller faire toucher son enfant du
Mal du Roy, et est des deniers des Pauvres."

CHAPTER XIII.

Story Telling.

"In winter tedious nights sit by the fire,
With good old folks, and let them tell thee tales."
—*King Richard II.*

WHEN, in former days, neighbours were in the habit of meeting together on such occasions as "*la grande querrue*," "*la longue veille*," or the more ordinary "*veillées*,"—at which the women of the neighbourhood, young and old, used to assemble in turn at each other's houses, and ply their knitting needles by the light of a single lamp and the warmth of a single hearth, thereby economising oil and fuel,—it was customary to break the monotony of the conversation by calling on each of the company in turn to relate some tale or anecdote. Most of these are simple enough, but in the mouth of a skillful story-teller are still capable of exciting a laugh among the unsophisticated audiences to whom they are addressed.

A favourite class of stories were those in which the inhabitants of the sister islands of Jersey, Alderney, and Sark, were held up to ridicule, and the following tales, trifling and absurd as they are, may suffice to give some idea of this sort of narrative,

How the Men of Alderney Sowed, and What Came of It.

Once upon a time, before the lighthouse on the dangerous reef of the Casquet rocks was erected, a vessel was wrecked on Alderney. Such occurrences in those days were not uncommon, but so cut off from intercourse with the rest of the world were the inhabitants of the island, that they were, for the most part, totally ignorant of the nature and value of the goods which the waves so frequently cast up on their inhospitable shores, and it is related that when a Dutch East Indiaman, laden with cinnamon, was wrecked on the coast, the people rejoiced in the seasonable supply of fuel that was afforded them, and employed the precious bundles of aromatic bark in heating their ovens.

On the occasion, however, to which our present story refers, among the articles saved from the wreck there was a barrel, which, on being opened, was found to contain a number of small packages carefully done up in paper. Some of these were opened and proved to be needles of various sizes, but the oldest inhabitant had never seen anything of the sort, and many were the speculations as to what they could possibly be. A general meeting of the islanders was called to deliberate, and many conjectures were hazarded. At last the opinion of an old grey-headed man prevailed. He expressed it to be his firm conviction that the strange commodity could be nothing else but the seed of some new kind of herb or useful root, and that the best thing to be done was to make choice of one of the most fertile spots on the Blaies, and to proceed forthwith to plough and sow.

His advice was received with acclamation, and immediately acted upon, but alas for their hopes! Spring came, and nothing but an unusually fine crop of weeds—always too common—appeared on the carefully-tilled land.*

How the Jerseymen Attempted to Carry off Guernsey.

It is not easy to understand why it should be so, but it is nevertheless a fact that the inhabitants of Jersey, although conceiving themselves a far superior race, have always looked with eyes of envy and jealousy on the smaller and less pretentious island of Guernsey. Perhaps the greater commercial prosperity which the possession of a good roadstead and port conferred on the latter at a time when Jersey could boast of neither, and the advantages arising in consequence from a freer intercourse with strangers, in days when these islands were almost cut off from the rest of the world, may have contributed to produce and keep alive these feelings. Certain it is that the Jerseymen have at all times had the reputation of being always ready, when an opportunity presented itself, to play a bad turn to their neighbours of Guernsey.

It is said that three audacious mariners, who had come over from the larger island with a cargo of agricultural produce, after disposing of their wares to good advantage, and having indulged perhaps a little

---

* " Semer des Aiguilles." See *Proverbes du Pays de Béarn*, page 17.

" Semia Agulhes—Semer des Aiguilles. Se donner une peine inutile, faire un travail qui ne produira rien. En Béarn, comme dans la Gascogne, (Bladé, Prov.) on attribuait aux habitants de quelques villages le fait d'avoir semé des aiguilles, dans l'espoir qu'elles multiplieraient comme du blé."

too freely in the excellent cider of the place, conceived the bold design of carrying away the island
with them and joining it on to Jersey! Could they
succeed in effecting the annexation, what credit
would they not gain for themselves! What advantages
would not accrue to their native isle!

Their hated rivals—for so, as true Jerseymen, they
looked on the quiet industrious inhabitants of
Guernsey—would be obliged to acknowledge their
superiority, and submit quietly to the supremacy of
the larger isle.

They were not long in putting their project into
execution. Maître Ph'lip, the captain of the boat,
gave directions to his cousin Pierre to make fast a
hawser to one of the needle-like rocks that stand
out so boldly from the extremity of St. Martin's
Point. The order was obeyed, the wind was fair, all
sails were hoisted and they steered towards Jersey,
singing out in full chorus :—

> " *Hale, Pierre ! Hale, Jean !*
> *Guernsi s'en vient !* "

They made sure that Guernsey could not resist
the tug, and that the morning light would find it
stranded in St. Ouen's Bay. But they had miscalculated
the strength of the hawser. It snapped short, and the
sudden jerk sent them all sprawling to the bottom of
the boat, too much bruised and discomfited to think
of renewing their bold attempt.[*]

The Jersey Gallows.

In Guernsey it is told as a joke against their
neighbours the Jerseymen, that when there was a

---

[*] See *Mélusine*, p. 321. Note (i).

Old Farm House at St. Saviour's,
From a Pencil Drawing, early in the Nineteenth Century.

question of rebuilding the gallows, hitherto a wooden structure, but falling to pieces from rottenness, the Procureur de la Reine recommended that the uprights should be of stone, as more desirable, and strengthened his argument by saying, "It will last for ever, and serve for us and for our children."

Proberbial Stories.

The terse form of an aphorism is not only one in which the proverbial philosophy of a people may be expressed. The idea is frequently expanded into a short tale or fable, and in this shape is often alluded to and understood, although perhaps the story or anecdote is unknown or forgotten.

To give an example. The meaning of the words " A Cat's Paw " is perfectly comprehended by many, who possibly have never heard or read of the fable of " The Cat, the Monkey, and the Chestnuts."

A few of these stories, as they are related in Guernsey, are given below.

LA DÉLAISSANCE.

Although scarcely a year passes without some fact coming to light which shows the folly and imprudence of the proceedings, it is by no means uncommon for old people to make over by a legal instrument, called "*Contrat de Délaissance*," the whole of their property to a child or other relative, on condition of being maintained for the rest of their days in a manner befitting their station in life. They have generally cause to repent the deed, for, even if kindly treated, there is a feeling of dependence, and a want of liberty of action, which cannot fail to be irksome to one who has hitherto been his own master, and free to act in any way he pleased.

It is related that a man who had given over his estate, and all that he possessed, to an only son, ordered, after a time, a strong coffer, with a secure lock, to be made. The son indulged him in the fancy, wondering what he could want the box for, but hoping perhaps that he might have kept back some hoard of money or other valuables he wished to secure. The old man kept his own secret. Not a soul but himself knew what the box contained. At last he died. The son hastened to open the coffer, hoping to find a treasure. What was his astonishment and disappointment at finding only a large mallet, such as is used for driving in the stakes to which the cattle are tethered. A writing attached to it explained the old man's meaning. The person who related the story had forgotten the exact words, but it was a rude rhyme, beginning thus :—

" *Ce maillot—ou un plus gros s'il le faut.*" *

The substance of the whole was that the mallet would be advantageously employed in knocking out the brains of the man who was fool enough to dispossess himself, during his lifetime, of the control of his own property.†

---

* From Rachel Du Port.

† " He that gives away all
    Before he is dead,
    Let 'em take this hatchet
    And knock him on ye head."

Notes and Queries, IV. Series, Vol. III., pp. 526 and 589. Vol. IV., p. 213. See *Gentleman's Magazine Library.* Popular Superstitions. *The Holy Maul*, p. 181. Compare representation of a hammer or pickaxe, sculptured on threshold of west door of Vale Church.

· The following legend, from the supplement to the *Illustrated News*, February 7th, 1874, seems to have a common origin with the preceding.

Jehan Connaxa was one of the merchant princes of Antwerp, who is supposed to have lived in the fifteenth century. His only children were two daughters, whom he had married to young noblemen. Not content with the handsome dowries he had given them on their marriage, and too impatient to wait for the time when all his vast wealth would become theirs by inheritance, they persuaded him to make it over to them during his life-time. For a short period he was treated with due consideration, but it was not long before he began to find that his presence in the houses of his sons-in-law was irksome to them and their wives; and at last he was plainly told that he must not expect any longer to find a home with them. Under these circumstances he hired a small residence, and turned over in his mind how he could manage so as to recover the position in his daughters' houses which he had formerly occupied. At last he hit on this expedient. He invited his sons-in-law and their wives to dine with him on a certain day, and, when he was quite sure they would come, he went to an old friend, a rich merchant, and borrowed from him the sum of one thousand crowns for twenty-four hours, telling him to keep the transaction a profound secret, but to send a servant to his house the next day at a certain hour to fetch it back. Accordingly, the next day, when his daughters and their husbands were seated at his table, a message came that his friend had sent for the sum of money he had promised. He pretended to be displeased at being interrupted in the midst of his meal, but left the table, went into an adjoining apartment, and returned with a sack of money, from which he counted out the full sum of a thousand crowns, and delivered it to the messenger. The astonishment of his guests, who were not aware of how the money had come into his possession, was extreme, and, believing him to be still the owner of unbounded wealth, his sons-in-law insisted on his taking up his abode with them alternately for the rest of his days. Each vied with the other in showing him every attention, hoping thus to secure the greater share of the inheritance. He always brought with him a heavy strong box with three locks, which was supposed to contain untold wealth. At last, the time when he was to quit this world arrived, and on his death-bed he sent for his two sons-in-law and the Prior of a neighbouring Convent of Jacobins, and delivered to them the three keys of the box, which, he said, contained his will, but with strict injunctions that it was not to be opened till forty days after his funeral had elapsed. Wishing, however, as he said, to do good while he was yet alive, he begged his sons-in-law to advance a large sum for immediate distribution among the poor, and also to pay another large sum to the Prior to secure the prayers of the Church for his soul. This was done willingly, in anticipation of the expected rich inheritance, and the old man was sumptuously buried. At the expiration of the forty days the box was opened with due formality, and was found to contain a heap of old iron, lead, and stones, on the top of which was a large cudgel, with a parchment rolled round it, on which was written the will in these terms :—" *Ego Johannes Connaxa tale condo testamentum, at qui sui curâ relictâ, alterius curam susceperit, mactetur hâc clavâ.*"

LE RATÉ.

When the means of education were not so good or so plentiful in Guernsey as they are in the present day, it was customary, with the better class of farmers, to send their sons to school in England for a year or two, in order that they might acquire, together with a more correct knowledge of the English tongue, such acquaintance with the ways of the world as might fit them to enter upon the active duties of life on their return home. This object, we may suppose, was to a certain extent gained, but, like the monkey who had seen the world, many of these youths returned to their native isle with an inflated idea of their own consequence, and affecting to despise and ignore all that had been familiar to them from their earliest childhood.

It is said of one of these young men, that, after a residence of no long duration in England, he pretended, on his return, to have completely forgotten the names of some of the most common farming implements, and, indeed, to have almost lost the use of his mother tongue. His father in despair, for it was evident that if the boy could not converse with the labourers, he would be of little or no assistance in directing the farming operations. A lucky accident set the father's mind at rest on this score. His son, in passing through the farmyard, put his foot on a rake that was lying on the ground, partly hidden by some straw. The handle flew up and hit him a smart blow on the forehead, upon which, forgetting his pretended ignorance, he exclaimed, in good Guernsey-French, "*Au Guyablle seit le râté,*" ("Devil take the rake.") His father, who was standing by, congratulated him on the miraculous recovery of his memory, and begged him henceforth not to forget "*sen râté.*" The proverbial saying "*Il n'a pas roublliaï sen râté,*" ("He has not forgotten his rake,") is still applied to a person who remembers what he learned in his youth.[*]

LE COTILLON DE RACHÉ CATEL.

The evils that may result from being over particular, and the wisdom of letting well alone, are exemplified by the story of Rachel Câtel and her petticoat. This respectable matron or spinster—for tradition gives us no clue to her state in life—was engaged in fashioning a petticoat. She cut it out, and found it somewhat too long. She cut again, and now it was too short. When, therefore, a thing has been spoilt by too much care or meddling, old people will shake their heads and say:—"*Ch'est coum le cotillon de Râché Câtel. A' le copit et il était trop long. A' le copit derechef, et il était trop court.*"

THE CAT AND THE FOX. A FABLE.

One day a cat and a fox were travelling together and chatting of one thing and another as they jogged on their way.

At last says the cat to the fox:

" You are always talking of your cleverness. How many cunning devices have you to escape from your numerous enemies? "

---

[*] See a story precisely similar in its incidents in that curious collection MacTaggart's *Scottish Gallovidian Encyclopædia*, under the word "Claut." The story must be an ancient one, to be told in places so far apart as Galloway and Guernsey, and speaking totally different languages.

" Oh ! " answered the fox, "*j'en ai une pouquie*, (I carry a whole sack full,) but you, Mistress Puss, pray tell me, how many have you ? "

" Alas," replied the cat, " I can boast but of one."

Shortly after this conversation they saw a large fierce-looking dog advancing towards them. It was but the affair of a minute for puss to climb into the nearest tree and hide herself among the branches, while Reynard took refuge in the entrance of a drain that was close at hand.

Unluckily the drain narrowed so suddenly that his body only was concealed, and his long bushy tail was left exposed. The dog seized on this, and caused poor Reynard to cry out pitifully for help. Puss, from her safe retreat among the branches, looked down, and called out to her unfortunate companion :

" Now's the time to make use of your many devices, *délie donc ta pouque* ! " (" Why don't you untie your sack ? ") *

The Farm Servant and the Weeds.

The Guernsey workman is industrious and thrifty, working hard when it is on his own account, but apt to be slow and disinclined to do more work than what is absolutely necessary to save his credit, when employed by others. There is a certain amount of calculation in this. Idleness or laziness are not the only motives. He knows that so long as the job in hand lasts, he will be paid his day's wages, and therefore he is not in a hurry to get it finished. His calculations go even a little beyond this ; for a master workman to whom an indifferent person made

---

* From John Rougier, Esq.
See also *Revue des Traditions Populaires*, Vol. I., p. 201.

Old Mill, Talbots.

the remark that the work he was executing was not of a quality to last many years, made the ingenuous reply, "Do you suppose I would willingly take the bread out of my children's mouths?" implying that if the work were done in too substantial or durable a manner, there would be nothing left for those who were to come after him to gain their living by.

A good story is told among the country people, of a farm labourer, who, when put to clear out the weeds from a field, was observed always to leave some of the most thriving standing. One day his master remonstrated with him, and got for answer, "Weeds are bread." No reply was made at the moment, but when meal-time came, and the soup was served out, a bowl full of weeds was handed to the workman with the remark :—"Since weeds are bread, eat that, for you get no more to-day." It is said that the lesson was understood, and that for the future the farm servant performed his allotted task in a more conscientious way. *

---

* From George Allez, Esq.

CHAPTER XIV.

Historical Reminiscences.

"Antiquities, or remnants of history, are, as was said, *tanquam tabula naufragii*, when industrious persons, by an exact and scrupulous diligence and observation, out of monuments, names, words, proverbs, traditions, private records and evidences, fragments of stories, passages of books that concern not story, and the like, do save and recover somewhat from the deluge of time."—Bacon's *Advancement of Learning*.

CADWALLA AND BRIAN.

LTHOUGH the following story is entirely forgotten in Guernsey, and indeed may possibly never have been popularly known in the island, it is entitled, from its legendary and romantic character, to a place in this collection. It is related by Geoffrey of Monmouth in his British History, Book XII. Ch. 4.

It is necessary to premise that Edwin, the first of the Anglo-Saxon Kings who embraced Christianity, having quarrelled with Cadwalla, Sovereign of North Wales, attacked and defeated him at Widdington, near Morpeth. Edwin pursued Cadwalla into Wales, and chased him into Ireland. These events happened about the year 630 A.D. The story itself shall be told in the words employed by Geoffrey in his account of Cadwalla's exile, as we find them translated in Bohn's "Antiquarian Library."

" Cadwalla, not knowing what course to take, was

almost in despair of ever returning. At last it came
into his head to go to Salomon, King of the
Armorican Britons, and desire his assistance and
advice, to enable him to return to his kingdom.
And so, as he was steering towards Armorica, a
strong tempest rose on a sudden, which dispersed
the ships of his companions, and in a short time
left no two of them together. The pilot of the King's
ship was seized immediately with so great a fear,
that, quitting the stern, he left the vessel to the
disposal of fortune, so that all night it was tossed
up and down in great danger by the raging waves.
The next morning they arrived at a certain island
called *Garnareia*,* where, with great difficulty, they
got ashore. Cadwalla was forthwith seized with such
grief for the loss of his companions, that, for three
days and nights together, he refused to eat, but lay
sick upon his bed. The fourth day he was taken
with a very great longing for some venison, and,
causing Brian (his nephew) to be called, made him
acquainted with it. Whereupon Brian took his bow
and quiver, and went through the island, that if he
could light on any wild beast, he might make booty
of it. And when he had walked over the whole
island without finding what he was in quest of, he
was extremely concerned that he could not gratify
his master's desire, and was afraid his sickness
would prove mortal if his longing were not satisfied.
He, therefore, fell upon a new device, and cut a
piece of flesh out of his own thigh, which he roasted

---

* As some readers may be unable to detect "Guernsey" in "*Garnareia*," it
may be as well to state that "*Ghernerhuia*," "*Gerneria*," "*Guernnerui*,"
and "*Gernereye*," are all names given to the island in ancient documents. The
last indeed is found on the ancient seal of the bailiwick.

upon a spit, and carried to the King for venison.
The King, thinking it to be real venison, began to
eat of it to his great refreshment, admiring the
sweetness of it, which he fancied exceeded any flesh
he had ever tasted before. At last, when he had
fully satisfied his appetite, he became more cheerful,
and in three days was perfectly well again. Then, the
wind standing fair, he got ready his ship, and, hoisting
sails, they pursued their voyage and arrived at the city
Kidaleta (St. Malo). From thence they went to King
Salomon, by whom they were received kindly and
with all suitable respect; and, as soon as he had
learned the occasion of their coming, he made them
a promise of assistance."

The chronicler subsequently relates how Brian killed
the second-sighted magician of Edwin. Cadwalla
returned to Britain, and, with the aid of the Saxon
Penda, King of Mercia, conquered and killed Edwin.
He was afterwards triumphant in fourteen great battles
and sixty skirmishes with the Angles, but finally
perished, with the flower of his army, in battle with
Oswald, ruler of the Saxon kingdom of Bernicia.

DUKE RICHARD OF NORMANDY AND THE DEMON.

As the inhabitants of Guernsey may be presumed
to be better acquainted with the chronicles of their
own Duchy of Normandy than with those of the
ancient Britons, it is not improbable that the following legendary tale, related of Duke Richard, surnamed
" Sans Peur," may be known to some of them. The
Chronique de Normandie, printed at Rouen in 1576,
gives it in words of which the following is a close
translation :—

" Once upon a time, as Duke Richard was riding

from one of his castles to a manor, where a very beautiful lady was residing, the Devil attacked him, and Richard fought with, and vanquished him. After this adventure, the Devil disguised himself as a beautiful maiden richly adorned, and appeared to him in a boat at Granville, where Richard then was. Richard entered into the boat to converse with, and contemplate the beauty of, this lady, and the Devil carried away the said Duke Richard to a rock in the sea in the island of Guernsey, where he was found."

Perhaps the marks of cloven feet, which have been found deeply imprinted in the granite * in more than one spot in the island, may be attributed to this visit.

Archbishop Mauger.

If the two legendary tales, which we have just related, are unknown to the present generation, it is not so with the well-authenticated fact of the temporary residence in Guernsey of that turbulent ecclesiastic, Mauger, Archbishop of Rouen, uncle of William the Conqueror.

All the Norman chroniclers agree in telling us that, although the Pope had granted a dispensation, this audacious prelate ventured to excommunicate his Sovereign for having contracted a marriage with Matilda, daughter of the Count of Flanders, an alliance within the degrees of affinity prohibited by the Church. Mauger's insolence did not remain unpunished. The Pope sent a Legate to Normandy,

---

* The stone at Jerbourg, which is said to bear the mark left by the Devil's claw, stands in a hedge on the right hand side of the road, where the rise towards Doyle's column begins. It is a large mass of white quartz, and has the black mark of the Devil's claw imprinted on it,—*From J. Richardson Tardif, Esq.*

the bishops of the province were assembled, and his treason to his Sovereign, and contempt of the Papal authority, were punished by his deposition from his archiepiscopal throne, and banishment to the island of Guernsey. Some historians assign, as a further reason for his disgrace, the immorality of his life, and his prodigal expenditure, which led him, not only to waste the revenues of the Church, but even to sell the consecrated vessels, and the ornaments of the sanctuary.

Tradition points out the spot in the neighbourhood of that romantic little creek, known by the anglicised name of Saints' Bay, but which, in ancient documents, is called "*La Contrée de Seing*," where the deposed prelate lived during his enforced sojourn in Guernsey. Here, it is said, he became acquainted with a noble damsel named *Gille*, by whom he had several children, one of whom, Michael de Bayeux, accompanied Bohemond of Austria to Palestine, and distinguished himself greatly.

Common report accused Mauger of being addicted to magical arts, and of having intercourse with a familiar spirit called "*Thoret*," a name which brings to mind the thunderer *Thor*, one of the principal deities of his Scandinavian ancestors. By means of this imp, it was believed, he had the faculty of predicting future events.

Having embarked one day, with the design of reaching the coast of Normandy, and having arrived at St. Vaast, he addressed the master of the ship in these words:—"I know for certain that one of us two will this day be drowned; let us land." The master paid no attention to what was said, but continued his course. It was summer, the weather was extremely hot, and the Archbishop was attired in very loose raiment. The vessel struck, Mauger endeavoured to leave the ship, but, becoming entangled in his garments, fell into the sea, and was drowned before any assistance could be given. When the tide retired, search was made for the body, and it was found wedged in between two rocks, in an upright position. The sailors carried it to Cherbourg, where it was buried.

It is possible that the prelate might have been entirely forgotten in the place of his exile, had it not been that a very numerous family, bearing his name, still exists in the island, and claims to be descended from him. No name indeed is more common in the parish of St. Martin de la Belleuse, and especially in the neighbourhood of Saint, than that of Mauger. An authentic document, the "Extent" of Edward III., proves that a family of this name held land in this parish in 1331.* All who bear the name, even in the humblest ranks of society, have heard of the Archbishop, and pride themselves in their supposed descent from him. Nor is this belief confined to Guernsey, for in Jersey also, where a branch of the family has long existed, the same idea prevails.

There is also extant an imperfect pedigree of the house of Mauger, of Jobourg, near Cape La Hague, in Normandy, which connects them with the insular family, but endeavours to get rid of the stigma of

EDITOR'S NOTE.—* And at the Assizes held in Guernsey in 1319, a "Rauf Mauger" appears among the landowners of St. Martin's parish. The same name—"Rauf Mauger"—appears in the Extent of 1331; "Richard Mauger" in a Perchage of Blanchelande, (undated, but made before 1364). In 1364 another "Rauf Mauger" appears among the Jurymen of St. Martin's summoned to adjudicate on the rights of the Abbot of Blanchelande; and a Richard Mauger, of St. Martin's parish, is mentioned in the "Bille de Partage" of Denis Le Marchant in 1393.

Ivy Castle.

illegitimacy, which would attach to the progeny of an ecclesiastic, by the invention of an imaginary brother, who accompanied Mauger in his banishment, and from whom, and not from the Archbishop, they pretend to deduce their descent. The family of Guille, long established in the island of Guernsey, and in the parish of St. Martin's, claims the questionable honour of having produced the fair Gille, whose charms captivated the unscrupulous prelate.

There is one fact, however, of which the family of Mauger, of Guernsey, has just cause to be proud, and that is the daring and successful exploit of one of them in the service of the descendant of their ancient Dukes. An extract from a manuscript register of the Cathedral of Coutances, said to be preserved in the British Museum, tells us how, on Midsummer Night, in the year of grace 1419, Jacques Mauger arrived from Guernsey with his men, at the port of Agon, at the entrance of the river, and took by escalade the fortress of Mont Martin, near Coutances, and how Henry V., King of England, then in possession of the greater part of Normandy, rewarded the gallant act by a gift of the Seigneurie of Bosques, and the permission to bear henceforth on his shield the cross of the blessed knight of St. George, in a field argent, with his own paternal arms, two chevrons sable, in the first and fourth quarters, and, in the second and third the arms of Bosques, a lion rampant, also sable.

It may not be uninteresting to some to know that the Hampshire and Isle of Wight family of Major were originally Maugers from one of the Channel Islands, and that Richard Cromwell, son of the Protector, married one of them.

It may be as well to give here a copy of the pedigree of Mauger, of Jobourg, in Normandy.

"Extrait de la Généalogie de la Famille du Mauger à Jobourg en Normandie au Cap La Hague.

"Le Duc de Normandie, nommé Guillaume le Conquérant, éleva son cousin d'Evreux, nommé Mauger, à l'Archevêché de Rouen en la troisième année de son règne en Normandie. Le Seigneur Archevêque, menant une vie non conforme à sa dignité, attira sur lui la haine du Duc, son bienfaiteur, qui le fit reléguer a l'île de Greneseye; il prit terre en ce lieu avec son frère Gautier Mauger, sur la côte et paroisse de St. Martin, et après avoir passé quelques années en ce lieu il péri au ras de Barfleur, après avoir prédit sa mort. Son frère Gautier eut plusieurs fils naturels, dont deux nommés Léopold et Théodore : Léopold épousa Pauline de Carteret, fille et seule héritière de Samuel de Carteret, Ecuyer, Seigneur du Castel, et Théodore ne maria point, et laissa deux fils et une fille naturels, l'un nommé Paul, l'autre nommé Rodolphe, et la fille nommée Cléotilde. Les deux fils furent mariés ; l'un épousa Sandirez Lampeirier ou Lampereur de Jersey, et Rodolphe épousa Marie Careye de Greneseye. Paul eut plusieurs fils, dont deux nommé Alexandre et Gautier, comme son premier père, lequel fut chassé de l'île de Jersey, avec deux des fils de Rodolphe qu'il avait eus de Marie Careye ; les autres enfans sortis de Rodolphe furent à Greneseye, demeurant sur l'héritage de leur mère en l'année 1399. Gautier fit plusieurs acquêts à Jobourg à la Hague, où il établit sa demeure, après avoir quitté Jersey, et fut marié à une des filles de Pierre de Mary, Seigneur de Jobourg, en l'année 1418. Gautier engendra

D D

Toussaint et Jacques, le dernier repassa à Greneseye pour prendre possession d'un héritage par succession, et Toussaint resta à Jobourg; de Toussaint naquit Fabien; de Fabien naquit Chaille; et Chaille engendra Pierre; de Pierre Chaille, qui vivoit encore en 1570; à l'egard de Léopold, qui avait epousé Pauline de Carteret, nous n'avons point, pour le present, de connaissance de sa généalogie.

" Les Armoiries des Mauger (descendant de Guillaume le Conquérant, Duc de Normandie) sont une ancre et des roses au dessus du dit ancre. Tiré de la Heraudrie, et approuvé du dit Duc." *

THE BALLAD OF IVON DE GALLES.

Before the invention of printing, oral tradition was almost the only way in which the people—generally ignorant of writing or reading—could transmit the recollection of facts and circumstances which they deemed worthy of being remembered; and it was soon discovered that versification afforded a very strong aid to memory. Hence arose that species of metrical tale which we call a ballad. These ballads, passing from mouth to mouth, soon became corrupted. Whole verses were sometimes omitted, by which the thread of the story was lost or rendered obscure, and others were supplied by borrowing from the work of another bard, or by the invention of the reciter. Nevertheless, in the historical ballads, facts and details were often preserved which had escaped the notice of the more regular chroniclers.

Whether, in former days, Guernsey could boast of any number of these metrical histories, it is now

EDITOR'S NOTE.—* The obvious inaccuracy of this pedigree can be judged by only nine generations being given to supply the interval of 515 years, 1055-1570. Thirty-three and a quarter years are generally allowed for a generation, so that to give any appearance of probability, at least sixteen generations would have to be accounted for.

impossible to say. Unless we include in this category, a sort of "complainte," written in 1552 by the Roman Catholic priests, whom the progress of the doctrines of the Reformation had driven out of their cures, the ballad of "*Ivon de Galles, ou la descente des Aragousais,*" is the only one which has come down to us.* Many copies of it have been preserved, differing but slightly from each other in the main, although there are one or two verbal differences of some importance. Most of the copies conclude with the twentieth verse, but some have a second part, consisting of six stanzas, and purporting to give an account of Ivon's adventures after he left Guernsey, and the subsequent melancholy fate of himself and his fleet. As this account is quite different from what has come down to us in history, it is probably the work of some later bard, who wished to make the story more complete than he found it, and by a sort of poetical justice to punish Ivon and his followers for the evil they had inflicted on the island.

The ballad agrees in the main with the account of the invasion as given by Froissart and Holinshed. The adventures in the second part probably relate to some other of the numerous descents on the island during the reign of Edward III., perhaps to that by Bahuchet, a French naval commander, about the year 1338. This Bahuchet landed in England, and committed great atrocities at Portsmouth and Southampton, for which, when he was taken prisoner in the great engagement off Sluys, in 1340, Edward ordered him to be hanged at the main-yard.

EDITOR'S NOTE.—* I have also met with an account of the destruction of the Tower of Castle Cornet by lightning in 1672, in some old MSS. dated 1719, where the visitation is ascribed to the sins of the people!

From Froissart's *Chronicles* we learn that Ivon, or as he calls him, Yvain de Galles, was the son of a Prince of Wales whom Edward III. had put to death, and whose possessions he had seized upon. Ivon, thus disinherited, took refuge in France, where he entered into the service of the King, Charles V., and was by him entrusted with the command of ships and three thousand men. It appears from another part of the Chronicle, that Henry of Trastamara, King of Castille and Aragon, had supplied his ally, Charles, with a large fleet, well armed and manned, and it is probable that the galleys which Ivon commanded formed part of this fleet. If so, the name of "Aragousais," or men of Aragon, given in the ballad to the invading force, is accounted for. With these troops he sailed from Harfleur and reached Guernsey.

Aymon, or Edmund, Rose, esquire of honour to the King of England, and Governor of the island, advanced to meet him with all the force he could muster,—about eight hundred men. The battle was long and hotly contested, but ended in the discomfiture of the insular force, with the loss of four hundred of their men, and in the retreat of Aymon Rose into Castle Cornet, to which Ivon laid siege. Several assaults were made on the Castle, but, as it was strongly fortified and well provisioned, they were not attended with success. How long the siege lasted we are not informed, but the French King, requiring the services of Ivon elsewhere, and believing Castle Cornet to be impregnable, sent orders for the siege to be raised. A few years afterwards, Ivon lost his life by the dagger of an assassin of his own nation, a Welshman of the name of Lambe, apparently at the instigation of Richard II.

According to the ballad, Ivon landed his troops early on a Tuesday morning in Vazon Bay. A countryman, who had risen early to look after his sheep, perceived the invaders and gave the alarm, upon which all the inhabitants assembled and endeavoured to repel them, but without success. A stand was at last made on the hill above the town of St. Peter Port, and a sanguinary engagement took place, in which five hundred and one of both sides were killed.

Tradition points to a spot near Elizabeth College as the scene of this encounter, and the locality to this day bears the name of "*La Bataille.*"

A deep lane, which formerly passed to the eastward of the strangers' burial ground, but which has been long filled up and enclosed within the walls of the cemetery, was said to owe its name of "*La Ruette Meurtrière*" to the same event.

Towards the evening, eighty English merchants,—probably the crews of some trading vessels—arrived, and lent their assistance to the islanders. By means of this reinforcement the enemy was prevented from penetrating into the town, but they reached the shore, and, the tide being low, crossed over to Castle Cornet, and attacked it.

Most of the copies of the ballad say that they took the Castle, "*par force prindrent le Chasteau,*" but one, which has been preserved in the registers of the parish of St. Saviour, where it is inserted about the year 1638, has these words—"*Il vouloient prendre le Chasteau,*"—which seem to agree better with the other statements in the ballad that Ivon's ships came round the island by the southward, that they received some damage from the peasantry at

La Corbière, and that they re-embarked their troops at Bec de la Chèvre, now known by the name of the Terres point, after which Ivon ordered them to make sail for St. Sampson's Harbour.

Here they landed. Negotiations were entered on with Brégart, the Prior or Commissary of St. Michel du Valle, a dependency of the famous Abbey of Mont St. Michel in Normandy, and Ivon laid siege to the Vale Castle, whither Aymon Rose, the Governor of the island, whom we hear of for the first time, had retreated and entrenched himself.

Summoned by Ivon to surrender, he refused, but agreed to sanction an arrangement which Brégart had made with the people, and which seems to have had for object to buy off the invaders by payment of a sum of money.

The ballad assigns this as the origin of the charge on land called "champart," but it is certain that this species of tithe existed long before this time.

Most of the copies end here, but some have a second part, of which we have already spoken, and which was probably written at a later period.

It is difficult to account for the discrepancy between the local account and that of Froissart and others as to the name of the Castle into which the Governor, Aymon Rose, retired, unless by the supposition that the historians knew Castle Cornet by name as a fortress deemed impregnable, and assumed, without further inquiry, that it must be the one in which the Governor entrenched himself.

An event of so much importance was well calculated to make a lasting impression on the people. And to this day "*Les Aragousais*" are spoken of, and various traditions relating to them are repeated. It is singular,

Houses formerly facing West Door of Town Church.

however, to find that with the lapse of time they have come to be looked upon as a supernatural race—in fact, to be confounded with the fairies. The form which this traditional remembrance of them has taken will be found on page 204, and tends in some degree to confirm the idea entertained by some writers on fairy mythology that many of the tales related of those fantastic beings may be accounted for by the theory that they refer to an earlier race of men, gradually driven out by tribes more advanced in civilisation.

The places called " *La Bataille* * " and " *La Ruette Meurtrière* " have already been mentioned as the spots where the great battle took place. The " *Rouge Rue*," leading down the hill to the westward of St. John's Church, is said to derive its name from the blood spilt on this occasion. If this really be the origin of the name, we may suppose that the islanders, retreating towards the Vale Castle, or perhaps the Château des Marais, were overtaken there, and that a second engagement took place. But there is reason to believe that the tradition relates to another locality in quite a different direction, which in times gone by bore also the name of " *La Rouge Rue*," but which has long ceased to be so called. We speak of the upper part of Hauteville, sloping southwards towards the valley of Havelet. According to the late Miss Lauga, who died at the advanced age of eighty-five, her mother, who had inherited from her ancestors property in this neighbourhood, always spoke of it as " *La Rouge Rue*," and said that a sanguinary battle had been fought in ancient days on this spot. And,

EDITOR's NOTE.—* On the slope of the hill rising to the south of Perelle Bay there is also a spot called " La Bataille," and about a quarter of a mile further inland another spot called " L'Assaut." This probably refers to some other conflict.—*From J. de Garis, Esq.*

indeed, this name appears in the old contracts and title-deeds, by which property in the neighbourhood is held. The consequence of its having ceased to be known popularly by its ancient appellation would naturally be that the traditionary tale of the name being derived from the blood spilt there would be transferred to another and better known locality, which chanced—perhaps simply from the colour of the soil—to bear the same name.

Firearms were of such recent invention that it is scarcely to be supposed that any had as yet found their way to Guernsey. If, however, any faith can be placed in tradition, their use and construction were not totally unknown in the island, for it is said that the trunk of a tree was hollowed out and bound round with iron hoops, but that when this deadly weapon was loaded, no one could be found bold enough to fire it, until a child, ignorant of the risk he was incurring, was induced, by the promise of a cake, to perform the dangerous feat.

It is also said that the women of the island contributed all their ear-rings and other jewels to buy off the invaders ; and it was very generally believed that a peculiar breed of small but strong and spirited horses—now unfortunately extinct—was derived from those that had escaped during the battle, and so had remained in the island after the Spaniards left.

The tradition, which confounds Ivon's forces with the fairies, relates how all the islanders were killed, except a man and a boy of St. Andrew's parish, who concealed themselves in an oven, over the mouth of which a woman spread her black petticoat, and so escaped ; and how the conquerors, who are described as a very diminutive race, married the widows and maidens, and so re-peopled the island. The small stature and dark complexion of some families are occasionally appealed to as proofs of this origin.

Perhaps this tradition may be an indistinct recollection of a far earlier invasion and possession of the island by some of the piratical hordes from the North, that began to infest the coasts of the Channel as early as the beginning of the fifth century. These were not unlikely to have subjugated the men of the island, and to have taken forcible possession of their wives, and any tradition of the event might very naturally be transferred from one invasion to another, and come finally to be fixed on the last and best known.

The ballad, of which an English translation is attempted, has evidently suffered much from the defective memory of reciters, and the carelessness of transcribers, so that some of the stanzas appear to be almost hopelessly corrupt. The main incidents of the story are, however, tolerably well defined. It seems to have been composed originally in French, and not in the Norman dialect used in the island. The stanzas consist of the unusual number of seven lines, of which the first and third rhyme together, and the second, fourth, fifth and sixth—the seventh rhyming occasionally with the first and third, but more frequently standing alone. In some verses assonances take the place of more perfect rhymes, which may be adduced as a proof of the antiquity of the ballad. Perhaps it would not be impossible, by comparing the various copies, choosing the readings which appear least corrupt, altering here and there the position of a line in the stanza, or the arrangement of the words that compose it, or even sometimes

changing a word where the exigencies of the rhyme
seem to require it, to produce a copy that would
offend less against the rules of prosody; but this is
a process which would require great care, and which
respect for antiquity forbids us to attempt.

We must take the ballad, with all its faults and
imperfections, as we find it.

EVAN OF WALES, OR THE INVASION OF GUERNSEY IN 1372.

Part the First.

I.

Draw near and listen, great and small,
　Of high and low degree,
And hear what chance did once befall
　This island fair and free
　　From warlike men, a chosen band,
　　Who roamed about from land to land,
　Ploughing the briny sea.

II.

Evan of Wales, a valiant knight,
　Who served the King of France,
In Saragossa's city bright
　Hired many a stalwart lance :
　　One Tuesday morn at break of day,
　　To land these troops in Vazon Bay,
　He bade his ships advance.

III.

At early dawn from quiet sleep
　John Letoc rose that day,
To tend his little flock of sheep
　He took his lonely way,
　　When lo ! upon the Vazon sands
　　He saw, drawn up in warlike bands
　The foe in fierce array.

IV.

A horse he met upon his way
  Trotting along the road,
Strayed from the camp—without delay
  The charger he bestrode,
    ·And soon from house to house the alarm
    He gave, crying out " to arms, quick, arm ! "
Through all the isle he rode.

V.

" To arms, to arms, my merry men all,
  To arms, for we must fight,
Hazard your lives, both great and small,
  And put the foe to flight ;
    Hasten towards the Vazon Bay
    Hasten our cruel foes to slay,
Or we shall die this night."

VI.

Evan of Wales, that vent'rous knight,
  Led the foe through the land,
But pressing forward in the fight,
  Upon a foreign strand,
    He won a garter gay, I ween,
    'Twas neither silk nor velvet sheen,
Though crimson was the band.

VII.

For near the mill at La Carrière,
  With halbert keen and bright,
Young Richard Simon, void of fear,
  Attacked the stranger knight.
    And gashed full sore his brawny thigh,
    Then smote his right hand lifted high,
To check the daring wight.

VIII.

Above Saint Peter Port 'tis said,
  The conflict they renewed,
Of friends and foes five hundred dead
  The grassy plain bestrewed :
    Our ladies wept most bitterly,
    Oh! 'twas a dismal sight to see
  Their cheeks with tears bestrewed.

IX.

Thoumin le Lorreur was in truth
  Our leader in the fray,
But brave Ralph Holland, noble youth,
  He bore the palm away ;
    Yet was he doomed his death to meet,
    The cruel foes smit off his feet,
  He died that dismal day.

X.

Hard blows are dealt on every side,
  The blood bedews the plain,
The footmen leap, the horsemen ride,
  O'er mountains of the slain.
    A deadly weapon, strongly bent,
    Against the foes its missiles sent,
  And wrought them death and pain.

XI.

But eighty English merchants brave,
  Arrived at Vesper-tide,
They rushed on shore the isle to save,
  And fought on our side :
    Our foes fatigued, began to yield,
    And leaving soon the well-fought field,
  To Heaven for mercy cried.

XII.

To'ards Galrion they bend their course,
  And range along the bay,
In hopes to make by fraud or force
  Into the town their way,
    But now the gallant Englishmen
    Return, and on our foes again
  Their prowess they display.

XIII.

But rallying soon, th'adventurous band
  Cornet's strong towers attack,
With ebbing tides, across the sand,
  They find an easy track,
    The beach is strewed with heaps of dead,
    The briny sea with blood is red,
  Again they are driven back.

XIV.

Many are killed, and wounded sore ;
  Meanwhile the hostile fleet,
Coasting along the southern shore
  A warm reception meet
    From peasants bold at La Corbière ;
    At Bec d'la Chèvre the land they near,
  And aid their friends' retreat.

XV.

But Evan's troops were mad with rage,
  Like lions balked of food,
Swear that their wrath they will assuage
  In floods of English blood ;
    Then suddenly their course they steer
    Towards Saint Sampson's port, and there
  They land in angry mood.

Old Cottage, Fermain.

XVI.

Saint Michael's Abbey soon they seek,
    Friar Brégard there had sway,
Who, full of fear, with prayers meek
    Meets them upon their way ;
        With presents rich and ample store
        Of gold, and promises of more
    Their fury to allay.

XVII.

To Eleanor, that lady fair,
    Sir Evan's beauteous bride,
The crafty monk gave jewels rare
    To win her to his side.
        At Granville, in the pleasant land
        Of France, Sir Evan sought her hand,
    Nor was his suit denied.

XVIII.

Near the Archangel's Castle then,
    Upon a rising ground,
Sir Evan camped—our countrymen
    Sure refuge there had found.
        Brégard, in hopes to increase his store,
        Advances to the Castle door
    And bade a parley sound.

XIX.

He counselled them to yield forthwith,
    But brave Sir Edmund Rose
Declared he'd sooner meet his death
    Than bend to foreign foes,
        But to the Abbot should they yield
        A double tithe on every field,
    He would it not oppose.

XX.

The Abbot to Sir Evan went,
  And soon a bargain closed;
The simple peasants gave assent
  To all the monk proposed,
    And bound their lands a sheaf to pay,
    Beyond the tithes, and thus, they say,
The Champart was imposed.

Part the Second.
I.

With spoils and presents not a few
  Sir Evan sailed once more
Tow'rds le Conquet, his ships with new
  Supplies of food to store;
    Before Belleisle (so goes the tale)
    They burnt a fleet of thirty sail,
The crews being gone on shore.

II.

The south wind rose, and cn the coasts
  Of Brittany they passed,
An English fleet to stop their boasts
  Appeared in sight at last:
    Full sixty men a footing found
    On board Sir Evan's bark, and bound
His crew in fetters fast.

III.

Sir Evan to the mast they tied,
  And then before his face
Insult his young and beauteous bride
  And load her with disgrace;
    They take him to Southampton town
    And on his head, in guise of crown,
A red-hot morion place.

E E

IV.

They dragged his men out one by one,
　And hung them up in chains,
And now not one of all the crew
　Save Eleanor remains.
　　A beggar's scrip her only store,
　　She roams about from door to door,
　And scarce a living gains.

V.

How fared the rest of Evan's fleet?
　Methinks I hear you say,
When raging winds for ever beat
　The strongest towers decay;
　　To bend these ships before the breeze,
　　And sinking 'neath the briny seas,
　In vain for mercy pray.

VI.

Our holy island's shores at last,
　One Tuesday morn they reach;
But on the Hanois rocks are cast,
　And soon on Rocquaine's beach
　　The waves their lifeless corpses threw,
　　That vengeance still will guilt pursue,
　Their dismal fate may teach.

THE RECAPTURE OF SARK.

At the beginning of the present century, when little
more was known of the Norman Islands than their
names, it might have been necessary, in speaking of
Sark, to describe where it is situated. Guernsey,
Jersey, Alderney, Sark, and Man, were always
associated together in Acts of Parliament and in
school books for teaching children geography; and

while there were many who believed the five to form but one group, there were many others who would have been very much puzzled to point out on the map the precise situation of any one of them. Now, thanks to the incessant intercourse with England by means of steam, and the attractions the islands present as resorts for tourists and excursionists, they are as well known as most watering places on the English coast.

Sark, though the smallest of the group, is by many considered the most beautiful of the Channel Islands, and, certainly in point of rock and cliff scenery, combined with the ever-varying effects of sea and sky, there are few lines of coast, of the same extent, that can compare with it. So precipitous are the shores on all sides, that there are very few spots where a landing can be effected, and in former days it would not have been difficult to repel an invader, merely by rolling down stones from the heights.

Of the history of Sark but little is known. St. Maglorius, a Briton from South Wales, who succeeded his kinsman, St. Samson, Bishop of Dol, about the year 565, in that see, gave up a few years afterwards his pastoral charge to his successor, St. Budoc, and retired to end his days in meditation and prayer in Sark, where he established a convent and college for training young men as missionaries to the neighbouring nations. As a priory, dependent probably on some one or other of the large monasteries in Normandy, this convent was still in existence in the reign of Edward III., but the wars between this monarch and the French king, seem to have been the cause of the monks withdrawing themselves

entirely from the island about the year 1349. After the
departure of the monks, Sark appears to have become
the resort of pirates, who did so much injury to the
trade of the Channel, that, in 1356, a vessel belonging
to the port of Rye was fitted out by the merchants of
that town and of Winchelsea to endeavour to expel
this band of marauders. This they succeeded in doing,
and are said to have effected an entry into the island
by means of a stratagem, which Sir Walter Raleigh,
sometime Governor of Jersey, where he may be
supposed to have gained his information, relates as
having occurred in the reign of Queen Mary, and
attributes to the crew of a Flemish ship.

We copy Sir Walter Raleigh's account of the
re-taking of Sark, from his *History of the World*,
Part I., Book IV., chapter XI., p. 18, but must
premise by saying that he is incorrect in stating that
Sark had been surprised by the French in the reign
of Queen Mary. It was in the year 1549, during
the reign of her brother Edward VI., that the
French, being at war with England, and finding the
island uninhabited, landed four hundred men and took
possession of it. The anonymous author of *Les
Chroniques de Jersey*, written apparently in the reign
of Queen Elizabeth, in noticing the recapture of
Sark by Flemings, says nothing of the stratagem,
but simply that, guided by some Guernseymen, they
landed at night and overpowered the French garrison,
which, at that time, was very much reduced in
numbers.

"The Island of *Sark*, joining to *Guernzey*, and of
that Government, was in Queen *Mary's* time surprized
by the *French*, and could never have been recovered
again by strong hand, having Cattle and Corn enough

upon the Place to feed so many Men as will serve
to defend it, and being every way so inaccessible
that it might be held against the *Great Turk*. Yet
by the industry of a Gentleman of the *Netherlands*,
it was in this Sort regained. He anchored in the
Road with one Ship, and, pretending the Death of his
Merchant, besought the *French* that they might bury
their Merchant in hallowed Ground, and in the
Chapel of that Isle; offering a Present to the *French*
of such Commodities as they had aboard. Whereto
(with Condition that they should not come ashore
with any Weapon, not so much as with a Knife),
the *French* yielded. Then did the *Flemings* put a
Coffin into their Boat, not filled with a Dead Carcass,
but with Swords, Targets and Harquebuzes. The
French received them at their Landing, and, searching
every one of them so narrowly as they could not
hide a Penknife, gave them leave to draw their
Coffin up the Rocks with great difficulty. Some part
of the *French* took the *Flemish* Boat, and rowed
aboard their Ship to fetch the Commodities promised,
and what else they pleased, but, being entered, they
were taken and bound. The *Flemings* on the Land,
when they had carried their Coffin into the Chapel, shut
the Door to them, and, taking their Weapons out of the
Coffin, set upon the *French*. They run to the Cliff,
and cry to their Companions aboard the *Fleming* to
come to their Succour. But, finding the Boat charged
with *Flemings*, yielded themselves and the Place."

Falle, the historian of Jersey, in citing this
anecdote says:—"I have seen Memoirs which confirm
the taking of this Island by such a Stratagem; but
the other Circumstances of Time and Persons do not
agree with the foregoing Story."

He then quotes, in a footnote, a passage from a MS. chronicle in Latin, which appears to have been in the possession of the de Carteret family, Seigneurs of St. Ouen, in Jersey, giving an account of the recapture of Sark by a vessel from Rye, by means of the stratagem related above, but he does not assign any date to the transaction.

It would be rash to assert that no such event ever occurred in the history of Sark, but it is curious to note that similar stories are told of Harold Hardráda, a Scandinavian adventurer who was in the service of the Byzantine Emperors, and of the famous sea-king, Hastings. The former fell dangerously ill while besieging a town in Sicily. His men requested permission to bury him with due solemnity, and, on bringing the coffin to the gates of the town, were received by the clergy. No sooner, however, were they within the gates than they set down the coffin across the entrance, drew their swords, made themselves masters of the place, and massacred all the male inhabitants.

Hastings, about the year 857, entered the Mediterranean with a large fleet, appeared before the ancient Etruscan city of Luna, professed to be desirous of becoming a Christian, and was baptised by the Bishop. After a time he pretended to be dangerously ill, and gave out that he would leave the rich booty he had amassed to the Church, if, in the event of his death, the Bishop would allow him to be interred in one of the churches of the city. This was conceded, and, shortly afterwards, his followers appeared, bearing a coffin, which they pretended contained his dead body. No sooner had they entered the church and set it down, than Hastings started

Old Mill, Talbot.

up, sword in hand, and slew the Bishop. His followers drew their swords, and, in the confusion, soon made themselves masters of the city.

These particulars are taken from Bohn's editions of Mallet's *Northern Antiquities*, pages 169 and 170. Perhaps the earliest known germ of this story is to be found in the famous Trojan horse; but it is curious to note that a tale, similar in all its incidents to that related of Sark, is told as having happened in the reign of William and Mary at Lundy, a small isle in the Bristol Channel. It will be found in *Murray's Handbook for Travellers in Devon and Cornwall;* and as the date assigned to it is long subsequent to the publication of Sir Walter Raleigh's *History*, the natural conclusion is that the incidents in the alleged taking of Lundy, have been borrowed from those of the recapture of Sark, as narrated by Sir Walter. In confirmation of this view of the case we would draw attention to the circumstance that the "Gentleman of the Netherlands," with his crew of Flemings, of the earlier narrative, becomes in the later edition of this story "A ship of war under Dutch colours."

With these preliminary remarks, we proceed to copy the account of the surprise of Lundy:—

"The principal event in the history of Lundy is its capture by a party of Frenchmen, in the reign of William and Mary. A ship of war, under Dutch colours, brought up in the roadstead, and sent ashore for some milk, pretending that the captain was sick. The islanders supplied the milk for several days, when at length the crew informed them that their captain was dead, and asked permission to bury him in consecrated ground. This was immediately granted, and the inhabitants assisted in carrying the coffin to the grave. It appeared to them rather heavy, but they never for a moment suspected the nature of its contents. The Frenchmen then requested the islanders to leave the church, as it was the custom of their country that foreigners should absent themselves during a part of the ceremony, but informed them that they should be admitted to see the body interred. They were not, however, detained long in suspense; the doors were suddenly flung open, and the Frenchmen, armed from the pretended receptacle of the dead, rushed, with triumphant shouts, upon the astonished inhabitants, and made them prisoners. They then quietly proceeded to desolate the island. They hamstrung the horses and bullocks, threw the sheep and goats over the cliffs, and stripped the inhabitants even of their clothes. When satisfied with plunder and mischief, they left the poor islanders in a condition most truly disconsolate."

No reference to any authority for the story is given, and it is difficult to conceive that such an unprovoked and barbarous outrage, leading to no useful end—for Lundy could be of little or no use to either in time of war—could have been perpetrated so lately as the reign of William III.; but in the case of Lundy, as well as in that of Sark, the date assigned to the event is extremely vague, some asserting that it happened in the time of the great rebellion, others that it is to be found related by one of the old chroniclers who wrote the history of that long period of civil strife known as the Wars of the Roses.

THE ALARM OF PULIAS.

A time of war between England and France would

naturally cause great anxiety and excitement in all the Channel Islands. Situated as they are, so near to the French coast that buildings of any size may be discerned in clear weather by the naked eye, and coveted by that nation ever since the time when King John, having lost Normandy, the islands, firm in their allegiance to the Duke, followed the fortunes of England, they were peculiarly exposed to a hostile attack.

England, fully aware of the importance of these islands, and knowing well what a command of the Channel the possession of them gives, has always been careful to have them well fortified and garrisoned in time of war, and to keep a fleet cruising in their waters. The local militia—a body of men which may be more correctly termed trained bands, for, by the ancient constitution of the islands, every male capable of bearing arms *must* be trained to the use of them, and is required to serve his country from the age sixteen to sixty—forms a subsidiary force, frequently and carefully drilled. In times when danger was to be apprehended, watch houses were erected on all the hills and promontories round the coast, where a vigilant lookout was kept up night and day; and near each of these was placed a large stack of dried furze, which might be set on fire at a moment's warning, and which would convey the intelligence of approaching danger to all parts of the island. The keeping of these guards was confided to the militia, or, to speak more precisely, to householders, who were told off by the constables of their respective parishes for this duty. Every house, in its turn, had to furnish a man, and even females living alone were not exempt, but were expected to find a substitute. These substitutes, being well paid for their trouble, were, of course, not difficult to be met with; but as they were for the most part idle fellows, and as they were enrolled under their employers' names, these last sometimes found themselves in an awkward predicament. It is said that two maiden ladies, householders, of most unblemished reputation, and belonging to two of the most aristocratic families in Guernsey, were reported one morning as having been drunk and disorderly on guard the previous night!

During the last wars between England and France there does not appear to have been, except on one occasion, any very serious alarm in Guernsey; but every now and then the sight of ships of war off Cape La Hague, in the neighbourhood of Cherbourg, gave rise to some uneasiness, and put the island on the alert. It is no wonder if some amount of fear was felt by the inhabitants on these occasions, when we remember the panic that Bonaparte's threatened invasion in flat-bottomed boats from Boulogne, occasioned in England.

It was during the American war, in the early part of the year 1781, shortly after the attempt made on Jersey by the French adventurer, de Rullecour, so gallantly repelled by a small body of the regular forces and the militia of that island, under the command of Major Pierson, who was killed fighting bravely at the head of his troops, that a drunken frolic of three thoughtless youths threw the whole island of Guernsey into a state of consternation, and was the unfortunate cause of the death of several sick persons.

On the night of Sunday, the 4th of March, these

men, officers in one of the militia regiments, after
attending a muster of the force, which, in those
days, generally took place on the Sunday, had
finished the day by dining together, and were
returning from the Castel parish to their homes in
the Vale and St. Sampson's. Their way was along
the sea-coast, at that time not nearly so thickly
inhabited as at present, and, on arriving at an almost
solitary house, situated near the marsh of Pulias,
just at the foot of the hill of Noirmont, on which
a watch and a beacon, ready to be fired, were always
in readiness, the fancy took them to knock at the
door of the cottage, and to represent themselves as
part of a French force, consisting of over ten
thousand men, who had just effected a landing. They
demanded that a guide should be furnished them
forthwith to shew them the most direct road to the
town, and to the residence of the Governor, promising that he should be amply rewarded for his trouble.
It so chanced that the only inmates of the house
were an old man and his wife. With admirable
presence of mind, the man replied that it was out
of his power to serve them as guide, as he had the
misfortune to be stone blind, but that if they went
a few hundred yards further in a direction which
he pointed out to them, they would find another
habitation, where, no doubt, the guide they were in
search of would be forthcoming. They took their
departure, going in the direction indicated to them,
and, no sooner were their backs turned, than the
old woman opened a window in the rear of the
house, and made her way across the fields, over
hedges and ditches, and through the thick furze that
covers the hill, to the signal station on the summit

of Noirmont. She told her story to the men on watch, and it was not many minutes before the beacon was in flames, and the signal taken up by all the others round · the coast. A swift messenger was sent into town with the unwelcome news. Before long, the alarm had spread into every part of the island. The troops in garrison were soon under arms, the militia regiments mustered at their respective places of meeting, and scouts were sent out to search for the enemy, and to find out where they had taken up their position. With the return of daylight, the reconnoitring parties came back to headquarters, bringing the reassuring intelligence that not a sign of an enemy was to be seen on any part of the coast. It was then evident that the whole community had been made the victim of a heartless hoax. A strict enquiry was set on foot to discover the authors of it, but, though suspicion pointed strongly in the direction of the real culprits, nothing definite could be brought home to any one in particular ; but the surmise was converted into certainty by the sudden departure from the island of the suspected parties, who did not venture to return to their homes till many years afterwards, when the affair was well-nigh forgotten, and when there was no longer any danger of their being called to account for their mad freak. A bitter feeling was, however, engendered in the minds of the people, which found vent in satirical songs, some verses of which are still remembered.

JEAN BRETON, THE PILOT.

From the · earliest times of which we have any authentic record, the · people ·of Guernsey appear to have been a seafaring race. Perhaps they inherit their disposition for maritime pursuits from their remote ancestors, those hardy Scandinavian adventurers, who, there can be no doubt, found these islands a very convenient resort in their early piratical incursions, and probably had settled in them long before they took possession of that fertile province of France, now known as Normandy, the land of the Northmen. But, however this may be, the inhabitants of these islands could scarcely be other than mariners, surrounded as they are by a sea abounding in an endless variety of fish, and especially when we take into consideration the small extent of land in them available for agricultural purposes compared with the teeming population which,—exclusive of that of the town, which has increased considerably since the beginning of the nineteenth century—appears from authentic documents to have been quite as dense in the rural districts in the early part of the fourteenth century as it is in the present day.*

Their situation gave the islands importance in a strategical point of view, and was favourable also to the development of commerce, possessing moreover, as they did, the extraordinary privilege of neutrality in times of war between England and France.

After the forfeiture of Normandy by King John, it was long before the inhabitants of that Province acquiesced cordially in their change of masters; and the district known as *Le Cotentin*, to which the islands naturally appertained, was last to give up their allegiance to their ancient Dukes. Indeed, it can scarcely be said to have been lost entirely to England, until the

EDITOR'S NOTE.—* This was true years ago when Sir Edgar MacCulloch wrote the above, but it has ceased to be true now.

Water Lane, Couture.

final expulsion of our kings from all their continental possessions in the reign of Henry VI. During the long wars between the two nations, the possession of these islands was of the utmost importance to England, commanding as they did so long a line of the French coast. Guernsey alone at that time possessed a tolerably secure haven, the early existence of which is proved by a charter of William the Conqueror, dated prior to his invasion of England, in which St. Peter Port is mentioned. Edward I. allowed of certain dues on merchandise being levied for the improvement of this harbour, and that an active trade was carried on between Guernsey and the English possessions in Acquitaine is undoubted. No wonder then that we find the names of Guernsey ships in the lists of those chartered for the conveyance of troops to France in time of war. But what, perhaps, more than anything else contributed to form a race of hardy and courageous seamen were the important fisheries, which, before the discovery of America and the banks of Newfoundland, gave employment to an immense amount of men, in catching, salting, and drying for exportation, the fish which abound in the neighbourhood of the islands. The dangerous nature of the coast, and the surrounding seas, is owing to sunken rocks, strong currents and tides, which vary from day to day. It requires a life-long apprenticeship to become well acquainted with all the hidden and open perils which threaten a seaman's life. No wonder then if some of our fishermen, brought up to the sea from their earliest youth, become experienced and fearless pilots, knowing every reef, every set of the tide, and able to reckon to a nicety, how long the current will run in one direction, and when it may be

expected to take a different course. In making their
calculations they are very much guided by the
bearings of certain marks on land, such as churches,
windmills, or other conspicuous buildings, and the
following anecdote, related of one of our pilots, Jean
Breton, is well worthy of being remembered, not
more for the skill he displayed under very trying
circumstances, than for the significant and touching
answer he gave when questioned whether he was sure
of his marks.

In the year 1794, Captain Sir James Saumarez
was at Plymouth, in command of H.M.S. *Crescent*
and a squadron consisting of two other frigates, the
Druid and the *Eurydice*, and two or three armed
luggers and cutters. He received orders to sail for
Guernsey and Jersey, to ascertain, if possible, the
enemy's force in Cancale Bay and St. Malo. On
the 7th of June he left Plymouth, having, a day
or two before, accidentally met Jean Breton, whom
he knew. He asked him what he was doing there.
" I am waiting, Sir, for a passage to Guernsey,"
was the reply. Sir James, whose active benevolence
always prompted him to do a kind action when it
was in his power, offered to take him across, and
his kindness to his poor fellow-countryman was
amply repaid in the sequel. The day after their
departure from Plymouth, when about twelve leagues
to the N.N.W. of Guernsey, and with a fresh N.E.
breeze, the English ships fell in at dawn with a
French squadron of considerably greater force. The
superiority of the enemy being much too great to
be opposed with any chance of success, it became
the imperative duty of the English commander to
effect, if possible, the escape of his ships. Observing

that his own ships, the *Crescent* and the *Druid*, had
the advantage in sailing, and fearing that the
Eurydice, which was a bad sailer, would fall into
the enemy's hands, he shortened sail, and, having
ordered the *Eurydice*, by signal, to push for Guernsey,
he continued, by occasionally showing a disposition
to engage, to amuse the enemy and lead him off
until the *Eurydice* was safe. He now tacked, and,
in order to save the *Druid*, closed with the enemy,
passing along their line. The capture of the *Crescent*
now seemed inevitable, but the *Druid* and the
Eurydice escaped in the meanwhile, and arrived safely
in Guernsey Roads, the smaller craft returning to
Plymouth.

But Sir James had, for his own preservation, a
scheme, to effect which required great courage, con-
summate skill in the management of his ship, and
an intimate knowledge of the intricate passages
through the reefs which render navigation, on that
part of the coast in particular, so very dangerous.
The providential presence of Jean Breton on board
enabled him to put this scheme into execution with
an almost certainty of success. Sir James knew
that if there was a man in Guernsey thoroughly
acquainted with every danger that besets that iron-
bound shore, Jean Breton was that man; and, making
a feint to run his ship on the rocks to avoid being
captured by the enemy, but trusting implicitly in
his pilot's skill, he ordered him to steer through a
narrow channel, a feat which had never before been
attempted by a vessel of that size. The result of
this manœuvre was watched with the utmost anxiety
from the shore, and remarks were made by the
lookers-on that Jean Breton alone, of all the pilots

in Guernsey, would venture on such a perilous feat,
little suspecting that it was indeed he, to whom,
under God, was to be attributed the safety of the
ship and her gallant crew. The frigate was soon
brought to in a secure anchorage under shelter of
the fire of the batteries on shore, and the French,
mortified at being baulked of a prize of which they
had made quite sure, had to retire from the contest.

The scene of this daring adventure was to the
westward of the island, off the bays known as Le
Vazon and Caûbo, on the shore of the former of
which Jean Breton's cottage was situated, and full
in view of Sir James Saumarez's own manorial
residence, a position truly remarkable, for on one
side was a prospect of death or a French prison,
on the other side home with all its joys! When in
the most perilous part of the Channel, Sir James
asked the pilot whether he was sure of his marks?
"Quite sure," was Jean Breton's reply, "for there
is your house and yonder is my own!"

CHAPTER XV.

Nursery Rhymes and Children's Games.*

CHILDREN'S GAME.

NUMBER of children seat themselves in a circle on the ground, as near to each other as possible, and one of the party is chosen to stand in the centre of the ring. Those who are seated keep their hands in their laps with their fists closed, and endeavour to pass a pebble or other small object from one to the other, without its being perceived by the child who is in the middle. While the game is going on they recite the following rhyme :—

> " Mon toussebelet va demandant,
> Ma fausse vieille va quérant,
> Sur lequel prends tu, bon enfant ? " †

---

* [Some of these I have found lying loose among Sir Edgar MacCulloch's MSS. I have put them together, and added to them a few I have collected among the old country people.—Ed.]

Editor's Note.—† All Guernsey nursery rhymes, etc., are naturally either in old French or Guernsey French dating as they do from the times when no other language was spoken in the island.

The child in the centre of the circle is in the meantime on the look out to discover into whose hands the pebble is passing, and, if he can succeed in arresting it in the possession of any one of the players, he takes his place in the ring, and the one in whose hands the pebble was caught, replaces him in the centre.

From Rachel du Port.

CHILDREN'S GAME.

A child stands in the middle and says :
> "J'ai tant d'énfants à marier."

Chorus frcm children standing round :
> "Ah ! Ah ! Ah ! "

The child again says :
> "Ah ! je ne sais qu'en faire."

One of the children then says :
> "Maman, maman, que voulez vous ? "

The first child replies :
> "Entrez dans la danse, faites la révérence,
> Chantez, dansez, et embrassez celui que vous aimerez."

This is repeated till all the children are brought inside the circle, then the "mother" says :
> "Tous mes enfants sont mariés,
> Je n'en ai plus un seul resté."

Then the first child says to the "mother" :
> "Entrez dans la danse, faites la révérence,
> Chantez, dansez, et embrasses celui que vous aimerez."

From Mrs. Jehan.

CHILDREN'S "COUNTING-OUT" RHYME.

The child in the centre says the first couplet and then "counts out" :

> "Un loup passant par le désert,
> La queue levée, le bec en l'air,
> Un, deux, trois,
> Vers le bois,
> Quatre, cinq, six,
> Vers le buis,
> Sept, huit, neuf,
> Vers le bœuf,
> Dix, onze, douze,
> Dans la bouze."

ANOTHER.

" Un " i " un " l," ma tante Michelle,
   Des roques, des choux, des figues nouvelles,
   Ne passez pas par mon jardin,
   Ne cueillez pas mon rosmarin,
   Crim! Cram ! Crue, ! Elysée, ! Henri! Va 't'en! "
Sometimes the last three ejaculations are omitted.
—*From Mrs. W. P. Collings.*

ANOTHER.

" A la grand' rue
   Les étoiles y sont suspendues ;
   Du vin blanc, et du vin noir,
   On le met à baptizer,
   Sur le dos de la cuiller.
   La cuiller se passe,
   L'enfant trépasse,
   Ainsi, par ci
   Mon cœur me dit
   Ceci, celà,
   Hors d'ici
   Hors de là ! "
  —*From Miss Harriet de Sausmarez, aged ninety.*
Used by children in her youth.

OTHERS.

" L'un de la lune
   Deaux, des ch'vaux
   Très des peis,
   Quâtre d'la grappe
   Chinq, des chelins,
   Six du riz.
   Sept du lait,
   Huit, de la gâche cuite,
   Neuf, du bœuf,
   Dix, pain bis,
   Onze de la congre,
   Douze de la bouze."
     —*From Mrs. W. Ozanne.*

Hautgard, St. Peter's, showing Pilotins.

" Hickory, Airy, Ory, Anne,
  Biddy, boddy, over San,
  Père, Père, Vierge et Mère,*
  Pit, Pout, out, one ! "

—*From Miss Annie Chepmell.*

ANOTHER VERSION.

" Eckary, airy, ory Anne,
  I believe in ury San,
  Père, père, what's your mère,
  Pit, pout, out, one ! "

—*From Mrs. Mollet, La Villette.*

ANOTHER.

" Onery, Twoery, Dickery, Davy,
  Arabo, Crackery, Jennery, Lavy,
  Wishcome, Dandy, Merrycome, Time,
  Humberry, Bumberry, Twenty-nine."

—*From Mrs. Durand, sen.*

Nurses' Rhymes.

NAMES OF THE FINGERS.

The nurse takes the child's hand, and beginning with the thumb says : " *Gros det*," " *Arridet*," (for the index finger.)

[Métivier, in his Dictionnaire Franco-Normand, says it comes from an obsolete word, " *arrer* " or " *arrher*," meaning to promise, to ratify, to buy; and quotes the " Speculum Saxonum II., 15, I." " Celui qui commence une cause devant le juge pour laquelle il est tenu de donner caution........du doigt."]

" *Longuedon*," or " *mousqueton*," the middle finger, " *Jean des Scéas*," the ring finger, or the finger which wears the signet. Métivier (page 443 of Dictionnaire Franco-Normand) gives as evidence of the signet being

---

* Or sometimes " Birds of the Air."

These words sound like a burlesque of Roman Catholicism, especially of the words of administration of the Mass.

worn on this finger, Macrobius VII., 13, p. 722. Edit.
de Lyon, 1560. " Dis-moi pourquoi on s'est déterminé,
par un assentiment universel, à porter l'anneau au doigt
qui avoisine le petit, qu'on a nommé aussi le doigt
médical : et cela presque toujours à celui de la main
gauche ? Voici la réponse de Disarius. ' Ayant
consulté les livres des anatomistes, j'en ai découvert
la vraie cause. Ils m'ont appris qu'un nerf passe du
cœur au doigt de la main gauche, qui avoisine le petit,
et que c'est là, enveloppé par les autres nerfs de ce
doigt, qu'il termine sa course. Voilà pourquoi les
anciens se sont avisés de ceindre ce doigt d'un
anneau, et, si j'ose m'exprimer ainsi, d'une couronne.' "

" *P'tit Coutelds*," the little finger.

The nurse puts the child on her knee and sings:—

" Sur les paires* et sur les poumes†
    Et sur le petit chevalot
    Qui va—le pas, le pas, le pas,
    Le trot, le trot, le trot,
    Le galop ! le galop ! le galop ! "

The nurse pretends to shoe the baby's feet and
sings :—

" Ferre, ferre la pouliche,
    Pour allaïr vée ma nourriche,
    Ferre, ferre le poulaïn,
    Pour allaïr vée mon parrain ;
    Ferre, ferre le cheval,
    Pour allaïr à Torteval.

Another version of this rhyme is given in Métivier's *Dictionary*. Vide *Pouliche*, namely :—
  " Ferre, ferre men poulaïn
    Pour allaïr à Saint-Germaïn ! ‡
    Ferre, ferre ma pouliche
    Pour allaïr cis ma nourriche."

---

* Poires.   † Pommes.

‡ Saint-Germain was a fountain with medicinal properties in the Castel parish.

Nurses' Rhymes.

The nurse tickles the baby's hands, and says :—

> " L'alouette, l'alouette a fait son nid
>
> Dans la main de mon petit,
>
> Et a passaï par ich n." (Here she tickles the baby's palm).

Then beginning with the thumb, she says :—

> " Ch'tinchin l'a tuaïe,
>
> Ch'tinchin l'a plumaïe,
>
> Ch'tinchin l'a rôtie,
>
> Ch'tinchin l'a mangie,
>
> Et le poure p'tit querouin,
>
> Qui a étai au fouar et au moulin,
>
> N'en a pas ieû un poure p'tit brin."

> (There are several slightly different versions of this rhyme.)

Nurses, while playing with a child's face, say : –

> " Menton fourchi " (pinch the chin)
>
> " Bouche d'Argent " (touch the lips.)
>
> " Nez de Cancan " (touch the nose.)
>
> " Joue rotie, joue fricassée " (touch the cheeks).
>
> " P'tit œillot, gros œillot " (touch the eyes.)
>
> " Craque Martel " (tap the forehead).
>
>   —*From Mrs. Kinnersly.*

> " En r'venant de S^t. Martin
>
> J' rencontri men p'tit lapin,
>
> Il sautit dans ma grand' chambre
>
> Et mangit toutes mes almandes ;
>
> Il sautit dans ma p'tite chambre
>
> Et mangit toutes mes noix ;
>
> Il sautit dans men chillier
>
> Et mangit toutes mes cuillers ;
>
> Il sautit dans men gardin
>
> Et mangit men rosmarin ;
>
> Il sautit dans men galetâs
>
> Et mangit tous mes râts ;
>
> Il sautit sur ma maison
>
> Et mangit mon p'tit garçon."

—*From Mrs. Dread, the old nurse in the service of Mr. Gosselin, at* **Springfield.**

> " L'alouette, l'alouette, qui vole en haut,
>
> Prie Gyu pour qu'il faiche caud,
>
> Pour ses poures p'tits aloutiaux,
>
> Qui n'ont ni manches ni mantiaux
>
> Ni alumettes ni coutiaux
>
> Pour copaïr les gros morciaux."

> " Tire-lire-li, ma cauche étrille,
>
> Tire-lire-li, ramendaïs la,
>
> Tire-lire-li, j' n'ai pas d'aiguille,
>
> Tire-lire-li, acataïs n'en,

Tire-lire-li, j' n'ai point d'argent,
Tire-lire-li, empruntaîs n'en
Tire-lire-li, j' n'ai point d' crédit,
Tire-lire-li, allou's-en."

" Corbîn, Corbîn, ta maison brule,
Va-t-en cueure ton pain et ton burre,
J'ai la cllai dans ma paoute,
Jamais tu n' la verras d'autre."
—*From Louise Martel, of the Vale.*

" Colin, Colimachon, montre mè tes cônes,
Ou je te tuerai ! "
—*From Louise Martel.*

Métivier in his *Dictionnaire* gives this version :—
" Limaçon, bône-bône
Montre-moi tes cônes ! "

ANOTHER VERSION.
" Coli, Colimachon, mourte mè tes cônes,
Et je te dirai où est ton père et ta mère.
Ils sont là bas, en haut du pré,
A mangier d'la gàche cuite et bère du lait ! "
—*From Mrs. Mollet.*

" Rouge bounet, veur-tu du lait ?
Nennin, ma mère, il est trop fred,
Rouge bounet, veur-tu d'la craîme ?
Oui, ma mère, caer je l'aîme."
—*From Mrs. Mollet.*

" Coquedicot, j'ai mal au det,
Coquedicot, qu'est qui-t-la-fait ?
Coquedicot, ch'tait men valet,
Coquedicot, où est qu'il est,
Coquedicot, il est à traire,
Coquedicot, dans qu'est qu'il trait ?
Coquedicot, dans son bounet,
Coquedicot, dans qu'est qu'il coule ?
Coquedicot, dans sa grand goule,
Coquedicot, dans qu'est qu'il ribotte ?

Coquedicot, dans sa grand botte?
* Coquedicot, dans qu'est qu'il fait le burre?
* Coquedicot, dans son grand verre!"

In summer a species of small black beetle, known
by the local name of "*pan-pan*," is found very
commonly in the hedges.   Children are in the habit
of laying these beetles on their backs, in the palms
of their hands, spitting upon them, and then repeating
the following words :—

" Pan-Pan,
    Mourte mé ten sang,
    Et je te dounerai du vin bllanc."

The insect thus tortured emits a drop or two of a
blood-red secretion, which is, of course, what the child
is looking for.

Compare " Les feux de la St. Jean en Berry," in
Revue des Traditions Populaires, Vol. I., p. 171.   " Il
existe une petite scarabée d'un noir bleu qu'on nomme
'*petite bête St. Jean*.'   Quand on le prend, il rend
par les mandibules (la bouche) un liquide rougeâtre ;
les enfants excitent cette sécretion en mettant de la
salive sur l'insecte, et en disant:—

' Petite bête Saint-Jean,
    Donne-moi du vin rouge,
    Et je te donnerai du vin blanc.' "

WHEN IT SNOWS.

" Les Français qui plument leurs ouaies
    Craquent leux puches et les font quée."
    —See Chambers' *Popular Rhymes of Scotland*.

" The men o' the East
    Are pyking their geese
    And sending their feathers here away, here away! "

---

* These two lines were omitted in the version known by Mr. de Garis, of the Rouvets.
See *Notes and Queries*, Vol. I., Series 1, January 26th, 1850.

" Margoton, mon amie, }
  Margoton, mon cœur,   } bis.
  Il te faudra du rôti,
  Pour et pour, et pour et pour,
  Pour te mettre en appetit."

———

" Patty Patoche, vendit la caboche
  Dans le marchi, pour des sous merquis."

———

Je fus par les châmps
Ma roulette roulânt.
J' rencontris Tchisette
Qui m' print ma roulette.
J' li dis " Tchisette,
Rends-mé ma roulette."
A' me répounit
" Je ne t'la rendrai poiut
Si tu n'me doune une croûte de lait."

Je fus à ma mère
J' li dis " Ma mère,
Doune mé une croûte de lait."
A' me répounit
" Je ne t' la dounerai poiut
Si tu n' me doune une cllavette."
Je fus à mon père
J' li dis, " Mon père,
Doune mé une cllavette."
I' me repounit
" Je ne t' le dounerai poiut
Si tu n'me doune un' tchesse de viau."
Je fus au viau
J' li dit " Viau,
Doune me un' tchesse."
I' me repounit
" Je ne t' le dounerai poiut
Si tu ne me doune du lait de la vâque."
Je fus à la vâque
J' li dit " Vâque,
Doune mé du lait."
A' me repounit
" Je ne t'en dounerai poiut
Si tu ne me doune de l'herbe de pré."
Je m'en fus au pré
J' li dis " Pré,
Doune mé de l'herbe."
I' me répounit
" Je ne t' la dounerai point
Si tu ne me doune une tranche de faux."
Je fus au faux
J' li dis " Faux,

Doune mé de la tranche."
I' me repounit
" Je ne t' la dounerai poiut
Si tu ne me doune de la graisse de porc."
Je fus au porc
J' li dis " Porc,
Doune mé de la graisse."
I' me repounit
" Je ne t' la dounerai poiut
Si tu ne me doune un glliand de quêne."
Je m'en fus au quêne
J' li dis " Quêne,
Doune mé un glliand."
I' me repounit
" Je ne t' le dounerai pouit
Si tu ne me doune du vent de maïr."
Je fus à la maïr
J' li dis " Maïr,
Doune mé du vent."
La maïr ventait—J'éventi men quêne
Men quêne glliandait—Je glliandi men porc
Men porc graissait—Je graissi men faux
Men faux tranchait—-Je tranchi men pré
Men pré herbait—Je herbi ma vâque
Ma vâque laitait—J'allaiti mon viau
Men viau tchessait—Je tchessi men père
Men paîre cllavettait—Je cllavetti ma mère
Ma maîre crôtait—Je crôti Tchisette
Par chunna j'eus ma roulette.

This, the local version of " The House that Jack Built," is widely known. Slightly different versions exist in the different parishes, but the above is as complete as I can make it.—*From Mrs. Mollet, Mrs. C. Marquand, Mrs. Le Patourel, and from a version collected in St. Peter-in-the-Wood, by Miss Le Pelley.*

" Haptalon * de la Vieille Nanon
Qui ribotait son cotillon."

Cradle Songs.

" Dindon, Bolilin,
Quatre éfants dans le bain de Madame.
Le petit, qui cri le bouille,
Dindon, bolilin ! "

" Chausseaton, berçeaton,
Ma grand'mère est au païsson,

---

* " Haptalon " is the Guernsey equivalent of " Hobgoblin."

Old Guernsey Farm House.

Si al'en prend j'en aïron
Tout sera plein à la maison !
Si non, j' nous en passerons ! "

" Ton père* a dit qui fallait dormir (bis).
Lo, lo, lo, le petit
Puisque ton père a dit." (bis).

" Makieu
Dors tu ?
Nennin, ma mère, quer je prie Gyu,
Quaille prière dis-tu ?
" Not' Père " et " Je cré en Gyu."

" Trop paresseuse, pourquoi te revaïr ?
Reveillez-vous joyeuse, et venez dansaïr."

ANOTHER VERSION.

" Crolloton, berchotton,
Ma grand'-mère est au païsson
S' al'en a j'en airon
S' a n'en a poiut, j' nous en passerons."
—*From John de Garis, Esq., of the Rouvets.*

Dancing Rhymes.

MON BEAU LAURIER.

It was formerly customary on holidays for the youth of both sexes to assemble in some tavern or private house to amuse themselves with dancing to the enlivening strains of the fiddle or *rote*, called in the local dialect the " *chifournie*." These assemblies were termed " *sons*," and were generally attended also by some of the older portions of the community,

---

EDITOR'S NOTE.—* This rhyme is repeated, bringing in " mère," " oncle," " tante," etc., till all the relations have been named.

whose presence was a guarantee for the orderly
conduct of the meeting. Things are now much
changed. The presence of a large garrison during
the wars that arose out of the first French
Revolution, and the influx of a mixed population
since the peace, altered the character of these
assemblies in town. They came to be regarded with
disfavour ; parents discouraged their children from
attending them ; the prejudice against them extended
to the country parishes, and the puritanical feeling
that grew up with the rapid spread of dissent
among the labouring classes was entirely opposed
to any species of amusement. Whether the cause
of morality has gained much by this over strictness
is questionable.

The dances at these meetings were of a very
primitive character, consisting almost entirely of a
species of jig, by two performers, or in joining
hands and moving round at a quick pace in a circle.
When a musician was not to be procured, recourse
was had to the united voices of the dancers, and an
ancient roundelay or "*ronde*," no doubt originally
imported from France, where such dances are still
common among the peasantry, helped to carry on the
amusement of the evening. It is still danced
occasionally by young people and children, and, as
the sole remaining specimen of this kind of diversion,
deserves to be recorded.

The performers, who must consist of an equal
number of either sex placed alternately, join hands
in a circle. They then dance round, singing in
chorus :—

" Saluez, Messieurs et Dames,
    Ah ! mon beau lau-ri-er ! " (bis)

One of the girls is then selected and placed in the middle of the circle, and the rest of the party continue to dance round her singing :—

"Ah! la belle, entrez en danse!
Ah! mon beau lau-ri-er!" (bis)

The next verse is :—

"Faites nous la révérence,
Ah! mon beau lau-ri-er!" (bis)

On this the damsel curtseys round to the company, who go on singing.—

"Faites le pot à deux anses,
Ah! mon beau lau-ri-er!" (bis)

The dancer must now set her arms a-kimbo, and so figure away in the centre of the ring until the strain changes to :—

"Jambe, enjambe en ma présence,
Ah! mon beau lau-ri-er!" (bis)

This figure generally causes much merriment, for the performer is expected to clasp both arms round one uplifted knee, and hop about on the other foot, the result of which is not unfrequently a fall. Then follows :—

"Prenez cil qui vous ressemble,
Ah! mon beau lau-ri-er!" (bis)

The maiden now makes selection of a partner among the youths, and both join hands in the middle of the circle, while the following words are sung to a different tune and measure :—

"Entr'embrassez-vous par le jeu d'amourette,
Entr'embrassez-vous par le jeu d'amour."

A tender embrace follows, and then the assistants sing :—

"Entr'embrassez-vous par le jeu d'amourette,
Entr'embrassez-vous par le jeu d'amour."

A kiss is now claimed from the compliant damsel, after which is sung :—

> " Entrequittez-vous par le jeu d'amourette,
> Entrequittez-vous par le jeu d'amour."

The girl now leaves the young man in the midst of the circle and returns to her original place, when the dance recommences with such verbal alterations as the change of the principal performers renders necessary.

The old-fashioned cushion dance, which delighted the romps of the Court of the merry-monarch, Charles II., is not altogether forgotten on these occasions.

There are several other dancing rhymes and snatches of dancing times in existence—such as the one quoted by Métivier in his *Dictionnaire*, page 148:—

> " Ma coummère, aquànd je danse, men cotillon
>   fait-i bien ?
> Ah ! vraiment oui, ma coummère, i va bien mûx
>   que le mien.
> I va de ci, i va de là ;
> I va fort bien, ma coummère,
> I va fort bien coumme i va."

Another version is :—

> " Ma coummère, aquànd je danse, men cotillon
>   fait-i bien ?
> Ah ! vraiment oui, ma coummère, i va bien mûx
>   que le mien.
> I va d'ici, I va de là, men cotillon,
> Vole, vole, vole, men cotillon vol'ra."

One dance consisted of a sort of see-saw in different corners of the room, the couple repeating :—

> " Dansez donc, ou ne dansez pas,
>   Faites le donc, ou ne le faites pas,
>   La-la-la." (bis).

Dance and repeat !

Sark Games.

EDITOR'S NOTE.—In a *Descriptive Account of the Island of Sark*, published in Clarke's *Guernsey Magazine* for September and October, 1875, the Rev. J. L. V. Cachemaille wrote :— "The public games and amusements of the Sarkese are few, and of a simple kind; and it is only children or young people who take part in them now-a-days Formerly they used to have a favourite amusement, consisting of six or eight men, or big boys, who placed themselves in a line, one behind the other, and held each other firmly round the waist, while two outsiders made every effort to pull them apart one after another, till one only remained. This game they called '*Uprooting the Gorse*,' and the last man represented the largest or principal root. Children still keep up this game, but not very universally, nor is it often played. It was one of the chief amusements of the '*Veilles*.'" Mr. Cachemaille also wrote :—"A person, either young or old, disguised himself in a manner to frighten people. At the end of a stick he carried the head of a horse or donkey, and this he placed on his own head, having first enveloped himself in a sheet. By means of cords, he made the jaws of this head to open and shut with a noise, then he ran after one or the other, endeavouring to bite them with the teeth of those horrible jaws; whereupon everybody ran away as fast as they could, and there was a general turmoil, the people either screaming with fright, or else laughing at the joke. This head made the round of all the "*Veilles*," followed by a crowd of people. and. until quite latterly, one of these heads was still to be seen in one of the principal farm houses."

CHAPTER XVI.

Superstitions Generally.*

> "Even a single hair casts a shadow."
> —*Lord Verulam.*

HE widely-diffused idea that the spirits of the dead sometimes return in the form of birds, is not altogether obsolete in these islands.

A widow, whose husband had been drowned at sea, asked the Seigneur of Sark whether a robin that was constantly flying round her cottage and alighting on her window-sill, might not possibly be the soul of the departed.†

The robin is a bird specially reverenced in Guernsey, as the widely-accepted belief is that it was the robin who first brought fire to the island. In bringing it across the water he burned his breast, and this is the reason why, to this day, the breast of the robin is tinged with red. "My mother," said the old woman who told me this, "had a great veneration for this little bird, which had been so

---

EDITOR'S NOTE.—* In this chapter are collected all the loose and unclassified bits of Folk-Lore scattered among Sir Edgar MacCulloch's manuscripts.

---

† See *Indo-European Folk-Lore.*

great a benefactor to those who came before us, for who can live without fire." * †

Soucique. This is the name given in Guernsey to the marigold, and also to the fire-crested or golden-crested wren, the word being derived from the Latin "solsequium." It is probably the same as the "heliotropium." The shape and colour of the flower, resembling the disc of the sun surrounded with rays, and the fact of the flower opening at sunrise and closing at sunset, would naturally cause it to be associated with that luminary, and considered sacred to Apollo. It is not quite so easy to account for the same name being given to the fire-crested and golden-crested wren, but we know that the wren plays a considerable part in the mythology of the Aryan nations, and is one of those birds which is believed to have brought fire from heaven for the use of man.‡ The story of its outwitting the eagle, in the contest for the sovereignty among birds, and getting nearer the sun by perching on its back, may have gained for it a name, which, as we have seen, signifies "a follower of the sun."

The willow-wren is known among us as "*Le Ribet*," from *Ri* (roi), and "*bet*," the form known in

---

* From Rachel Du Port.

EDITOR'S NOTES.

† "Another version of this story is: The robin redbreast brought fire to the Island, and by so doing burnt his breast, as he had been carrying a lighted torch in his beak. When he arrived with his breast-feathers burnt and raw and red, all the other birds were so sorry for him that they each gave him a feather, except the owl, who would not, so that is why he no longer dares show his face by day."—*Told me in 1895 by the late Miss Annie Chepmell, who had heard it from an old servant.*

"Quand la rouge-gorge alla chercher le feu, ses plumes furent toutes brulées, alors les oiseaux en eurent pitié et ils résolurent de lui donner chacun une plume pour la réhabiller. Seul le chat-huant, oiseau orgueilleux et peu compatissant, refusa. C'est pour cela que, lorsqu'il se montre au jour, tous les petits oiseaux crient après lui, et la rouge-gorge en particulier, qui, par son cri, lui reproche son orgeuil."—*Traditions et Superstitions de la Haute Bretagne*, Tome II., p. 201.

‡ One country tradition says that the wren brought water to Guernsey.

Portion of the Old Town House (on the left) of the de Sausmarez Family,
situated where St. Paul's Chapel now stands.

the province of Bearn of "bel." Vallancey says:—
"The Druids represented this as the king of birds,
hence the name of this bird in all the European
languages. Latin, *Regulus*; French, *Roitelet*; Welsh,
Bren (or "king"); Teutonic, *Konig Vogel*; Dutch,
Konije, etc.

A magpie crossing one's way is of evil augury,
portending vexation, or trouble of some kind. Crows
cawing much in the neighbourhood of a house is
also a sign of impending trouble.*

When the cuckoo is heard for the first time in the
year one ought to run a few steps forward in order
to ensure being light for the rest of the year. If
you have money in your pocket, and turn it, or shake
it, it will ensure good luck, and you will not want
money throughout the rest of the year.†

"Money should be turned in the pocket when the
cuckoo is heard for the first time."

An old woman, living at the Vale used to say:—
"*En Guernesi nous a coutume de dire en oyant le
coucou pour la première fais:—'Si tu ne cuers pas
tu seras lourd toute l'annâie.' Nous remue étout
l'argent qu'nous peut aver dans les paoutes, en les
secouant—et il y a des gens qui se mettent à
genouaïx. La première fais que nous-ôt le coucou il
faut metire une grosse roque sus sa tête, arroûtaïr à
courre, et nou sera légier toute l'annâie.*"

CUCKOO RHYMES.

"*En Avril
Le coucou crie
S'il est vif.*"

---

* From J. R. Tardif, Esq.

† See "Folk-Lore of the North of England," in the *Monthly Packet*, February,
1862.

" *Le coucou*
S'en va en Août
La barbe d'orge
Li pique la gorge."

" *Coucou-Varou*
Bave * *partout.*"

(See *Notes and Queries*, 4th Series, Vol. III., 1869.)

It is thought lucky to shake one's pockets and run a few steps, the first time one hears the cuckoo sing. The following lines are also repeated by some, and the number of times the cuckoo utters his note is taken as an answer to the question.

" *Coucou, cou-cou, dis mé*
Combien d'ans je vivrai." †

I remember when I was a child, my aunt, Miss de Sausmarez, making me remark how chickens, when they drink, lift up their heads at every sip, and telling me that they did so to thank God. ‡

The bone of the cuttle fish, which is found at times thrown up on the beach, is called in Guernsey " *Pépie.*" It is supposed to possess the quality of healing the " pip " in chickens, also known as " la pépie."

A stye in the eye is called in Guernsey " *un laurier,*" and is to be cured by bathing the eye with an infusion of laurel leaves or " lauriers."

If a fisherman, on setting out, sees a humble bee flying in the same direction as he is going, he considers it a good omen, and that he is sure of a plentiful catch. If, however, the insect meets him,

---

* *Bave*—The cuckoo spittle.

† See Thorpe's *Northern Mythology*, and Chambers' *Popular Rhymes*, p. 193.

‡ See *English Folk-Lore*, p. 95.

it is quite the reverse. The ill-luck, however, may be averted by spitting thrice over the left shoulder. Omens of good or bad luck are also derived from sea-birds. All depends on whether a gull or a cormorant is seen first, as, if a cormorant, no fish is to be expected that day. All fishermen also know how unlucky it is to count one's fish until the catch has been landed, as, however freely they may be biting, counting them would inevitably stop all sport for the day.*

If a pair of bellows is put on a table, some great misfortune is sure to happen in the household.†

Richard Ferguson, fisherman, of the Salerie, tells me that there is a great objection against taking currant cake with them when they go a-fishing, it is sure to bring bad luck.

Guernsey Local Nick-Names.

ALDERNEY	=	Vâques (Cows).
SARK	=	Corbins (Crows).
JERSEY	=	Crapauds (Toads).
GUERNSEY	=	Anes (Donkeys).

* From the late Colonel de Vic Tupper.
† From J. R. Tardif, Esq

EDITOR'S NOTE.

The following scraps of Folk-Lore I have gathered from old people in St. Martin's parish, in the years 1897-99.

THE MAN IN THE MOON.

" *J'ai ouï dire à ma gran'mère i'y a be'tôt chinquante ans qu'l'bouan homme que nou veit dans la lune enlevit un fagot de bouais le Dimanche, et pour chut fait le Bon Gyu'le condamnit à s'en allair dans la lune jusqu'au Jour du Jugement. V'la l'histouaire de chut poure Mâbet que nou vait si souvent perqui là-haut.*"—From Mrs. Le Patourel.

A robin flying to the window or in the house is a sign of death. Crows flocking together and cawing over the house are most unlucky. To go out and meet three crows or three magpies means good luck, all other numbers mean misfortune.

None should ever cut their finger nails on either a Sunday or a Friday if they wish to prosper. A baby's first nails should never be cut, but bitten.

On being given a present of scissors or a knife, a double * should always be given in exchange. Parsley should never be taken as a gift, but it is very lucky to steal some (!).

No berried plants such as ivy, etc., should be brought into the house before Christmas, and it is especially unlucky if, when they are brought in, they are allowed to touch the

* The smallest local coin, value one-eighth of a penny.

Guernsey Parish Nick-Names.

St. Pierre Port = Les Cllichards (See Métivier's *Dictionnaire,* p. 134.)

St. Samson = Raines (Frogs.)

Le Valle = Ann'tons (Cockchafers.)

Le Catel = Le Câtelain est un âne-pur-sang.

St. Sauveur = Fouarmillons (Ant lions.)

St. Pierre-du-Bois = Equerbots (Beetles).

Torteval = Anes à pid de ch'vâ (Asses with horses' feet.)

La Forêt = Bourdons (Drones.)

St. Martin = Dravants (Large Ray-fish.)

St. André = Craînchons (siftings) "Ce qui reste dans le crible." *

---

mantel shelf. May should *never* be brought into a house, and many people, especially in Alderney, consider that to bring in furze or gorse means to introduce sorrow.

Should an unmarried woman go in and out of a house through a window which is not destined as a means of entrance or exit, she will never marry.

An umbrella should never be opened in a house, or placed upon a table, quarrelling and strife are sure to follow.

It is supposed to be very unlucky when going out of the house, if the first person you meet is a woman. Never pass her if you can avoid it, but stand still and let her pass you.

To keep witches from entering a stable and molesting the cattle a piece of naturally pierced flint-stone should be tied to the key of the stable door. On going down to a beach it is considered lucky to pick up a small stone and bring it away with you. Never give away money with a hole in it.

If you think you are bewitched or that any one has a spite against you, throw a lump of salt on the fire, and as it burns blue the spite will evaporate.

Fanny Ingrouille, of the Forest parish, from whom the foregoing was obtained, also repeated the following formula, which apparently was a programme for the week of a Guernsey country girl.

"*Au matin—Pierre Martin* †
Au ser—Jean Mauger †
Lundi, Mardi—Fêtes
Mercredi—Mâ à la tête
Jeudi, Vendredi—Fort travâs
Samedi—A la ville
Dimanche—Vée les filles."

---

* *Criblure,* Métivier, p. 152.—"In sifting corn the *craînchons* are the light and defective grains and husks that gather in the *middle* of the sieve, as it is worked with a circular motion. St. Andrew's is the *middle* parish of the island."—*From Mr. Linwood Pitts and* "*Bad'la goule.*"

---

† "*Martin*" and "*Mauger*" are two of the most widely spread of the country names,

EDITOR'S NOTE.

The following is a rhyme describing the girls of each parish, given me by the late Mr. Isaac Le Patourel, of St. Martin's.

LES FILLES DES DIX PAROISSES.

" *Ce sont les filles de la Ville*
Elles sont des jolies Belles !
Ce sont les filles de Saint Samson
Elles sont bonnes pour le lanchon ! *
Ce sont les filles du Valle
Elles sont prêtes pour faire du mal !
Ce sont les filles du Câtel
Elles sont prêtes pour la gaieté !
Ce sont les filles de Saint Sauveur,
Elles sont toutes de bouane humeur !
Ce sont les filles de Saint Pierre
Ah ! qu'elles sont terjous à braire ! †
Ce sont les filles de Tortevâ
Elles ont vraiment les pids de ch'vâ !
Ce sont les filles de la Forêt
Dame ! ch'est qu'elles sont bien laides !
Ce sont les filles de St. Martin
Elles sont niais comme des lapins !
Ce sont les filles de Saint André
Elles seront toutes des delaissées ! "

* Lanchon = Sand-eels.   † A braire = To weep.

CHAPTER XVII.

Proverbs, Weather Sayings, etc.

"They serve to be interlaced in continued speech. They serve to be recited upon occasion of themselves. They serve, if you take out the kernel of them, and make them your own."
—*Lord Verulam.*

NO nation is without its proverbs; but while in many cases these pithy sayings are the same in all languages, and merely literal translations from one dialect to another, in other instances the idea only is present, and the words in which the proverb is expressed have little or nothing in common, as, for example, the English saying:— "A bird in the hand is worth two in the bush," appears in French in the far less picturesque form of "*un* '*tiens*' *vaut mieut que deux* '*tu l'auras.*'" Sometimes, from the peculiar circumstances of the people using it, a proverb takes a local tinge, and, in so doing, may change considerably from its original wording, while continuing at the same time to convey a similar lesson. Thus the pastoral saying:—"To lose one's *sheep* for a penn'orth of tar," becomes, very naturally, among a nautical population, "to lose one's *ship*, etc."

Some few proverbs are so thoroughly local as to

appear to have originated in the place where they are used.

Guernsey is not rich in proverbs properly so called; but, as might be expected among an agricultural and maritime people, weather-sayings are not uncommon. Many of these could no doubt be traced to the mother-country, Normandy, but some few may be indigenous, and the result of local observation.

We will give specimens of each class of these proverbial expressions, with such remarks as may be necessary to explain them as far as they can be explained; and, although many of them might be put into modern French, we have preferred retaining the old Norman dialect still preserved as the language of all the rural parts of the island.

Proverbs.

Nou (on) ne va pas au jàn (àjonc) sans ses gànts.— No one goes to cut furze without gloves. If you would undertake an arduous matter, be well prepared for it.

Ch'est la coue (queue) qui est la pière (pire) à écorchier (écorcher).—It is the tail that is the hardest to flay. It is often more difficult to bring an affair to a successful end than to begin it.

Qui sent mànjue (démangeaison) se gratte.—He who itches scratches himself. Nearly equivalent to the English saying, "The cap fits."

Quand le bouissé (boisseau) est pllein, i' jette.—When the bushel-measure is full it runs over. The last straw breaks the camel's back.

Building the south arm of the Town Harbour, connecting Castle Cornet with the Island.

Nécessitaï fait la vieille trottaïr.—Need will make an
old woman trot.

Au broue (brouille, embarras) est le gan (gain, profit).
—No exact equivalent is to be found for this
proverb, but it means that profit, in some way
or other, may be made where there is much
doing. The English saying "No pains, no gains,"
comes near it.

Pûs (plus) de broue que de travâs (travail).—More
bustle than work. Much cry and little wool.

Mettre daeux guerbes (deux gerbes) en un llian (lien).
—To bind up two sheaves with one wisp. To
kill two birds with one stone.

*Biautaï (beauté) sans bountaï (bonté), ne vaut pas
vin évantaï.*—Beauty, without goodness, is not
worth stale wine.

L'amour hâle (tire) pûs (plus) que chent (cent) bœufs.
—Love draws more than a hundred oxen.

A p'tit pourche (pourceau) grosse pânais.—The little
pig gets the big parsnip. The youngest child is
the most petted.

Qui paie s'acquitte; qui s'acquitte s'enrichit.—He
who pays his way keeps out of debt; he who
keeps out of debt gets rich. No comment is
needed on this thoroughly practical proverb.

*Si nou (on) lli dounne ùn peis (pois) i' prend une
faïve.*—If you give him a pea, he'll take a bean.
Give him an inch, he'll take an ell.

*Ch'n'est pas ôve (avec) du vinaigre que nous (on)
attrâpe des mouques (mouches).*—Flies are not caught
with vinegar. Nothing is to be gained by roughness.

Qui peut volaïr (voler) ùn œuf, peut volaïr ùn bœuf.
—He who would steal an egg would steal an
ox. Be honest in the smallest matters.

F"rine du guiablle (diable) s'en va en bran (son).—
The devil's flour turns to bran. Ill-gotten wealth
never prospers.

*Chàngement d'herbage est bouan (bon) pour les jânes
viaux (jeunes veaux).—*Change of pasture is good
for young calves. Variety is necessary for the
young. " Home-keeping youth have ever homely
wits."

*I' ne faut pas faire le cottin (cabane, crêche) d'vànt
que le viau seit naï.* (Avant que le veau ne soit
né).—One must not make the crib before the calf
is born. Do not count your chickens before they
are hatched.

*S'il ne l'a en breuf, il l'aira (l'aura) en soupe.—*If
he does not get it in broth, he'll get it in soup.
If he cannot obtain his end by one means, he
will by another.

*Apprins au ber (berceau), dure jusqu'au ver.—*What
is learnt in the cradle goes with one to the
grave—literally " to the worm."

*La bète d'un poure (pauvre) houme (homme) mourrait
pûs-à-caoup (plus tôt) que li (lui).—*He would die
more opportunely than a poor man's beast, is said
of a person whose death would not leave much
cause for regret.

*Les p'tits tchiens (chiens) ont de longues coues
(queux).—*Is the equivalent of the French proverb,
" dans les petites boîtes les bons onguents ; "
precious ointments are in small boxes.

*Ch'est une querrue à tchiens (charrue à chiens).—*It
is a plough drawn by dogs, is said of any affair
which is badly conducted—where those who ought
to work in concert are pulling different ways,
like two dogs on a leash.

H H

Un mouisson (oiseau) à la main vaut mûx que daeux qui volent.—A bird in the hand is worth two on the wing.

Il n'y a fagot qui n'trouve sen lliàn (lien).—There is no faggot but what at last finds a band. Every Jack has his Jill; every dog has his day.

I' n'y a fagot qui n'vaut sa lliache (liasse).—There is no faggot so bad as not to be worth a band.

Qui mange la craïme ne rend pas du burre (beurre).—He who eats his cream makes no butter. You cannot eat your cake and have it.

I' ne vaut pas grànd burre (beurre).—He or it is not worth much butter; meaning, such an one is not worth much, the matter is not worth going to any expense about; an allusion to a worthless fish on which the butter used in cooking it is so much thrown away.

Ecoute-paret (paroi) jamais n'ot dret (n'ouit droit).—An eavesdropper never hears good.

I' n'y a rien itaï (tel) que sé (soi) sa qu'minse (chemise) lavaïr (laver).—There is nothing like washing your own shirt. If you wish a thing well done, do it yourself. It is also used in the sense of "Wash your dirty linen at home."

Nou (on) ne tràche (cherche) pas de la graïsse dans le nic (nid) d'ùn tchien (chien).—No one thinks of looking for fat in a dog's kennel. Look not for qualities where they are not likely to be found, as generosity in a miser, or honesty in a thief.

Si ùn cat (chat) s'amord (s'adonne) au lard, nou ne sairait (saurait) l'en d's'amordre.—If a cat takes a liking for bacon you can't break her of it. It is difficult to get rid of bad habits.

P'tit à p'tit l'ouaisé (oiseau) fait sen nic (nid).—Little by little the bird builds her nest. Rome was not built in a day.

Tout neû g'nêt (neuf balai) néquie (nettoie) net.—A new broom sweeps clean.

I' n'y a itäils (tels) qus les féniêns (fainéants) quand i' s'y mettent.—There are none like idlers when they once set to work.

Ch'est cauches (bas, chausses) grises, et grises cauches.—This is the equivalent of the French proverb "C'est bonnet blanc, et blanc bonnet," and the English, "Six of one, and half-a-dozen of the other."

Ch'n'est pas les ciens (ceux) qui labourent le pûs près du fossaï (de la haie) qui sont les pûs riches.—It is not they who plough nearest the hedge who are the richest. Economy may be carried too far.

I' s'y entend coume à ramaïr (ramer) des chaoux (choux).—He understands as much about it as about putting pea-sticks to cabbages. The meaning conveyed being: he knows nothing at all about it.

Tout chu (ce) qui vient de flot se retournera d'èbe.—All that comes with the flood will return with the ebb. Riches too rapidly acquired, or ill-gotten, will disappear as quickly as they came—nearly equivalent to the French proverb "Ce qui vient de la flûte s'en va par le tambour."

Si l'houme aïme autre mûx que sé (mieux que soi) au moulin i' mourra de set (soif).—If a man loves others more than himself, he will die of thirst even were he in a mill. The mill spoken of in this selfish proverb, which is equivalent to "Look after number one," is, of course, a water-mill.

Biauture (beau-temps, beauté) d'hiver ; santaï (santé) de vieil homme ; parole de gentilhomme ; ne t'y fie, homme !—A fine day in winter, the health of an old man, the word of a nobleman ; trust to none of these, O man ! The marked distinction of "noble" and "rôturier," if such ever existed in Guernsey, died out many centuries ago ; and this proverb has all the appearance of an importation from Normandy, or some other part of France, where the peasantry were oppressed by the feudal system. The word "biauture" does not belong to the Guernsey dialect, and when the saying is quoted in the present, it is generally with reference to the two first clauses.

Un tchien (chien) vaut bien p'tit qui ne vaut pas ùn caoup de suffllet (coup de sifflet).—A dog that is not worth whistling for is not worth much.

Les grands diseurs sont de p'tits faiseurs.—Great talkers are little doers.

Où 'est qu'il y a du crottin, il y a du lapin.—Where you see their droppings, you may expect to find rabbits. Used both literally and metaphorically. There is no smoke without fire.

Il y a terjoûs (toujours) un épi qui mànque à la guerbe (gerbe).—There is always a spike of corn lacking in the sheaf. Nothing is ever perfect.

I' n'y a bouais (bois) dont nou (on) n'fait buche.—There is no wood but what will serve for firing, meaning that everything can be put to some use or other ; but the latter half of the proverb is sometimes varied to "*dont i' n' fait buche,*" and it is then equivalent to the English saying "All is fish that comes to his net."

Va où tu peux, meurs où tu deis (dois).—Go where
you can, die where you must. Dispose of your
life as you please, death is inevitable.

*Il est niais coume Dadais qui se couachait (couchait)
dans l'iaue (eau) d'paeur (peur) d'être mouailli
(mouillé).*—He is as foolish as Dadais who
lay down in the water to avoid getting wet in a
shower.

*Il est niais coume Dadais qui tâte l'iaue pour vée
(voir) s'a bouit (bout).*—He is as stupid as Dadais
who puts his hand into the water to feel if it is
boiling.

*Il est pûs (plus) niais que Dadais qui se fouittait
de crêpes.**—He is more simple than Dadais who
flogged himself with pancakes. The word "Dadais"
is used in the sense of simpleton. In the three
sayings that we have just quoted "Dadais" bears
a strong family resemblance to the "Simple
Simons" and "Silly Billies" of English nursery
tales.

*Ch'tait du temps du Rouai (Roi) Jehan. Ch'était
du temps des Scots.*—Are used in speaking of events
which took place beyond the memory of man. It
is easy to understand how the reign of King
John came to form an epoch in the history of
Guernsey; for it was then that the connexion
with the mother-country, Normandy, was severed,
and the islands, until then part and parcel of
that Duchy, became attached to the Crown of
England, and have so continued ever since. But
it is not so easy to say when or how the latter
saying originated. It may refer to an invasion

---

* EDITOR'S NOTE.— The version I have heard of this proverb is : "Il est niais coume
Dadais qui se fouittait de crêpes et tout-le-temps mourait de faim."

of the island by David Bruce, about the tenth
year of Edward III., (A.D. 1336); when great
atrocities appear to have been committed on the
inhabitants; but some old people seem to think—
and probably with reason—that the "Scots" were
a Scotch regiment sent here in the early part of
last century on a fear of hostilities breaking out
between England and France. It is right, however,
to notice that in the Guernsey dialect "*Ecossais*"
and not "*Scots*" is used to designate Scotchmen.

I' mànge coum' un varou.—He eats like an ogre,
is the exact English equivalent of this saying;
but there are few who use the saying who could
say what is meant by "*un varou.*" It is, undoubtedly, the same as the French "loup-garou"
in English—a were-wolf; and may have reference
to the old superstition of men and women being
turned into wolves.

I' s'en est allaï (allé) les pids (pieds) d'vànt.—
He has gone feet foremost. He has been carried
to his grave.

*Il a étaï enterraï la tète ès tchiens (aux chiens)
dehors.*—Is used in the same sense as "being
buried like a dog."

Il a tète et bounet (bonnet).—He has a head, yea,
and a cap, is said of an opinionated man.

I' n'en reste ni tchiesse (cuisse) ni aïle.—There
neither remains leg nor wing. All is lost, nothing
remains.

I' quient (tient) d'la chouque (souche).—He's a
chip of the old block.

I' fait rille (raie) de gras.—He is making a streak
of fat, is said of a man who is prospering in his
affairs, in allusion to a pig that is being fattened,

I' peut mànger sa gâche (galette) dorâïe (beurrée) des daeux bords (des deux côtés).—He can eat his cake buttered on both sides. He is rich enough not to be obliged to spare himself any indulgence.

I' mànge sa dorâie (tranche de pain beurré) grajie (grattée).—He spares the butter on his bread, either from poverty or from avarice. It is "bread and scrape."

I' prend les cauches (chausses, bas,) pour les sôlers (souliers).—He mistakes the stockings for the shoes. He is a blunderer who does not know one thing from another.

Il a paeux (peur) des p'tits sôlers (souliers).—He is afraid of the little shoes, is said of a man who is unwilling to enter into the estate of matrimony for fear of the additional expenses that it will entail—shoes for the children being a considerable item in the disbursements of a poor family.

I' n'en prend ni compte ni taille.—He takes no account nor tally. He lets matters take their course.

V'là une fière perruque à débouquèr (démêler).—There's a fine wig to comb out! Is said of an affair which is almost hopelessly involved.

Il a fait pertus (pertuis, trou) sous l'iaue (eau).—He has made a hole in the water. He has disappeared furtively. Compare with the French saying "Il a fait un trou à la lune."

I' vêt (voit) sept lieues dans la brune.—He sees seven leagues through the fog, is said derisively of a man who boasts of being more clearsighted than his neighbours.

Il est montaï (monté) sur ses pontificaux.—He is in his pontificals, is equivalent to the English saying "He is riding the high horse,"—asserting his dignity when there is no need to do so.

Ch'est le bouâine (borgne) qui mène l'aveuglle. —The one-eyed man is leading the blind man.

Nou (on) ne saït pouit (point) où il puche (puise).— One knows not what well he draws from, is said of a man who manages to get on without any very visible means of existence.

Trop de cuisiniers gâtent la soupe.—Too many cooks spoil the broth.

I' n'y a pas de rue sâns but.—There is no road but has an ending. Equivalent to "It is a long lane that has no turning."

S'il y avait un démarieur, il airait (aurait) pûs (plus) à faire que tous les marieurs.—If there were an "un-marryer" he would have more work to do than all the "marryers."

Ce n'est pas tout que les chaous, faut de la graïsse à les cuire.—Cabbages alone are not sufficient, one must have grease to cook them with. Generally applied to "*parvenus*," who have money but no manners.

Nou' n'engraisse pouit les p'tits cochons d'iau fine.— Little pigs are not fattened by pure water.

Vieille pie a plus d'un pertus à son nic (nid).—An old magpie has more than one hole in her nest. Said of a man who is skilful at evasion.

T'as acouare les jaunes talons.—You have still got yellow heels, is said to youngsters who are too presuming in giving their opinion in the presence of their elders. Compare the French "blanc-bec" and "béjaune."

Ch'est la vermeïne (vermine) qui mànge (mange) l'tàs (le tas).—It is the vermin that eats up the stack. Said of a father who has a large family of children drawing upon him and eating up all his savings.

––––––

Popular Sayings.

There are certain popular sayings which contain a comparison, and which, although in a strict sense they cannot be called proverbs, may yet be classed with them. Some of these contain words which have become obsolete, or, at least, antiquated. "*Vier (vieux) comme suée*" equivalent to "As old as the hills," may be quoted as an example, for not only is the word "*suée*" obsolete, but its very meaning is forgotten and unknown. Mr. George Métivier, a learned philologist, author of the *Dictionnaire Franco-Normand, ou Recueil des Mots particuliers au Dialecte de Guernesey*, is inclined to refer it to the old French *suée* signifying *sueur*, sweat, used in the sense of labour. The conjecture is ingenious, but not quite satisfactory.

I' s'est maniaï (manié) coume un albroche.—He has conducted himself like a boor. Roquefort in his "*Glossaire de la Langue Romane*" explains the word *Allobroge* as "un homme grossier, un rustre, etc.," and gives *Adlobrius, Allobrox*, as the Latin forms. According to Ducange, these words signify a citizen or native of Gaul. The Allobroges, however, in the time

of the Roman Empire, were the tribes inhabiting
Savoy and Piedmont.

I' bét (boit) coume ùn alputre.—Is used in the sense of
"He drinks likes a fish," but why the *alputre*,—
rockling, or sea-loach,—should be singled out among
fishes for bibulous propensities, it is impossible to guess.

I' plleut coume cis (chez) Pierre de Garis.—Is used
in the sense of "raining cats and dogs." A
certain Pierre de Garis, a merchant of Bayonne,
in the time when Aquitaine was governed by
English Princes, was appointed to the responsible
office of Bailiff of Guernsey, about the year 1325.*

EDITOR'S NOTE.

* The following short pedigree of the first members of the de Garis family in the island may
prove interesting :—It is extracted from the proceedings of the law suit re the Fief Handois
in 1497. See Additional MSS. British Museum, 30, 188.

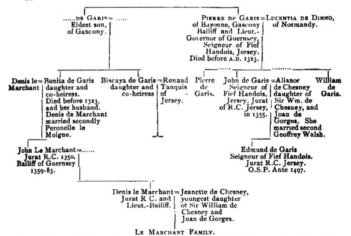

LE MARCHANT FAMILY.

In the "Extente" of 1331, Pierre and John de Garis held land in the parishes of St. Peter
Port, St. Andrew's, St. Peter's-in-the-Wood, and St. Sampson's. In the "Calendars of Patent
Rolls" for the years 1328-36, we find Nicholaa, Abbess of the Holy Trinity, Caen, nominating
Peter and William de Garis her Attorneys in the Channel Islands, and in 1332 a Commission was
given to Robert de Norton, William de la Rue, and Peter de Garis to survey the King's Castles
and Mills in the islands of Jersey and Guernsey which are reported to be greatly in need of
repair, and to certify by whose default, and by whom they fell into decay. In 1380, a William
de Garis, described as being "de l'isle de Guerneseye," sold to "Sire Pierre Payn" the Manor
of Malorey in St. Laurent, Jersey, to which parish the Fief Handois also belonged.

In all probability he derived his name from a small town called *Garis*, about half-way between Bayonne and St. Jean-de-Luz. He became the founder of a family of importance, not only in Guernsey, but also in the neighbouring island of Jersey, and of which there are still numerous descendants. It is not very likely that the saying dates so far back as the fourteenth century, although it has no doubt a very respectable antiquity. We can only conjecture that it must have derived its origin from some well-known Pierre de Garis of indolent or miserly habits, who allowed the roof of his dwelling to fall into decay and let in the rain, and so became a by-word with his neighbours.

Ill' y en a assaï (assez) pour tous les Tostevins.—There is enough for all the Tostevins—is said when there is an abundance of anything—enough and to spare. The name is extremely common in the western parishes of Guernsey, especially in St. Pierre-du-Bois and Torteval, where many of those who bear it are stone-masons who walk every day into town—a distance of five or six miles—to their work. Perhaps the good appetite they acquire in so long a walk may have had something to do in originating the saying.

Jaune coume q'zette.—As yellow as a daffodil, is equivalent to the English saying "As yellow as crow's foot." It is sometimes varied to "*jaune coume du murlu,*" this last word being the local name of the corn-marigold and the ox-eye daisy.

Vert coume ache.—As green as smallage—a herb closely allied to celery and parsley, and, like them, intensely green—is used where we should say in English "As green as grass."

Chièr (cher) coume paivre (poivre).—As dear as pepper, is a comparison which must have originated when this useful condiment, now within the reach of the poorest, was a luxury brought from far and obtainable only by the rich. Quit-rents payable in pepper were not unknown in the middle-ages; and in the Extente, or account of the revenues and obligations of the Crown in Guernsey, drawn up in the fifth year of the reign of King Edward III., A.D. 1331, there is an item of a quarter of a pound of pepper to be paid annually at Michaelmas, by a tenant of lands situated in the parish of St. Martin's. The money payment for which this rent was commuted at that time was twelve deniers tournois, which would make the value of a pound four sols tournois, no inconsiderable sum in those days.

I' chànte coume ùn orateur.—He sings like an orator. A loud voice is certainly desirable in one who attempts to *speak* in public. Our countrymen seem to consider it equally necessary and admirable in a *singer.*

Orguillaeux (orgueilleux) coume ùn pouáis (pou) sûs v'louss (velours).—As proud as that insect which Shakespeare calls "a familiar beast to man" may be supposed to feel when it finds itself on velvet.

Caûd (chaud) coume braïze.—As hot as embers, needs no explanation.

Ch'est coume un bourdon dans une canne.—It is like a humble bee in a can—is said of a droning monotonous style of preaching or speaking.

*Ch'est coume les prières de Jacques Ozanne qui
n'ont pas . de fin.*—It is like James Ozanne's
prayers which never come to an end. This is
said of any matter which is prolonged to an
unreasonable extent; but nothing seems now to
be known of the individual whose lengthy suppli-
cations gave rise to the saying.

T'es coume Jean Le Tocq.—You are like Jean Le Tocq.
This is addressed to a man who is seen abroad
at an earlier hour than usual, and contains an
allusion to two lines in the old Guernsey ballad
of the invasion of the island by Evan of Wales
in 1373, where it is said :—

> *" Jean Le Tocq sy se leva*
> *Plus matin qu'a l'accoutumée."*

Indeed this last line is generally added.

*Il a la conscience de la jument Rabey qui mangit
s'en poulain.*—He has the conscience of Rabey's
mare, who ate her foal. Said of an utterly hard-
hearted and unscrupulous man. The Rabeys are a
well-known country family, and it is possible that
this proverb refers to some domestic tragedy, the
details of which have long been forgotten.

Avoir le corset de Maître George.—To wear the
corset of Maître George. An allusion is here
meant to a certain George Fénien. The Féniens
were a family who owned property in Fountain
Street, and seem to have become extinct towards
the middle of the eighteenth century. This
expression is applied to an indolent man, so that
the "Maître George Fénien" * here alluded to

EDITOR'S NOTE.—* A "George Fenien" was in existence at the end of the sixteenth
century, and his daughter Collette Fenien, was married to William Brock, ancestor of the
Brocks of Guernsey. William Brock died in 1582.

must have lived up to his name, Fénien—
Fainéant—a sluggard. We have seen in some of
the preceding proverbs and sayings, allusions to
individuals and families. Here are two or three
more of the same kind :—

I' fait de sen· Quéripel.—Is untranslatable literally,
but may be rendered " he acts like a Quéripel."
and is said of a man whose vanity leads him to
give himself airs, and take too much upon
himself. The name existed in Guernsey as early
as the fourteenth century, at which time it was
written *Carupel*, but there is not the slightest
clue when or how the saying originated. It may
possibly be a corruption of some proverbial expression current in Normandy.

Il est dans les Arabies de Mons. Roland.—" He
has got into Mr. Roland's Arabias," is a remark
made when a preacher, a public speaker, or any
one who sets up for a talker, has got beyond his
depth, and is discoursing on a subject which he
does not understand. The Rolands, now extinct,
are believed to have been a Huguenot family
that took refuge in Guernsey in the sixteenth
century.* The Monsr. Roland who figures in the
saying is supposed to have been a schoolmaster. †

*Ch'est prendre de Pierre Chyvret pour dounaïr à
Monsieur Careye.*—" It is taking from Pierre

EDITOR'S NOTES.

* In the "Placita Coronæ" held in the reign of Edward III., William, son of Robert Roland,
held land in the Vale parish. In a deed of 23rd of August, 1517, dealing with land in St.
Sampson's parish, south of the "Grand Pont" the *"Rue Roland"* is mentioned; in 1569,
there was living in St. Sampson's parish a Richard Roland and Collenette Le Retylley, his
wife, and (2nd November, 1569) Thomas Roland and Jeanne Blondel, his wife, bought a house
in St. Peter Port from Jean Le Montés; so the probabilities are that the Rolands, if they
migrated from France, did so before the Huguenot persecutions, and had been domiciled in
Guernsey long anterior to the sixteenth century.

† Or he may have been the "Monsieur Jean Roland," son of Thomas and Elizabeth
Bailloul, who was Rector of S. Pierre-du-Bois, and imprisoned in the Tower of London in
1665, for his refusal to submit to the Act of Uniformity.

Old Guernsey House.

Chyvret to give to Mr. Carey," is used in the sense of "sending coals to Newcastle," or "taking from the poor to give to the rich;" but who the particular individuals were whose names figure in this saying it is impossible to say. In the reign of Queen Elizabeth a Mr. Nicholas Careye was farmer of most, if not all, the mills in Guernsey situated on the Crown domain, he being then Her Majesty's Receiver. At a time when all persons residing on a manor were obliged to bring their corn to be ground at their Lord's mill, under severe penalties, such a monopoly in the mills as Mr. Carey possessed, must have tended to make him a very wealthy man.[*] It is not unlikely that he, or one of his immediate descendants, who enjoyed the same privilege, may have been the person whose name became proverbial for riches. The name of Peter Chyvret occurs in another saying too coarse to be quoted, but which suggests the idea that he may have been an idiot, and, if so, probably living on charity. It is, however, worth noting that a certain Peter Chyvret was, about the beginning of the present century, in possession of property situated in the neighbourhood of one of the mills of which we have spoken. He is reported to have been one of those eccentric characters of whom it is difficult to say whether they have all their mental faculties—a mixture, in fact, of shrewdness and simplicity. As he was by no means in indigent circumstances it is scarcely probable that he can be the same man alluded to in this saying.

EDITOR'S NOTE.—[*] It was this Monsieur Careye, who in September, 1563, bought the Fief Blanchelande from Her Majesty's Commissioners; he married Collette de la Marche and was buried 15th of July, 1593.

Tenír à pinche-beleïne.—Means to hold lightly,
without a firm grasp. It is used in the following
proverbial saying :—

> "*A pìnche-beleïne—sû la haute épeine,*
> *Si je m'déroque—je n'en dirai mot.*"

—Which may be freely translated :—" Holding on
too lightly, if I fall from the tree I shall say
nothing about it." If I suffer from my own
negligence I must not complain.

Proberbial Sayings.

We now come to a class of proverbial sayings
which might almost claim an exclusive right to the
title of " Folk-Lore,"—those relating to the weather
and other natural phenomena; and which, being the
result of long experience on the part of the people,
are religiously believed in by them. Many of these
sayings are common, in spirit if not in form, to the
greater part of Europe; some of them are confined
to certain districts; and, although a few may have
a superstitious aspect, such as those which profess
to predict what events will happen in the course of
the year from an observation of the weather on a
particular holy day, yet some of them may be worthy
the notice of meteorologists, who have discovered
that, in many cases, the probable character of the
weather in a particular month may be guessed at
by that which prevailed at an earlier season.

Janvier a daeux bouniaux (deux bonnets), Février en
a treis (trois).—January wears two caps, February

I I

wears three. As a rule February is the coldest month in the year. In a curious old MS. of the sixteenth century, containing memoranda of household accounts, copies of wills, and various entries of more or less interest, written between the years 1505 and 1569 by various members of a family of the name of Girard, landed proprietors in the parish of Ste. Marie-du-Castel in Guernsey, we find the following weather prognostications for St. Vincent's Day (January 22nd), and the Feast of the Conversion of St. Paul, (January 25th).

" *Prens garde au jour St. Vincent*
Car sy se jour tu vois et sent
Que le soleil soiet cler et biau
Nous érons du vin plus que d'eau."

———

" *Sy le jour St. Paul le convers*
Se trouve byaucob descouvert,
L'on aura pour celle sayson
Du bled et du foyn à foyson ;
Et sy se jour fait vant sur terre ;
Ce nous synyfye guerre ;
S'yl pleut ou nège, sans fallir,
Le chier tans nous doet asalir ;
Sy de nyelle faict, brumes ou brouillars,
Selon le dyt de nos vyellars,
Mortalitey nous est ouverte."

Similar sayings are to be found in Latin, English, German, Italian, and other languages.

February, as every one knows, is the shortest month in the year; but few know why. This is how it is accounted for by old people in Guernsey :—" *Février dit à Janvier :*—' *Si j'étais à votre pièche (place) je f'rais gelaïr (geler) les pots sus le faeu (feu) et les*

p'tits éfàns (enfants) aux seins de leurs mères'—*et pour son impudence i' fut raccourchi (raccourci) de daeux jours, et Janvier fut aloigni (alongé).'* "
February said to January :—If I were in your place I would cause the pots to freeze on the fire, and babes at their mothers' breasts, and for his insolence he was shortened of two days, and January was lengthened.

The most intense cold in the year generally sets in with February; and this saying reminds me of what is told in Scotland, and in many parts of the north of England, of the *borrowing days*, the three last days of March (See Brand's *Popular Antiquitics*, Bohn's edition, Vol. II., p. 41-44). It appears, however, according to this authority, that in the Highlands of Scotland the *borrowing days* are the three first days of February, reckoned according to the old style, that is, the days between the eleventh and the fifteenth.

February 2nd, Candlemas Day. Fine weather on this day is supposed to prognosticate a return of cold. The following lines were communicated by a country gentleman, but they have not quite the same antique ring as those relating to St. Paul's and St. Vincent's Days, and may, possibly, be a more recent importation from France.

" *Selon les anciens se dit :*
   Si le soleil clairement luit
   A' la Chandeleur vous verrez
   Qu' encore un hiver vous aurcz."

———

" *Quànd Mars durerait chent àns l'hiver durerait autànt.*—If March were to last for a hundred years, winter would last as long.
Mars qui entre coume ùn agné (agneau) sortira coume

ùn touaré (taureau).—The Guernsey form of this saying substitutes a bull in the place of a lion.

Mars a enviaï (envoyé) sa vieille trachier (chercher) des bûquettes (buchettes).—When, after a spell of comparatively mild weather, March comes with blustering winds, breaking off the small dry branches from the trees, the country, people say that he has sent out his old wife to look for sticks ; and predict that, as he is laying in a store of fuel, the cold is likely to last.

Pâques Martine—guerre, peste, ou famine.—Easter happening in March, forebodes war, pestilence, or famine.

A Noué à ses perrons, à Pâques à ses tisons.—If at Christmas you can sit at your doorstep, at Easter you will be glad to sit by your fire.

Avril le doux—quànd il s'y met le pière de tous.—Or, as the Norman antiquary, Pluquet, gives it :—" *Quand il se fâche, le pire de tous.*"—When the weather is bad in April, it is the worst of all the months.

En Avril, ne quitte pas ùn fil.—In April leave not off a stitch of clothing—a piece of advice which is well warranted by the sudden and extreme changes in the temperature in this month. On the other side, this advice holds good a month later—" Till May be out cast not a clout."

Caud (chaud) Mai, gras chimequière (cimetière), fred (froid) Mai, granges pllaïnes (pleines).—A warm May, a fat churchyard, a cold May, fat granaries.

A' la mié Acût, l'hiver noue.—About mid-August there is usually a marked change in the weather, gales of wind and heavy rain generally occurring at this season, and any long continuance of settled fine weather, is scarcely to be hoped for. This has led to the remark that winter "*sets*" at this time; as the blossoms in Spring set for fruit.

A' la mi-S'tembre, les jours et les nits s'entre ressemblent.—In the middle of September, days and nights are alike.

Six s'maïnes avant Noué, et six s'maïnes après, les nits sont les pûs longues, et les jours les pûs freds.—Six weeks before Christmas and six weeks after, the nights are the longest and the days the coldest. This saying is scarcely correct in Guernsey, as very cold weather about the end or the beginning of the year is rather the exception than the rule in this climate.

Si le soleil liet à méjeur, le jour de Noué, il y aura bien des faeux l'annaïe ensuivant.—If the sun shines at noon on Christmas Day, there will be many fires lighted in the ensuing year.

Aube gelaïe est biétôt lavaïe.—Hoar-frost is soon washed away, or, as another weather proverb says:—"*Après treis aubes gelaïes vient la pllie.*"—After three hoar-frosts comes rain, a saying which experience amply bears out.

Vent d'amont qui veur duraïr, au sér va se reposaïr.—An east wind that intends to last, goes to rest in the evening.

Vent d'amont ôve (avec) pllie, ne vaut pas un fllie (patelle).—An east wind with rain is not worth a limpet.

Quand i' plleut ôve vent d'amont, ch'est merveille si tout ne fond.—Rain from the east is rare; but when it does occur it is so heavy and continuous as to give rise to the saying that it is a wonder that everything does not melt.

Cherne (cerne) à la lune, le vent, la pllie, ou la brune—When there's a circle round the moon, wind, rain, or fog, will follow soon.

Cherne de llien (loin), tourmente de près; cherne de près, tourmente de llien.—If the halo round the moon is large and at a distance, it denotes that a storm is at hand, if, on the contrary, it is small and near the moon, the storm will not arrive for some time.

Cherne à la lune, jamais n'a fait amenaïr mât d'hune. —A circle round the moon has never caused topmast to be struck. It is difficult to reconcile this saying with the preceding, unless by supposing that sailors are so convinced that a circle round the moon portends bad weather that they are careful to shorten sail before the gale comes on.

Cherne au soleil i' ne fera pas demain bel.—A solar halo means bad weather to-morrow.

> *Si le soleil est rouage (rouge) au sèr (soir),*
> *Ch'est pour biau temps aver (avoir),*
> *S'il est rouage au matin,*
> *Ch'est la mare au chemin.*

If the sun sets red, it is a sign of fine weather, but when he rises red, you may expect to see pools of water on the road.

Rouage ser, gris matin, ch'est la jouaie (joie) du pèlerin.—A red evening and a grey morning are the pilgrim's joy, but this saying is sometimes varied to :—

Rouage sèr, bllanc matin, ch'est la journaïe du pèlerin. —A red evening and a white morning is the day for the pilgrim.

En Avril, le coucou crie, s'il est en vie.—In April, the cuckoo sings, if he is alive. · The cuckoo

generally arrives in Guernsey about the 15th of
April.

> *Le cou-cou s'en va en Août,*
> *L'épi d'orge li pique la gorge.*
> The cuckoo departs in August,
> The barley-spike pricks his throat.

Agricultural Sayings.

It is not easy to draw a clear line between those
sayings which have reference to the weather, and those
which relate to agricultural pursuits and experience;
but the following appear to fall more naturally under
the latter head :—

> *Quànd i' plleut ôve vent d'aval,*
> *Nourrit l'houme et sen cheval ;*
> *Quànd i' plleut ôve vent d'amont,*
> *Ch'est merveille si tout ne fond.*

When it rains with a westerly wind it feeds man and
beast; but when it rains with an east wind, it is
a marvel if everything does not melt.

> *L'arc d'alliance du soir, bel à voir,*
> *L'arc d'alliance du matin, fait la mare à chemin.*

Rainbow in the evening, fair to see; rainbow in the
morning, there will be pools on the roads.

*Si tu vois le soleil le jour de la Chandeleur, sauve le
foin, car tu en auras besoin.*—If you see the sun on
Candlemas Day, save your hay for you will want it.

A' la Paintecoûte, les grouaïsiaux se goûtent.—Green
gooseberries are in perfection at Whitsuntide.

*De la St. Michel à Noué (Noel) une pllante ne sait pas
chu (ce) que nou (on) li fait.*—From Michaelmas

to Christmas a plant does not know what you do
to it.

*De la Toussaint à Noué un arbre ne sait pas chu
que nou li fait.*—From All Saints' Day to
Christmas a tree knows not what is done to it.
The autumnal quarter is supposed to be the best
for transplanting trees or shrubs, as at that time
the vigorous growth that had been going on in
spring and summer has ceased, and there is less
danger of their suffering from the change.

*Noué n'est pas Noué sàns pâcrolle (paquerette prime-
vère).*—Christmas is not Christmas unless there be
primroses.

*Noué est pûtôt Noué, sans pâcrolle, que sans agné
(agneau).*—A Christmas without primroses is more
rare than a Christmas without lambs. Another
version is :—

*Nou ne vit jamais Noué, sans pâcrolle ou p'tit
agné.*—This saying, as well as the preceding,
seems to refer particularly to the occurrence of
that harbinger of spring, the primrose, at this
season. With the exception occasionally of a few
very cold days about the beginning of November,
the weather in Guernsey up to Christmas, and
frequently far into January, is remarkably mild;
vegetation is scarcely checked, and many summer
flowers continue to bloom freely up to this time.
It is a well-known fact that the primrose, like
many other plants and most bulbs, has its period
of repose during the hot and dry weather of
summer, the flowering ceasing about the end of
May, and the leaves withering away. In the
autumn there is a fresh growth of leaves, and
the flower buds, which had been already formed

towards the end of spring, but had been prevented
by the drought from expanding, are ready to
burst into bloom with the mild days that generally
usher in Christmas, the earliest blossoms being
invariably found on the north sides of the hedges,
where the latest flowers of the preceding summer
lingered, the plants with a south aspect having
exhausted their bloom in the hot weather.

A flleur de Mars—ni pouque (poche) ni sac ;
A flleur d'Avril—pouque et baril ;
A flleur de Mai—barrique et touné (tonneau).

Blossom in March requires neither bag nor sack ;
Blossom in April fills bag and barrel ;
Blossom in May fills hogshead and tun.

This saying refers to the apple crop, and the quantity
of cider that may be expected, judging from the
month in which the trees come into bloom.

> *Sème tes concombres en Mars,*
> *Tu n' airas qu' faire de pouque ni de sac ;*
> *Sème-les en Avril, tu en airas ùn petit ;*
> *Mé, j' les semerai en Mai ;*
> *Et j'en airai pûs que té (toi).*

Sow your cucumbers in March, you will want neither
bag nor sack ; sow them in April, you will have a
few ; I will sow mine in May, and I shall have
more than you.

Pouit (point) de vraic, pouit de haugard.—No sea-
weed, no corn ricks. The sea-weed, *vraic* or
varech, which grows in such abundance on all the
rocks round the islands, is of the utmost importance to the farmer. It is almost the only
dressing used for the land, stable manure being
scarce and expensive. Hence the saying quoted
above ; for without sufficient manure the crops are

sure to fall short. The *haugard*, or, more
correctly, *haut gard*, (high yard) is the enclosure
near a homestead on which the ricks are erected.

*Débet (dégel) de pllie, ne vaut pas une fllie (patille);
débet de sec, vaut demi-fumaeure (fumier).*—A thaw
with rain is not worth a limpet; a thaw with
dry weather is worth half a load of manure.

Un essaim en Mai—vaut une vaque (vache) à lait.—A
swarm of bees in May is worth a milch cow.

*Où est qu'll y a un cardon (chardon) ch'est du pain;
où est qu'ill y a du laitron, ch'est la faim.*—
Where thistles grow there will be bread, where
the sow-thistle grows it is famine. The latter is
mostly found in very poor land.

*Il vaut mâx pour un houme d'aver un percheux
(paresseux) dans son ménage qu'un frêne sur s'n
héritage.*—It is better for a man to have a lazy
fellow in his service than an ash-tree on his estate.
The shade of the ash is believed to be destructive
of all vegetation over which it extends; and it is
this belief that has in all probability given rise
to this saying. This proverb sometimes takes the
following form :—

> *Bâtard dans sen lignage
> Vaut mâx qu'un frêne sur s'n héritage.*

Piscatory and Maritime Sayings.

The following sayings may be termed piscatory and
maritime.

A quànd le bœuf est las, le bar est gras.—When the
ox is weary, that is, when ploughing has come

to an end for the season, the bass is in good condition. This fish is decidedly best in summer.

A quànd l'orge épicotte, le vrac est bouan sous la roque.—When the barley comes into ear, the wrasse or rock-fish, is at its best.

L'àne de Balaam a pàlaï (parlé) j'airon du macré (maquereau).—Balaam's ass has spoken, we shall soon have mackerel. The mackerel, it is almost needless to say, is a migratory fish, arriving on our coasts in the spring, and remaining with us till late in the summer. Formerly the reading of the First Lesson at Evensong on the first Sunday after Easter, in which the story of Balaam and his ass is told, was considered a sure indication that the welcome shoals would soon make their appearance. The Cornish fishermen have the same saying.

Old fishermen pay great attention to the direction of the wind at sunset on old Michaelmas Day (10th October), for they firmly believe that from whatever point it blows at that time, the prevailing winds for two-thirds of the ensuing twelve months will be from that quarter.

> *Grànd maïr (mer) ou morte iaue (eau),*
> *La lune au sud, il est basse iaue.*

Whether it be spring tides or neap tides, when the moon is due south it will be low water.

EDITOR's NOTE.—Another version : " Vive iaue ou morte iaue, La lune au sud, il est basse iaue."—*From John de Garis, Esq.*

Various Sayings.

A few sayings omitted may find a place here :—

Alle ira sù le coquet de l'Eglise ramendaïr (racommoder) les braies (culottes) des viers garçons.—She will get a seat on the weather-cock of the church and mend old bachelor's breeches, is said of old maids, and is equivalent to the English saying, "She will lead apes in hell."

Ch'est une autre pàire (paire) de cauches (bas, chausses).—That's another pair of stockings, is used in the sense of "That's quite another affair."

A quànd les filles sufflent (sifflent) le guiablle (diable) s'éluque.—When girls whistle the devil laughs outright. Whistling is not generally reckoned among feminine accomplishments, and by many would certainly be considered as a symptom of what, in the present day, is termed "fastness" in the fair sex. According to the Northamptonshire proverb :—

"A whistling woman and crowing hen,
Are neither fit for God nor men."

In Normandy they say :—"Une poule qui chante le coquet, et une fille qui siffle, portent malheur dans la maison." *

And in Cornwall :—"A whistling woman and a crowing hen, are the two unluckiest things under the sun."

Trachier (chercher) la Ville par Torteval.—To seek for the Town by way of Torteval, is said of one who goes a round-about way to work. The rural parish of Torteval, situated at the south-west corner of Guernsey, is, of all the parishes in the island, the one furthest removed from the town of St. Peter Port. Compare the French "Chercher midi à quatorze heures."

Editor's Note.—* In *Traditions et Superstitions de la Haute Bretagne*, Tome II., p. 29., are various sayings to the same effect, such as :—

"Fille siffler.
Poule chanter,
Et coq qui pond,
Trois diables dans la maison,"

Il ôt (ouit, entend) fin coume une iragne (araignée).
—His sense of hearing is as quick as that of a
spider. Whether the abrupt retreat of the common
wall-spider into the inner recesses of its web, at
the approach of anything that alarms it, is to be
attributed to the sense of hearing, sight, or feeling,
would be difficult to determine. The fact, however, has been noticed, and has given rise to
this saying.

> *Entre le bec et le morcé,*
> *Ill y a souvent du destorbier.*

T'wixt cup and lip—there's many a slip.

> *Qui épouse Jerriais ou Jerriaise,*
> *Jamais ne vivra à s'n aise.*

In all countries and in all ages jealousies and dislikes
have existed between neighbouring communities.
The inhabitants in Guernsey and Jersey are not
exempt from these feelings, which find vent in
malicious tales told of each other. The saying
quoted above is common in Guernsey ; probably its
counterpart exists in Jersey, substituting " Guernesiais " for " Jerriais." It by no means follows,
however, that the want of comfort in these mixed
marriages may not be quite as attributable to the
one side as the other.

Il y a terjoûs quiqu'ùn qui a sa qu'minse à sequier.—
There is always some one wanting to dry his
shirt. The weather never suits everybody's wants.

I' n'a que vie d'alàngouraï (languissant).—Equal to
the English saying "A creaking door hangs
longest."

*Si un houme n'a pas le sens de pâlaïr (parler)
il est bien sàge s'il a le sens de se taire.*—A
man who has not the sense to speak is still

a wise man if he has the sense to hold his
tongue.

I' faut savèr ouïr, véer, et se taire. One should
know how to hear, see, and be silent.

La s'maïne qui vient—is the equivalent of the English
"To-morrow come-never."

*Chu qu' nou n'a jamais veu, et jamais ne verra,
Ch'est le nic d'une souaris dans l'oreille d'un cat.*—
In the *Folk-Lore Record*, Vol. III., Part I., p. 76,
we find the Breton equivalent of this saying :—
"One thing you have never seen, a mouse's nest
in a cat's ear." We are not told, however, whether
the proverb is found in the French patois of
Upper Brittany, or in the Celtic dialect still spoken
in Lower Brittany—la Bretagne bretonnante.

I' va d'vànt ses bètes, or *I's'met d'vànt ses bètes.*—
He is going before his team, is said of a prodigal,
one who is out-running his income.

Ch'est une pouquie (pochée) de puches (puces) or *de souaris.*
—Is a sackful of fleas, or of mice, is said of a
person who is very lively and always on the move.

*Il n'est si bouane (bonne) bête qui n'ait quiqu' (quelque)
ohi.*—There is no beast so good but that it has
some fault or vice. It is worthy of notice that
the word "*ohi*" is gone entirely out of use except
in this proverb.

*I' vit d'amour et de belles chànsons—coum' les alouettes de
roques (pierres, cailloux).*—The first part of this saying
—He lives on love and fine songs—is frequently
used alone, but it is often capped by the concluding words, "As larks do on stones," meaning that
something more nourishing is needed to keep body
and soul together.

" *Un mouisson (oisseau) dans la main vaut mûx que daeux*

qui volent." " *Un mouisson à la main en vaut daeux
sur la branque (branche.)* ". " *Un pourché (pourceau)
dans sen parc en vaut daeux d' par les rues."* All these
are equivalent to the English proverb: "A bird
in the hand is worth two in the bush," but the
last must have originated in days long gone by,
when swine were allowed to roam at their will
about the streets.

I ' n' y a pas de cousins à Terre-Neuve.—There are no
cousins at Newfoundland. This somewhat selfish
proverb, indicating that where one's own interest
is at stake the ties of consanguinity go for little,
although occasionally heard in Guernsey, originated
most probably either in Jersey or St. Malo, both
which ports are largely engaged in the cod fisheries
on the banks of Newfoundland. Jersey, indeed,
owes her commercial prosperity almost entirely to
this branch of industry, to which, it is said, the
attention of the inhabitants was directed by Sir
Walter Raleigh during the time that he held the
office of Governor of the island. During the
Middle Ages the fisheries in the Channel Islands
were very productive, and a source of considerable
revenue to the Crown, but the discovery of
Newfoundland, and the superior quality of the
codfish caught on its shores, drove the salted conger
and mackerel of the island out of the market.

Le cul d'un sac et la langue d'une femme gagnent terjoûs.
—In former days, when horses were more employed
in carrying loads than they are at the present
time when carts are in universal use, it was
observed that a sack thrown across the back of
a horse had a tendency to slip down gradually
in the direction opposite to its mouth. This

explains the first part of the proverb; the second part is equivalent to the saying that a woman will always have the last word and gain her end at last.

Nou veit bien pûs de meïnes de gâche crue que de biaux musíaux.—One sees many more pasty, doughy looking faces than pretty ones. Said in very cold weather.

Ch'n'est que faeu et flâmme.—It is nothing but fire and flame, said of a boaster, and also of a passionate man, whose temper quickly rises, and as quickly dies down.

Pêle-mêle gabouaré.—Pell-mell, as merry-makers tumble out of a village inn. This word "gabouaré," derived from the Bas Breton "*gaborel,*" is only found in this phrase.

Il est coume le pourché du negre, petit et vier.—He is small and old, like the negro's pig.

Cope le cô, i.e., "coupe le cou," is a common asseveration among children. They pronounce the

EDITOR'S NOTES.

The following are a few local proverbs and sayings which I have met with at different times, and which I do not find included in Sir Edgar MacCulloch's collection.

Il est si avare, il ne dounera pouit daeux p'tits œufs pour un gros.—He is such a miser that he would not give two little eggs for one big one.

Coume St. Paterne, tu feras pâlir le Diable.—Like St. Paterno, you would turn the Devil pale, said of a man whom nothing will daunt. St. Paterne was one of our local saints, who was specially noted for the conversion of the inhabitants of the Forest of Scissy—the submerged forest which lies off our western coasts. He was induced to do so by a pious Seigneur of the Forest, and began his work there by going into a cavern where the idolaters were celebrating a great feast presided over by the Devil himself. Armed only with his pilgrim's staff he routed them all, Satan included. He was specially beloved by birds, who followed him wherever he went. He was made Bishop of Avranches, and died in the year A.D. 495.

La s'maine de treis (trois) Jeudis ou il n' y a pas de Vendredi.—The week of three Thursdays and no Friday. This is used when talking of an event which will never come off. Then they say " Ça, se fera, etc."

Haut coumme un béguin.—As high as a beacon. The Guernsey "béguins" were tall stacks of furze placed on prominent points so that they could be lit in case of an alarm.

Ecoute-paret (paroi) jamais n'ot dret.—He who listens through partitions never hears correctly.

Faire pertus (trou) sous l'iaue.—To make a hole in the water, said of a man who is ruining himself.

I' vaut mûx pillaïr (plier) qu' rompre.—It is better to bend than break

Il ne faut pas queruaïr trop près des fossaïs.—One should not plough too close to the hedges. Said of people who have no tact and say the wrong things at the wrong times—" Dancing on the edge of precipices."

Maujeu au naïr, signe d'être guervaï, ou baisi d'un fou. Tickling in the nose shows that you will either be worried or kissed by a fool!

Daeux petites paûvretaïs en font une grande.—Two small paupers make one big one ; said when two impecunious people marry each other.

words, drawing their right hand at the same time
towards their throat, as if cutting it, and the
action is meant to imply that they wish their
throats may be cut if they do not tell the truth,
or perform what they have promised.

Vaque (*vache*) *d'un bouan égrùn* (*croissance*).—A cow that
does credit to her food, and that feeds close.
Etre d'un bouan égrùn—is also said of children who
look fat and healthy.

In conclusion, we will give a story which is often
told in the country, as a warning to those who are
apt to laugh at fools. A half-witted fellow, who
had gone to the mill with his corn, was asked
by the miller, who wanted to laugh at him :—
"John, people say that you are a fool and know

WEATHER PROVERBS, ETC.

Quànd tu veis la fieille (feuille) à l'orme
Prends ta pouque et sème ton orge.
When you see the leaf on the elm
Take thy bag and sow thy barley.

Quand il fait biau, prend ton manteau,
Quand il pleut fais coume tu veus.
When it is fine take your cloak.
When it rains do as you like.

Vent perdu, se trouve au sud.
A lost wind is found in the south.
(This is a Sark proverb, and was found by the Rev. G. E. Lee in the Rev. Elie Brevint's MSS).

Hardi des hâgues sus l's épines
D'un rude hiver ch'est le signe.
Many hips and haws on the trees,
Is the sign of a severe winter.

Le dix de Mai des sardes au Gaufricher.
On the 10th of May, sardans (a kind of fish) are to be found at Le Gaufricher—a rock north
of Fermain.

La maïr qui roule au Tas de Peis
Ch'est coumme nous verrait de l'iaue quée.
The sea that rolls at the Tas de Pois (the rocks at the end of St. Martin's Point) look to the
beholder like falling rain.

" *La lune levante*
La maïr battante."
At moon rise
It is high tide.

" *Fin nord et epais sud*
Ne s'entrefont jamais d'abus
Fin sud et epais nord,
Ne sont jamais d'accord."
A fine north and a lowering south, have no occasion to quarrel, but a fine south and lowering
north, will never agree.—*The two last " dictons " are from John de Garis, Esq.*

nothing. Now, tell me what you know and what you don't know ? " " Well ! " answered John, " I know this, that millers have fine horses." " That's what you know," said the miller. " Now tell me what you don't know." " I don't know on whose corn they are fattened," said John.

—*From Denys Corbet.*

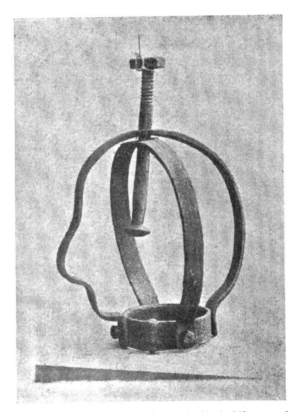

Gibbet from which pirates were suspended in the Island of Herm, now in possession of H.S.H. Prince Blücher von Wahlstatt, who kindly allowed it to be photographed for reproduction in this book.

Part III.

Editor's Appendix.

" Dear Countrymen, whate'er is left to us
Of ancient heri·age —
Of manners, speech, of humours, polity,
The limited horizon of our stage—
Of love, hope, fear,
All this I fain would fix upon the page :
That so the coming age,
Lost in the Empire's mass,
Yet haply longing for their fathers, here
May see, as in a glass,
What they held dear—
May say, " 'Twas thus and thus
They lived ; and as the time-flood onward rolls,
Secure an anchor for their Celtic souls."
    (Preface to *The Doctor and other Poems*, by the Rev. T. E. Brown).

CHAPTER XVIII.

Guernsey Songs and Ballads.

HAVE added this chapter to Sir Edgar MacCulloch's book, as I thought it a good opportunity of preserving a few of the old ballads and songs which, for generations, amused and interested our forefathers, and which now, alas, are all too surely going or gone from among us,—swept away by the irrepressible tide of vulgarity and so-called "Progress," by which everything of ours that was beautiful, picturesque, or individual, has been destroyed. As descendants of the Celtic trouvères, menestriers, and jongleurs, as well as of the Norse Skalds, the bards from whose early songs and chants, the literature of Europe has sprung, we, Normans, should specially treasure the old poems which have been handed down for so many successive generations, and which, in the rapid extinction of the old language in which Wace, Taillefer, Walter Map, and Chrestien de Troyes sang, are doomed to oblivion.

In most places the old ballads can be divided into two classes— the Religious and the Secular. The first of these classes, except in the form of the metrical version of the Psalms by Ronsard, does not seem to have existed over here. I can find no trace of any Noëls, or of any Easter songs. The Secular songs may be divided into the Historical and the Social.

The Historical deserve precedence. The *Ballade des Aragousais* of which a translation has already been given, and of which I append the original, is by far the oldest and most interesting. Then comes a ballad descriptive of the Destruction of the Spanish Armada in 1588, which I found in a manuscript book compiled by a Job Mauger in 1722. In it he has copied the *Dedicace des Eglises*, and such poems which apparently were current in his day, and which he deemed worthy of preservation. Of his collection this is the most distinctive, and I have included it in this chapter, although it is evidently defective in parts, as these old ballads, handed down orally from generation to generation, are so apt to be. The *Complaint of the dispossessed Roman Catholic Clergy*, written in March, 1552, and copied into the Registers of St. Saviour's parish in 1696 by Henry Blondel, is already in print, being included in Gustave Dupont's *Histoire du Cotentin et de ses Iles*, Tome III., p. 311-313.

Job Mauger's MSS. also comprise a long and monotonous ballad of twenty verses describing the destruction by lightning of the Tower of Castle Cornet in 1688, and various poems, conspicuous more by the loyalty of their sentiments than by the merits of their versification, on contemporary events in England, such as —"La mort du Roy Guillaume III.," written in 1702; "Cantique Spirituel à la mémoire de la Royne Marie IIme., et sur l'oiseau qu'on voit sur son Mausolée;" "Sur la mort de son Altesse Royale Guillaume, Duc de Glocestre, decedé au Château de Windsor le 30me Juillet, 1700;" and "Vive le Roy George," written in 1721. He also copies a "Chanson Nouvelle de l'Esclavage de Barbarie," doggerel verses "composée par dix pauvres hommes, esclaves en Barbarie, où ils sont," viz.: "Edouard Falla, Edouard Mauger, Phelipe le Marquand, Richard Viel, et ses camarades, Pierre le Gros et Jean Aspuine," written in the reign of William III.

In the year 1736 the bells of the church of S. Peter Port, being no longer fit for service, were taken down for the purpose of being melted and re-cast. This circumstance gave rise to a piece of poetry composed by the Rev. Elie Dufresne, Rector of the Town parish, of which many manuscript copies are in existence.

But by far the most popular and widely known of all our local ballads is "Les vers de Catherine Deslandes," by an unknown author, descriptive of the trial and execution for infanticide, of an unhappy woman called Catherine Deslandes in 1748. These verses have been repeatedly copied and printed, and are to be found in almost every old farm-house.

The Secular ballads were undoubtedly all, or nearly all, importations from the mainland. Of these I have made a selection, and have striven to record those which do not appear to have been already printed, or which, like "La Claire Fontaine," vary considerably from the continental models. Thus "Malbrouck," which is one of the most widely known of all our old ballads, appears in every French "Recueil de Chansons," and the verses of "Le Juif Errant" and "Geneviève de Brabant" of which copies are also found in all our old farm houses, have also been repeatedly printed on the Continent, so are not included here.

YVON DE GALLES.

"Surprise de l'Ile de Guernesey l'an 1370, sous le Règne d'Edouard III., Roy d'Angleterre, et de Charles V., Roy de France." *

"Or, grands et petits entendez
Lai¹ d'allure² fort'ment rimée,³
Sur nombre de gent ramassée,
Qui va sillant⁴ la mer salée,
Du Roy de France la mesgnée,⁵
Par Yvon de Galles guidée,
Si mauvaisement mis à mort.⁶

Par un Mardy s'est comparée
La gendarmerie et l'armée,

NOTE.

* This poem is copied from a version compiled by Mr. Métivier, and said by him to be the revised text of seven mutilated manuscript copies. I have also included most of his notes.

NOTES.

1. *Lai*—Chant, mélodie, complainte.
2. *Allure*—pas continu, mesuré.
3. *Fort'ment rimée*—dont la rime est riche, roulante.
4. *Sillant* v. fr : fendant, coupant.
5. *Mesgnée*—guern' *mégnie*,—maisonnée, troupe.
6. *Mis à mort*—assassiné par le traître gallois John Lambe, soudoyé par Richard II.

Faite de grands Aragousais[1]
Gens enragés à l'abordée.
Dans le Vazon fut addressée
Cette pilleuse[2] marinée
Pensant nous mettre tous à mort.

Un Jean L'Estocq si se leva,
Plus matin qu'à l'accoûtumée ;
Et à sa bergerie alla,
Sur l'ajournant[3] à la brunée.
Telle compagnie a trouvée
Sur le grand Marais arrêtée,
Ce qui grandement l'étonna.

Vit un cheval sur son chemin,
Faisant marche de haquenée,[4]
Qui, pour vray, étoit un guildin,[5]
Qui lors échappoit de l'armée.
Toute l'isle en a chevauchée,
Criant à la désespérée,
Sus ! aux armes, en un moment ! "

" Et vous trouvez sur les Vazons ![6]
L'armée est dessus arrêtée ;
Diligentez-vous, bons garçons,
Ou toute la terre est gâtée !
Mettez tout au fil de l'épée,
Hasardez-vous, à bonne heurée,
Ou vous mourrez griève mort ! "

Yvon de Galles, vrai guerrier,
Était conducteur de la guerre,
Homme grand'ment adventurier,
Dessus une terre étrangière,
Ne se donnant garde en arrière,
Il reçut la rouge jarr'tière
Qui n'étoit ni soye, ni velours.

NOTES.

1. *Aragousais*—Chez les Gascons, nos compatriotes alors, *Aragons*, espagnol. L'Aragon était le royaume principal.
2. *Pilleuse*—pirates.
3. *Ajournant*—v. fr.. ajornant, faire *jor* ou jour.
4. *Haquenée*—cheval qui va l'amble, hobin.
5. *Guildin*—Anglais *gelding*.
6. *Les Vazons*—Marais, tourbières, aujourd'hui Vazon. Il y avait le Vazon d'Albecq et le Vazon du Marais.

C'est qu'il fut frappé d'un garçon
D'une alebarde[1] meurtrière,
Il se nommoit Richard Simon
Sur le moulin, en la Carrière,
Tant qu'il eut la cuisse hachée
Aussi la main dextre tranchée
Par ce glorieux compagnon.

Sur le mont de St. Pierre Port
Fut la dure guerre livrée ;
Cinq cents et un fur' mis à mort,
Tant de l'isle[2] que de l'armée,[3]
C'étoit pitié, cette journée
D'ouïr les pleurs de l'assemblée
Des dames de St. Pierre Port.

Thoumin le Lorreur,[4] tout le jor
Fut, de vrai, notre capitaine ;
Rouf Hollande[5] fut le plus fort,
Il eut l'honneur de la quintaine,[6]
Sa vie, hélas ! fut hasardée,
Car, sa jambe étant fracassée,
Force lui fut de souffrir mort.

Frappant à travers et à tors,
Le sang courait dans les vallées,
On marchait dessus les corps morts
Qui chéaient[7] au fil des épées.

NOTES.

1. *Alebarde*—sans aspiration, comme l'Ital: *alabarda*.
2. *L'isle*—les habitants de l'île
3. *L'armée*—la flotte étrangère.
4. *Le Lorreur*—surnom d'une famille câtelaine dont les traces se retrouvent au commencement du dix-septième siècle. *Le lourreur* était un joueur de cornemuse, Normand *lourre*, Danois *luur*. C'est tout un alors pour nous autres Anglais, que *Thoumin le Lorreur*, et "Tommy the Piper."

The first mention of a "Le Lorreur" in the Channel Islands I have found, occurs in the Calendar of Patent Rolls for 1316. where Philip L'Evesque, Bailiff of Jersey, witnesses (June 25th, 1311) a demise by Macie Le Lorreur, clerk, to Richard le Fessu, his brother, Viscount of Jersie, of the escheat of Pierres du Mouster, for twelve cabots of wheat rent yearly, for three virgates of land in the parish of Grouville. The Richard le Fessu mentioned above was also known as Richard *de Jersey*, he married Elizabeth de Burgo, described as the King's kinswoman, and in 1317 the King gave, as a grant for life, to "John de Jereseye" his son, the Viscounty of Jersey, which his father had held during his life-time.

5. *Rouf Hollande*—On August 26th 1338, a warrant was issued against a *Richard de Holand*, who had absconded with £40 delivered to John Godefelawe of Southampton, by John de Harleston, for payment of the wages of the garrison of Jersey. (Calendar of Patent Rolls).

6. *Quintaine*—espèce de tournoi.

7. *Chéaient*—tombaient guern: et norm: queyaient,

Une meurtrière[1] fut lancée,
Qui, à grand' force débandée,
Aux Aragousais fit grand tort.

Quatre-vingt bons marchands anglais
Arrivèrent sur l'avesprée;[2]
A notre secours accouraient,
Mais l'armée étant fort lassée,
Leva le siège, tout de voir,[3]
Ne sachant quel remède avoir,
Sinon crier à Dieu mercy.

Furent contraints de s'enfuir
Prenant leur chemin gaburon,[4]
Par les Bordages sont allés,
Pour passer dedans ils se rue';
Mais les Anglais sans retenue,
Remplissent de corps morts la rue,
Sur cette troupe de bedots.[5]

Par force espreindrent les châtiaus,[6]
La mer étant fort retirée,
On les tuait à grands monceaux,
Taillant tout au fil de l'épée;
La mer étoit ensanglantée
De cette troupe ainsi navrée,
De lez la chair et les corps morts.

Ces navires et ces bateaux
Ceignirent l'isle par derrière;
Bons paysans leur firent grands tosts,[7]
Vers le château de la Corbière,[8]
Vindrent par le Bec-à-la-Chièvre,[9]
Pour à l'armée faire estère,[10]
Avec le reste des lourdauds.

NOTES.

1. *Meurtrière*—Catapulte, machine qui lançait des pierres et des dards.
2. *Avesprées*—Commencement du soir.   3. *Voir*—Vrai.
4. *Gaburon*—Ce serait pêle-mêle, a la manière de goujats, des manants. Telle serait, osons le croire, l'origine du guernesiais "*pêle-mêle gabouaret.*"
5. *Bedots*—étrangers, trompeurs. L'acceptation française de *bedos*, selon Roquefort, était autrefois "forain."
6. *Espreindrent*—serrèrent, assaillirent. Selon les annales du temps, le château ne fut pas pris.
7. *Tosts*, pour *tostes*, soufflets. "good thrashings."
8. *La Corbière*—The point underneath "Village de Putron," just north of Fermain Point, is called "La Corbière," but this line probably refers to the Vale Castle, in the parish of St. Michel de l'Archange du Valle.
9. *Bec-à-la chièvre*—Just underneath Fort George, the southern boundary of Petit Fort Bay.
10. *Estère*—passage.

Rembarquèrent leurs matelots,[1]
Puis soudain mirent à la vèle,
Tous marris comme lionceaux
D'avoir perdu telle bredelle.[2]
Le général[3] fort ce repelle,[4]
Commandant de remettre à terre
Dans le havre de St. Samson.

À l'Abbé St. Michel s'en vont,
Dont Brecard étoit commissaire ;
Il les reçut, à grand cœur-jouaie
Donnant présents et fort grand chère
Donnant or à la gente amée,[5]
Qui était dame dans l'armée
Nommée Princesse Alinor.

Car Yvon l'avoit épousée
En France au pays de Gravelle,
Dont il fut riche à grands monceis[6]
Des biens de la grand' mariée.
L'abbé fit grand joie à l'armée
D'or et d'argent et de monnoye
Qu'il leur donna bien largement.

Yvon, l'ennemy, s'en alla
Sur une montagne voisine
Du pauvre Château St. Michel,
Là où Yvon faisait ses mines.[7]
Frère Brecart,[8] par courtoisie
S'adresse au château par envie
De faire croître ses trésors.

NOTES.

1. *Matelots*—camarades, guern : *matnots*, mot franc-tudesque. Ici ce n'est [pas un marinier exclusivement, c'est un *mess-mate*.

2. *Bredelle*—morceau.

3. *Général*—l'Amiral, celui qui commande la générale, angl : *flag-ship*.

4. *Repelle*—rejette, oppose.

5. *Gente amée*—gentille amie.

6. *Monceis*—monceaux.

7. *Mines*—Semblant de vouloir assaillir le Château (de Néel de St. Sauveur, aujourd'hui Chateau des Marais ou Ivy Castle).

8. *Brecart*—The Brecarts, Bregearts, or Briards, were a comparatively influential family in the parishes of the Vale and St. Sampson's up to the sixteenth century ; they then bought land in the town, in the district of Vauvert, and became known as " Brégart alias Vauvert," and finally as " Vauvert," *pur et simple*, they seem to have become extinct in the eighteenth century.

Mais Aymon ₂ Rose, retranché
Au puissant Chasteau de l'Archange
Dit qu'il serait avant tranché.

Que de se rendre à gent estrange ;
Mais si ses gens se veulent rendre
A Brecàrt, pour leur terre vendre,
Par compos,[1] il estoit d'accord.

Le pauvre peuple se rendit
A cet Abbé pour leur grand perte
Qu'il avoit pour eux accordé
Aux ennemis par ses finesses
Dont assoujettirent leurs terres
La plupart à payer deux gerbes
Nommez aujourd'hui les champarts.*

Quand Yvon fut bien soudoyé
S'est rembarqué dans ses navires
Dans le Coquet s'en est allé
Se refournir de nouveaux vivres,
En passant par devant Belle Isle
Mit le feu dans trente navires
N'ayant que les garçons à bord.

Le vent du sud étant venu
Sillant la côte de Bretagne

---

* Here Mr. Métivier's version ends, the remainder is from an old Guernsey Almanac dated 1828.

NOTES.

1. *Compos*—Composition.
2. *Aymon Rose*—"Edmund de Ros ou Rous" était d'origine Normande.

"It appears that Edmund Rose, who defended Castle Cornet on this occasion was only Lieut.-Governor, as, in the previous year, Walter Huwet appears as governor of all the islands. There is a letter from the King to Edmund Rose, dated the 14th of August, 1372, as Constable of the Castle of Gorey in Jersey ; so that within two months after Yvon had raised this siege of Castle Cornet, he, Edmund Rose, must have been sent to that of Gorey."—(*Some Remarks on the Constitution of Guernsey*, by T. F. de H., p. 119.)

Champarts—The "Camparts"—or the eleventh part of the grain grown upon the land of the fief, is described by Warburton thus :—"The first dukes of Normandy granted several parcels of land in the island, to such as had served them in their wars, and granted likewise a very considerable part to some religious houses. These, whether soldiers or churchmen, not being themselves skilled in agriculture, let out these lands to tenants under them, reserving such rents and services as they thought most convenient ; such was the "Campart," and such were the "chef-rentes," and these have been in use ever since Richard I., duke of Normandy, and possibly they may yet be of more ancient date. ., . In the Clos du Valle, out of extraordinary respect for the Abbot who resided among them, they paid both the *tenth* and the *eleventh* sheaf, both as *tithe* and *campart*." Camparts were owed on many fiefs, if not on all. Many owners of land have redeemed them. Others have *affranchis* their land, which is done by Act of Court, on proof that the land has been under grass for forty years, and lasts as long as the land is tilled yearly.

Un navire Anglois est venu
Dont ils eurrent bien de la hoigne[1]
Saillit soixante hommes ensemble
À bord Yvon, sans plus attendre
Qui les lièrent tous à bord.

Puis violèrent Alinor,
En la présence de son homme
Lui étant lié au grand mat
Les amenèrent à Hantonne[2]
Yvon étant un mauvais homme
Eut sur sa tête une couronne
Savoir ung mourion tout chaud.

Puis pendirent toutes ces gens
Portez à chartez[3] couple à couple
Et Alinor eut un présent
Pour gueuser une belle poche
Et avec peines et travaux
Cherchant son pain de porte en porte
Après plaisir eurent grands maux.

Les dix-neuf autres vaisseaux
Voulez-vous ouïyr leur destinée
Ils se dissout de grands châteaux
De tourments bien agittée
Or voilà donc leur destinée
C'est qu'ils burent la mer salée
Brisant dessus les Hanouets.

Au matin coume des porceaux
Estoient au plein cette journée
Où ils avaient fait leurs grands maux
En Guernesey la bienheurouse
Ils estoient là en grands monceaux
Dessus les sablons de Rocquaine
Après plaisir eurent grands maux.

FIN.

NOTES.

1. *Hoigne*—Haine.
2. *Hantonne*—Southampton.
3. *A chartez*—En charrettes.

L'Armée d'Espagne, Defaitte en l'an 1588.

Puissant Roy d'Espagne,
Combien riche tu es
Pour l'entreprise vaine
Que tu fis sur les Anglois,
Ton entreprise vaine,
Fut bientôt rebroussée. [1]

Vindrent sur l'Angleterre,
Au beau mois de Juillet,
Pour voir la bienheureuse
Ma Dame Elizabeth,
Mais ce fut à leur honte
Que sentir grand reveil.

La grande Armée Angloise
Commence a s'apprêter,
Tous leurs soldats embarqués
La poudre et les bullets,
C'est pour joüer au quille [2]
Avec les Portuguées.

Qui eust vue l'armée,
D'Elizabeth s'en va
De voir les grands bigots [3]
Et flâquées [4] sur leurs mâts
Des tambours et trompettes
Apprêtés au combat.

La puissante avans garde
A l'ancre n'étoit pas
Comme fut "La Revanche"
La vaisseau de Dras [5]
Qui sortoit de Plymouth,
Sillant sur sa plumas. [6]

NOTES.

1. *Rebrousser*—Retourner sur ses pas.
2. *Quille*—" C'est un morçeaux de bois tourné, plus gros par le bas que par le haut, dont on se sert pour joüer."
The English captains were playing bowls when the Spanish ships were announced as being in sight.
3. *Bigots*—Terme de Marine. C'est une petite pièce de bois percée de deux ou trois trous, par où l'on passe le bâtard pour la composition de racage.
4. *Flagner*—Jetter.
5. Sir Francis Drake commanded the ship *Revenge* during the fight with the Armada.
6. *Plumas*—Plumage.

Tous les plus grands navires
Qui furent haut et bas
De toute l'Angleterre
Vindrent vers l'Amiral
Luy supplier la grace
D'aller sur les guayhards *(sic)*.

L'Amiral d'Angleterre [1]
Leur répond d'un voix quas [2]
Enfans, donnez vous garde
Ne vous hasardez pas,
Car l'armée est puissante
Et nos vaisseaux sont trop ras. [3]

Ces gens de grand courage,
Disoient à l'Amiral
Seigneur, gardez la terre,
Nous allons avec Dras [4]
Nous aurons la vengeance
De l'armée des Pillards.

La " Revanche " d'Angleterre
Sous ses voiles s'en va,
Chargeans ses coulverines
Et tirans ses coutelas,
Au grand tyran s'entraine
Et luy couppa ses mats.

Quand le Duc de Mydine,
Sit ses grands arbres bas,
Dit à sa compagnie
Enfans—ne tirez pas,
Mais rondez les navires,
Ou vous mourrez tous plats. [5]

NOTES.

1. *L'Amiral d'Angleterre*—Lord Howard of Effingham.
2. *Quas*—Brisé.
Ras—Terme de Mer. C'est un bâtiment qui n'a ni pont, ni tillac, ni couverture.
4. *Dras*—Drake. Motley, in his *History of the Netherlands*, Vol. II., p.p. 498-9, says : There were many quarrels among the English admirals at this period, and much jealousy of Drake.
5. *Duc de Mydine*—The Duke of Medina-Sidonia, leader of the Spanish Armada, who, when the great hulk *Satana* and a galleon of Portugal were attacked by the *Triumph* and some other vessels, on the flag-ship, (the *St. Martin*) tried to repel Lord Howard on the *Ark Royal* and other men-of-war, and thence arose the hottest conflict of the day. He had previously, when Don Pedro de Valdez, commander of the Andelusian squadron,—having got his foremast carried away close to the deck,—lay crippled and helpless, calmly fired a gun to collect his scattered ships, and abandoned Valdez to his fate. . . . The next day Valdez surrendered to the *Revenge.*—Motley's *Netherlands*, Vol. II., pp. 456-7.

Sept navires de guerre,
Lièrent au grand " Arc "
Abordent cette vermine
Sur le " Satanas "
Pour porter pillage
Avec le Seigneur Dras.

Un noble gentil homme
Grand Seigneur des Estats
S'en va rompant les coffres
Et bahuts [1] hauts et bas,
Où il trouva des lettres
D'un fort merveilleux cas. [2]

Le grand Dauphin de Naples [3]
De ça ne ryoit pas,
Le Flamen se presente
Sur un de ses boulevards
De cette nef horrible, [3]
Du grand " St. Matthias." [4]

S'informe par enquête
Des gens d'armes en bas
Touchant une lettre
Quy portoit de grand mal
En contre l'Angleterre
Et tout le sang Royal.

Le peuple luy déclaroit
Seigneur ne fâchez pas
Que l'adresse de ça
C'est au Prince Farnése [5]
De par le Roy d'Espagne
Qui de ça chargera.

NOTES.

1. *Bahut*—Coffre couvert de cuir orné de petits clous.
2. *Cas*—Terme de Pratique, Matière, Crime.
3. *Nef*—Navire.
4. *Le Grand Dauphin, etc.*—Don Diego de Pimental, nephew of the Viceroy of Sicily, and uncle to the Viceroy of Naples, was captured in his ship the *St. Matthew*, by Admiral Van der Does, of the Holland fleet.—*Motley*, Vol. II., p. 473.
5. Alexander, Prince Farnèse, and Duke of Parma, was commandant of the Spanish Army, and was waiting in Flanders for an opportunity of co-operating with the Spanish fleet. He was suspected of having a secret treaty with Queen Elizabeth, (*Motley*, Vol. II., p. 273-4), but these verses are so very obscure, it is impossible to identify the incidents to which they allude. It may be that they, as well as the last verse of this poem are interpolations from some other ballad, which has got confused with this one.

Demande au grand de Naples
Ce qu'il disoit de cela
Encontre sa maitresse
Quoi penser en tel cas.
En disant deux cu trois paroles,
Le grand Prince le tua.

Puis luy fendit le ventre,
Jusqu'à l'estomac,
Son pauvre cœur luy tira
Qui soudain luy trancha
Devant la compagnie
Qui beaucoup soupira.

Lors l'Amiral d'Espagne
Soudain apparreilla
Avec sa compagnie
A vau la mer s'en va
Mettant basse enseigne
Par grand deuil s'en va.

Sortant vers Irlande
Sous tout leur appareil
Sur la haute mi-été[1]
Le vent leur prend su-est
Qui les mis sur la terre
D'Irlande et y reste.

Les prudens Irlandois
A leurs secours venoient
En plaignant leurs misères
Aux maisons les portaient
Faisant au grands d'Espagne
Plus qu'ils ne méritoient.

Le général d'Espagne
Ses mourtres fits dresser,
Appeller ses gens d'armes
Et tous ses centeniers,
Fit en grand' diligence
Sa grande troupe marcher.

---

1. *Mi-été*—le milieu de l'été.

L L

Au peuple d'Irlande,
Rendit tous ses bienfaits,
Mit par toute la terre
Gens d'armes en harnois,[1]
Tuant homme et femme
Sans merci ni délai.

Tous les Irlandois s'adressoient
Au Comte de Tyrone
Qui tenoit pour la Reine
Contre la nation,
Luy priant donner aide
Contre les Castillons.

Le Comte met en ordre
Ses princes et barons,
Tous au fil de l'épée[2]
Leur ordonner la fronde,[3]
La douleur redoublée
Qui les déconfit tous.

Lors voilà la ruine
Des meurtriers Espagnols
Qui faisoient tant de mines
Dans de bien grands flibots,[4]
Pensant prendre Angleterre
Comme de fols idiots.

À Dieu soit la louange
Qui de son bras tout fort,
De tous leurs grands vaisseaux
De nous pris la revanche
Nous pensant détruire
Et démembrer nos corps.

Les braves gens d'Espagne
Partant de leurs maisons
Pensant en Angleterre

---

1. *Harnois*—signifie l'habillement d'un homme d'armes.
2. *Fil de l'epée*—est en usage depuis long tems. Ronsard a dit parlant de Henri III., ..
"devant le *fil* de son epée."
3. *Fronder*—Attaquer quelque chose.
4. *Flibot*—Terme de marine. C'est un moïen vaisseau qui est armé en course.

Sarcler[1] tous les chardons,
Mais leurs gens et leurs moufles
N'étoient pas assez bons.

Quand on va par les villes
Pour vendre les moutons,
Chacun se donne à croire
Que les viandes vaudront
Mais c'est bien le contraire
La plupart en donneront.[3]

FIN.

Secular Poems.

BELLE ROSE AU ROSIER BLANC.

J'ai cueilli la belle rose
Qui pendait au rosier blanc,
    Belle Rose
Belle Rose au rosier blanc !

Je la cueillis feuille à feuille
Et la mis dans mon tablier blanc
    Belle Rose
Belle Rose au rosier blanc.

Je l'ai portée chez mon père
Entre Paris et Rouen
    Belle Rose
Belle Rose au rosier blanc.

---

1. *Sarcler*—Terme de Laboureur. Couper les méchantes herbes avec le sarcloir.
2. *Moufles*—Garnie de poulies de cuivre, de boulons, et de cordages pour monter les pièces d'artillerie à l'elesoir.
3. That this poem is very defective, and therefore obscure, is obvious, but I thought even this mutilated fragment was worth preserving. Many of the statements made in it are not borne out by history, though they probably formed part of the gossip of that day, and had filtered over to the Islands from sailors who had themselves had a share in some of the events narrated. This last verse seems to have no connection with the rest of the poem, but I have copied it as Job Mauger wrote it, nearly two centuries ago.

Las !—je n'ai trouvé personne
Que le rossignol chantant
    Belle Rose
Belle Rose au rosier blanc.

Qui me dit dans son langage
Mariez vous à quinze ans
    Belle Rose
Belle Rose au rosier blanc !

Hélas comment me martrai-je ?
Moi qui suis baisse * pour un an,
    Belle Rose,
Belle Rose au rosier blanc !

Combien gagnez vous, la belle ?
Combien gagnez vous par an ?
    Belle Rose
Belle Rose au rosier blanc !

Je gagne bien cent pistoles
Cent pistoles en argent blanc
    Belle Rose
Belle Rose au rosier blanc.

Venez avec moi, ma belle,
Vous en aurez bien autant
    Belle Rose
Belle Rose au rosier blanc.

Je ne vais avec personne
Si l'on ne m'épouse avant
    Belle Rose
Belle Rose au rosier blanc.

Si l'on ne me mène à l'église
Par devant tous mes parents
    Belle Rose
Belle Rose au rosier blanc ! †

---

* Baisse—servant girl.
† There are many versions of this song to be found among the country people, I have compared this with five or six others, and it is, I think, the most generally received.

A LA CLAIRE FONTAINE.

À la claire fontaine
Dondaine, ma dondaine
Les mains me suis lavé
Dondaine ma lou-lou-la
Les mains me suis lavé,
Dondaine m'a dondé.

A la feuille d'un chêne
Dondaine, ma dondaine
Je les ai essuyées
Dondaine ma lou-lou-la
Je les ai essuyées
Dondaine m'a dondé.

A la plus haute branche
Dondaine, ma dondaine
Un rossignol chantait
Dondaine ma lou-lou-la
Un rossignol chantait
Dondaine m'a dondé.

Chante, rossignol, chante
Dondaine, ma dondaine,
Toi qui as le cœur gai
Dondaine ma lou-lou-la
Toi qui as le cœur gai
Dondaine m'a dondé.

Le mien n'est pas de même
Dondaine, ma dondaine,
Il est bien affligé
Dondaine ma lou-lou-la
Il est bien affligé
Dondaine m'a dondé.

Pierre, mon ami Pierre,
Dondaine, ma dondaine,
A la guerre est allé
Dondaine ma lou-lou-la
A la guerre est allé
Dondaine m'a dondé.

Pour un bouton de rose
Dondaine, ma dondaine
Que je lui refusai
Dondaine ma lou-lou-la
Que je lui refusai
Dondaine m'a dondé.

Je voudrais que la rose
Dondaine, ma dondaine
Fut encore au rosier
Dondaine ma lou-lou-la
Fut encore au rosier
Dondaine m'a dondé.

Et que mon ami Pierre
Dondaine, ma dondaine
Fut ici à m'aimer
Dondaine ma lou-lou-la
Fut ici à m'aimer
Dondaine m'a, dondé.

Qui Veut Ouïr.

Qui veut ouïr, qui veut savoir } bis.
Comment les maris aiment ? }
Ils aiment si brutalement
Ils sont de si brutales gens,
Qu'on les entend toujours disant
(Parlé) "Ah Madame allez gardez
Le ménage et les enfants !"
    Fal-la-la.

Qui veut ouïr, qui veut savoir } bis.
Comment les filles aiment ? }
Elles aiment si discrètement
Elles sont de si discrètes gens,
Qu'on les entend toujours disant
(Parlé) "Ah Monsieur ne parlez pas si haut
Car Maman nous entendra."
    Fal-la-la.

Qui veut ouïr, qui veut savoir } bis.
Comment les veuves aiment ? }
Elles aiment si sensiblement

Elles sont de si sensibles gens, ·
Qu'on les entend toujours disant
(Parlé) "Ah! le beau jeune homme!
Comme il ressemble à feu mon mari."
     Fal-la-la.

Qui veut ouïr, qui veut savoir } bis.
Comment les soldats aiment? }
Ils aiment si cavalièrement
Ils sont de si cavaliers gens
Qu'on les entend toujours disant
(Parlé) "Ah! Madame m'aimez vous?
Ne m'aimez vous pas? dictes moi,
Car il me faut rejoindre mon régiment."
     Fal-la-la.

Qui veut ouïr, qui veut savoir } bis.
Comment les Français aiment? }
Ils aiment si frivolement
Ils sont de si frivoles gens,
Qu'on les entend toujours disant
(Parlé) "Ah! Madame depuis que je vous ai vue
Je ne songe qu'a vous!"
     Fal-la-la.

Qui veut ouïr, qui veut savoir } bis.
Comment les Anglais aiment. }
Ils aiment si stupidement
Ils sont si stupides gens
Qu'on les entend toujours disant
(Parlé) "Tantôt la chasse, tantôt la
Gazette, tantôt l'amour!"
     Fal-la-la.

Qui veut ouïr, qui veut savoir } bis.
Comment les Guernesiais aiment }
Ils aiment si prudemment,
Ils sont de si prudents gens
Qu'on les entends toujours disant
(Parlé) "Mademoiselle à-t'elle de l'argent!"
     Fal-la-la.

I have to thank Mr. J. T. R. de Havilland, of Havilland Hall, for kindly supplying me with a copy of this song.

Marguerite s'est Assise.

Marguerite s'est assise—Tra-la-la.
À l'ombre d'un rocher
À son plaisir écoute—Tra-la-la
Les mariniers chanter,
 Tra-la-la. Tra-la-la.

Elle fit un' rencontre—Tra-la-la
De trente matelots
Le plus jeune des trente—Tra-la-la.
Il se mit à chanter.
 Tra-la-la. Tra-la-la.

Qu'avez vous la belle—Tra-la-la.
Qu'avez vous a pleurer?
Je pleure mon anneau d'or—Tra-la-la.
Qui dans la mer est tombé
 Tra-la-la. Tra-la-la.

Que donnerez-vous la belle—**Tra-la-la**
A qui le pêcherait?
Un baiser sur la bouche—Tra-la-la.
Ou deux s'il fallait
 Tra-la-la. Tra-la-la.

Le galant se dépouille—**Tra-la-la.**
Dans la mer a plongé
La première fois qu'il plonge—**Tra-la-la**
Il n'en a rien apporté
 Tra-la-la. Tra-la-la.

La seconde fois qu'il plonge—**Tra-la-la**
Les cloches vont ric-tin-té
La troisième fois qu'il plonge—**Tra-la-la.**
Le galant s'est noyé!
 Tra-la-la. Tra-la-la.

Nous l'ferons enterrer—Tra-la-la
Et puis dessus sa tombe
Un rosmarin planter—Tra-la-la.
Sur ce pauvre jeune homme!
 Tra-la-la. Tra-la-la.

Nous dirons à sa mère—Tra-la-la
Qu'il s'est embarqué
Sur un vaisseau de guerre—Tra-la-la.
Qui de loin est allé !
 Tra-la-la. Tra-la-la.

LA MEUNIÈRE.

Je vais épouser la Meunière
Dont on voit le moulin là bas
Mais j'aime une pauvre bergère
Comprenez-vous mon embarras,
Ma Fanchette est si jolie
Mais la Meunière a du bien
S'il faut faire une folie
Que cela ne soit pas pour rien.
Bah ! j'épouserai la Meunière
Qui me fait toujours les yeux doux
En me disant " Beau petit Pierre
Mais quand donc nous marierons nous ? "

Uninstant—n'allons pas si vite,
Suis je bien certain d'être heureux
Avec la femme du moulin
Dont je ne suis pas amoureux ?
Il s'agit de mariage
C'est hélas ! pour plus d'un jour,
Oui ! mais pour vivre en ménage
C'est bien maigre de l'amour !
Bah ! j'épouserai la Meunière
Qui me fait toujours les yeux doux
En me disant " Beau petit Pierre
Mais quand donc nous marierons nous ? "

Cependant mon cœur s'inquiète
Et me dit que c'est mal à moi
De trahir la pauvre Fanchette
A qui j'avais donné ma foi
Elle est si tendre et si bonne
Comme son cœur va souffrir.
Hélas ! si je l'abandonne
 Elle est capable d'en mourir

Ma foi ! tant pis pour la Meunière,
Je ne serai pas son époux
Qu'elle dise "Beau petit Pierre !
Petit Pierre n'est pas pour vous ? "

Le Glaneur.

Sur nos grands blés déjà le soleil brille
Quels lourds épis—en fût il de pareils !
Va ! travaillons, vite, en main la faucille
Mais suivrez vous, suivrez vous mes conseils.

Chorus :

Enfant, de chaque gerbe
Que mûrit le Seigneur
Laissez tomber dans l'herbe
Quelques épis pour le glâneur
Pensez au pauvre glâneur
Faites le bien—vous porterez bonheur } bis

Notre ministre dit que le bien qu'on donne
Est le meilleur qu'on pense récolter
Il dépose lorsqu'il disait aux hommes.
Donner aux pauvres, à Dieu n'est que prêter.
Chorus.—Enfant, etc.

Aux pauvres içi le peu qu'on abandonne
Dieu pour beaucoup ailleurs le comptera
Des grains donnés, la moisson sera bonne
Pour nous au Ciel, Dieu les centuplera."
Chorus.—Enfant, etc.

Les Trois Tambours.

Trois jeunes tambours, revenant de la guerre,
Le plus jeune des trois avait un bouquet de roses
Au ron-ron-ron-te-tan-plan.

La fille du roi étant par sa fenêtre
" Ah ! jeune tambour, veux tu me donner tes roses ? "
Au ron-ron-ron-te-tan-plan.

" Mes roses sont pour mon mariage
La fille du roi, veux tu être ma femme ? "
Au ron-ron-ron-te-tan-plan.

"Và jeune tambour, demander à mon père"
"Sire le Roi, veux tu me donner ta fille ? "
  Au ron-ron-ron-te-tan-plan.

"Ah ! jeune tambour dis moi qu'est tes richesses ? "
"Mes richesses sont mes caisses₁ et mes balletes,₂ "
  Au ron-ron-ron-te-tan-plan.

"Và ! jeune tambour, demain je te ferai pendre "
"Six cent mille canons dans ce cas vont me défendre "
  Au ron-ron-ron-te-tan plan.

"Ah ! jeune tambour, dis moi qui est ton père ? "
"Mon père il est le roi—le roi d'Angleterre ! "
  Au ron-ron-ron-te-tan-plan.

"Ah ! jeune tambour, voudrais tu bien ma fille ? "
"Ah ! je m'en moque de vous et de votre fille,
Dans mon pays y' en a de bien plus gentilles."
  Au ron-ron·ron-te-tan-plan.

Si j'avais le Chapeau.

Si j'avais le chapeau
Que ma mie m'avait donné
Mon chapeau est bel et beau

Chorus :
Adieu ma mignonne
Adieu donc mes amours

Si j'avais la casaque³
Que ma mie m'avait donné
Ma casaque est zic et zac
Mon chapeau est bel et beau.
  Chorus.—Adieu, etc.

Si j'avais le corselet
Que ma mie m'avait donné
Mon corselet est fort bien fait

---

1. *Caisses*—Coffres.   2. *Ballettes*—Petites Valises.
3. *Casaque*—"Habillement qui est plus large qu'un juste-au-corps et qui se porte sur les épaules en forme de manteau."—*Richelet.*

Ma casaque est zic et zac,
Mon chapeau est bel et beau
       Chorus.—Adieu, etc.

Si j'avais la cravate
Que ma mie m'avait donnée
Ma cravate est ric et rac
Mon corselet est fort bien fait
Ma casaque est zic et zac
Mon chapeau est bel et beau.
       Chorus.—Adieu, etc.

Si j'avais la culotte
Que ma mie m'avait donnée
Mes culottes débotes [1] et botes,
Ma cravate est ric et rac,
Mon corselet est fort bien fait
Ma casaque est zic et zac,
Mon chapeau est bel et beau.
       Chorus.—Adieu, etc.

Si j'avais les blancs bas
Que ma mie m'avait donnés
Mes blancs bas sont de damas,
Mes culottes débotes et botes,
Ma cravate est ric et rac
Mon corselet est fort bien fait,
Ma casaque est zic et zac,
Mon chapeau est bel est beau.
       Chorus.—Adieu, etc.

Si j'avais les souliers
Que ma mie m'avait donnés
Mes souliers sont de cuir doux,
Mes blancs bas sont de damas,
Mes culottes débotes et botes,
Ma cravate est ric et rac,
Mon corselet est fort bien fait,
Ma casaque est zic et zac,
Et mon chapeau est bel et beau.
       Chorus.—Adieu, etc.

---

1. *Débotes*—Tirer les botes de quelqu'un,

Venez Peuples Fidèles.

Venez peuple fidèle pour entendre chanter
Un jeune militaire qui revient de la guerre,
Qui revient de la guerre, muni de son congé
En entrant dans son isle sa sœur l'a rencontré.

La sœur avec tendresse, de la joie qu'elle avait
Vint embrasser son frère, et lui donner des baisers
Le frère avec tendresse dit à sa chère sœur
Ne m'y fais pas connaître, garde cela dans ton cœur.

Et le jeun' militaire tout de suite est allé.
Chercher son père et mère, en gardant son secret,
Bonjour Monsieur et Dame aurez vous chambre à louer
A un jeune militaire de la guerre retourné.

Ah oui ! notre bon jeune homme, nous avons logement,
Sur le lit de notre fils, nous te ferons coucher
Les affaires de la guerre, tu nous raconteras
Le soir à la table, après avoir soupé.

Il donne à la dame son argent à garder,
Tenez ma très-chère dame, gardez moi cet argent,
C'est pour soulager les peines de mes parents,
Et la méchante femme de là s'en est allée.

Trouver son mari, lui dire, " C'est une fortune
Faut le tuer de suite, nous aurons son argent."
Les deux méchants armés des gros couteaux
Ont trainé dans la cave son corps tout sanglant.

Le lendemain matin la pauvre fille arrive,
Ah ! bon jour père et mère, je voudrais bien parler
A ce beau jeune militaire,
Que je vous ai amené.

La méchante mère, lui répond hardiment,
Mais que dis tu ma fille? Est ce de nos parents ?
Ah ! oui, ma très chère mère, c'est mon frère arrivé,
Il revint de la guerre, mon cœur en est content.

La cruelle mère, si tôt elle écria
J'ai égorgé ton frère, hélas ! n'en parle pas.
Mais la fille tout de suite les fit être emmenés
Devant les justiciers, hélas ! pour être jugés.

Les justiciers s'empressent de juger le procès
Et les condamnent, tous les deux d'être brulés
Oh vous pères et mères oyez ces malheurs
Que les biens de ce monde ne vous tiennent point au cœurs.

Par la barbarie et l'ambition d'argent,
Ces deux dans les flammes passent leurs derniers moments.*

JEAN, GROS JEAN.

Jean, gros Jean, marie sa fille,
Grosse et grasse et bien habile,
A un marchand de sabots,
Radinguette et radingot

CHORUS :
A un marchand de sabots
Radinguette et radingot.

Pour dîner ils eurent des peis
Entre quatre ils n'eurent que treis
Ah ! dévinez si c'est trop
Radinguette et radingot.
Chorus.—A un, etc.

Pour souper ils eurent des prunes
Entre quatre ils n'en eurent qu'une
Et la quervaie d'un escargot
Radinguette et radingot.
Chorus.—A un, etc.

Ils firent faire une couachette
De deux secs buts de bûchette
Et l'oreiller d'un fagot
Radinguette et radingot
Chorus.—A un, etc.

Ils firent faire des courtines
Creyant que c'était mousseline

---

* This legend, which is found with slight variations in the Folk-Lore of almost every European nation, seems to be deeply impressed on the older St. Martinais, in fact some say that the two rocks between Moulin Huet and Saints' Bays, which look like two kneeling figures, are the petrified forms of the man and the woman, condemned there to kneel and expiate their crime till the end of the world.

Mais c'était Calaminco
Radinguette et radingot.
Chorus.—A un, etc.*

*   *   *   *   *

I have concluded this chapter of Guernsey songs with this one, though it is of an entirely different style and class to any of the others, but the tune to which it is set, is said to be the national air of Guernsey.

When the Duke of Gloucester landed here on the 18th of September, 1817, this song, as the Guernsey National Air was struck up by the band which came to meet him ; the militia-men, knowing the song, all burst out laughing, much to the astonishment of the Duke and his suite !

Jean, gros Jean, ma-rie sa fille, Grosse et grasse et bien ha-bile, À un marchand de sa-bots,

Radinguette et ra-din-got; À un marchand de sa-bots, Ra-dinguette et ra-din-got.

---

* From Mrs. Kinnersly, to whom I am also indebted for the music.

The Clameur de Haro.*

THE "Clameur de Haro," abolished in Normandy, A.D., 1583, is, perhaps, the most ancient and curious legal survival in the Channel Islands.

Should a Channel Islander consider his estate to be injured, or his rights to be infringed, by the action of another, in the presence of two witnesses he kneels on the ground and says :—

"Haro! Haro! Haro! à l'aide mon Prince! on me fait tort!" and he then repeats the Lord's Prayer in French.

This formula, which is tantamount to an injunction to stay proceedings, causes all obnoxious practices to be suspended until the case has been tried in Court, when the party who is found to be in the wrong is condemned to a fine and a "Regard de Château," which, in former times, meant a night's imprisonment. All "Clameurs," according to an ordonnance of October 1st, 1599, have to be registered at the Greffe within twenty-four hours, on penalty of being "convict en sa clameur," and, should no proceedings be taken within a year of the clameur, it is considered to have lapsed.

An order of Queen Elizabeth relative to Guernsey, given at Richmond, October 9th, 1580, decides that "yt shall not be lawfull to appeale in anie cause criminell, or of correction, nor from the execution of anie order taken in their Courte of Chief Pleas, nor in cries of Haro." †

---

* It has been suggested that the Clameur de Haro should be included among the civic customs peculiar to the Channel Islands. (See p.p. 59-77) so, as Sir Edgar MacCulloch had not mentioned it in his MSS. I have ventured to include a short description of it in the Appendix.

† *Livres des Jugements*, etc., Vol. II., p. 16, (transcribed from British Museum, Lansdowne MSS., No. 155, fol. 426).

One of the most important occasions on which this prerogative was used happened in the year 1850, when it was in contemplation to demolish the ancient fortifications of Castle Cornet, but the late Mr. Martin F. Tupper, who was then on a visit to Guernsey, had recourse to this form of appeal, and saved the oldest parts of the fortress from demolition. An extraordinary instance of a "Clameur" took place in the Church of Sark on the 14th of December, 1755. A great dispute had arisen between Dame Elizabeth Etienne, widow of Mr. Daniel Le Pelley, Seigneur of Sark, and the ecclesiastical authorities of Guernsey, as to in whose gift was the living of the Church of Sark. She appointed a Mr. Jean Févot to the Church, and when Mr. Pierre Levrier, who had been appointed by the Dean of Guernsey to this post, arrived in Sark to perform the service, he found Mr. Févot in the pulpit. He then and there, in the words of various scandalized eye-witnesses, "interjetta une Clameur de Haro, environ les deux heures d'après-midi, dans le tems qu'il avoit commencé à lire le service Divin." * This of course led to many disputes, and for over a year Dame Le Pelley locked up the Church of Sark, and allowed no one to enter it. Finally, after much litigation, and threats of major excommunication from the Guernsey Ecclesiastical Court, the Bishop of Winchester intervened, Pierre Levrier was forcibly ejected from the island, and, in 1757, Mr. Cayeux Deschamps was given the living.

Four cases of "Clameurs" were registered between the years 1880-90, and an instance occurred as recently as 1902.

There has been much controversy as to the origin of the word "Haro." Terrien, (*Coutûme de Normandie*, Edition 1684, p. 104), ascribes it to Rollo, Duke of Normandy, Ha-Ro, and says "La seule prononciation de son nom, même après tant de siècles a cette vertu, qu'elle engage ceux contre lesquels ou s'en sert à cesser leurs entreprises et atenter rien au-de-là." Laurence Carey, in his essay on the Laws and Customs of the Island, and all the other old writers say likewise, but modern philologists, such as Le Héricher and George Métivier have disputed this theory, and have resolved the word "Haro" into a "cri de charge," which has survived as such in the English "Hurrah." Froissart employs it frequently as the sound of combat : "Le *Haro* commença à

---

* From Colonel Ernest Le Pelley's MSS.

monter," and, in the description of the battle of Bouvines, won from the Germans and English in 1214, by Guillaume Guiart, who died in 1306 we find :—

> " La vois de nuls n'i est oïe
> Fors des heraux qui *harou* crient,
> Et par le champ se crucefient
> *Harou*, dient-ils, quel mortaille !
> Quelle occision ! quelle bataille ! " *

---

* See *Dictionnaire Franco-Normand*, by G. Métivier, p. 280.

APPENDIX A.*

Ghosts.*

THE GHOST OF MR. BLONDEL.

T "Les Mourains" we have seen that the ghost was "laid" by the means of the clergy of the parish, (see page 288) and it is evident by the following stories that the laying of spirits frequently formed part of the duties of the clergy in Guernsey in the last century.

The house Colonel Le Pelley now inhabits at St. Peter-in-the-Wood, was formerly owned by an old Mr. Blondel, who, on his death bed, gave instructions to Mr. Thomas Brock (then Rector of the parish and grandfather of the present Rector, Mr. H. Walter Brock), to toll the big bell to announce his decease.

This was not done, but Mr. Blondel's spirit determined to show that promises to the dying were not to be trifled with ! All the parish of St. Pierre-du-Bois were ready to affirm that the ghost was to be seen climbing up the Church tower ; and in the Rectory kitchen the china on the dresser would make a clattering noise and finally be swept by the unseen hands on to the floor.

Life at the Rectory became so unendurable under these circumstances that Mr. Brock finally decided to "lay" the ghost, and confine it to its own house. So he went to "Prospect Place," as the house is now called, with twelve others of the local clergy. They shut every door and window, and blocked up every crevice, key-hole, etc., through which the spirit might pass. They then prayed in every room, after which having driven the spirit out of

---

each room in succession, they locked it up in a cupboard, with either the key of the Church door or a specially-made silver key (Miss Le Pelley could not find out which, some say one, and some another), but the ghost has not troubled the Brock family since.

The old servants now living in the house firmly believe that the ghost still inhabits the cupboard, and affirm that its groans can still be heard.[*]

The Old House at St. George.

Judith Ozanne, an old woman, who is servant at the Le Pelleys', tells the following story.

Her uncle, an old Mr. Ozanne, remembered the last Mr. Guille who inhabited the original " St. George," the old house which has been replaced by the modern building which is now known as " St. George."

This Mr. Guille left instructions that the old house was never to be pulled down, as a spirit had been shut up in one of the cupboards; but his son found the old house quite unsuitable for his bride to live in, so he pulled it down, and built the present house, and the consequence was that the poor homeless spirit was forced to wander about the garden. Judith's uncle saw him often on moonlight nights, wandering among the trees around the pond.

All the family saw him too, and decided that something had to be done. So they had a " conjuration " as they call a laying of the spirit, and tried to induce it to enter an underground cellar, and shut it down by means of a trap door.

But Mr. Ozanne would never say whether or no they were successful. Judith Ozanne finishes the story by saying, " And I should like to know what would happen to Mr. Blondel's spirit if this house were burnt down ? "[*]

Many of the old Guernsey " haunted houses " had their ghosts locked up in cupboards. Mrs. Le Poidevin, who in her youth had been an " ironer," and had gone round from house to house ironing after the weekly washing at home had taken place, related that the famous haunted house at the Tour Beauregard was also in possession of a ghost locked up in a cupboard, a cupboard whose doors, in spite of many efforts, would not open, and from which the most fearful groans and dismal wailings were heard to

---

arise. Mrs. Le Poidevin also used to go as ironer to the old house at the top of Smith Street, now pulled down, belonging to the de Jersey family. In this house also was a ghost locked up in a cupboard, and Mrs. de Jersey, a very strong minded old lady,—in defiance of superstition—insisted on having this cupboard door forced open, and the ghost escaped! After that the house was rendered almost uninhabitable by the frightful noises that were heard all over it. No one could get any sleep, and not a servant could be found to stay in the house. So finally Mrs. de Jersey decided to have the clergy called in, and one of the maids described to Mrs. Le Poidevin the ceremonies that ensued.

She said that every outer door was locked, all the crevices between the window sashes were wedged up, and every keyhole was plugged up. Then the minister of St. James' and some of the other clergy prayed in every room, and she thought they read something about "casting out devils." Finally the ghost was locked up with the key of the Church door.*

The Ghosts of La Petite Porte.

La Petite Porte is the sandy bay immediately underneath Jerbourg. Tradition derives its name "the little door" from an incident which is said to have occurred in 1338. In those days the French had made one of their periodical inroads on the island, and were in possession of its principal fortresses. Eighty-seven men of St. Martin's parish, headed by l'honorable "Capitaine Jean de la Marche," † attempted to disloge them, but were defeated at Mare-Madoc, in the Hubits, and fled down to La Petite Porte,

---

* From Mrs. Le Poidevin.

In Moncure Conway's book on *Demonology and Devil-Lore*, Vol. I., p. 102, he says :—" The key has a holy sense in various religions." I have not been able to find out the exact formula used by the clergy, but in the Sarum Office, and also in the first Prayer Book of Edward VI., an exorcism is given to be used at the Baptism of Infants, in which the evil spirit is addressed as follows :—" Therefore, thou accursed spirit, remember thy sentence, remember thy judgment, remember the day to be at hand, wherein thou shalt burn in fire everlasting, prepared for thee and thy angels," etc. This was founded on the ancient exorcisms, and was only left out in the revis.on of 1552, in deference to the criticisms of Bucer.

† " L'honorable Jean de la Marche, du bas, Commandant-en-Chef de la paroisse de St. Martin. voyant l'isle de Guernesey révoltée contre son Roi, et servant de préférence sous les drapeaux Français ; ce vaillant homme, dis-je, ému par un esprit vraiment loyal, et secondé par l'honorable Messire Pierre de Sausmarez, James Guille, Jean de Blanchelande, Pierre Bonamy, Thomas Vauriouf, et Thomas Etibaut, qui allèrent partout chercher des secours, et tàchant de détruire tous les factieux, et animês d'un désir d'assister à leur bien-faiteur pour reprendre le Château Cornet, assistés par les braves habitants de la petite

where they embarked for Jersey, and founded a colony at St. Ouen's. An old Jersey manuscript goes on to say that Charles II., during his sojourn in Jersey, was so touched by the recital of the bravery and fidelity of these men, that he granted to the "South" Regiment of Militia, the old "Regiment Bleu," a special "aiguillette d'argent." Later authorities disprove this, on the grounds that there were not, at this epoch, either regiments or uniforms, and that the "royal blue facings and silver lace" quoted as "being borne at present by the South Regiment of Militia" did not exist two centuries ago!

But among the old country people, to the present day, the bay known as "Moulin Huet" is invariably called "Vier Port" (old harbour), and if one mentions "Moulin Huet *Bay*" they will tell you that the name "Moulin Huet" only applies to the old mill, (now destroyed, and the site turned into a picnic house), and that it was "Les Anglais" who transferred the name of the mill to the bay just below, so that "La Petite Porte," being just the other side of the bay, might easily have been originally "Petit Port"—(Little Harbour.)

Bounded by the "Tas de Pois," the most magnificent rocks in the Channel Islands, it is noted for its beauty, and, from its long expanse of sand, is the best place for sand-eeling. But about the beginning of last century no sand-eelers dared approach this spot by night. Screams, shrieks, and groans were heard there, night after night, and finally it was shunned after dark by the whole island. There was no difficulty in the people's minds in accounting for these sounds. Two such awful tragedies were connected with this bay and its environs that it was an "embarras de richesse"

Césarée ; la paroisse de St. Martin leva et envoya quatre-vingt-sept hommes, qui se joignirent aux dites honorables personnes, sous le commandement du dit noble Jean de la Marche, du bas ; ce nombre était autant que la paroisse de St. Martin pût en fournir dans ce temps là. Ayant été attaqués au Mont Madau (dit les Hubits) ils firent retraite et s'embarquèrent à la petite Porte (qui porte ce nom à cause de cette aventure) sur de frêles barques, parmi les rochers, et arrivèrent enfin à Jersey, et se joignirent sous le commandement de Messire Renaud de Carteret, Grand Gouverneur des Iles, et se battirent vailleusement sous les drapeaux de sa Majesté, après avoir échappé à la fureur d'une mer orageuse. St. Martin était la seule paroisse de cette isle de Guernesey, qui se garda sous l'obéissance du Roi, pour lesquels bons services, il plut à sa Majesté Charles II., leur accorder à leur requête le galon d'argent comme le plus noble. C'est alors que plusieurs habitants de St. Martin donnèrent leurs services pour leurs vies au susdit Renaud de Carteret, Gouverneur-en-Chef, et conçurent un tel mépris pour leurs pays qu'ils habitèrent Jersey. Lisez pour cela le discours que Charles II. donna au Parlement à son retour, et l'estime et l'éloge qu'il fait de ces héros."—*From an old document entitled* "*Touchant La Préséance d'Honneur chalengée, par Guernesé.*"

to decide which of the ghosts of the two men who had been murdered in this vicinity it could be!

The first of these stories has already been published in a little book, now out of print, called *Anglo-Norman Legends* or *Tales of the Channel Islands*, N.D., under the title of "John Andrew Gordier," and has also been taken as the foundation of "Rachel Mauger, a Guernsey Tragedy," published some years ago in Clarke's *Guernsey Magazine*, where also, in the number for May, 1883, the same story is given in a condensed form, as taken from a newspaper cutting, and is preceded by the following note, signed "J. Y."

"The following striking narrative, relating to the origin of a drama celebrated in its day (the tragedy of "Julia)," became known to the writer through an old newspaper cutting preserved in a family scrap book. The newspaper of which we speak must be at least fifty years old (in 1883), and it related events which were then long past."

A book called *The Locket*, by Mrs. Alfred Marks is based on the same tradition.

Though these events must have happened nearly two hundred years ago, there are still some recollections of them lingering in the minds of the very old people, who preface them by saying "*J'ai ouï dire à ma gran'mère !*"

The story runs thus :—"About the end of the seventeenth century there was an extremely beautiful girl, living at the Varclin, in St. Martin's parish, called Rachel Mauger. The Maugers were of a good old Guernsey family, and were, in those days, extremely well-to-do. She was engaged to John Andrew Gordier, a native of Jersey, though of French extraction. One day he sent her word that he was going to sail over from Jersey to see her, and intended landing at La Petite Porte, which was the nearest place to her house. She started to go to meet him. But he never appeared, and she had to return home, fearing that some accident had happened to him. What really had happened was this : There was a wealthy merchant, in St. Peter Port, named Gaillard, who had long wished to marry Rachel ; he had formerly been her father's clerk, so they had been much thrown together, but she did not reciprocate his affection.

The day Mr. Gordier sailed over to Guernsey, Gaillard was down in the bay of La Petite Porte, having previously been

refused admission to the Mauger's house, on the ground that Mr.
Gordier was expected, and they were all busy preparing for his
reception. Brooding over his wrongs, he looked up, and saw his
rival just on the point of landing. . Mad with jealousy he waited
behind the rocks till he saw him preparing to ascend the winding
path which leads to the top of the cliff, then he rushed out, and
stabbed him twice in the back with the knife he always carried,
and, doubling him up, thrust the body into a cave close by with
a particularly small entrance. The cave is still pointed out, and
is on the western side of the bay, just below the path, leading
from La Petite Porte to Moulin Huet. Before leaving the body,
Gaillard searched it, and abstracted a peculiarly-shaped locket from
one of the pockets, which Gordier was bringing as a present to
his *fiancée*.

Of course the disappearance of Gordier led to a search, and
his body being finally discovered in this cave by some boys, his
murder was made manifest. His mother finally resolved to come
over and visit her intended daughter-in-law, whom she found in a
most depressed and excitable condition, and evidently dying of a
broken heart. United to the shock of her lover's death, she had
been exposed to the incessant persecution of her relations, who
were determined that she should marry Gaillard, and had insisted
that she should accept the locket that he had stolen from Gordier's
corpse, and, with a refinement of malice, had pressed on her. So
unstrung was the unfortunate Rachel that she did nothing but
sink into one fainting fit after another on seeing Mrs. Gordier,
and when the latter, struck with horror on seeing this jewel on
her watch-chain, asked her how she had come into possession of
a locket which had, she knew, been made specially for her in
Jersey by her son's orders, the unhappy girl turned deadly pale,
and, murmuring the word "clerc," fell in a dead faint to the
ground. The final shock, and sudden conviction that they had
been harbouring her lover's murderer, being too much for her in
her enfeebled condition, she died in a few moments.

Mrs. Gordier misinterpreted the poor girl's grief, and, thinking
it proceeded from a guilty conscience, intimated that it evidently
shewed that Rachel was an accomplice in the murder. Naturally
the Maugers were most indignant at such an unworthy aspersion
on their daughter, and, after a violent scene, asked her to prove
her statements. She replied that the jewel their daughter was

then wearing was one which was purchased by her son before leaving Jersey, and she proved the fact by touching a secret spring and shewing his portrait concealed in the locket. The Maugers, knowing that Gaillard had been the donor of this jewel, and connecting "clerc," the last word Rachel's lips had uttered, with him, as being her father's clerk, immediately sent for him. On being confronted with the jewel, and asked to explain how it came into his possession, he replied that he had purchased it from a Jew, named Levi, who had for years paid periodical visits to the island as a pedlar. So Levi was then considered to be undoubtedly guilty, and was taken into custody, but then, remorse, the fear of public shame, and also the conviction that, Rachel being dead nothing made life worth living, so wrought on the miserable Gaillard, that the morning of the day on which Levi was to be brought before the Royal Court, he was found dead, stabbed by his own hand.

A letter was found on the table in his room confessing his guilt and reading thus : " None but those who have experienced the furious impulse of ungovernable love will pardon the crime which I have committed, in order to obtain the incomparable object by whom my passions were inflamed. But, Thou, O Father of Mercies ! who implanted in my soul these strong desires, wilt forgive one rash attempt to accomplish my determined purpose, in opposition, as it should seem, to thy Almighty Providence." *

Le Seigneur de Damèque.

This second story is not at all well known, except among some of the very old people at St. Martin's. I will not mention the names of the murderers, as descendants of the family still survive, and are among the most respected of the country people.

At the end of the eighteenth century many French noblemen fled over here, to escape the terrors of the French revolution. Among them was a Seigneur de Damèque. (I have no idea whether or not whether this is the correct spelling of his name, but it represents the pronunciation of the people). He came out to St. Martin's parish, and took a house at Le Hurel, just above Le Vallon. He was very proud and reserved, made no friends, and was always

---

* From Mrs. Le Patourel, Mr. Tourtel, and from my father, who had heard it from his father, and collated with the printed versions of the story.

seen going for long solitary walks, or pacing down " Les
Olivettes," (the old name for what is now known as " the water
lane ") or underneath " Les Rochers," the cliffs on which the
Manor House of Blanchelande now stands, and resting by the
" douït " where the pond at Le Vallon now is, but which, in
those days, was public property.

He was always very richly dressed, and was supposed to have
hidden hoards of wealth, as well as to carry large sums of
money on his person. There were two or three brothers who
lived together in a house near Le Varclin, who, tempted by his
supposed riches, and thinking that his isolation would prevent his
disappearance being noticed or enquiries being made, decided on
following him on one of his solitary rambles and on murdering
him. These brothers had always borne a bad reputation ; they
gambled and drank, and were the "vauriens" of an otherwise
respectable family.

So, one evening, they followed him, as, passing above La Petite
Porte, he entered into the narrow lane, overgrown with trees and
thorn bushes, which leads to Jerbourg Point. There they closed
upon him, and, being two or three to one, murdered him, and,
after having robbed the body of his watch, rings, etc., buried the
corpse under some of the heaps of stones which lie on the
waste lands at the top of the cliff.

Some wonder was caused at Le Hurel when he failed to
appear, but the rumour was started that he had been seen sailing
away in a little fishing boat he used to hire for the season,
from Bec du Nez, and which the murderers had had the
forethought to scuttle and sink. The country people thought he
had returned to his native land, and all interest in the matter
dropped.

But there was one man to whom M. de Damèque's disappearance meant much. In Paris he had left a dear friend, a
Dr. Le Harrier. These two men wrote to each other regularly,
and when M. de Damèque's letters suddenly ceased, letters came
to Le Hurel from this doctor, asking for explanations—letters
which were never answered. Among M. de Damèque's jewellery
was a beautiful and most uncommon watch, with either his coronet
and monogram or his coronet and arms displayed on the case.
One day, some years after his disappearance, Dr Le Harrier,
walking through the streets of Paris, saw this unmistakable

Haunted Lane near Jerbourg.

watch hanging in a jeweller's shop. He went in and asked the
man how it had got into his possession, and the man told him
it had been brought by some men from Guernsey, who had been
trying to sell it in England, Holland, and Belgium, and finally
had left it with him to dispose of. Dr. Le Harrier bought the
watch, and, taking the men's address, started at once for Guernsey.
When he arrived he made enquiries, and, finding that these men
bore a bad reputation, took some constables with him and went
to the house. There they found them sodden with drink, and,
haunted by fear and remorse when they saw the watch, they
sank down on their knees and confessed everything, and were led
off then and there to prison.

The next thing to be done was to disinter the bones of the
murdered man and give them Christian burial. Heavily handcuffed
the brothers were taken to the spot, accompanied by various
members of the clergy, a doctor, who had to certify that every
bone was there, (this is a point much dwelt upon by every teller
of the story), Dr. Le Harrier, and all the people of St. Martin's.
Then the bones, being found, were placed in a coffin, and reverently
buried in St. Martin's churchyard.

After the last spadeful of earth had been put in the grave, and
while handcuffed prisoners and all the bystanders were still present,
an old St. Martin's man, named Pierre Jehan, got up and made
the following speech, which I have written down word for word as
the people still tell it.

"*Autrefois quand on enterrait des dépouilles mortelles on y envoyait
des rameaux et des bouquets de fleurs. Aujourd'hui on ne voit rien
de tout ça.*"

"*Autrefois on aurait donné un quartier de froment en fonds
d'héritage pour porter le nom de ——. Aujourd'hui on en donnera
quatre pour ne le pas porter.*"

("Formerly when burying a corpse one sent branches of trees
and bouquets of flowers. To-day there is nothing of that."

"Formerly one would have given a quarter of wheat rent to bear
the name of ——. To-day one would give four not to bear it.")

The shock and the shame were such that the brothers were
seized by what the people call "a stroke," and to the relief of
their relations died in prison before being brought for trial.

That the ghosts of these two murdered men should revisit the
scenes of the crime was only to be expected, but finally, when La

Petite Porte was shut to sand-eelers by reason of *"ces cris terribles,"* some of the neighbours and fishermen began to wonder whether nothing could be done to lay these unquiet spirits and free the bay from its supernatural visitants.

There was a man called Pierre Thoume, who lived at Les Blanches, most popular in the parish, being ready to go everywhere and join in everything, though he was emphatically a "bon Chrétien." He was a distant relative of the murderers of M. de Damèque, and, having heard these noises at various times, it was borne in upon him that perhaps if he could find out what the ghost wanted, he could fulfil its wishes, and so let it rest in peace. He even prayed for guidance, and more and more he felt it to be his duty to go and meet the ghost face to face. At first some other men said they would join him, but when the appointed night came their spirits failed them, and no one arrived at the rendezvous. Undaunted, and armed only with his Bible, Mr. Thoume sallied forth alone at midnight. I think it is difficult to realise what moral and physical courage it must have involved to go forth alone to encounter the supernatural, fully persuaded of its unearthly character.

Early in the morning he returned to his home, looking very white, and with a curiously set expression on his face. His wife and daughters, who had waited up for him, rushed at him to know what had happened, but he said, "You must never ask me what has happened, what I have seen, what I have done. I have sworn to keep it a secret, and as a secret it will die with me, but this I can tell you, you may go to La Petite Porte at any hour of the day or night, and never again shall any ghost haunt it, or noise or scream be heard." And to this day the noises have utterly ceased.

Pierre Thoume kept his vow, though his family, friends, and neighbours, implored him time after time, even on his death bed, to tell them what he had seen. His invariable reply was, "I have given my word, and I will not break it." *

LES CACHES.

There are two houses called Les Câches in St. Martin's parish, situated one behind the other in the district so called, between

---

* From Mrs. Rowswell, Mr. Thoume's daughter, Mrs. Le Patourel, Mrs. Charles Marquand, Margaret Mauger, Mr. Tourtel, and many others, inhabitants of St. Martin's parish.

the blacksmith's forge at St. Martin's and the Forest Road. Tradition says that they all formed part of one property, which extended as far as St. Martin's Church, and was a nunnery, the nuns having a private lane of their own by which they could go to the church without the fear of meeting any men *en route*. There is a pond situated to the left of a long avenue which now leads to the front door of one of the houses, and for years it was believed that on a certain night of the year, a woman's figure, dressed in grey, is seen walking up and down the avenue, weeping and wringing her hands, and then rushing to the pond. The story the people tell to account for this appearance is, that one of the nuns was discovered at the dead of night trying to drown her child and herself in the pond. They were rescued, but only for a worse fate, for the unfortunate woman and child were bricked up in a cupboard which is now situated in one of the outhouses, but is supposed to have been the old refectory. The people also tell in confirmation of this story that the night the ghost is seen this cupboard door flies open of itself though it is quite impossible to force it open at any other time.

It is possible that if this was an ecclesiastical establishment, it was one of those alien priories of which Sir Edgar MacCulloch says :—

" After the loss of Normandy the inconvenience of having so many valuable possessions in the hands of the enemy, led to the suppression of these priories, and in these islands, whenever there was war between England and France, alien ecclesiastics were compelled to leave."

So probably the old conventual buildings, if there were any, were allowed to fall into ruins, and the land passed into the hands of the Patrys, and thence, through the marriage of Marguerite Patrys and Pierre Bonamy, into the possession of the Bonamys, who owned it for many centuries. There is an old document which tells the story of how the Bonamys first came to Guernsey.

" On their return from the Holy Land, whither they had accompanied the King of France, two brothers were driven by a violent storm, and thrown into a little bay, where their bark went to pieces. In gratitude for their preservation they made a vow to remain where Providence had placed them. One, a priest, founded a church, and the other married and founded the Bonamy family." In 1495, John Bonamy, son of Pierre and

Marguerite l'atrys, was "Procureur du Roi" in Guernsey, and his old MS. memorandum book still survives, in which he describes a pilgrimage to Rome he made in 1504, through France and Italy.

The following extracts relative to building Les Câches have been deciphered from the old crabbed manuscript by Colonel J. H. Carteret Carey:—

1468.—M° des gans quy mont aydy a caryer la pere .... et des grant roquez .... de le Cluse Luet—premez Gylome robert j jor &c.

1498.—M° que je marchande de Colas Fyquet po' ma meson, le but deverz le nort .... par la some de viij escus .... Il comencest le xiij^{eme}* jo' du moys de Maye—le Mardyt.*

1504.—M° que Gylome le Corvar et Colin Savage comancer acovyr ma grange landeman du jo, Saint Appolyne. Acevest le jo' Saint Aubin lan vc quatre," which may be translated:—

(1468.—Memo of the people who helped me to quarry the stone.... and the big rocks.... of "l'Ecluse Luet" [the Ecluse was the mill-dam in connection with the old watermill which gave its name to Moulin Huet Bay. It was situated in the hollow at the bottom of the water-lane of "Les Olivettes," just above the old Mill House] first William Robert, one day, &c.

(1498.—Memo. That I bargain with Colas Fyquet about my house, the end (to be) towards the north. ... for the sum of eight escus. They began the 18th of May—on Tuesday.)

(1504.—Memo. That William Le Corvar (&) Colin Savage, began to cover my barn the day following the day of Saint Appolyne [Feb. 9,] finished the day of St. Aubin [March 1,] 1504.)

In the parish of St. Martin's they still tell a story of the old days when the Bonamys yet occupied Les Câches.

"Years and years ago, there was an old Helier Bonamy,* who lived at the Câches. He was one of the richest men in Guernsey, and kept, as well as cows and horses, a large flock of sheep, there being much demand for wool in those days on account of the quantity of jerseys, stockings, &c., knitted over here. One night he and his daughter went to a ball in the town. Tradition even goes so far as to say that Miss Bonamy was dressed in white brocade.

---

* On referring to the Bonamy pedigree, the only Helier Bonamy who appears to have owned Les Câches. is a "Hellier, fils Pierre." Peter Bonamy being a Jurat in 1548. Helier does not seem to have borne the best of reputations, for Nicholas Bermis writes of him to Bishop Horn: "Guernsey, December 13, 1575. He is a disorderly character, notorious for impiety and obstinacy. . . . Finally publicly excommunicated from the commune of the Church of God and of His Saints and given over to Satan until he should repent."—*Zurich Letters,* Vol. II., p. 224.

Before starting, Helier Bonamy summoned his herdsmen, and told them to keep a sharp look out after his sheep, for that there were many lawless men about. Helier and his daughter * walked home that night earlier than was expected.

As they turned into the avenue, between high hedges and forest trees, they heard the bleatings of sheep in pain. "*Écoute donc, ce sont mes berbis*" (Listen, those are my sheep), said Helier, and drew his daughter under the hedge to listen. Peeping through the bushes they saw his herdsman and farm labourers calling each other by name, drinking, talking and laughing, and, while cutting the throats of the defenceless sheep, chanting in chorus :—

> "*Rasons ! rasons ! les berbis*
> *Du grand Bonamy,*
> *S'il était ichin d'vànt,*
> *Nou l'i en feraït autant !*"
>
> (Shear ! shear ! the sheep,
> Of the great Bonamy,
> Were he here before us,
> We would do as much to him).

They crept up the avenue unobserved to the house, for Helier was afraid to confront all these men who had evidently been drinking heavily, alone and unarmed. The next day his herdsman came to him with a long face, and said that robbers had broken into the sheepfold in the night and killed all the sheep, and brought up the other men as witnesses. Mr. Bonamy said nothing, except that he would like all these men to accompany him down to the Court to there testify to the robbery. This they did, and when they got there and told their story, Mr. Bonamy and his daughter then turned round and denounced them. They were taken into custody, and hanged shortly afterwards at St. Andrew's. *

There are several stories illustrating the re-appearance of people whose dying wishes had been disregarded by their survivors, and also of people wishing to tell their heirs where their treasure had been hid.

At the King's Mills, a Mrs. Marquand died, and left instructions with her husband that her clothes were to be given to her sister

---

* Even into the nineteenth century the old ladies would tell you how they walked home, lit by a three-candled lantern from " the Assembly " and how the last dance was always given to the favourite partner, so that he might have the privilege of accompanying them.

* From Miss C. Tardif, who was told the story by her grandmother.

Judith. After her death the widower did not do it, so every night her ghost came and knocked at her husband's door. One night she rapped so loudly that all the neighbours opened their windows, and heard her say :—

"*Jean, combien de temps que tu me feras donc souffrir, donne donc mes hardes à ma sœur Judi.*"

(John, how much longer wilt thou make me suffer, give then my clothes to my sister Judy).

He gave the clothes the next day, and the spirit returned no more.*

Almost the same story is told of a Mrs. Guille, who gave orders that after her death a certain amount of clothes were to be bought and yearly distributed amongst the poor. This her husband neglected to comply with, so Mrs. Guille visited him one night, and told him that she would do so every night until the clothes were given. Mr. Guille hurriedly bought and distributed the clothes, and continued to do so yearly until he died.†

Miss Le Pelley also contributes the following ghost stories which are told at St. Pierre-du-Bois :—

"About the beginning of the century a man went to Gaspé (which the narrator said was Newfoundland, but is really on the mainland). While there, his father died suddenly, and the son came back to Guernsey to work the farm. One night his father appeared to him and told him that he would find "*une petite houlette*" (a little mug) on the barn wall, with something of value in it. Next morning the son went to look, and found a mug full of five franc pieces."

"A widow in Little Sark had sold her sheep advantageously and hidden the money in the "*poûtre*" (the large central rafter which runs along the ceiling of the kitchen). Quite suddenly she died. Whenever her son walked about in Little Sark he met his mother, which made him feel very frightened, so one day he made his brother come with him, and together they met her, and plucked up courage enough to say:—'In the name of the Great God what ails you,' so then, having been spoken to first, she could tell them where her hoard of treasure was, and then disappeared, and was never seen again."

The whole country-side is full of shreds of ghost stories and

---

* † Collected by Miss E. Le Pelley.

N N

beliefs; many of these were probably due to, and encouraged by, the smugglers of olden days.

For instance a funeral procession was supposed to issue from an old lane south of Le Hurel—now blocked up—and no St. Martin's man or woman would dare pass the place at night. But smugglers, creeping along between the overhanging hedges, with kegs and bundles on their shoulders, would have had just the same effect, especially to people who would have been far too frightened at an unexpected nocturnal appearance to stop and investigate the matter.

At the corner between Les Maindonneaux and the Hermitage, a tall figure was said to appear, and hover round the spot. When the road was widened and the wall round the Hermitage was built, a stone coffin was found full of very large bones. These bones were taken to the churchyard, and the burial service read over them, and since then no ghost has been seen.

Then, a little further on, around the pond of Sausmarez Manor, was seen an old man, dressed in a long grey coat, and a grey felt plumed hat. This is supposed by the people to be old Mr. Matthew de Sausmarez—" Le Grand Matthieu " as he is called,—but why he is supposed to return is unknown.

Even now-a-days, in quite modern most unghostly-looking houses, you hear tales of little old women, former inhabitants, being seen. In another house, where a suicide is known to have occurred, soft finger knocks are heard against the walls of one of the rooms, as of some one shut up in the room and seeking release; the door is opened, and nothing is to be seen. And in St. Martin's the ghost of a woman, who only died a few years ago, is said to haunt the garden of the house in which she lived. Her daughter saw the appearance and was picked up in a dead faint from fright, but then the woman was supposed by all the neighbours to have been a witch, and, of course, as they say, the spirit of " une sorcière " could not rest quiet in consecrated ground.

I will close this chapter on ghosts with a story which is firmly believed and told by many of the country people. For obvious reasons I suppress all names.

At the beginning of the nineteenth century, a very rich widower had a house in Smith Street. His first wife had left many small children, to whom in her lifetime she had been devoted, and spent many hours of her day in the nursery. The widower, after a short interval, married again, a young, pretty, and frivolous girl, who utterly neglected her step-children. Then the spirit of his first wife came back for a short time every morning, and washed and dressed them, the curtains of their beds were found pushed back in the mornings, and her silk dress was heard rustling up the stairs, and the children used to say " Mamma dressed us." *

A man residing on the north-west coast had a brother who was drowned whilst out fishing. This man, wishing to do his best for his brother's family, was sore perplexed some years afterwards, as the family ran great risk of losing their property, owing to the absence of a title deed which he knew to have existed, but which unfortunately had not been registered.

One day, when out fishing, he was greatly surprised to see his brother's boat coming full sail close to him and just rounding to, with his brother at the tiller, and exclaimed :—" La ! te v'lo et ta femme qu'est r'mariaïe ! " (Lo ! there you are and your wife married again !) The answer he received was :—" La papier que tu trache est dans un taï endret sus la poutre," (the paper you are looking for is in such a room, on the beam). Immediately everything disappeared.

Arrived ashore, he searched in the place indicated and found the missing document.†

---

* From Mrs. Le Patourel, and also told to Miss Le Pelley by an old woman at St. Pierre-du-Bois.

† From John de Garis, Esq., of the Rouvêts, whose father was told the story by the man himself.

APPENDIX B.*

Witchcraft.*

MARIE PIPET.

THERE are many stories still told and firmly believed by the country people, of Marie Pipet, who was a noted "sorcière" of the early part of the nineteenth century. She came of a race of witches and wizards, thus described in Redstone's *Guernsey and Jersey Guide*, by Louisa Lane Clarke, (Second Edition, 1844), p. 86.

" On the road past St. Andrew's Church, one of the lanes to the right leads to the village called " Le Hurel,"† a collection of mere huts; rude, dirty looking cottages, but remarkable from the people who tenant it. They are a kind of half gipsy, half beggar race, bearing the name of Pipet; and kept totally distinct from every other family, because no person would intermarry with them upon any consideration. Their appearance and features are quite unlike the rest of the Guernsey peasantry, who are extremely good-looking, clean, and active; whereas those Pipets may be found basking in the sun, with anything but a prepossessing exterior. The country people consider them as wizards and witches, and, at certain times of the year, about Christmas, when they are privileged to go round and beg for their *Noël*, or " *irvières* " (New Year's gifts), no one likes to send them away

---

* Referred to on page 386.

† *Hure, Hurel,* and *Huret,* all frequently met with as place-names in Guernsey, mean " rocky ground."—Métivier's *Dictionnaire*.

empty handed for fear of the consequences to themselves, their cattle, or their children." Even to this day the country people have a great dread of "Les Pipiaux." *

My father's old nurse, Margaret Mauger, told me that the cook at old Mr. Fred Mansell's, of the Vauxbelets, (about the year 1850), was a great friend of hers, and told her that one day Marie Pipet came into the Vauxbelets kitchen, and demanded some favour which was refused. "*Tu t'en repentiras*," she said, and went out of the door and sat on the adjoining hedge to await developments. Meanwhile the sirloin which was being cooked for Mr. Mansell's dinner refused to be cooked! For hours she turned it round and round on the jack in front of the fire. The heat had apparently no effect on it, and it was as raw as when she first put it there. Finally, in despair, the cook went to her master, and told him what had happened. So he sent for Marie Pipet, and told her if she did not disenchant his dinner she would spend the night in gaol, (he was a Jurat of the Royal Court). With a curtsey she replied that if he would go into his kitchen he would find his sirloin ready for eating, and, at that moment, the cook declared, it suddenly turned brown!

There are many stories told of Marie Pipet in St. Pierre-du-Bois. One old woman, Judith Ozanne, told Miss Le Pelley that Marie Pipet, "la sorcière," once asked her grandmother, old Mrs. Ozanne, for some milk. This was refused her, so she prevented the cows from eating, and they were all pining away. So then her grandfather took his pitchfork, and, going straight to the witch, compelled her, under the fear of corporal punishment, to undo the spell.

Judith Ozanne also tells the following story of Marie Pipet, which she affirms is true. One day Marie took her corn to the Grands Moulins (the King's Mills) to be ground. The two young men who were in charge of the mill said "Oh dear no, they were not going to grind her corn," and so she returned home, but the mill-stones turned round and round and round so quickly that no corn would grind, and nothing would stop them, so they had to call back Marie Pipet and promise to grind her corn for her, and, as soon as her corn was put in, the millstones worked as usual.

---

* The Guernsey people have a way of making plurals of many words ending in "et" or "ert" or "el," by substituting "iaux," as:—Pipets=Pipiaux, Robert (a very common surname) Robiaux, Coquerel=Coqueraulx, bouvet, bouviaux, touffet, touffiaux.

Mr. Métivier gives a story of Marie Pipet which was current in his day, in his *Souvenirs Historiques de Guernesey.*

"The incomparable Marie, so dreaded by the millers of the King's Mills, because she often amused herself by unhinging our mills, rests in peace on the good side (au bon côté) of the Castel churchyard.* It is firmly believed, and frequently told, how she, and other members of her family, could metamorphose themselves as "cahouettes"—red-legged choughs. One day, in the form of one of these birds, she was discovered in a cow stable, and run through the thigh by the proprietor of the stable, with his pitchfork. The bird managed to escape, but the woman Marie Pipet was obliged to keep her bed for six months with a terrible and mysterious wound in her leg, by which of course the metamorphosis was proved." †

Possibly a bird of such evil omen, having red legs, accounts for the fact that to this day our country people tell you that all witches who go to dance at the Catioroc wear red stockings. ‡

All witches are supposed to be endowed with the faculty of keeping the person they have bewitched walking—walking, for hours perhaps, in a circle, to which they cannot find a clue.

Marie Pipet, one day being offended with a man, made him walk backwards and forwards one whole night between the Vauxbelets and St. Andrew's Church. §

The Wizard of Sark.

About the end of the eighteenth century there lived in Sark a very notorious wizard called Pierre de Carteret. An old Sark woman called Betsy Hamon, now Mrs. de Garis, has given Miss Le Pelley, whose servant she is, the following particulars concerning him :—

Pierre de Carteret, called "le vieux diable," lived in Sark. He

---

* In Guernsey the south side of our churchyard was "le bon côté." The north side, (according to the old Norse mythology, where hell and its attendant demons were situated in the *north*) was reserved for criminals, suicides, etc.

† The "Cahouettes" or red-legged choughs, have always, according to Mr. Métivier (see his *Dictionnaire*, art. "Cahouettes"), played a prominent rôle in the Néo-Latin mythology. According to the Council of Nismes, 1281, witches and wizards metamorphosed themselves into "Cahouets" and "Cahouettes." Raphaël, Archbishop of Nicosia, capital of the island, excommunicated all *cahouets* and *cahouettes*, as well as all who maintained and encourage games of chance.

‡ From Margaret Mauger, who also said that in her youth if one met an old woman in the the town wearing red stockings, it was always said "*V'là une des sorcières du Catioroc !*" In Holbein's *Crucifixion*, 1477, now at Augsberg, a devil which carries off the soul of the impenitent thief has the head of an ape, bat-wings, and *flaming red legs*.

From Margaret Mauger.

always worked at night, and when the fishermen passed by his house at night they heard him talking to the little devils who worked for him. They could not understand, for it was the devil's language they talked. He built a boat in a barn in one morning, and the Sark people were amazed to see it launched in the Creux harbour. This was Black Art, for the boat was too large to go out of the door, and also his house was not quite close to the sea.

He was very rich, partly owing to his having no expenses, as he had no workmen to pay, everything being done for him by these little devils, and partly from his first wife, whom he courted in France. Pierre went over to France alone, in a small open boat. The girl he married, who was herself a lady, thought he was of gentle blood. After he married her he was most cruel, and spoilt all her furniture. For instance, her parlour was mirrored from ceiling to floor, and he brought her horses up into the room, and the poor things became excited when they saw other horses, and kicked the looking-glasses and broke all the other furniture. This wife died of a broken heart, and for his second wife Pierre married a Sark girl, little more than a child.

If Pierre wanted his hedges repaired he simply gave the order to his little helpers, and the next morning they were done. Pierre's daughter—"la petite Betsy"—used to feed the cow at night in the churchyard, and she was seen returning home at daybreak with the cow, looking thoroughly well fed. Consequently nobody would buy butter or milk from him.

When Pierre had nothing else to give his workers to do they used to forge money, and their hammers could be heard by the passers by.*

Old Mrs. Le Messurier, in Sark, also confirmed a great many of these details in 1896. She said he, Pierre de Carteret, was well known to be a famous sorcerer. He had pictures of the Devil on his walls, and little images of Satan were found in his house after his death, and promptly burnt by the incomers. He could build a boat, alter a loft, or build a wall in a single night, because he had "des esprits malins" to help him. He was an excessively bad man and used to smuggle ball and ammunition to France, to help the French against the English in

---

* From Miss Le Pelley, who wrote it down word for word as it was said.

the war. The English found him out and came over with bayonets to take him, but he hid down his well, and could not be found.

Out at St. Pierre-du-Bois they still tell the tale of a Frenchman, who was a "sorcier," and in league with the Devil.

One day he entered a farm kitchen, where he found all the young people playing a game, in which they used a number of doubles, placed in a jam pot, for counters.

He said "I can turn all those doubles into mice."

They did not believe him, so he took the pot, shook it, and turned it upside down on the table. Then he turned to one of the girls standing by and said "Now, take up that pot." She did so, and numbers of mice ran out of it, all over the table, with their tails cocked up!

Of the same man another story is told. One morning he wanted some of his neighbours to play cards with him, but they said they could not spare the time, for they must weed their parsnips.

He replied—" If you will come, your parsnips shall be weeded by dinner time."

So they played, but one man looked up, and saw through the window numbers and numbers of little demons weeding very quickly, and by mid-day the work was done.*

Mr. J. Linwood Pitts has also collected two stories bearing on the subject of the transformation of witches, both of which were related to him in perfect good faith by reliable witnesses.

Many years ago a Guernsey gentleman went over to Sark. While sitting on the cliffs above the Havre Gosselin he noticed a flock of birds, principally wild duck, circling round and round. He fired off his musket, but did not succeed in hitting any of them, or even, much to his astonishment, in frightening them away.

He thought there must be something mysterious about them, as wild duck are generally such shy birds, so he consulted a noted wizard, who told him that if he loaded his musket with a piece of silver having a cross on it it would take effect on any transformed witch. So he went over to Sark again with this silver bullet, and on returning to the Havre Gosselin again saw the birds. He picked out one, which seemed the finest of the flock, and apparently their leader. On firing at it he succeeded

---

* Collected by Miss Le Pelley.

in winging it, though it disappeared, and he thought it had escaped.

That evening, on the return boat to Guernsey, a girl on board, who used to pay almost daily visits to Sark, and about whom there were many mysterious reports, appeared with a bad wound in her hand, about which she would vouchsafe no explanation, but looking very white and frightened. The man identified her in his own mind as the mysterious bird, but did not speak about the affair till long after.

The Witch of Alderney.

A very respectable Alderney man used to tell old Mr. Barbenson, Wesleyan minister, about a noted Alderney witch.

He declared that one night, passing by her cottage, he looked in, and saw a blue flame blazing up, and the witch dancing in the middle of it, surrounded by little devils, also dancing.

"But how do you know that they were devils?" Mr. Barbenson asked:—"Because they were just like the pictures of Apollyon in my old *Pilgrim's Progress*" was the reply. Another day, he said that, coming home from milking, he saw two large black birds revolving over his head. They both sank, almost at his feet, behind a small furze bush. Suddenly this woman rose up from behind the same bush, and ran away. He said the bush was made too small to hide the woman, and that it was quite impossible that she could have been concealed there. The man vouched for the truth of these stories.

Mr. Pitts has also kindly allowed me to include the following extract from an old MS. which was communicated to him by Mr. E. P. Le Feuvre, a gentleman of Jersey extraction, residing in London, and connected with some of our Guernsey families.

"He also gave me the details of a remarkable local witch story, which he had found in a curious old MS. in the library of Dr. Witham, of Gordon Square, London. This MS., which is in two volumes folio, is entitled '*Icones Sacræ Gallicanæ et Anglicanæ*," and contains seventy biographies of ministers and clergymen. Among them is a sketch of the life of the Rev. Daniel Fautrat, of Guernsey, who was minister of the Câtel parish; then of Torteval; and who afterwards, in 1633 (in the reign of Charles I.), succeeded Mr. de la Marche, at St. Peter-Port. This MS. is by a John Quick (born 1636—died 1706). There were two Fautrats, Helier and Daniel, father and son, and the biographer somewhat confuses them.* This story of the witch—who was burnt alive in the Bordage during Daniel Fautrat's ministry at the Town Church—is a very curious one, and is a decided acquisition to the witch-lore of the island. It is as follows :—

THE WITCH AND THE RAVEN.

" After Monsieur [Daniel] Ffautrat had spent some years at Torteval and St. Andrew's [Guernsey] he was, upon the death of Monsr. de la Marche, called to succeed him in ye Pastorall charge of St. Peters Port, [in 1634, in the reign of Charles I.]

---

* The following is an abbreviated pedigree of the Fautrat family, showing what close connections there were between the leading families in Guernsey and Jersey before the wars of the Commonwealth, when—the islands taking different sides—was established a feud which has never properly been healed.

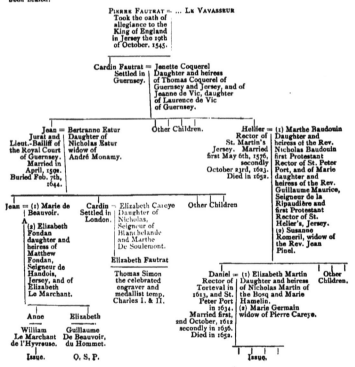

which is ye Towne of this Island, a fair Markett Towne and priviledged with ye Sessions of ye whole Island, where all caisses Civill and Criminall are finally tryed and determined in ye Playderoye,* by ye Bayliffe and Jurates.

" During his ministry in this Towne, and about ye year 1640 [Charles I.] there happened a most remarkable event. Divines do say that it is a very rare thing for witches under Gospell Light to repent; and some have given this reason of their assertion — because they have committed that unpardonable sin against ye Holy Ghost. I cannot tell, but that this following story seems to confirm it.

" There was a certain woman of this Island, above four-score years of age, who had been imprisoned, indicted and found guilty upon full evidence, of that abominable sin of witchcraft, and for it was condemned to death. She gave out confidently that she should not dye. However, she is carried from prison to ye appointed place of Execution to be burnt alive.

" All the way, as she was going thither, a great Black Raven was seen hovering, and heard croaking after a dolefull manner over her head, till she came to ye stake. And now, while they be fastening ye chain, she begs of one of the Bystanders to give her a clew of thread, which having received, she fastens one end of it to her girdle, and taking ye other end, she flings it with her hand up into ye aire. The Raven, stooping down, catcheth at it with his Beak, and, mounting, carrys with him ye old witch from ye bottom of ye vale up into ye air. A young man of that Island, seeing her flying, being on ye top of ye hill, flings his Halbard so exactly betwixt her and ye raven, that it cuts ye thread asunder, and ye old witch is taken by him, but with many fearfull imprecations upon him, she vomityng out whole cartloads of curses against him.

" However, she is once again carryed down to ye stake, and there accordingly executed, being burnt to ashes. But this poor officious wardour, whose name was Gosslin—ye holy wise provi-

---

* The Court House used to be situated in the Plaiderie before the present Court House was built.

" About two centuries ago, public justice was administered in a building, which, like those still used in many country towns in England, was both Corn Market and Court House, which by a special ordinance was to be cleared by noon that the Market might commence ; and after that a Court House was erected near Pollet Street, near a place called from the circumstance " La Plaiderie." This, however, was soon found too small and inconvenient, and the present building was erected in 1799, at the expense of about £7000, paid by the States, and further improved in 1822."—Redstone's *Guernsey and Jersey Guide*, 2nd Edition 1844, p. 13.

dence of God so permitting it—felt a short time after, ye bitter consequences of her rage and dying curses; for he grew sick of an incurable disease, lying under most exquisite torments, of which he could never be relieved by any means or medicines, till having languished some years he was at last released from his sufferings by death."

" A girl was very ill, and the doctor did not know what was the matter with her, and, though he tried many remedies, none succeeded. One day a friend from the Vale, their native parish, called, and told the girl's mother privately that the girl was bewitched, and that it was Mrs. ———— who had done it, but that he could, with certain herbs, boiled in a particular manner, cause the witch to die, and then the girl would be well. The herbs were boiled, and a few days afterwards the witch died. During the funeral the girl jumped joyfully out of bed, quite well. This occurred within the last twenty years."

" One day, two boys, well on in their teens were chaffing an old witch, when suddenly she got very angry, threw dust in the air, and gabbled some words very quickly. The boys went home and found they were covered with vermin. They were near neighbours. One of the boys was so angry that he took his gun and went to the old witch and said, " Now, take away the vermin, or I shoot you," and he levelled his gun at her. They parleyed a little, but the boy was so determined that the witch suddenly took fright, threw dust in the air, repeated some words, and the vermin disappeared. The other boy was covered for three days." *

The following story illustrating the widespread belief in these special powers of witches and wizards was told me by Mrs. Le Patourel, of St. Martin's, who was told the story by the heroine, and who vouched for its authenticity.

Mrs. Le Patourel's mother-in-law was a Miss Mauger, of Saints, very handsome and very well-to-do. In fact, she and her sister went to school in England, which was considered very grand in those days. On her return from school she, her sister, and a friend, all went together to one of the country dances then frequently held in the various parishes. They all " held their heads very high," dressed very well, and would only dance with those whom they considered the " best" partners. They were dressed on this occasion in silk dresses with large white lace collars and ruffles. At the beginning of the dance, as they were all sitting in a row together, some man came up and asked each of them in turn to dance, but they all considered him unworthy of the honour, and each refused to dance with him. As the last refused he turned on his heel muttering that they would repent their rudeness. A minute or two later one of the girls leaned forward and cried to her sister, "Oh, Marie, what have you got there?" and pointed to an insect crawling on her lace. Covered with confusion the girl killed it, only to see swarms more crawling after it. The other two girls then discovered to their horror that they were likewise covered with swarms of vermin, and covered with shame and confusion they all had hurriedly to leave the dance. For three days they all remained in this condition, and then the vermin disappearred as suddenly as they came.

"The shame of it I can never forget," Mrs. Le Patourel says was the way her informant always ended the story. "But," said Mrs. Le Patourel, "that is nothing to what people can do who use the bad books."*

She thinks it is the French people who have brought these evil arts to Guernsey, and in proof of her theory told me this story which happened to one of her own friends, "who has told it to me many a time."

A Guernsey farmer living in St. Saviour's parish had a French manservant, who slept on the premises. Suspicion being aroused by his haggard looks he was watched, and seen to leave the house every night and not come back till the morning. When asked where he had been and what he had been doing he returned evasive answers. So one night his master determined to follow him. He tracked him across some fields till he reached the Catioroc, and there he saw him lie down in the middle of a field, and then, in a few moments, a clear, bluish flame, like the flame of a candle, was seen issuing out of his mouth, and wandering off like a will-o'-the-wisp across the fields. When the astonished farmer went up to the body he found it lying rigid and lifeless, and no amount of shaking or calling could make any impression on it. After some time the flame was seen returning, and settled on the man's mouth, and there

---

* "I have heard of too many instances of this power of giving vermin being exercised to admit of doubt. The surprising part is the removal. I have not heard of a case for more than thirty years."—*Note by John de Garis, Esq., of Les Rouvêts.*

disappeared, and shortly after the man sat up, looking dazed and tired, and absolutely declined to answer any of the questions with which his master greeted him.

On pp. 305 to 351 (ante) are given various trials for witch-craft, which took place in Guernsey during the sixteenth and seventeenth centuries, but Sir Edgar MacCulloch has not included the following, which I have found cited in an old MS. book compiled by Eleazar Le Marchant and Pierre Careye between the years 1728 and 1743.

"Le 26me Juillet 1594, pardevant Louis de Vick, baillif, et Messrs. Nicholas Martin, sen., Guillaume de Beauvoir, André Henry, Jean Andros, Jean de Sausmarez, Pierre de Beauvoir, Pierre Careye, William le Marchant, Nicholas Martin, jun., and François Allez, jurez.

"Marie Martin, alias Salmon, fille Osmond, deubment atteinte et convaincue d'avoir usé d'Art de Sorcelerie, dont elle a empoisonné, tourmenté et fait mourir jouxte sa propre et volontaire confession, Anne Careye*, fẽme de John de Vick, la fẽme de Pierre Vodin, l'enfant de son oncle, Thomas Breton, l'enfant de John Briart, et deux enfants à Collas Nouell, et plusieurs bestes et autres maux, par elle commis par le. dit art de Sorcelerie, comme apparoist par les procédures et enquestes sur ce passées. Est ajugée d'être aujourd'huy brulée tant que son corps soit reduit en cendres, et ses biens, meubles, et héritages confisquées à la Majesté de la Royne, et est comandé aux officiers de sa Majesté de voir la ditte execution être faitte, ainsi qu'ils en voudront répondre : et est après avoir en sur ceu l'advis et opinion de Henri de Beauvoir et John Effart, jurez."

There are many other instances, which, did space permit, I could mention, of belief in witches and wizards, extending even down to the present day. Animals dying from no visible cause, bread turned sour and uneatable, wounds mysteriously inflicted and incurable by physicians, but at once healed by crossing running water, a woman sent mad by smelling a harmless-looking bouquet of flowers, and so on. Many involving the names of persons still

---

* John de Vick, King's Procureur, son of Richard, married first, the 15th of March, 1579, Anne Careye, daughter of Nicholas Careye, Seigneur of Blanchelande, and Collette de la Marche. I do not know the date of her death, but he married, secondly, December 15th, 1594, Elizabeth Pageot, and their son, Sir Henry de Vic, Knight, Baronet, and Chancellor of the Garter, was one of the most distinguished Guernseymen in our history. He was buried in Westminster Abbey the 24th of November, 1672.

living. For underneath the veneer of civilisation and education found in the island are the same old beliefs and superstitions, as deeply cherished and ingrained as they were in the days of Queen Elizabeth—" Plus ça change, plus c'est la même chose."

In conclusion, I will give a few extracts respecting witchcraft from Elie Brevint's note book. Elie Brevint was born in 1586, became minister of Sark in 1612, and died in 1674.

" Quelques uns tesmoignent avoir veu une nuée se lever d'Erm, et de là s'en aller sur le dongeon du Chasteau Cornet, où un certain Maugier depuis bruslé pour sortiléges estoit lors prisonnier, et ladite nuée s'estre dissipée et esvanouie sur le dit Chasteau, et que les bateaux pescheurs sur lesquels elle avoit passé avoyent cuide renversés." . . . .

" Histoire d'un juge, qui ne croyoit point qu'il y eust de sorciers ; il advint qu'il luy mourut soudain plusieurs vaches et brebis. Pourtant depuis cette perte, laquelle il imputoit à belles personnes, il fist rigoureuse justice de sorciers." . . . .

" On dit que quelqu'un va à la graine de Feugère* quand par un livre de magie, ou par quelque autre voye il a communication avec le Diable, qui luy baille des poudres pour attenter et commettre diverses meschancetés, comme ouvrir serrures, violer femme et fille, &c., et faut bailler à ce m͡r͡e pour ces drogues une beste vive, comme chien ou chat, autrement il poursuit N. pour le faire mourir."

---

* Graine de Feugere (fougère) = Fern seed.

APPENDIX C.*

Charms and Spells.*

VERY old lady remembers, when a child, seeing some small bits of stick, shaped like slate-pencils, which old women wore sewn up in their stays as charms against witchcraft, on the homœopathic principle, for they called them "*Des Bouais de Helier Mouton*," Helier Mouton being himself a noted sorcerer.

When I mentioned this to Sir Edgar he told me that a hundred years ago a man named Colin Haussin was put in the stocks for witchcraft and using "*des petits bouais.*"

The following charms, etc., were collected for me in 1896-7, as still current in the parish of St. Pierre-du-Bois, by Miss E. Le Pelley.

St. Thomas' Day.

If a girl wishes to knew whom she will marry, on the eve of St. Thomas' Day she puts her shoes in the form of a T under her bed, and says, in getting in :—

> "*Saint Thomas, Saint Thomas,*
> *Le plus court, le plus bas,*
> *Fais moi voir en m'endormant*
> *Celui qui sera mon amant,*
> *Et le pays, et la contrée.*
> *Où il fait sa demeurée,*
> *Et le métier qu'il sait faire.*
> *Devant moi qu'il vienne faire.*

---

* Referred to on page 421.

Qu'il soit beau ou qu'il soit laid
Tel qu'il sera je l'aimerai.
Saint Thomas, fait moi la grâce
Que je le voie, que je l'embrasse."
"Ainsi soit il."

MIDSUMMER EVE.

A girl makes a dumb cake and puts it on a gridiron over the fire, and watches it in silence between twelve and one o'clock at night, during which time the girl's future husband arrives and turns the cake. The narrator tried this, and when the cake was cooked on one side she heard someone walking clumsily upstairs. She was so frightened that she threw the cake away and got into her mother's bed and held tight on to her! Years afterwards she married and often recognised her husband's step as the one she heard that Midsummer Eve. She very much repented having done it, for she said it gives the poor man so much suffering being under the charm.

Another charm for Midsummer Eve is this:—If a girl wishes to know the profession of her future husband she must melt some lead in an iron spoon between twelve and one o'clock at night, and pour it in a tumbler of cold water, and then watch the shapes it takes, such as a sword would denote that he would be a soldier, an anchor a sailor, etc., etc. Should she wish to know whether she is to be married or not, she must kill two pigeons, take out their hearts and roast them on skewers, also between twelve and one o'clock. If she is to be married she will see her intended, if she is not to be, some men will bring in a coffin. There must be perfect silence the whole time. It once happened that, as a girl was doing it, a coffin appeared. She screamed aloud, and the men came up to her and began to put her in the coffin. But fortunately for her she fainted, and was quiet, and the men with the coffin could go away as they came.

Another charm against witchcraft is *"vif argent"* or quicksilver, but camphor, white salt, or heather, are all good. The charm must be put in a small cotton or linen bag, two inches long by one and a half inch wide, and attached by a ribbon round the neck, so that the charm rests above the heart. Red salt is used by witches in their incantations.

The following written charm was lent me to copy by Mr. Guille,

O O

one of the founders of the Guille-Allès Library. It is in the form of a letter, and he told me, when he was a boy, a copy existed in almost all the old Guernsey farm houses.* I have transcribed it verbatim, with all its faults of spelling, punctuation, etc.

" L'Ettre Miraculeuse.

"Trouvé depuis peut par un Etudians au pied d'un Crusifix Miraculeux de la Ville d'Arrass Escritte en Lettres d'Or de la propre main de notre Sauveur et Redempteur Jesus Christ.

Jesus—Marie.

Les Dimanches vous ne ferez aucune œuvre n'y travail sur peine d'être maudits de Moy. Vous yrez à l'Eglise et priez Dieu qu'il vous fasse Misericorde et qu'il vous pardonne vos péchés. Je vous ai donné six jours de la semaine pour travaille, et au septième me servir et vous Reposer ayant entendu le Service divin. Vous ferez la charité et vous donnerez de vos biens aux pauvres et vos champs seront fertille et vous serez remplis de Benediction. Au contraire si vous ne croyez à la presente l'Ettre Malediction viendra sur vous et sur vos Enfants, et vos Bestiaux seront maudits, je vous envoierez Guerre, Peste, et Famine et Douleur, et l'Angoisse de Cœur, et pour Marque de ma juste colère et dure Vengeance vous voirez signes prodigieux dans les Astres et Elements avec grands tremblements de Terre. Vous jeunerez cinq Vendredis en l'honneur des Cinq Plaies qui iai souffert pour vous sauver sur l'Arbre de la Croix. Vous donnerez cette L'Ettre sans aucun interêt que celuy de ma Gloire. Ceux qui murmuront sur cette L'Ettre seront aussy maudits et confis ; qui la tiendra dans la maison sans la publier sera aussy maudits au Jour Terrible Epouvantable du Jugement. Mais s'y vous gardez mes comandements et pareillement ceux de ma Sainte Eglise faisant une veritable penitence vous aurez la Vie Eternelle. Celuy qui la lira ou publiera ycelle est écrite de Ma Sacré Main et dictes de Ma Sacrée Bouche. S'il a comis autant de Péchés qu'il y a de Jours en l'an ils luy seront Pardonnés étant veritablement constrit, se confaisant, et satisfaisant au prochain. Sy on luy a fait tort. Sy vous ne croyez Pieusement en Ycelle Lettre je vous envoirez des Bestes Monstreuses qui

---

* In reading this proof Mr. de Garis notes that in his young days he had sometimes heard of a "Lettre d'Or" but had never seen the contents.

dèvoreront vous et votres Enfants. Bienheureux sera celuy qui prendra une copie de cette L'Ettre, qui la portera sur Soi, qui la lira, ou fera lire ou la gardera en sa Maison. Jamais aucun Feu Malin, on autre feu ni foudre ne la touchera. Et toutes Feme enceinte qui sur Elle qui la lira ou fera lire en Bonne intention etant en Travail d'Enfans sera incontinent heureusement délivré. Gardez mes comãndements et ceux de Ma Sainte Église Catolique, et vous serez bien heureux.

Avec 'Aprobation et Permission de Superieur de la Ville d'Arrase.

Nous Vicaire Generale certifions avoir lut la presente Copie et nous n'avons rien vus qu'il ne soit Utile et Capable de faire réussir le Pêcheur dans la Voie du Salut."

" À NICHOLAS GUILLE."

I will conclude by giving an instance of "Folk Medicine" which was sent me the other day by one of the most prominent of our local physicians.

"As you are interested in Guernsey Folk-Lore I send you the following :—

A patient of mine at St. Pierre-du-Bois suffered from an affection of the brain which has led to total loss of sight. It was supposed by the wise people around her that she was suffering from "Mal Volant," so a black fowl was waved three times round her head on three successive days, to the accompaniment of a prayer (? incantation). On the ninth day the fowl ought to have died and the woman recovered.—As this did not happen they concluded that their diagnosis was wrong !

E. LAURIE ROBINSON

Melrose, Guernsey, December 11th, 1902."

Index.

PRINTED IN GUERNSEY, BY FREDERICK CLARKE, STATES ARCADE.

Milton Keynes UK
Ingram Content Group UK Ltd.
UKHW022357221123
433098UK00005B/93